Metadata for Digital Collections:
A How-To-Do-It Manual®

Steven J. Miller

HOW-TO-DO-IT MANUALS®

NUMBER 179

Neal-Schuman Publishers, Inc.
New York   **London**

Published by Neal-Schuman Publishers, Inc.
100 William St., Suite 2004
New York, NY 10038

Library of Congress Cataloging-in-Publication Data

Miller, Steven J., 1954-
    Metadata for digital collections : a how-to-do-it manual / Steven J. Miller.
      p. cm. — (How-to-do-it manuals ; no. 179)
    Includes bibliographical references and index.
    ISBN 978-1-55570-746-0 (alk. paper)
    1. Cataloging of electronic information resources—Standards. 2. Metadata—Standards. 3. Dublin Core. I. Title.

Z695.24.M55 2011
025.3—dc22

                2011012594

Contents

Contents

11. Metadata, Linked Data, and the Semantic Web

List of Illustrations

Figures

Tables

Foreword

Back in the dark ages of the past decade, when first talking to publishers about putting together my own contribution to the metadata canon, it was suggested to me that I write more of a how-to book, but I demurred, largely because of the enormous effort required. As it happens, I broke my right arm early in the process of creating *Metadata in Practice*, so it's just as well that my actual writing effort was somewhat limited, as I could do the recruiting of contributors (and the inevitable herding) by telephone.

With that as background, I was really happy to hear that Steve was writing the book I hadn't the fortitude to attempt back then, and particularly pleased that he's done such a nice job of it. The metadata community needs this book—at all levels, from the beginner to the practitioner to the teacher. As it is, when those of us who teach about metadata these days go about gathering material, it's something of a treasure hunt, and each discovered resource needs to be presented with a map of where it fits in the pantheon, a bunch of caveats about age and suitability for particular purposes, and apologies for the fact that there is not a single resource that covers it all. Steve has relieved us of all that, for which we are very, very grateful. He's also included in the book the kinds of pointers to the important work of others that expands on his more comprehensive approach.

The other great news about this book is that Steve has been paying close attention to the Semantic Web, and he understands well that though we may be building our metadata using current technology we *must* pay attention to where our world is shifting. I predict that in the future we will look upon that shift as the most important change in our corner of the profession since Henriette Avram started thinking about automating the printing of catalog cards. Steve's approach—sensible and accessible to his audience—is to include that information in the relevant beginning portions and as a separate chapter. The reality is that we are on a moving sidewalk of transition that will be a part of our lives for most of (if not all of) our careers.

There is no shortcut—no one-size-fits-all template—available to us as we plan today for a tomorrow that will be rife with change, not all of which we can predict. But readers of this book will be as prepared as it is possible to be for whatever the future hands us. Thanks, Steve; we're in your debt.

Diane I. Hillmann
Director of Metadata Initiatives
Information Institute of Syracuse
Syracuse, New York;
Partner
Metadata Management Associates

Preface

Good quality metadata is critical for providing intellectual access to the ever-increasing number of digital collections being created by libraries, archives, museums, and other organizations today. Without good metadata, the digital resources would be sadly underutilized because most potential users would never discover their existence. Information professionals charged with organizing these collections need guidance. *Metadata for Digital Collections: A How-To-Do-It Manual* and its companion website (http://www.neal-schuman.com/metadata-digital-collections) introduce readers to fundamental concepts and practices in a style accessible to beginners and LIS students, as well as experienced practitioners with little formal metadata training.

Metadata for Digital Collections does not presume that readers come to the book with any cataloging experience. Instead, it guides students and working professionals through the basics of digital resource description, raising their awareness of commonly encountered challenges, along with common solutions, regardless of the specific metadata scheme being used, and it suffuses every chapter with numerous illustrative examples.

When turning to specific metadata schemes, rather than give a cursory survey overview of a large number of them, as many texts do, this book covers only three of those most commonly used for general digital resource description—Dublin Core, MODS, and VRA—allowing for each to be addressed in greater depth. Because Dublin Core is by far the most widely used metadata scheme for digital collections today, this book provides detailed, practical guidance on applying each of the Dublin Core elements and qualifiers, taking special care to clarify those most commonly misunderstood in order to assist readers in creating better quality, more functional, sharable, and interoperable metadata. The book uses MODS in large part for purposes of giving readers some practical familiarity with a hierarchical XML-based scheme, as a basis for informed comparison and contrast with Dublin Core, and for gaining hands-on experience with mapping between diverse element sets.

The book culminates in a step-by-step guide on how to design and document a metadata scheme or application profile for local institutional needs and digital collection projects. Unlike many other metadata texts, this book takes into account the widespread use of digital collection management systems such as CONTENTdm. *Metadata for Digital Collections* also covers such topics as XML encoding, OAI harvesting, metadata sharing and aggregation, metadata quality control, and the emerging environment of Linked Data and the Semantic Web, explaining their relevance to current practitioners and students.

Two central themes run throughout the text: the primary theme of metadata *functionality* and secondary theme of metadata *interoperability*. Each chapter emphasizes that practitioners design and create metadata to perform specific *functions* for their users and that they also often need to merge metadata from diverse sources and make it *interoperate* and function together effectively for those users. The book covers the topics of resource description, application of standardized metadata elements and controlled vocabularies, and consistency in metadata creation all from the perspective of how they function to serve end users' information discovery needs and how they facilitate metadata interoperability for the same purposes.

The companion website (http://www.neal-schuman.com/metadata-digital-collections) includes review questions, ideas for exercises, and additional practical and reference sources useful for educators, students, and practitioners. Those who complete this book will be well equipped for engaging in concrete metadata work and entering the professional marketplace, as well as for learning additional metadata topics and schemes such as Encoded Archival Description (EAD).

This book is intended primarily, but not exclusively, for the following audiences:

- Practitioners and students who need a practical introduction to metadata for practical implementation and a detailed guide to applying Dublin Core in practice

- Practitioners in small to medium-sized libraries, museums, archives, and other institutions, rather than the largest, most well-funded research and academic institutions

- Practitioners who are short on time, staff, budget, programming expertise, professional reading, or formal metadata education

- Users of out-of-the-box digital collection software packages, such as CONTENTdm, Insight + LUNA, or Greenstone

- Students and instructors in schools of library and information studies and continuing education courses and workshops, as an introduction to the world of metadata practice experienced by these audiences

Organization and Scope

Metadata for Digital Collections is organized into 11 chapters that progressively build on one another in order to introduce fundamental concepts and practices. The book's design also facilitates independent chapter consultation by practitioners who need on-the-run guidance.

Chapter 1 introduces basic metadata concepts, definitions, functions, and types. This chapter, and indeed the entire book, emphasize the creation of metadata to perform *functions* for users of digital collections, such as searching, browsing, navigating, identifying, and interpreting digital texts, images, and other resources. Chapter 1 goes on to give an overview of the larger digital collection creation process, of which metadata is but one piece, followed by a brief overview of the process of designing a metadata scheme for local use.

The next section of the book explores the most common kinds of information needed to describe and provide access to digital resources and gives practical guidance on understanding and applying the Dublin Core Metadata Element Set. **Chapters 2**, **3**, and **4** accomplish this and dig into the nitty-gritty challenges faced by metadata designers and creators, addressing such common questions as these:

- What is a "digital object" or "resource," and what aspects of it should a good metadata record describe and represent?

- How do I balance the meaning of local elements devised for a specific collection with the meaning of standardized elements, such as Dublin Core, to which they are mapped?

- How do I deal with information about both the digitized and the original physical versions of a resource, when each has its own creator, date, identifier, and other characteristics?

- What does each of the 15 Dublin Core metadata elements mean, what qualifiers can be used with each, and how do I correctly apply them in practice?

- What is the meaning of, and difference between, the Dublin Core *Type* and *Format* elements and the *Relation* and *Source* elements?

- How should I devise titles for resources such as local photographs that have no pre-assigned titles?

- How do I analyze the subject content of a resource, such as an image, and represent it using metadata terms?

Chapter 2 introduces fundamental resource description concepts and issues encountered when creating metadata for digital collections. This chapter also introduces the Dublin Core Metadata Element Set, including simple (unqualified) as well as qualified Dublin Core (DC).

Metadata professionals face many practical challenges in the application of elements needed to address user needs and system functionality related to titles, identifiers, dates, languages, names, responsibility, and intellectual property. **Chapter 3** delves into these issues. After looking at general needs and practices, it goes into detail on how to apply the relevant Dublin Core elements for each of these aspects. **Chapter 4** continues this approach, but turns to more complex and challenging elements and practices, including resource types and formats, subject analysis and representation by means of subject terms and descriptions, and relationships among resources. After looking at each of these in general, it details how to apply the relevant Dublin Core elements for each.

Controlled vocabularies improve resource discovery for users. **Chapter 5** provides an overview of different types of vocabularies, such as lists, taxonomies, and thesauri. It examines some of the most commonly used established vocabularies, as well as the creation of an institution's own local vocabularies.

Chapter 6 provides a very simple introduction to the basics of XML, focusing on those aspects needed to "read" and understand an XML-based metadata record. It includes examples of Dublin Core and MODS XML records, and concludes with a guide to the anatomy of an XML metadata record.

MODS, the Metadata Object Description Schema, is the subject of **Chapter 7**. This chapter gives an overview of the MODS elements, subelements, and attributes; illustrative examples of MODS records; and issues in mapping from Dublin Core to MODS. The chapter makes points about the value of learning something about MODS even if not using it in practice. Studying MODS provides an opportunity to compare Dublin Core with a more complex, XML-based general resource description scheme, and to directly experience the complexities of mapping between different element sets, among other uses.

Chapter 8 surveys the Visual Resources Association (VRA) Core Categories for works of art and architecture, including overviews of both the relatively DC-like VRA 3.0 and the relatively MODS-like VRA 4.0, with record examples of each. VRA is covered in much less detail than DC or MODS and is included primarily for purposes of further comparison and contrast with those two schemes.

In the current and future metadata environments, practitioners need to be concerned about the usability of their local metadata outside of its original context. **Chapter 9** investigates a set of interrelated topics having to do with interoperability, including viability of metadata for future system migration; sharing metadata within an institution or with a consortium or a third-party aggregator; issues of metadata harvesting, especially the use of the OAI harvesting protocol; metadata ingestion, processing, and conversion; crosswalks and mapping among different element sets; and metadata quality indicators and assessment methods. The chapter concludes with five concrete practices that readers can follow to improve their metadata quality and interoperability.

Metadata project managers often need not only to create metadata, but also to design and document their own local metadata schemes or application profiles. **Chapter 10** details a step-by-step process of assessing the context, content, and users of the collection, developing a set of functional requirements, selecting or creating a set of metadata elements and determining the element and database field specifications to meet those functional requirements, as well as examples of, and best practices for, documentation of one's scheme. The chapter looks at two basic models of metadata design: (a) selecting and adapting an established scheme such as Dublin Core to serve for multiple collections within an institution or consortium, and (b) creating collection-specific elements and mapping them to an established scheme such as Dublin Core (the typical CONTENTdm method).

Chapter 11 serves as a beginner's-level, step-by-step introduction to the *Resource Description Framework* and other aspects of metadata in the context of the currently developing *Linked Data* and *Semantic Web* environments. This includes the formal registration of metadata elements on the Internet using URIs, some basics of the Resource Description Framework (RDF), selected concepts from the DCMI Abstract Model, and recent developments in formalized Dublin Core Application Profiles. The working assumption is that most readers of the book will not be directly working with metadata in this context, but that some familiarity with these topics is valuable both for current awareness of new developments in the field and for possible future directions in which many current practitioners may eventually work.

Not all of the information in all chapters will be relevant to all practitioners. For example, the chapters on MODS and VRA may be of little interest to practitioners using only Dublin Core. But a study of a hierarchical, XML-based scheme such as MODS has great value for better understanding a simpler, flatter scheme such as DC for getting a better sense of the strengths and limitations of DC, for better understanding hands-on issues of mapping from one scheme to another, and for gaining insight into the types of metadata schemes that could possibly supersede DC in prominence for digital collections in the future. Learning some basics about topics such as XML, interoperability, harvesting, and aggregating will help broaden and deepen metadata practitioners' knowledge of their field of practice and might also suggest unforeseen practical applications.

One aspect of the book's organization deserves special note. When creating a digital collection, the first step is to design a metadata scheme or application profile. Yet *Metadata for Digital Collections* covers this topic in the second-to-last chapter rather than in the second chapter. Experience has shown that, in order to design a well-developed and effective metadata scheme, the designer needs a solid foundational knowledge of resource description and controlled vocabulary issues, the meaning and application of the standard scheme (such as Dublin Core, MODS, or VRA) selected as the basis for the local scheme, and some familiarity with issues of interoperability, harvesting, and mapping for metadata shareability and long-term usability.

Metadata for Digital Collections provides a practice-oriented approach to learning about and applying metadata based on the author's many years of practical experience and of teaching both students and working professionals. Readers will come away with a solid working knowledge of metadata for digital resources that they can put to use in their jobs or take with them into today's professional marketplace.

Acknowledgments

I gratefully acknowledge the University of Wisconsin–Milwaukee School of Information Studies and Dean Johannes Britz for their support of my work on this book. I would like to extend special thanks to David Bloom for his thorough and academically skilled assistance with the preparation of the text. I am highly grateful to Debbie Cardinal and Krystyna Matusiak for being excellent colleagues from whom I have learned a great deal about digital collections metadata in practice over many years prior to undertaking this writing. I want to acknowledge the UWM Libraries and Janet Padway for their support over many years of conference and workshop attendance, travel, and other activities that have contributed invaluably to my background for this work. Thanks also to my editor at Neal-Schuman, Sandy Wood, who has patiently and expertly helped shepherd this text into existence. I finally want to thank my partner Shawn for his tremendous patience and forbearance during the past year as I worked on this book.

Introduction to Metadata for Digital Collections

Metadata is a broad generic term that encompasses a wide variety of specific types of information that is either created or captured about information resources. Various kinds of metadata are used today in a wide variety of contexts, including government, research, education, health care, law, business, and e-commerce. This book focuses on one particular type of metadata, usually called descriptive metadata, and on its application in one particular type of context—namely, online collections of digital objects, such as digital images, texts, sound files, and video files, within cultural heritage institutions such as libraries, archives, historical societies, and museums.

1.1. What Is Metadata?

Metadata is a term used to refer to a particular kind of data or information. It is data or information that is *about* other data or information resources, such as a book, an audio file, a scientific data set, or a digital image. Metadata is data or information that enables people to perform certain *functions* in relation to the information resources that the metadata is about. Metadata is information that is distinct from the resource which it is about, even when the metadata is embedded within a digital resource. The term *metadata* itself is a combination of the Greek prefix *meta* and the Latin word *data*.

- **Meta**: *about, after, higher, relating to* or *based on; on an abstraction level higher than the current*, that which is *about* something else
- **Data**: bits of information processable by computers, but may also refer to any kind of information object or resource composed of data, even non-digital data, such as print or film
- **Metadata**: data about data, or information about information

Many knowledgeable writers have composed concise definitions of the general concept of metadata. Here are some examples.

- "Metadata is structured information that describes, explains, locates, or otherwise makes it easier to retrieve, use, or manage an information resource. Metadata is often called data about data or information about information" (NISO, 2004).

- "Metadata is data that describes the content, format, or attributes of a data record or information resource. It can be used to describe highly structured resources or unstructured information such as text documents. Metadata can be applied to description of: electronic resources; digital data (including digital images); and to printed documents such as books, journals and reports. Metadata can be embedded within the information resources (as is often the case with web resources) or it can be held separately in a database" (Haynes, 2004: 8).

- "In essence, metadata is the extra baggage associated with any resource that enables a real or potential user to find that resource; to decide whether or not it is of value to them; to discover where, when, and by whom it was created, as well as for what purpose; to know what tools will be needed to manipulate the resource; to determine whether or not they will actually be allowed to access to the resource itself and how much this will cost them. Metadata is, in short, a means by which largely meaningless data may be transformed into information, interpretable and re-usable by those other than the creator of the data resource" (Miller, 2004: 4; as cited in Cwiok, 2005: 104–105).

- "...the sum total of what one can say about any information object at any level of aggregation" (Gilliland, 2008: 2).

D. Grant Campbell explains that "metadata is difficult to define as an activity for two primary reasons. First, unlike library cataloging, metadata development involves a large number of varied stakeholders.... Second, metadata evolved from several different communities, each with its own disciplinary background and objectives" (2005: 59). According to Campbell, these include but are not limited to libraries, database design, records management, and computer science and programming.

A good way to demystify the meaning of *metadata*, for those who are completely new to the concept, is to look at some concrete examples. All of us have encountered metadata in one form or another many times in our lives, although most of us have never called it by that name. In its broadest sense, metadata can include the information on the title page and other preliminary pages of a book, giving information *about* the book, such as title, author, publisher, date, and so forth. Product information printed on a packaged grocery item that lists its contents could be considered metadata; it is data or information *about* the food contained in the package.

To take another example, Microsoft Word automatically generates some metadata about a document at the time of creation, often including its author and sometimes its title, which can be further edited. Table 1.1 gives an example of some of the kinds of metadata that may be included in a Word 2007 document. Author, Title, Subject, and Keywords are metadata elements, fields, or properties, and the information in the boxes is the content or value of each element. In this example, the data or information object is the Word document. The information shown in Table 1.1 is data *about* that document, namely, *meta*data.

Table 1.1. Metadata in a Microsoft Word Document	
Document Properties	
Author:	**Title:**
Steven J. Miller	The One-To-One Principle
Subject:	**Keywords:**
Metadata	metadata, Dublin Core, one-to-one principle

The textual information that appears in Apple iTunes and on the iPod consists of nothing but pure metadata: data *about* each song or piece of music, as illustrated in Table 1.2. This information is separate from the music itself, but it enables a user to find songs by several different properties, such as name, album, and composer; to identify information about each song; to navigate through the user's collection of digital music; and to pull together sets of songs by the same performer, in the same genre, published in the same year, and so on. These are all classic functions of metadata. The key thing about metadata is what it is intended to do. People create metadata to help themselves, their family, friends, customers, or users to find, identify, sort, gather, and navigate collections of music, texts, images, and other resources, among various other functions.

Digital cameras, to take another example, automatically generate various pieces of technical information *about* digital images they've created. These pieces of information may include filename, date created, resolution, file size, make and model of the camera, exposure time, and

Table 1.2. Metadata for an Album of Songs in iTunes

Name	Album	Composer	Artist	Genre	Year	Track #	Time
Changing Opinion	Songs from Liquid Days	Glass, Philip, 1937–	Michael Riesman & Philip Glass Ensemble	Classical	1986	1 of 6	9:56
Lightening	Songs from Liquid Days	Glass, Philip, 1937–	Janice Pendarvis, Michael Riesman, & Philip Glass Ensemble	Classical	1986	2 of 6	6:42
Freezing	Songs from Liquid Days	Glass, Philip, 1937–	Kronos Quartet	Classical	1986	3 of 6	3:16
Liquid Days (Part I)	Songs from Liquid Days	Glass, Philip, 1937–	Michael Riesman, Philip Glass Ensemble & The Roches	Classical	1986	4 of 6	4:46
Open the Kingdom (Liquid Days, Part II)	Songs from Liquid Days	Glass, Philip, 1937–	Douglas Perry, Michael Riesman, & Philip Glass Ensemble	Classical	1986	5 of 6	6:59
Forgetting	Songs from Liquid Days	Glass, Philip, 1937–	Kronos Quartet, Linda Ronstadt, Michael Riesman, Philip Glass Ensemble, & The Roches	Classical	1986	6 of 6	8:10

Table 1.3. Technical Metadata about a Digital Photograph

Properties - Metadata	
Filename	IMG_8-31-2010.jpg
Image Format	image/jpeg
Date Created	8/31/2010 3:25 PM
Date Modified	9/02/2010 10:11 AM
Color Mode	RGB
Resolution	1900.00
File Size	6.2 MB
Width	4416
Height	1969

so on. This kind of information is commonly called *technical metadata*. In the example in Table 1.3, the information resource is the digital photograph, and the information in the table is data *about* that photograph, called *meta*data.

The information in a library catalog is a well-known kind of metadata: data or information *about* a book, video, map, or the like that stands as a concise, humanly constructed surrogate for the actual information resource. It allows users to find, identify, select, and obtain these resources without having to examine every physical item residing in a library or every digital resource licensed by a library. Figure 1.1 shows part of an online library catalog record for a book. In this context, the data or information object is the book, and the *meta*data is the data in the catalog record *about* the book.

Finally, in an example very similar to that of a library catalog record, Figure 1.2 shows a digital image of women suffragists picketing in front of the White House in 1917, and Table 1.4 gives the metadata *about* that image from one of the Library of Congress's American Memory collections.

As diverse as these examples are, they have several things in common. First, they all consist of a set of **properties** (elements or fields) and a set of **values** for each property. In most of the examples, the properties are displayed to the left of each value. The properties have been invented or selected by human beings because they have been judged to be useful for people to perform some kind of function in relation to the resource. Functions might include finding resources in a database or catalog based on the value of a single property, such as Title or Date, or gathering together many resources that share the same value for a given property, such as all books by the same author, all songs by the same performer or composer, all images about the same subject or depicting the same location or time period, or all items in the same file format. Metadata allows

Figure 1.1. Library Catalog Record: Metadata about a Book

LC Control No.: 2008015176
LCCN Permalink: http://lccn.loc.gov/2008015176
Type of Material: Book (Print, Microform, Electronic, etc.)
Personal Name: Zeng, Marcia Lei, 1956-
Main Title: Metadata / Marcia Lei Zeng and Jian Qin.
Published/Created: New York : Neal-Schuman Publishers, c2008.
Related Names: Qin, Jian, 1956-
Description: xvii, 365 p. : ill. ; 23 cm.
ISBN: 9781555706357 (pbk. : alk. paper)
1555706355 (pbk. : alk. paper)
Contents: Introduction -- Current standards -- Schemas : structure and semantics -- Schemas : syntax -- Metadata records -- Metadata services -- Metadata quality measurement and improvement.
Notes: Includes bibliographical references (p. 327-353) and index.
Subjects: Metadata.
LC Classification: Z666.7 .Z46 2008
Dewey Class No.: 025.3 22

Source: Library of Congress Online Catalog: http://catalog.loc.gov/.

Figure 1.2. Digital Image in an Online Digital Collection

Source: Library of Congress, Prints and Photographs Division, LC-USZ62-31799.

people to perform various other kinds of functions as well, including managing, structuring, preserving, authenticating, and exchanging those resources. The collection of properties (elements or fields) used in any particular context are often called a metadata scheme or element set.

Second, the metadata stands *apart from* the information resource it is about. It is something extra, in addition to, and logically separate from the data or information it is about. This is obviously true when the metadata resides in a database or catalog record completely separate from the information resource itself, but it is also true when the metadata is embedded within the information resource itself, as in the examples of the Word document and the digital photograph file.

Third, in each example the metadata properties and values for each information resource are grouped together in what is traditionally called a **record**, each record representing selected attributes or properties about one information resource. The metadata record as a whole is about the information resource it describes or represents. Another way to look at metadata is to take each property and value pair by itself as making up a **statement** about the information resource. For example, the metadata in Table 1.4 includes the implied statements:

- Digital image cph3a32338 **has title** *The first picket line - College day in the picket line.*
- Digital image cph3a32338 **has subject** *Suffragists--1910-1920.*

Table 1.4. Metadata about the Digital Image

The first picket line - College day in the picket line.

CREATED/PUBLISHED
1917 Feb.

SUMMARY
Women suffragists picketing in front of the White house.
SUBJECTS
White House (Washington, D.C.)--1900-1920.
Demonstrations--Washington (D.C.)--1910-1920.
Suffragists--1910-1920.
Women's suffrage--Washington (D.C.)--1910-1920.
Photographic prints--1910-1920.

MEDIUM
1 photographic print.

CALL NUMBER
Item in National Woman's Party Collection

REPRODUCTION NUMBER
LC-USZ62-31799 DLC (b&w film copy neg.)

REPOSITORY
Library of Congress Manuscript Division Washington, D.C. 20540 USA

DIGITAL ID
(b&w film copy neg.) cph 3a32338

Source: Library of Congress, Prints and Photographs Division, American Memory, "By Popular Demand: 'Votes for Women' Suffrage Pictures": http://memory.loc.gov/ammem/vfwhtml/vfwhome.html.

In this view, metadata is a set of statements made about information resources. Each statement is made up of a property-value pair consisting of one property and one value. This view is compatible with the Linked Data and Semantic Web approach to metadata, currently growing in importance, and discussed in Chapter 11 of this book. Traditionally, catalogers and metadata specialists have viewed the *record* as the basic unit of metadata, but in this *semantic* view, the basic unit of metadata is a *statement* (Sutton, 2007: slide 9; Zeng and Qin, 2008: 152).

Karen Coyle defines metadata as follows:

- **Constructed**: Metadata is not found in nature. It is entirely an invention; it is an artificiality.

- **Constructive**: Metadata is constructed for some purpose, some activity, to solve some problem. . . .

- **Actionable**: The point of metadata is to be useful in some way. This means that it is important that one can act on the metadata in a way that satisfies some needs. (Coyle, 2010: 6)

Coyle uses the examples of latitude and longitude and subway maps to illustrate her definition. Both are artificial human constructions that help human beings more efficiently accomplish certain tasks such as precisely referencing a specific point on the earth or efficiently identifying a needed subway line and connections (Coyle, 2010). Coyle's approach makes clear some important points about metadata. It is invented by human beings in particular contexts for particular types of resources and users to accomplish particular functions. For example, the Dublin Core Metadata Element Set consists of 15 simple elements or properties, such as *Title*, *Creator*, *Subject*, *Date*, *Type*, and *Format*. These elements were invented by a group of people who met and agreed on a simple core set of properties for describing web resources for the purpose of improving resource discovery on the web.

1.2. What Is a Digital Collection?

A **digital collection**, as the term is used in this book, is a collection of digital resources, along with metadata about those resources, made available online through an interface that allows users to search and/or browse the contents of that collection. A digital collection is often explicitly labeled as a *collection* and is often centered around a particular topic, a resource type, or some other common characteristic. Especially common resource types include digital still images, digital texts, digital audio files, and digital moving image files. Most frequently, these resources are digitized versions of rare or unique resources that would otherwise be unknown outside of the local institution and inaccessible without physically visiting the institution. They may include born-digital resources—that is, resources originally created in digital format—but most frequently they are composed of digitized versions of resources that were originally in physical (analog) form.

Some Common Types of Digital Collection Content

Subject Matter
- *Topical*: resources about a similar subject, group of people, etc.
- *Geographical*: resources about or created in a particular country, state, region, or city
- *Chronological*: resources about a particular time period or historical event
- *Creator*: resources created by a particular author, photographer, artist, or composer

Resource Types, Genres, and Formats
- *Text*
  - Books and pamphlets (often rare or locally published)
  - Letters, diaries, personal papers
  - Yearbooks
  - Newspapers and newspaper articles (often rare or locally published)
  - Journal articles (often from locally published journals)
- *Still Image*
  - Photographs
  - Slides
  - Maps
    Depicting:
    - People, places, things, events
    - Museum objects such as paintings, sculptures, clothing, furniture, natural objects
    - Architectural works
- *Music*
  - Scores, song sheets, broadsides
- *Sound*
  - Music: studio or live performance
  - Spoken word: poetry, drama, literary readings
  - Oral history interviews
  - Radio broadcasts
- *Moving Image*
  - Films (often locally produced)
  - Oral history interviews
  - News clips

Figures 1.3 through 1.5 illustrate a small random sampling of the wide diversity of digital collections consisting of various resource types, covering various subject matter. While many, perhaps most, individual digital collections consist of a single resource type, the American Variety Stage collection (Figure 1.3) is an example of a digital collection that includes digitized texts, still images, moving images, and sound files.

Digital collections may be created by a single institution or by a consortium of institutions. Consortia or collaboratives are usually composed of member institutions sharing some common characteristics, such as being located in the same state or geographic region; dealing with resources in a common subject area such as educational or scientific resources; or being of the same institution type, such as a consortium of large research libraries.

Digital collections can also consist of a large repository of many smaller, diverse collections. For example, all of the individual digital collections of a particular university or museum may be made cross-searchable and

---

Figure 1.3. American Variety Stage: Vaudeville and Popular Entertainment, 1870–1920

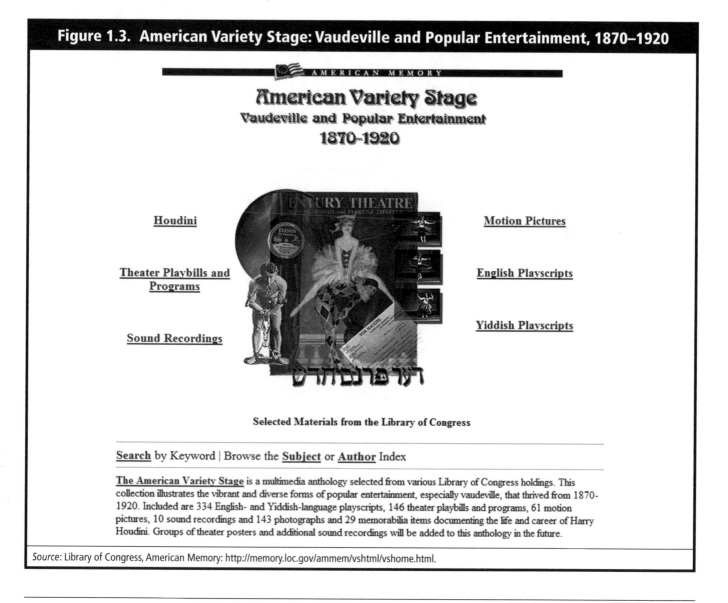

Source: Library of Congress, American Memory: http://memory.loc.gov/ammem/vshtml/vshome.html.

Figure 1.4. Southern Oral History Program Interview Database

Southern Oral History Program | INTERVIEW DATABASE

Home | About this Database | About the Southern Oral History Program

The Southern Oral History Program Interview Database provides detailed information for each oral history interview in the Southern Historical Collection conducted under the auspices of the Southern Oral History Program. The oral histories described here are available in the fourth floor search room at The Louis Round Wilson Special Collections Library at the University of North Carolina at Chapel Hill. Digital transcripts and audio for some interviews are available through this database. For more information about the Southern Oral History Program Collection (#4007) at the Southern Historical Collection, please see the SOHP finding aid.

KEYWORD SEARCH:

[   ] Across all fields ▼ Search

*Abstracts and transcripts are not available for every interview.
Advanced Search

BROWSE BY:

Interviewee ▼ Browse

Southern Oral History Program | Southern Historical Collection | SOHP Finding Aid

UNC UNIVERSITY LIBRARY

Source: University of North Carolina at Chapel Hill Libraries: http://www.lib.unc.edu/dc/sohp/.

Figure 1.5. Smithsonian American Art Museum George Catlin Indian Paintings

UNIVERSITY of VIRGINIA LIBRARY

Digital Collections
UVa Library Home | Digital Collections | Texts | Images | Finding Aids | Feedback | Questions | VIRGO

Smithsonian American Art Museum George Catlin Indian Paintings   Advanced Search Help

Over 400 portraits of Native Americans and cultural documentation landscapes by American artist George Catlin (1796-1872) from his travels with William Clark and on his own through the western frontier in the early 1830s. Of particular note is the authoritative identification of the tribal affiliations.

Browse the Images by Thumbnail

Browse the Images by Title:

- A'h-sha-la-cóots-ah, Mole in the Forehead, Chief of the Republican Pawnee. (1832)
- A'h-tee-wát-o-mee, a Woman. (1830)
- Ah'-kay-ee-pix-en, Woman Who Strikes Many. (1832)
- Ah'sho-cole, Rotten Foot, a Noted Warrior. (1834)
- Ah-móu-a, The Whale, One of Kee-o-kúk's Principal Braves. (1835)
- Ah-sháw-wah-róoks-te, Medicine Horse, a Grand Pawnee Brave. (1832)
- Ah-tón-we-tuck, Cock Turkey, Repeating his Prayer. (1830)
- Ah-yaw-ne-tah-cár-ron, a Warrior. (1831)
- Aih-no-wa, The Fire, a Fox Medicine Man. (1835)
- An-nó-je-nahge, He Who Stands on Both Sides, a Distinguished Ball Player. (1835)

Search This Collection

Smithsonian American Art Museum Catlin Indian Paintings Collection

[   ]

Present results as:
☑ Images
☑ Titles

Search

Source: Smithsonian American Art Museum George Catlin Indian Paintings, Special Collections, University of Virginia Library: http://www.lib.virginia.edu/digital/collections/image/catlin_smithsonian.html.

thus treated in effect as one large digital collection for this particular function. Many consortia and collaboratives harvest and aggregate diverse sets of metadata contributed by their member institutions rather than creating collections and metadata themselves. The variations are many, but the basic concept is the same.

The terms *digital collection*, *digital library*, *digital archive*, and *digital repository* are quite often used synonymously in current literature and practice. Sometimes, however, these terms carry different nuances or even different meanings. The term **digital library** is sometimes used to mean an online extension of a physical library, presenting users with a wide variety of digital resources and services above and beyond only the types of digital collections covered in this book. The term **digital archive** may refer specifically to an online repository or collection of archival resources, or the term *archive* may simply refer to a repository of any kind of resources that are being preserved and made accessible online. The term **digital repository** sometimes implies a centralized place where various individuals or institutions deposit their resources or metadata about their resources, or where an organization stores metadata harvested from various sources. At other times all of these terms are used to refer to digital collections of the type covered in this book.

The term **institutional repository**, on the other hand, almost always refers to something more specific—namely, an online space for collecting, preserving, and making accessible the intellectual and research output, in digital form, of a specific institution or group of related institutions. These are most frequently universities and other academic and research institutions. These repositories also require metadata, but institutional repositories per se are outside of the scope of this book. Nonetheless, most of the principles and practices covered in this book can be easily translated to the content of digital institutional repositories.

This book focuses on digital collections created by what are commonly called **cultural heritage** or **cultural memory** institutions, chief among these being libraries, archives, historical societies, and museums. The term *cultural heritage* is a convenient umbrella term for grouping together types of institutions concerned with collecting, preserving, and making available various kinds of resources of current and historical value. *Cultural* in this sense is not restricted to so-called high culture, art, scholarly research, and the like, but also includes resources of everyday life, folk culture, and popular culture.

1.3. What Does Metadata Do?

Descriptive metadata is important because it provides *intellectual access* to the contents of a digital collection. Without metadata, the collection would be virtually useless. Users would have no way to find and identify the digital objects within the collection. This is especially true for collections of digital images, sound files, and video files that are not made up of text that can be made searchable as text. Descriptive metadata can be seen as serving the two overarching functions of *identification* and *retrieval.* It allows users to identify the content, context, and meaning of digital resources, both individually and in relation to one another, and it allows users to retrieve individual resources and sets of related resources based on any number of shared characteristics. Metadata supports both the *searching* and *browsing* methods of information retrieval. With *search*, the user thinks up terms to enter into a search engine and retrieves results that happen to match his or her terms. With *browse*, the user is presented with terms used in the metadata, from which he or she selects.

Without the metadata, the user would need to examine every information object individually. Depending on the specific type of object, the user may have no idea about its subject content or what is depicted in an image, when and by whom it was created, and the like. Without even such a basic metadata element as *Title*, there would be no way to browse alphabetically through an index or list of resources in the collection. Metadata provides the basis for users to be able to interact with the collection's content, to browse through meaningful groupings such as topical categories, geographic areas, and time periods. Metadata provides the basis for searching the collection, by uncontrolled keyword, but also by restricting keyword searches to specific metadata fields, such as title, author, or subject, and by narrowing search results by aspects such as date range, resource type, and genre. Chapters 2–4 will go into more detail on this topic, which is in many respects the central point of this entire book.

Figure 1.6 is a schematic representation of one kind of functionality that can be provided for users of a digital collection based on the underlying metadata. Among other things, the metadata provides the ability for users to narrow their search results by selecting specific values from the categories displayed on the left side of the screen. Each of these category names, such as *Resource Type*, *Country*, *Decade*, and *Language*, is a metadata element, and the clickable choices under each of them are controlled values entered into those elements in the underlying metadata records. Each of these categories may be considered a *facet* of the content of the collection, and this method of information retrieval is called *faceted navigation*, *faceted browsing*, or *faceted search*. This method of metadata-driven navigation has been common in e-commerce websites for many years, and it is gradually becoming more common in cultural heritage websites, including some online library catalogs. A good example of faceted navigation in practice, as of this writing, is in the University of North Texas Digital Library (http://digital.library.unt.edu/help/guide/facets/).

1.4. Types of Metadata

Creators and managers of digital resources usually create different types of metadata to accomplish different kinds of functions. The functions in all of the examples in this chapter up to this point fall into the category of what is usually called *descriptive metadata*, except for Table 1.3, which falls into the category of *technical metadata*. Descriptive metadata serves the functions of providing users with intellectual access to digital

Figure1.6. Functionality: Faceted Navigation

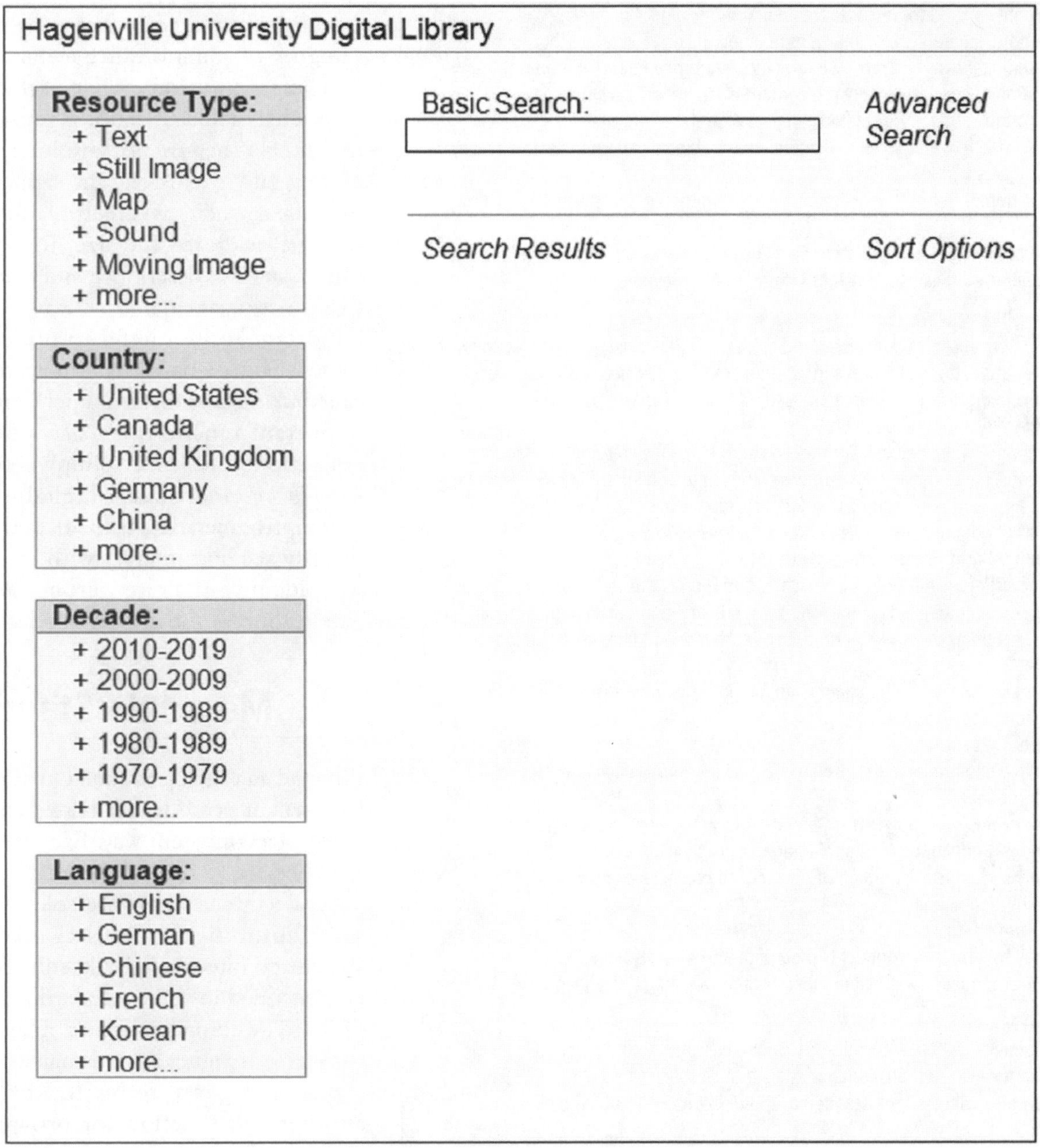

Hagenville University Digital Library

Resource Type:
+ Text
+ Still Image
+ Map
+ Sound
+ Moving Image
+ more...

Country:
+ United States
+ Canada
+ United Kingdom
+ Germany
+ China
+ more...

Decade:
+ 2010-2019
+ 2000-2009
+ 1990-1989
+ 1980-1989
+ 1970-1979
+ more...

Language:
+ English
+ German
+ Chinese
+ French
+ Korean
+ more...

Basic Search:

Advanced Search

Search Results

Sort Options

resources by searching and browsing. Although this book deals almost exclusively with descriptive metadata, it is important to be aware of other types of metadata that perform other types of functions. For example, some kinds of metadata serve such functions as management, administration, and preservation of digital resources, as well as internal structuring of complex digital objects. The literature on cultural heritage metadata most frequently divides metadata into three broad categories: *administrative*, *structural*, and *descriptive* metadata. Some experts

Types of Metadata

Descriptive Metadata

- Data elements used to describe, catalog, or index digital resources
  - The same general type of information found in library catalogs, but following different standards (library bibliographic data is one kind of metadata)
- Information needed to identify the content of an image, text, map, etc.
  - For example: title, date created, subject, digital file format
- Terms needed for retrieval of individual digital objects and sets of related digital objects within a database
  - For example: creator names, resource types, geographical place names, time periods
  - Must be entered in a consistent form, usually taken from a controlled vocabulary, to ensure consistent information retrieval

Administrative Metadata

- Data elements used to administer and manage digital objects and collections
  - For example: the name of the institution creating the digital objects, date digitized, digitization equipment used, filename of master digital file, display file, and thumbnail file
  - Information lifecycle data, such as dates of digital file creation, subsequent revisions, time of review for retention, archiving, or disposal, names creators and revisers of the resource, and authorization levels for a given function
- Subtypes of administrative metadata include the following:
  - **Technical and preservation metadata**
    - Two different subtypes, but much information is the same for each
    - Information needed for the long-term preservation of the digital object, migration to other digital formats as software and hardware change over time
    - For example: type of scanner used, original scanning resolution, image editing specifications
  - **Rights metadata**
    - Information on ownership, copyright, restrictions on use and reproduction
    - For example, a copyright statement, information on restrictions on use and reproduction of a digital image, restrictions on access if limited to only certain users, method of payment to purchase or download a full-resolution image
  - **Use metadata**
    - May be separate from rights metadata, but may also overlap with it
    - For example: data about number of times an image has been viewed

Structural Metadata

- Data elements used to internally structure a complex digital object or provide structure for the relationships among a set of closely related digital objects
- For example: a single book scanned as multiple image files (complex digital object)
  - Metadata needed to label each image, to relate them to each other as part of the same complex digital object, to structure them sequentially to allow users to navigate through them
  - Example: The bestiary: a book of beasts (University of Wisconsin): http://digicoll.library.wisc.edu/cgi-bin/HistSciTech/HistSciTech-idx?type=header&id=HistSciTech.Bestiary
  - Allows the user to jump to different parts of the book from the selected list, to enter a page number and go to that page, or to proceed page by page, backward and forward, and so on
- Multiple views of the same object, such as front, back, and side views of the same sculpture, captured in separate digital image files

include *technical*, *preservation*, *rights*, and *use* metadata as categories on the same level as these three, while others more frequently subsume these under the umbrella category of administrative metadata.

These distinctions, while useful, can be somewhat artificial, and it is important to realize that they are not absolutely distinct or mutually exclusive. The same piece of metadata, such as creator, digital file format, or digital file size, for example, can serve both descriptive and administrative functions at the same time. It is also important to be careful to not interpret these labels too narrowly. For example, so-called *descriptive* metadata performs many important functions for users of digital collections beyond simply passively *describing* individual digital objects. Descriptive metadata is the data that users directly see and interact with in order to find, identify, interpret, group, and navigate resources and collections.

1.5. Metadata Standards

If metadata is going to function as intended for users, it needs to be created and structured in a consistent way. Even in a purely *closed-system*, local database (that is, a single database intended for use solely within a single institution), metadata needs to be structured into a standardized set of fields and encoded in some standardized way in order to be computer processable. In order for element values such as names, subject terms, and genre terms to link to one another and function for browsing and search limits, the values of those elements need to be entered in a consistent, standardized format, often using a predefined set of acceptable terms called a *controlled vocabulary*. If metadata is to be shared beyond a single collection or database within the same institution, cross-searched among diverse collections or institutions, exposed for harvesting and aggregating by consortial or national digital resource repositories, or made viable for migration into future systems and services, it is all the more necessary that it follow more widely established community standards.

Standards in the broadest sense can range from purely local, informally established guidelines in a single institution, or even for a single digital collection, at the one extreme, to formally established, widely shared national and international standards, at the other extreme, with many gradations in between. In this book, the term *standards* is understood to include this wide range of formality, but the term will more often refer to those relatively more formal, widely shared standards issued by formal standards agencies and other organizations such as The International Organization for Standardization (ISO), the American National Standards Institute (ANSI), the Dublin Core Metadata Initiative (DCMI), the Library of Congress (LC), the Getty Research Institute, the World Wide Web Consortium (W3C), and the like. This latter use of the term *standards* is the most common in the wider professional metadata community. In actual practice, most digital collection implementations use a combination of formal national/ international and informal local standards and specifications, as will become clearer throughout the course of this book.

Various cultural heritage metadata communities have developed a large, sometimes confusing array of formally established standards. Almost every one of them has an acronym that is commonly used for easier reference to the standard. It can be very helpful to categorize these standards into groups to better make sense of them and understand how different kinds of standards serve different purposes for digital collections. A fourfold typology has been used in one form or another in a number of publications on the topic, distinguishing metadata (1) structure, (2) content, (3) value, and (4) encoding/exchange standards (Gilliland, 2008; Zeng and Qin, 2008; Elings and Waibel, 2007; RLG, 2005; Boughida, 2005). The exact terminology varies somewhat among these sources, but the four categories are primarily the same. This typology is equally useful for purely local metadata scheme design, because all four types of specifications are needed even when designing the metadata scheme for a single digital collection not intended to be shared outside of the local system. Each of these types of standards will be introduced and illustrated throughout this book.

Typology of Metadata Standards

1. Data Structure Standards

- These are standardized sets of metadata elements such as *Title, Name, Identifier, Technique, Coverage, Location,* and *Style/Period*, apart from any input guidelines or encoding format.
- Structure standards are commonly called metadata *schemes, schemas,* or *element sets*.
- In databases, elements are called *fields*. In other contexts, elements are called *tags*. In a Linked Data and Semantic Web context, elements are called *properties*.
- Examples include the Dublin Core Metadata Element Set (DCMES or DC), the Metadata Object Description Schema (MODS) elements, and the Visual Resources Association Core Categories (VRA).

2. Data Content Standards

- Content standards are rules or usage guidelines for how to input data into the elements.
- For example, such guidelines might instruct metadata creators to omit initial articles in a title, capitalize only proper names in a title, use a particular set of abbreviations for certain common terms, prefer a publication date over a copyright date, enter personal names with surname first, and so forth.
- Examples include the core content of *Cataloging Cultural Objects* (CCO); the *Anglo-American Cataloguing Rules, Second Edition* (AACR2); *Describing Archives: A Content Standard* (DACS); and much of the content found in less formal consortial metadata guideline documents such as the Cooperative Digitization Program (CDP) "Dublin Core Metadata Best Practices."

3. Data Value Standards

- Value standards are lists of established, standardized terms and codes, such as lists of terms for resource types or genres, lists of codes for languages, authority files of names for persons, thesauri and subject heading lists for topical subject terms, geographic names, and the like.
- Examples include the Library of Congress *Thesaurus for Graphic Materials* (LCTGM or TGM); the Getty *Art and Architecture Thesaurus* (AAT), *Thesaurus of Geographic Names* (TGN), and *Union List of Artist Names* (ULAN); the *Library of Congress Subject Headings* (LCSH); the LC/NACO *Name Authority File* (LCNAF or NAF); and the ISO 639-2 "Codes for the Representation of Names of Languages."

4. Data Format, Technical Interchange, or Encoding Standards

- Technical specifications for encoding metadata for machine-readability, computer processing, and exchange among systems.
- The most common data encoding and interchange format in the current metadata environment is Extensible Markup Language (XML) in general, which must be realized in specific XML languages, defined by XML schemas or document type definitions (DTDs), such as MODS-XML or VRA-XML.

1.6. Creating a Digital Collection

Although this book focuses on understanding, creating, and designing *metadata* for digital collections, it is important to understand that metadata is only one part of a much bigger picture. Designing a metadata scheme and creating metadata for individual digital objects is one component of a larger process of bringing a digital collection to life and making it available to the public. Michael Chopey, in his article "Planning and Implementing a Metadata-Driven Digital Repository" (2005), gives an excellent overview of the steps and functions that need to go into this larger process and the types of people and expertise required. One noteworthy aspect of this article is how much time is devoted to planning before the actual work begins on digitizing and cataloging the resources. Chopey identifies the following areas of functional expertise needed to plan and implement a repository managed and organized with metadata: curatorial, digital object formatting, web design and programming, database and retrieval system design, cataloging and indexing, and administrative/managerial (Chopey, 2005: 267). The following is an adaptation of his list:

- Project planning, management, and administration
- Digital collection development (selection and compiling of the resources to be digitized)
- Digitization, formatting, and storage of the digital objects
- Database and retrieval system design
- Web-based user interface design and programming
- Metadata design and creation (resource description/cataloging/indexing)

Depending of the type and size of institution, and of the individual project, one or more persons or teams may be responsible for each of these functions. In smaller and medium-sized institutions, a single person may be primarily responsible for most or even all of them. Work may be done within different units or within a single digitization or digital collection unit within an institution. Such a unit may consist of one or more staff members, and perhaps also student workers, interns, and/or volunteers. In some libraries, archives, museums, and other types of institutions, especially larger ones, these functions are spread out among various staff with specialized expertise. In many of these, the metadata design and indexing functions are performed by professional catalogers or metadata librarians, who may reside in the Technical Services or equivalent division of the library. Large numbers of institutions use some kind of digital collection management software or digital asset management system, such as CONTENTdm, Insight + LUNA, Greenstone, or PastPerfect, that will integrate many of these components and functions into a single system.

Project planning, management, and administration. Often an individual digital collection is created as part of a distinct project with its own personnel, budget, and timeline for digitization, metadata creation, and online user interface development. This requires someone to coordinate the project and exercise good project-planning skills. The importance of the project planning and management component of the greater whole cannot be overestimated, and it runs through all of the other components and functions.

Digital collection development. Typically, a librarian, archivist, museum curator, subject expert, or institution-wide committee made up of representatives from various units decides on a group of resources to be digitized and made available as an online collection. Subject specialists, researchers, faculty, donors, or resource collectors external to the institution might have a hand in selecting the resources to be digitized. Digital collections can include *born-digital* resources, *digitized* versions of analog resources, or a combination of both. This book focuses on digitized versions of analog/physical resources. Resources to be digitized may come from an archive, special collection, external donor, subject expert, department on a university campus, and other such sources.

There is an almost limitless number of possible scenarios in which an institution decides to create a digital collection. An organization or a donor may own an existing collection of rare or one-of-a-kind photographs, slides, maps, texts, or sound or video recordings that the institution wants to make widely accessible across the Internet. Preservation of decaying physical materials is another common motivation for digitization. Developers frequently organize individual digital collections around a common unifying theme, a particular subject area, a specific artist or photographer, and so on. An organization might decide to digitize the entire contents of a physical collection to make an online collection that parallels that original physical collection. Alternatively, it might select a subset of a physical collection, or it might create an entirely new collection of digital resources that has no physical counterpart.

Digitization, formatting, and storage of the digital objects. Digitization requires investment in equipment, software, time, and expertise. Specific types of scanning and other digitization hardware and software need to be purchased and configured for different types and sizes of objects such as bound books and journals, flat sheets, photographs, slides, small and large maps and charts, sound recordings in vinyl and cassette formats, or moving images in film reel and videocassette formats, any of which might be fragile materials that require special handling. Each type of material has its own challenges. Staff need to be trained in how to use the digitization equipment. The digital objects resulting from the scanning or other digitization processes often need further processing and formatting in order to make them into good-quality digital objects. For example, many institutions will use software such as Adobe Photoshop to improve the quality of digital images. Project managers need to make decisions about digital file formats, file storage, preservation, and so on. Quite often, the *master* files for digital images are of a much higher resolution and file size than the *access* file versions to be displayed on the website for the collection. The project may also create smaller thumbnail versions of each image. The project manager needs to store and keep track of each of these versions. He or she will also need to be concerned with storing the digital files, including master copies, in a safe location or in more than one location, planning for long-term preservation of the digital files, and capturing, creating, and storing administrative and technical metadata associated with each object. The project manager will usually create and maintain administrative, technical, and preservation metadata as a part of these activities.

Descriptive metadata design and creation. After the resources have been selected and digitized, they need to be cataloged, organized, and made accessible online. This requires some kind of database software capable of storing and associating the digital files with the metadata about them, and some kind of web interface software capable of making the digital collection searchable, browsable, and navigable by end users. The design of the metadata scheme, the database, and the user interface should ideally all go hand-in-hand with each other. *Metadata scheme design*, which entails the selection of an element set and specifications made about each element, can be distinguished from *metadata creation*, which entails the cataloging or indexing of each individual digital object based on that metadata scheme. Metadata creation is often the single most time-consuming piece of the digital collection creation process. It may take one-half to two-thirds of the time of the entire project, with implications for project planning, staffing, training, timelines, workstations, and the like. It often requires training of staff and review of their work. Chapter 10 goes into some detail on the components of designing and documenting different metadata schemes for a specific digital collection project or a single scheme for all of an institution's collections and projects. Chapters 2, 3, and 4 give an overview of metadata creation, also called resource description, and also provide a foundation for knowledgeable metadata scheme and application profile design. Chapters 3, 4, 7, and 8 deal with creating metadata according to four widely used standardized element sets. Although logically metadata design and documentation precede metadata creation, an understanding of resource description and standardized element sets is critical for good metadata scheme design. For that reason, this content is covered in the order it is in this book.

Database and retrieval system design; web-based user interface design and programming. Digital collection projects may also require some amount of programming, database design, web design, and information architecture knowledge. Some larger institutions have local programmers who can do original database and interface design in-house. Large numbers of medium-sized to smaller organizations, however, need to rely on other solutions. They may create their metadata in a program such as Microsoft Access and tie it to a searchable web interface using an application such as Adobe ColdFusion. Many organizations today, however, use so-called out-of-the-box, turnkey, or plug-and-play software solutions, such as OCLC's CONTENTdm digital collection management software. CONTENTdm will be referenced many times in this book because it is probably the most widely used multipurpose software for digital collections today, at least within the United States. It provides for digital text and image storage, metadata creation, and web interface functionality, all in one ready-to-go package that does not require programming knowledge. That is its great strength, which is counterbalanced by the relative weaknesses of a lower level of flexibility and customization. Other common digital collection software products include Insight + LUNA and Greenstone digital library software. Greenstone is free, open-source software. Some integrated library system vendors have also added digital collection management systems to their suites of products. Even when using such software, there is still often a need for some amount of design of the architecture of the web-based user interface, including the main HTML page for the collection; an *About* page; other hard-coded HTML pages; the graphical look and feel of the site; the search, browse, and navigation functionality; and so forth. Some knowledge of HTML, JavaScript, and the like can be quite useful even when working with these software packages.

A first major point here is that, one way or another, all of these pieces need to come together to make a digital repository happen, and that the expertise and people involved will vary from one institution to another. Larger institutions with more specialized professional staff will often advertise for and hire people with some knowledge and experience in one or more of these areas. In many institutions these knowledge and skills are learned and developed on the job. New graduates from library and information studies programs may come into the job marketplace with coursework and internships in one or more of these areas. It is increasingly common to see job advertisements for metadata librarians, metadata specialists, or combination cataloger/metadata librarians, who need a broad range of skills in selecting, applying, and designing metadata schemes and standards for different projects, and mapping data among those different schemes.

A second major point, one of the most important, is that the design of the metadata scheme and the selection or creation of controlled vocabularies ideally always go hand-in-hand with the design of the search, browse, and navigation functions and of the record displays in the user interface. Each is dependent on the other and informs the other. And each of these should go hand-in-hand with the curator/subject expert's identification of key pieces of information that the primary users of the collection will need in order to identify and access the objects in the collection. The article by Chopey (2005) referenced earlier in this chapter does an excellent job of discussing how all of these are intertwined with one another.

1.7. Metadata for Digital Collections

This section provides a summary introduction to the metadata aspects of digitization projects and digital collections, which is the focus of the remainder of this book. Since many readers may be catalogers or work in libraries, it is worth noting first off that the approach to creating metadata for digital collections is rather different from the approach to cataloging resources for a library catalog. In the library cataloging world, catalogers

---

Common Digital Collection Software Solutions

Digital Collections for Libraries, Museums, and Archives
- CONTENTdm Digital Collection Management Software by OCLC: http://www.contentdm.org/
- Insight + LUNA Software Suite by Luna Imaging: http://www.lunaimaging.com/insight/index.html
- Greenstone Digital Library Software (open source): http://www.greenstone.org/

Integrated Library System Vendor Products
- DigiTool by Ex Libris: http://www.exlibrisgroup.com/category/DigiToolOverview
- Content Pro by Innovative Interfaces: http://www.iii.com/products/content_pro.shtml

Museum Database Software and Digital Asset Management Systems
- Filemaker Pro database management software: http://www.filemaker.com/products/filemaker-pro/
- PastPerfect museum software: http://www.museumsoftware.com/

Institutional Repositories
- DSpace software (open source): http://www.dspace.org/
- Fedora Commons Repository Software (open source): http://fedora-commons.org/

consult and apply a set of common, shared, and well-established standards within an established infrastructure for sharing bibliographic records nationally and internationally. All catalogers work with mostly the same set of structure, content, value, and encoding standards—namely, MARC, AACR2, LCSH, DDC, LCC, or other parallel international standards. Catalogers create highly standardized resource descriptions that can be widely shared among MARC-based systems. This is not the case when it comes to creating metadata for digital collections. Metadata creation in most digital projects places a strong emphasis on the particular digital collection, the specific types of resources it contains, and selecting metadata elements and standards needed for the specific end users' anticipated information retrieval needs.

1.7.1. Designing and Documenting a Metadata Scheme

As resources are selected for digitization, those responsible for selection, especially subject experts, will often also develop a list of elements or fields that they judge will be important for identification and access for the particular subject matter of that digital collection. This may go hand-in-hand with the development of a list of functional requirements that the metadata should serve. At that point, the project developers must also decide on which established metadata standards to use that best suit the content and retrieval needs for that particular collection. The development of the metadata elements and vocabularies for the project results from this interplay between locally specific elements and retrieval needs, on the one hand, and nationally or internationally established standardized element sets such as Dublin Core, VRA, or MODS, on the other hand. If the local elements are to interoperate in the wider Internet world, they need to conform to one or more shared, established standards. The people who design the metadata scheme may or may not be the same people who create the actual metadata conforming to that scheme. Good metadata scheme design and documentation will help metadata creators (catalogers) create good-quality metadata. Chapter 10 details the following steps or components of metadata scheme design:

1. Analyze context, content, and users, and determine functional requirements
2. Select and develop an element set
   a. A general, cross-collection element set
   b. A collection-specific element set
3. Establish element and database specifications
4. Establish controlled vocabularies and encoding schemes
5. Develop content guidelines
6. Document the scheme

Metadata scheme documentation is a critical aspect of metadata design. Documentation may range from the informal to the formal, from the general to the specific, from a simple table to a document of several dozen or hundred pages. Such documentation is commonly known by several different names in the cultural heritage metadata environment. Common names include *metadata/user/usage guide/guidelines*, *best practices*, *data dictionaries*, and *application profiles*. For purposes of this book, all of these terms are understood refer to some kind of metadata scheme documentation. This book will use the terms *best practice guide* and especially *application profile* in their broadest sense to include the full range of metadata scheme design and documentation. Chapter 10 goes into this topic in much greater detail. In addition to the article by Michael Chopey (2005), another excellent resource covering metadata and systems design within the larger context of digital collection development is Muriel Foulonneau and Jenn Riley's book *Metadata for Digital Resources* (Foulonneau and Riley, 2008).

1.7.2. Creating Metadata for Digital Objects

Once the metadata scheme has been designed and documented, the database configured according to that scheme, and the metadata creation interface finalized, work can begin on analyzing each individual digital object and creating the descriptive metadata for each. This process, which is part art, part science, part data entry, is variously also known as cataloging, indexing, and resource description. Who creates metadata for digital collections? This varies greatly from one institution and project to another. The person responsible for coordinating the project, selecting the metadata elements and vocabularies, and designing the metadata template may or may not also be the person who creates the metadata for the individual digital objects in the collection. This is the distinction already made between *metadata design* and *metadata creation*. Metadata creators may range from professional catalogers or metadata specialists, to a single or small number of metadata or digital project staff, to interns, student workers, and volunteers. Volunteers may range from subject specialists with an interest in contributing to the collection, at one extreme, to a retired person volunteering a few hours a week at a museum, at another extreme. This diversity poses challenges for the consistency and quality of the metadata, and the resulting usefulness for end users. Ultimately, the quality of the metadata that is input into the fields is what determines the findability and interpretability of the resources in the digital collection. The old adage *garbage in, garbage out* is all too true.

Metadata creators most often work with some kind of user-friendly interface and do not usually directly code the metadata in XML or some other coded format such as MARC tagging. Those metadata creators who do work directly with XML will do so using XML editor software that will include the allowable elements, prompt for them, and validate the resulting XML. Since a large number of readers of this book are likely to use the CONTENTdm digital collection software, this section includes two CONTENTdm examples. Chapter 10 will include several additional CONTENTdm screen capture examples. Figure 1.7 shows

Figure 1.7. CONTENTdm "Collection Field Properties" Screen Example

CONTENTdm Administration

admin home | server | collections | items

:: configuration : fields : viewers : reports : export : view collection : help ::

Current collection: Polar Expeditions - Images from the American Geographical Society Library | change

Metadata fields

View and configure collection and administrative fields.

Collection field properties

View, add, edit and delete fields. Enable full text searching and controlled vocabulary. After you have added, changed, or deleted fields, index the collection to update changes.

	Field name	DC map	Data type	Large	Search	Hide	Required	Vocab		add field
1	Title	Title	Text	No	Yes	No	Yes	No	move to	edit | delete
2	Date of Photograph	Date-Created	Text	No	Yes	No	No	No	move to	edit | delete
3	Caption	Description	Text	No	Yes	No	No	No	move to	edit | delete
4	Verso Description	Description	Text	No	Yes	No	No	No	move to	edit | delete
5	Photographer	Creator	Text	No	Yes	No	No	No	move to	edit | delete
6	Source of Descriptive Information	Description	Text	No	Yes	No	No	No	move to	edit | delete
7	Subject TGM	Subject	Text	No	Yes	No	No	Yes	move to	edit | delete
8	Expedition	Subject	Text	No	Yes	No	No	No	move to	edit | delete
9	Subject LC	Subject	Text	No	Yes	No	No	Yes	move to	edit | delete
10	Continent	Coverage-Spatial	Text	No	Yes	No	No	Yes	move to	edit | delete
11	Country	Coverage-Spatial	Text	No	Yes	No	No	No	move to	edit | delete
12	Region	Coverage-Spatial	Text	No	Yes	No	No	No	move to	edit | delete
13	State/Province	Coverage-Spatial	Text	No	Yes	No	No	No	move to	edit | delete
14	City or Place	Coverage-Spatial	Text	No	Yes	No	No	No	move to	edit | delete
15	Geographic Feature	Coverage-Spatial	Text	No	Yes	No	No	No	move to	edit | delete
16	Type	Type	Text	No	No	No	No	Yes	move to	edit | delete
17	Original Collection	Relation-Is Part Of	Text	No	Yes	No	No	No	move to	edit | delete
18	Original Item Size	Format-Extent	Text	No	Yes	No	No	No	move to	edit | delete
19	Original Item Medium	Format-Medium	Text	No	Yes	No	No	No	move to	edit | delete
20	Original Item ID	Identifier	Text	No	Yes	No	No	No	move to	edit | delete
21	Provenance	Contributors	Text	No	No	No	No	No	move to	edit | delete
22	Repository	Relation-Is Part Of	Text	No	No	No	No	No	move to	edit | delete
23	Rights	Rights	Text	No	No	No	No	No	move to	edit | delete
24	Digital Publisher	Publisher	Text	No	No	No	No	No	move to	edit | delete

Source: CONTENTdm screenshots are used with OCLC's permission. CONTENTdm® is a registered trademark of OCLC Online Computer Library Center, Inc.

an example of a CONTENTdm *Collection field properties* screen. In this particular example, the metadata designer has taken the Dublin Core *Creator* element and renamed it with the local element name *Photographer* to point out only one such instance. This creates the local *Photographer* element and maps it to the DC *Creator* element behind the scenes. This figure also shows some of the other field properties that can be set, including whether or not a controlled vocabulary will apply to any particular field.

Figure 1.8 shows an example of the screen for creating and editing a metadata record for a specific digital object in CONTENTdm, in this case a digital image and map collection having to do with a toy store display in Japan. The cursor in this screen capture is in the *Subject LC* field, which brings up the list of controlled vocabulary terms selected for this field in the pane on the right side of the screen. The metadata creator only needs to scroll to the appropriate term and click on it, and then the software automatically adds that term to the *Subject* field. More than one term can be selected. Not all institutions follow this model for metadata design and creation in which unique local field names are created and mapped to generic Dublin Core elements. Many institutions use a

Figure 1.8. CONTENTdm Metadata Record Creation/Editing Screen Example

Field Name	Field Values	Controlled Vocabulary
Title	Japan, toy store display	Alexandria (Egypt)
Part of Set	Enami glass lantern slide collection	Alley, Rewi, 1897-1987
		American Geographical Society of New York
Notes		Aswan Dam (Egypt)
		Ataturk, Kemal, 1881-1938
		Babylon (Extinct city)
		Badshahi Masjid
		Baghmati River (Nepal and India)
Date of Photograph	[ca. 1900-1920]	Bamian (Afghanistan)
		Bamiyan Region (Afghanistan)
		Bang Khen (Bangkok, Thailand)
Photographer's Note		Bangkok (Thailand)
		Bani Hasan Site (Egypt) 1860-1900
		Bechard, Henri
		Bedouins Egypt
		Bhaktapur (Nepal)
Photographer	Enami, T., 1859-1929	Blue Mosque (Istanbul, Turkey)
		Cairo (Egypt)
		Cairo (Egypt) 1860-1890
Description		Chamundeswari Temple (Mysore, India)
		Chamundi Hill (India)
		Changdokkung (Seoul, Korea)
		Changsha (Hunan Sheng, China)
Source of Descriptive Information		Cheops, Pyramid of (Egypt)
		Chiang Dao (Thailand : Amphoe)
Related Resources		Chiang Kham (Phayao, Thailand)
		Chiang Mai (Thailand)
Subject TGM	Stores & shop; Daggers & swords; Toys; Balls (Sporting goods); Merchandise displays	Chiang Rai (Thailand)
		Chiang Saen (Thailand)
Subject LC		Chiang, Ching-kuo, 1910-1988
		Chinese New Year
Continent	Asia	Chongqing (China)
		Citadel (Cairo, Egypt)
Subcontinent		Cochin (India)
		Coimbatore (India)
Country	Japan	Coonoor (India)
		Damascus (Syria)
Region		Dandara (Egypt)
		Dandara (Egypt) Antiquities
State/Province		Darjeeling (India)
		Deir el-Bahri Site (Egypt)
City/Place		Dhaka (Bangladesh)
		Djoser, King of Egypt
Geographic Feature		Evans, Charles, 1918-1995
Type	Image	Forman, Harrison, 1904-1978

Source: See Figure 1.7.

broader, more generic set of elements, such as Dublin Core, MODS, or VRA, and perhaps add some additional local elements. Both of these general models of metadata will be taken into account throughout this book and addressed specifically in Chapter 10.

1.7.3. Metadata Sharing, Harvesting, and Aggregating

Metadata is first and foremost created for use in its individual local context. But in addition to its original context, which is often designed for a specific collection, cultural heritage metadata is also often shared among multiple collections within an institution, among different institutions, and among various external metadata services and repositories. In many of these cases, the institution exposes its own local metadata for automated harvesting by a consortium or other third-party agency into a shared metadata repository, where it is aggregated with metadata from many other institutions. Once harvested and aggregated into an external repository, the rich, collection-specific local element names, along with most of the original context of the metadata itself, are lost. This complicates the process of metadata design. It is very important to keep metadata harvesting and aggregation in mind when designing the metadata standards for a digital collection. This is one reason why it is important for projects to include a mapping of each local metadata element or field to one of the 15 simple Dublin Core elements. This point will be made again at several points throughout this book, and this topic covered in greater detail in Chapter 10.

1.8. Summary

Metadata is data that performs a function in relation to other data or information resources. The key thing about metadata is what it is intended to *do*. People create metadata to help themselves or their family, friends, customers, or users to find, identify, sort, gather, and navigate collections of music, texts, images, and other resources, among various other functions. Metadata provides *intellectual access* to the resources in a digital collection by making them findable and identifiable. Metadata provides information that allows users to interpret and understand those resources, as well as the basis for the searching and browsing functionality within an online digital collection user interface. Digital collections come in many shapes and sizes, consisting of a wide range of resource types and subject matter. Metadata also comes in different varieties depending on the functions it is intended to serve and includes descriptive, administrative, technical, preservation, rights, and structural metadata. This book focuses on descriptive metadata for digital collections created by cultural heritage institutions, most notably libraries, archives, historical societies, and museums.

In order to be useful in any context, metadata needs to be structured according to various kinds of standards: informal, locally established guidelines; formal, internationally established standards; or a combination of both, with many gradations in between. All metadata applications require some form of data *structure*, data *content*, data *value*, and data *encoding and exchange* standards. Metadata design and creation are one part of a larger process of creating a digital collection, a process that consists of several components or functions, including project planning, management, and administration; digital collection development; digitization, formatting, and storage of digital objects; metadata design and creation; database and retrieval system design; and web-based user interface design and programming.

The design and documentation of a metadata scheme precedes actual metadata creation, which is done according to the scheme and its specifications. Metadata scheme design also consists of several components or steps. Metadata scheme documentation is commonly called by various names, including metadata guidelines, best practice guides, data dictionaries, and application profiles. A common software solution for digital collections and their metadata is CONTENTdm. Good metadata scheme design and creation need to take into account the larger metadata sharing, harvesting, and aggregating environment in order for the metadata to be interoperable and viable over time for future systems and uses.

> ▶ **Companion Website**
>
> See this book's companion website at **http://www.neal-schuman.com/metadata-digital-collections/** for Chapter 1 review questions, suggestions for exercises, and other resources.

References

Boughida, Karim. 2005. "CDWA Lite for Cataloging Cultural Objects (CCO): A New XML Schema for the Cultural Heritage Community." In *Humanities, Computers and Cultural Heritage: Proceedings of the XVI International Conference of the Association for History and Computing, September 14–17*. Amsterdam: Royal Netherlands Academy of Arts and Sciences. http://www.knaw.nl/publicaties/pdf/20051064.pdf.

Campbell, D. Grant. 2005. "Metadata, Metaphor, and Metonymy." In *Metadata: A Cataloger's Primer*, edited by Richard P. Smiraglia, 57–73. Binghamton, NY: Haworth Press.

Chopey, Michael A. 2005. "Planning and Implementing a Metadata-Driven Digital Repository." In *Metadata: A Cataloger's Primer*, edited by Richard P. Smiraglia, 255–287. Binghamton, NY: Haworth Press.

Coyle, Karen. 2005. "Understanding Metadata and its Purpose." *Journal of Academic Librarianship* 31, no. 2 (March): 160–163.

Cwiok, Jennifer. 2005. "The Defining Element—A Discussion of the Creator Element within Metadata Schemas." In *Metadata: A Cataloger's Primer*, edited by Richard P. Smiraglia, 103–133. Binghamton, NY: Haworth Press.

Elings, Mary W., and Günter Waibel. 2007. "Metadata for All: Descriptive Standards and Metadata Sharing across Libraries, Archives and Museums." *First Monday* 12, no. 3 (March). http://firstmonday.org/issues/issue12_3/elings/index.html.

Foulonneau, Muriel, and Jenn Riley. 2008. *Metadata for Digital Resources: Implementation, Systems Design and Interoperability*. Oxford: Chandos.

Gilliland, Anne J. 2008. "Setting the Stage." In *Introduction to Metadata*. 2nd ed., version 3.0, edited by Murtha Baca, 1–19. Los Angeles: Getty Research Institute.

Haynes, David. 2004. *Metadata for Information Management and Retrieval*. London: Facet.

Miller, Paul. 2004. "Metadata: What It Means for Memory Institutions." In *Metadata Applications and Management*, edited by G.E. Gorman and Daniel G. Dorner, 4–16. Lanham, MD: Scarecrow Press.

NISO (National Information Standards Organization). 2004. *Understanding Metadata*. Bethesda, MD: NISO Press. http://www.niso.org/publications/press/UnderstandingMetadata.pdf.

RLG. 2005. "Terminology." In *Descriptive Metadata Guidelines for RLG Cultural Materials,* 3–5. Mountain View, CA: RLG. http://www.oclc.org/programs/ourwork/past/culturalmaterials/RLG_desc_metadata.pdf.

Sutton, Stuart. 2007. "Tutorial 1: Basic Semantics." Presentation at DC-2007: International Conference on Dublin Core and Metadata Applications, Singapore, August 27–31. http://dublincore.org/resources/training/dc-2007/T1-BasicSemantics.pdf.

Zeng, Marcia Lei, and Jian Qin. 2008. *Metadata*. New York: Neal-Schuman.

Introduction to Resource Description and Dublin Core

Following the design of a metadata scheme and its application to local database specifications, as briefly summarized in Chapter 1, work begins on creating the metadata for the individual digital objects in the collection. This is the core activity that provides users with intellectual access to the contents of the collection. This chapter deals with foundational aspects of, and challenges in, creating metadata for digital resources, also called *resource description*. Almost every metadata designer and creator will encounter these issues in one form or another. This chapter also provides an introduction to the *Dublin Core Metadata Element Set*, the most commonly used scheme for digital resource description.

In covering these topics, this chapter thereby also gives readers a solid initial foundation for designing a local metadata scheme or application profile, especially one based on Dublin Core. In practice, most resource description for digital collections is done by following the local metadata scheme, best practice guide, or application profile. Chapters 3 and 4 address further the topics covered in this chapter and explore the most common kinds of information needed to describe and provide access to digital resources, along with the corresponding Dublin Core elements, digging into nitty-gritty challenges faced by metadata designers and creators. Chapter 5 goes on to deal with the topic of controlled vocabularies, including those commonly used in metadata for digital collections. Thus Chapters 2 through 5 provide a core foundation for both metadata scheme, or application profile, design and metadata record creation, or cataloging.

2.1. Resource Description Fundamentals

Before looking at how to deal with specific types of information such as titles, dates, names, and subjects in Chapters 3 and 4, it is important to have a basic understanding of terminology and overarching issues involved in creating metadata for digital objects in online collections.

2.1.1. Resource Description

What do you call the process of creating metadata for digital objects? Metadata literature and working documents use various terms for this process, including *metadata creation, cataloging, indexing,* and *resource description.* The word *cataloging,* while perfectly usable in this context, tends to be associated with creation of AACR2/MARC records for library catalogs, while *indexing* more often refers only to analyzing the subject content of, and assigning subject terms to, a resource. The cultural heritage metadata communities, especially the Dublin Core and digital library communities, have commonly used the phrase *resource description* for this process. You will often encounter this term when reading other documentation. This book will use the phrases *resource description* and *metadata creation* more or less interchangeably and will also occasionally use the terms *cataloging* and *indexing* to describe the same process.

Unfortunately, there are sometimes misconceptions and misunderstandings when using the term *description.* For one thing, metadata creation entails much more than simply describing the characteristics of a resource. It includes, for example, analyzing a resource's subject content and assigning subject terms to represent that content. Metadata creation also takes into account the various functions of different metadata elements within a database beyond only those that are purely *descriptive* in the narrower sense. The term *description* can also be misleading when you deal with the inevitable question of whether you are *describing* an original analog resource or a digitized format of the same resource in a metadata record. Section 2.1 seeks to help clarify these and other difficulties frequently encountered in practice.

2.1.1.1. Resources

First of all, what is it that you are describing, cataloging, or creating metadata for? In order to talk about this in general, it is useful to have a general or generic term for what is being described. Different communities use the terms *items, content items, objects, resources, information resources,* and *bibliographic resources,* among others. This book will use the terms *resource* and, to a slightly lesser extent, *object* as basic generic terms, alternating between the two for the sake of variety in the text. So, then, what is a *resource?* A resource is any object or collection of objects that is of interest to you or your users and that can be described in some way. Normally, resources are entities that individuals or institutions such as libraries, museums, and archives collect and own.

A resource can be a physical item such as a book, letter, document, map, photograph, slide, sound recording, film, video recording, painting, sculpture, and so on. These are often called *physical* or *analog* resources, in contrast to *digital* resources. A digital resource may be a text file, a still image file, a moving image file, a sound file, or the like, or in some cases a collection of such files. A digital resource may be a digitized version of an original analog resource, or it may be *born digital*: that is, created originally as a digital object with no analog equivalent. A *resource* can also be a collection of digital files that together make up one whole logical resource, such a single book that has been digitized as multiple image files, one image having been made of each page of the book.

The term *resource* is also used to refer to collections of resources, such that an analog or digital collection taken as a whole may also be considered to be a *resource*. A hypothetical digital image collection of Bridges of Wisconsin, for example, can be thought of as a *resource* of interest to users and can be described as a whole. At the same time, each image within that collection can also be described individually. Understanding a collection as a describable resource becomes important when looking at relationships among different resources. An individual digital image, for example, has a relationship with the online collection of which it is a part. They are both *resources*, one being a part of the other. This will be explored more than once again in this chapter.

Figures 2.1 and 2.2 provide examples of two different kinds of digital resources. The digital image in Figure 2.1 is fairly straightforward. It is a single resource in a single digital file, in this case a JPEG image file. An original analog 35 mm photographic print was digitized to create this JPEG file.

Figure 2.2 is more complicated. It represents what is often called a *complex digital object*. In this case, the covers and each set of pages of an analog book have been photographed and digitized as separate image files. The navigation on the left side shows the digital image files that the user may select in order to view the different pages of this digital

Figure 2.1. Digital Image

Source: From the Archives Department and Digital Collections, University of Wisconsin–Milwaukee Libraries. Image reproduced with permission.

Figure 2.2. Digital Text: Book Digitized as Separate Image Files (Complex Digital Object)

Source: Special Collections and Digital Collections, University of Wisconsin–Milwaukee Libraries. Image reproduced with permission.

book. Although each of these image files can also be considered to be a *resource*, you would virtually never create a complete descriptive metadata record for each individual page. Instead, you normally create one metadata record for the digital book as a whole.

2.1.1.2. Metadata Descriptions and Records

This leads to the concept of the metadata *description* or *record*. In the context of metadata residing in a database, a metadata record is identical to a database record. A database record is a collection of fields, each consisting of a field name (also often called an element, tag, or property) and a field value, which is the content of that element as it pertains to the specific resource being described in the metadata record. The basic unit of metadata is the combination of a *property* (element or field) name and its *value* (or content), often referred to as a *property-value pair*. Each property-value pair constitutes a *statement* about a resource, and a collection of such statements constitutes a *description* or a *record*. In the library cataloging tradition, a *record* functions within a catalog as a *surrogate* for the resource it describes. That is, it stands in place of the actual resource in the catalog and consists of selected pieces of information about that resource, pieces of information judged especially important for identifying and finding that resource. In many ways, understanding a metadata record as a *representation* of a resource is more helpful than talking about it as a *description*. This use of language can help clarify common misunderstandings that will be discussed elsewhere in this chapter. Nonetheless, the word *description* has come to be frequently used in practice.

Figure 2.3 shows a display of both a digital image and the metadata record for that image. The terms in the left hand column are the metadata *properties*, *elements*, or *fields*, while the data in the right hand column are the *values* of each of those properties, elements, or fields. This record

Figure 2.3. Metadata Record for Digital Image

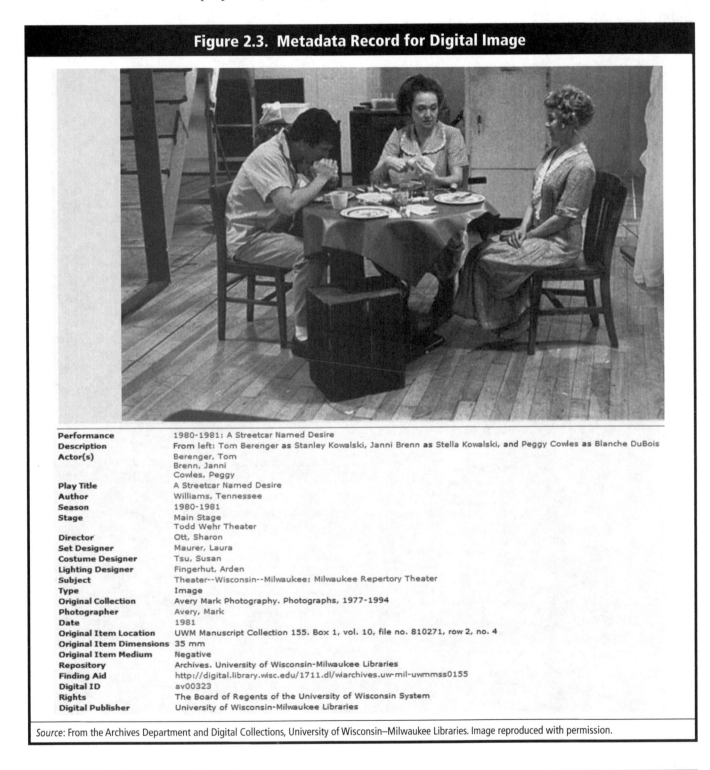

Performance	1980-1981: A Streetcar Named Desire
Description	From left: Tom Berenger as Stanley Kowalski, Janni Brenn as Stella Kowalski, and Peggy Cowles as Blanche DuBois
Actor(s)	Berenger, Tom
	Brenn, Janni
	Cowles, Peggy
Play Title	A Streetcar Named Desire
Author	Williams, Tennessee
Season	1980-1981
Stage	Main Stage
	Todd Wehr Theater
Director	Ott, Sharon
Set Designer	Maurer, Laura
Costume Designer	Tsu, Susan
Lighting Designer	Fingerhut, Arden
Subject	Theater--Wisconsin--Milwaukee; Milwaukee Repertory Theater
Type	Image
Original Collection	Avery Mark Photography. Photographs, 1977-1994
Photographer	Avery, Mark
Date	1981
Original Item Location	UWM Manuscript Collection 155. Box 1, vol. 10, file no. 810271, row 2, no. 4
Original Item Dimensions	35 mm
Original Item Medium	Negative
Repository	Archives. University of Wisconsin-Milwaukee Libraries
Finding Aid	http://digital.library.wisc.edu/1711.dl/wiarchives.uw-mil-uwmmss0155
Digital ID	av00323
Rights	The Board of Regents of the University of Wisconsin System
Digital Publisher	University of Wisconsin-Milwaukee Libraries

Source: From the Archives Department and Digital Collections, University of Wisconsin–Milwaukee Libraries. Image reproduced with permission.

was created in CONTENTdm and illustrates the collection-specific metadata design model using field names tailor-made for this particular digital collection.

Figure 2.4 illustrates the metadata record for the digital book shown in Figure 2.2 as an example of a complex digital object. A single descriptive

Figure 2.4. Metadata Record for Complex Digital Object (Book Digitized as Set of Image Files)

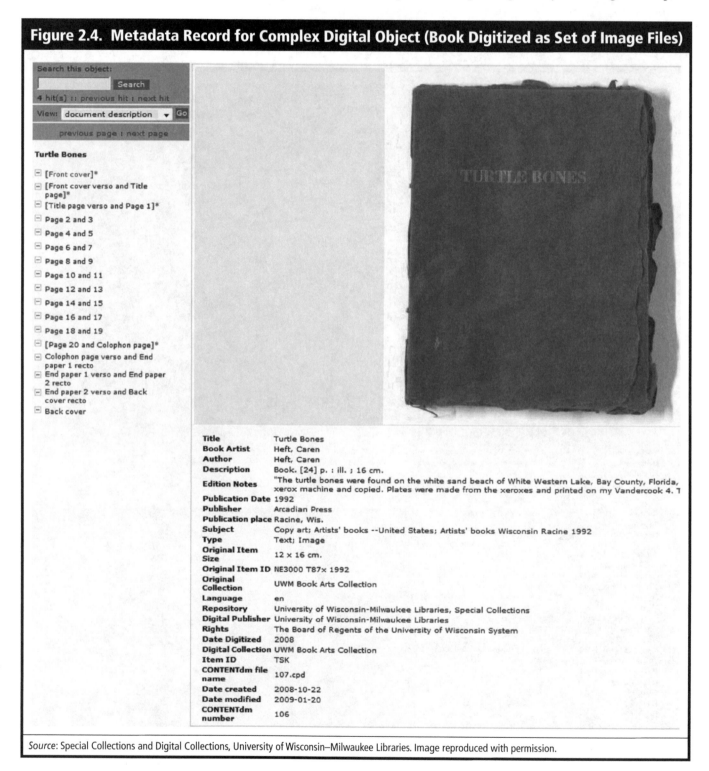

Title	Turtle Bones
Book Artist	Heft, Caren
Author	Heft, Caren
Description	Book. [24] p. : ill. ; 16 cm.
Edition Notes	"The turtle bones were found on the white sand beach of White Western Lake, Bay County, Florida, xerox machine and copied. Plates were made from the xeroxes and printed on my Vandercook 4. T
Publication Date	1992
Publisher	Arcadian Press
Publication place	Racine, Wis.
Subject	Copy art; Artists' books --United States; Artists' books Wisconsin Racine 1992
Type	Text; Image
Original Item Size	12 x 16 cm.
Original Item ID	NE3000 T87x 1992
Original Collection	UWM Book Arts Collection
Language	en
Repository	University of Wisconsin-Milwaukee Libraries, Special Collections
Digital Publisher	University of Wisconsin-Milwaukee Libraries
Rights	The Board of Regents of the University of Wisconsin System
Date Digitized	2008
Digital Collection	UWM Book Arts Collection
Item ID	TSK
CONTENTdm file name	107.cpd
Date created	2008-10-22
Date modified	2009-01-20
CONTENTdm number	106

Source: Special Collections and Digital Collections, University of Wisconsin–Milwaukee Libraries. Image reproduced with permission.

metadata record has been created to describe or represent the digitized book as a whole.

2.1.1.3. Granularity of Description

As discussed earlier, for purposes of resource description, individual analog and digital objects as well as collections of such objects are considered to be *resources* that can be described or represented by means of a metadata record. This raises the topic of **granularity** of resource description. The term "granularity" refers to the level of detail at which an information resource is viewed or described. The more granular the level, the smaller the chunks of information. For example, you can view and consider the characteristics of a series of books as a whole, or of each individual book in the series, or of each chapter in each book, progressing from a lower to a higher level of granularity.

In creating metadata for resource description, granularity most commonly refers to the level at which you create a metadata record representing an information resource. You may, for example, choose to create a **collection-level** metadata record that describes or represents an entire online collection as a whole. Many practitioners in libraries choose to create collection-level records in MARC for inclusion in their online catalog. In such a case, you need to be sure to enter values in the metadata elements that are applicable to whole collection. The primary type of resource description for digital collections, however, is creating **item-level** metadata records representing each individual resource within a collection. This is resource description at a relatively high level of granularity, a higher level than is usually done within a library catalog. Again, the critical point is that the values entered into the individual elements in the metadata records must be applicable to the individual item and not to the collection as a whole.

Table 2.1 illustrates a partial collection-level metadata record. Compare this carefully with Table 2.2 illustrating a partial item-

A Linked Data/Semantic Web Approach to Metadata Description and Records

More recent metadata developments, especially within the international Dublin Core and other cultural heritage metadata communities, are looking for ways to talk about and use metadata in the larger *Linked Data* environment, also known as the *Semantic Web*. Chapter 11 deals with these topics, but it is worthwhile mentioning a few basic points here. In this context, the term **description** refers to a collection of statements about a resource. A **statement** consists of an assertion such as *Resource X has the title Turtle Bones*. This statement is represented in Figure 2.4 by the first metadata field, in which the **property** called *Title* is associated with the **value** *Turtle Bones*, and both are associated with the digital resource being described. The metadata record as a whole is a collection of statements about this resource.

In order to make metadata more flexible and reusable in an open web environment, *the statement, rather than the record, is considered to be the basic unit of metadata* (Sutton, 2007: slide 9; Zeng and Qin, 2008: 152). In a Semantic Web of Linked Data environment, each statement can stand on its own and be dynamically linked to other statements to form an ever-growing web of data. When following the DCMI Abstract Model, discussed in Chapter 11, a set of statements about a single resource is called a *description*, while several descriptions may be combined together into a *description set*. A description set is equivalent to a *record* in traditional terminology. While these technical distinctions may seem overly abstract and of little concern to many practitioners, they do relate to concrete problems in metadata creation and in sharing metadata outside of one's local closed system.

Table 2.1. Collection-Level Record (Selected Elements)		
Element	**Value**	**Explanatory Notes**
Title	Bridges of Wisconsin	Name of the digital collection
Identifier	http://www.uxyz.edu/wisbridges/index.html	URL for the collection home page
Resource Type	Collection	The general type of resource applicable to the collection as a whole
Date	2009	The date the collection as a whole was created and made available online
Creator	Jones, Jane A.	Names of staff members primarily responsible for creating the digital collection as a whole
Creator	Smith, John J.	
Publisher	Hagenville University	The institution responsible for making the collection available online
Topical Subject	Bridges	Terms representing the general subject content of the collection as a whole
Geographic Subject	Wisconsin	

Table 2.2. Item-Level Record (Selected Elements)

Element	Value	Explanatory Notes
Title	Manchester Street Bridge, Sauk County, Wisconsin	Name given to one specific image within the collection
Identifier	WB0078736	The unique file name for this specific digital image
Resource Type	Still Image	The general type of resource applicable to this specific resource
Date	1955	The date on which the original photograph of this bridge was taken
Creator	Kramer, Paul Jacob	The person who took the photograph of this bridge
Topical Subject	Truss bridges	Terms representing the subject content of this specific image
Geographic Subject	Sauk County	
Part of Collection	Bridges of Wisconsin	The name of the collection of which this image is a part

level record for a specific image within the hypothetical Bridges of Wisconsin image collection. Observe how the values of the elements are consistent with the level of granularity of the resource being described or represented in each record.

Granularity also relates to the description of complex digital objects, such as the one illustrated in Figure 2.4. Although some simple metadata does usually need to be created for each individual image file (at an even higher level of granularity than the book level), that is mostly technical, structural metadata, often consisting of nothing more than the page name or number for each image file and a designation for sequencing each image in the correct order. The primary descriptive metadata record is created for the digital book as a whole.

Collections of digital images, especially for museums, sometimes include images showing multiple views of the same work: for example, front, back, and side views of a three-dimensional sculpture. Similarly, an image of a whole painting or a map may be accompanied by several images of detailed views of subsections of the painting or map. Each of these may require descriptive metadata, often in separate records. This is a higher level of granularity of description than a description of the sculpture, painting, or map taken as a single whole. These separate records also need to be linked to one another in the database.

You encounter similar granularity issues if you are digitizing, for example, individual articles from a periodical or individual short stories from a book of collected short stories. You may create a metadata record for the periodical and the book as a whole, as well as records for each individual article and short story. This is a local resource description decision based on the desired functionality for users.

The important thing in all of these cases is to keep carefully in mind what level you are describing in your metadata record and to keep the descriptive elements consistent with that level. You do not want, for example, to mix elements representing an entire digital collection with those representing a single digital object within that collection, or a record representing an image of the dome of St. Peter's Basilica with a record representing an image of the Basilica as a whole.

2.1.1.4. Element Repeatability

Metadata designers and creators will quickly run into the issue of what to do when they have several values to be entered for the same element within a single metadata record. For example, what do you do when you have more than one author of a text and you want to include all of their names in your metadata record? Should you make the author or creator element *repeatable* and enter each person's name in a separate *Creator* field, repeating the field as many times as needed within a record? Or should you enter all of the individual people's names in a single *Creator* field?

To a large extent, the answer depends on the particular software and retrieval system you are using. Some systems allow for, and may even require, entering multiple names, subject terms, and the like, in a single field. In such cases, the software specifies a standardized way of demarcating one name or subject term from another in order for the system to be able to search and index each name or term separately. A common demarcator is a semicolon followed by a space, as illustrated in Example A in Figure 2.5. This is the case in CONTENTdm. Most current best practice guides for sharing metadata across systems, however, recommend separate terms in separate fields, as illustrated in Example B in Figure 2.5. This is an example of a repeatable *Creator* element or field. This makes the differentiation among separate names and terms unambiguous to computers, since it does not rely on software-specific punctuation conventions.

This practice generally increases the interoperability of the metadata, because it increases the chances that different computer systems will be able to process, search, and index each name separately. Outside of its original environment, a system might process the complete character string *Washington, Tamara; Garcia, Carlos; Moretti, Frank* as one single creator name, making all three names unindexed and un-hyperlinked in the system. The same principles apply to any other element for which there will be multiple values per record, such as a *Subject* element, because metadata creators will most often assign more than one subject term per record. But metadata creators using systems such as CONTENTdm will need to follow the practice of entering multiple names and subject terms in a single instance of an element or field. It is possible to machine process the metadata to parse these into separate fields or elements if necessary, such as when the metadata is harvested by an external aggregator service.

A Linked Data/Semantic Web Approach to Element Repeatability

When looking at a metadata record as a *description set* consisting of reusable *statements*, having a separate statement for each person's name increases interoperability and the ability to link multiple statements in different descriptions from different sources having to do with the same person. For example, Tamara Washington might be the author of another article on her own, without coauthoring it with Carlos Garcia and Frank Moretti. Therefore the statement equivalent to *Resource Z has Creator Washington, Tamara* allows the character string *Washington, Tamara* to be also linked to any other resource with which she is associated, whereas the character string *Washington, Tamara; Garcia, Carlos; Moretti, Frank* cannot be so linked and reused for each of the three different persons. It is attempting to express three logically separate statements in one syntactical statement. Chapter 11 will explore these issues, including the use of URLs in place of character strings.

Figure 2.5. Element Repeatability: Multiple Values in a Single Field versus Separate Fields

Example A: Multiple values in a single element/field:

Creator	Washington, Tamara; Garcia, Carlos; Moretti, Frank

Example B: Each value in a separate element/field, repeatable as many times as needed within any record:

Creator	Washington, Tamara
Creator	Garcia, Carlos
Creator	Moretti, Frank

2.1.1.5. Element Functionality

Different metadata elements serve different types of functions within an online digital collection interface. Not all metadata elements are created equal; they do not all serve the same functions. A key part of the metadata design process is the identification of functional requirements for the metadata, the database, and the user interface. For an imaginary Bridges of Wisconsin image collection, the following might be among the functional requirements established:

Users should be able to search Bridges of Wisconsin images by any of the following:

- Date or date range of photograph
- Type of bridge
- County name

These functions can be accomplished for the user only if you have established separate database fields for each of these aspects and only if the metadata creators enter consistent values into those fields, such that the system can link them together for search and browse retrieval. Figure 2.6 offers a rough approximation of how a user interface might look that accomplishes the desired functionality based on the metadata design and creation. Users may choose to limit their searches to the content of specific fields in the metadata records and to also limit any search by an individual date or range of dates from the Date field.

Figure 2.7 shows how drop-down browse menus can be generated from the underlying metadata. *Type of Bridge* is the element/field name, and the selections available to the user are the values entered into that field in different metadata records. Selecting *Truss bridges* will retrieve all metadata records in which that value resides in the *Type of Bridge* field. The same is true for the list of Wisconsin counties in the *County* field in the metadata.

To take another set of examples from an actual collection, Figure 2.8 depicts a digital image and its metadata record in a Milwaukee Neighborhoods collection.

At the point of designing the metadata scheme for this collection, the collection development team and metadata designer might have established the following among the various functions they wanted to enable for users.

Users should be able to search Milwaukee Neighborhoods images by the following:

Figure 2.6. Search Options Based on Metadata Fields

Advanced Search

Find results with:

Words: [   ] in: | Title ▾ | Field(s)
Creator
Type of Bridge
County

Limit results by:

Date or Date Range:
Single Year: [   ]
Beginning Year: [   ] Ending Year: [   ]

Figure 2.7. Drop-Down Browse Menus Based on Metadata Fields and Values

Browse by:

Type of Bridge: ▾	County: ▾	
Aqueducts	Adams	Manitowoc
Arch bridges	Ashland	Marathon
Bailey bridges	Barron	Marinette
Bascule bridges	Bayfield	Marquette
Cable-stayed bridges	Brown	Menominee
Cantilever bridges	Buffalo	Milwaukee
Continuous bridges	Burnett	Monroe
Covered bridges	Calumet	Oconto
Deck truss bridges	Chippewa	Oneida
Drawbridges	Clark	Outagamie
Footbridges	Columbia	Ozaukee
Girder bridges	Crawford	Pepin
Inhabited bridges	Dane	Pierce
Lift bridges	Dodge	Polk
Military bridges	Door	Portage
Multispan bridges	Douglas	Price
Pile bridges	Dunn	Racine
Pontoon bridges	Eau Claire	Richland
Railroad bridges	Florence	Rock
Road bridges	Fond du	Rusk
Single span bridges	Lac	Saint Croix
Skew bridges	Forest	Sauk
Skybridges	Grant	Sawyer
Stress ribbon bridges	Green	Shawano
Suspension bridges	Green	Sheboygan
Swing bridges	Lake	Taylor
Toll bridges	Iowa	Trempealeau
Transporter bridges	Iron	Vernon
Truss bridges	Jackson	Vilas
	Jefferson	Walworth
	Juneau	Washburn
	Kenosha	Washington
	Kewaunee	Waukesha
	LaCrosse	Waupaca
	Lafayette	Waushara
	Langlade	Winnebago
	Lincoln	Wood

Figure 2.8. Metadata Record for a Digital Image

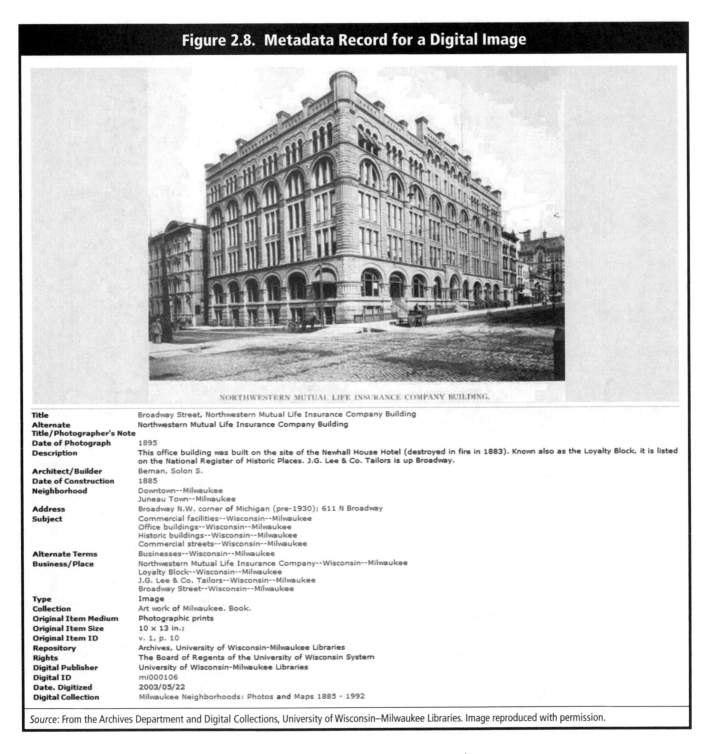

NORTHWESTERN MUTUAL LIFE INSURANCE COMPANY BUILDING.

Title	Broadway Street, Northwestern Mutual Life Insurance Company Building
Alternate Title/Photographer's Note	Northwestern Mutual Life Insurance Company Building
Date of Photograph	1895
Description	This office building was built on the site of the Newhall House Hotel (destroyed in fire in 1883). Known also as the Loyalty Block, it is listed on the National Register of Historic Places. J.G. Lee & Co. Tailors is up Broadway.
Architect/Builder	Beman, Solon S.
Date of Construction	1885
Neighborhood	Downtown--Milwaukee Juneau Town--Milwaukee
Address	Broadway N.W. corner of Michigan (pre-1930); 611 N Broadway
Subject	Commercial facilities--Wisconsin--Milwaukee Office buildings--Wisconsin--Milwaukee Historic buildings--Wisconsin--Milwaukee Commercial streets--Wisconsin--Milwaukee
Alternate Terms	Businesses--Wisconsin--Milwaukee
Business/Place	Northwestern Mutual Life Insurance Company--Wisconsin--Milwaukee Loyalty Block--Wisconsin--Milwaukee J.G. Lee & Co. Tailors--Wisconsin--Milwaukee Broadway Street--Wisconsin--Milwaukee
Type	Image
Collection	Art work of Milwaukee. Book.
Original Item Medium	Photographic prints
Original Item Size	10 x 13 in.;
Original Item ID	v. 1, p. 10
Repository	Archives, University of Wisconsin-Milwaukee Libraries
Rights	The Board of Regents of the University of Wisconsin System
Digital Publisher	University of Wisconsin-Milwaukee Libraries
Digital ID	mi000106
Date. Digitized	2003/05/22
Digital Collection	Milwaukee Neighborhoods: Photos and Maps 1885 - 1992

Source: From the Archives Department and Digital Collections, University of Wisconsin–Milwaukee Libraries. Image reproduced with permission.

- Subject
- Collection
- Date or date range of photograph

Figure 2.9 shows an advanced search screen that allows users to restrict their search terms to a specific metadata field, including *Subject* and *Date of Photograph*, among many others.

Figure 2.9. Search Options Based on Metadata Fields

From the Collections at UWM Libraries

UWM

Milwaukee Neighborhoods
Photos and Maps 1885 -1992

Home : About : Browse: Advanced Search : Map : Picturing Milwaukee : Preferences : My Favorites : Help

Search: Across all fields | **Selected fields** | By proximity

Find results with:

All of the words ▾ [_____] in Title ▾ field(s) show terms

The exact phrase ▾ [_____] in [_____] Search options. w terms

Title
Photographer
Date of Photograph
Map Publisher
Map Publication Date
Architect/Builder
Date of Construction
Neighborhood
Address
Subject
Alternate Terms
Business/Place
Period
Collection
Original Item ID
Original Item Location
Digital ID
Digital Collection
All

+ more fields | - fewer fields

Search clear all

© University of Wisconsin Board of Regents | UWM Libraries | Digital Collections | (| powered by
CONTENTdm ®

Source: From the Archives Department and Digital Collections, University of Wisconsin–Milwaukee Libraries. Image reproduced with permission.

Figure 2.10 shows how browse menus can be generated from the underlying metadata. The *Subject* metadata element in each record for each image has been populated with terms such as *Historic Buildings* that can be used to create categories by which users may browse a subsection of the collection based on a specific topical focus, thus narrowing their search results. Dates may be gathered into date ranges for the same purpose. Selecting *Historic Buildings* will retrieve all metadata records in which that exact term resides in the *Subject* field of each record.

Figure 2.11 shows one specific example pointing out *Date* and *Subject* metadata fields and their values that allow for this functionality.

Another way to look at differences in metadata functionality is to differentiate between metadata elements that contain purely or primarily descriptive information that can be entered in a *free text* form, on the one hand, and those elements that contain values that will be indexed and must be entered in a *standardized* or *controlled* form, on the other hand. Indexed fields are used for fielded searching, browsing, search limits, and navigation, and are usually hyperlinked to each other in the user interface. The contents of these fields also appear in system-generated indexes, such as indexes of names, places, and subject terms, usually arranged alphabetically. The example in Figure 2.12, from the Library of Congress's American Memory collections, further illustrates this distinction.

Notice that the content of the photographer's name and the subject elements in Figure 2.12 appear as hyperlinks (indicated by underlined text in a different font color than the rest of the record). These names and subject terms have been entered into the underlying metadata database

Figure 2.10. Browse Options Based on Metadata Fields and Values

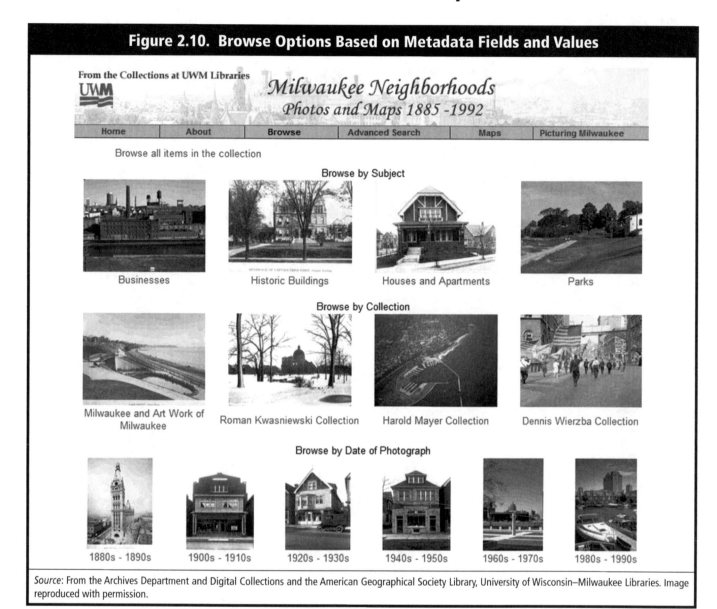

fields in a *controlled* form, following a standardized vocabulary, allowing them all to be linked to each other in the database and to be indexed for user browsing. Contrast these with content of the title and medium elements. The metadata there is entered in a *free text* way—that is, in a free-flowing, natural-language way that does not follow a set of preestablished, standardized terms. Clicking on the subject phrase *Indians--Montana* in Figure 2.12 takes the user to an index of all the images in the collection that include that phrase in a *Subject* field in the metadata, as illustrated in Figure 2.13.

2.1.2. Local versus Standard, Shareable Element Sets

Chapter 1 briefly mentioned two basic models for metadata scheme design, and Chapter 10 covers them both in greater detail. In one

Figure 2.11. Metadata Fields and Values That Underlie Functionality

Title	Broadway Street, Northwestern Mutual Life Insurance Company Building
Alternate Title/ Photographer's Note	Northwestern Mutual Life Insurance Company Building
Date of Photograph →	1895
Description	This office building was built on the site of the Newhall House Hotel (destroyed in fire in 1883). Known also as the Loyalty Block, it is listed on the National Register of Historic Places. J.G. Lee & Co. Tailors is up Broadway.
Architect/Builder	Beman, Solon S.
Date of Construction	1885
Neighborhood	Downtown--Milwaukee Juneau Town--Milwaukee
Address	Broadway N.W. corner of Michigan (pre-1930); 611 N Broadway
Subject	Commercial facilities--Wisconsin--Milwaukee Office buildings--Wisconsin--Milwaukee Historic buildings--Wisconsin--Milwaukee Commercial streets--Wisconsin--Milwaukee
Alternate Terms	Businesses--Wisconsin--Milwaukee
Business/Place	Northwestern Mutual Life Insurance Company--Wisconsin--Milwaukee Loyalty Block--Wisconsin--Milwaukee J.G. Lee & Co. Tailors--Wisconsin--Milwaukee Broadway Street--Wisconsin--Milwaukee

Source: From the Archives Department and Digital Collections, University of Wisconsin–Milwaukee Libraries. Image reproduced with permission.

model, for example, which is commonly used in CONTENTdm, the scheme designer develops a set of elements for one particular collection at a time, with many element names specific to that collection and not to others. These elements are then mapped to a standard shared scheme such as Dublin Core in the underlying database. The Dublin Core elements provide the basis for cross-collection searching within the institution. They can also be exported or made available for harvesting by consortia or third-party aggregators. In the other model of metadata scheme design, the designer uses a standardized shared scheme such as Dublin Core as the base set of elements to be used for all collections within the institution or consortium.

The point here is that metadata creators should have a sound understanding of the meaning of the Dublin Core (or other standard scheme) elements in order to enter good quality metadata into those elements in accord with their established definitions and scope. Those using local elements should have an understanding both of the local element definitions and of their underlying Dublin Core elements.

Table 2.3 illustrates mapping between customized local elements to standard Dublin Core elements for an image in the imaginary Bridges of Wisconsin digital collection. Compare and contrast the element names. Notice especially that several different local elements need to be mapped to the same Dublin Core element, since Dublin Core consists of a relatively small set of generic elements, in contrast to the much larger set of local elements in the metadata scheme developed specifically for this collection.

In all cases, metadata designers and creators need to balance local needs for searching individual local collections with current or future needs for cross-collection searching, consortial sharing, or harvesting

Figure 2.12. Functionality: Description versus Indexing

Display Images with Neighboring Call Numbers

Cheyenne Indian and son. Tongue River Reservation, Montana.

Rothstein, Arthur, 1915-1985, photographer.

CREATED/PUBLISHED
1939 June.

NOTES
Title and other information from caption card.

Transfer; United States. Office of War Information. Overseas Picture Division. Washington Division; 1944.

More information about the FSA/OWI Collection is available at http://hdl.loc.gov/loc.pnp/pp.fsaowi

SUBJECTS
Indians--Montana
Safety film negatives.
United States--**Montana**--Rosebud County--Northern Cheyenne **Indian** Reservation.

MEDIUM
1 negative : safety ; 3 1/4 x 4 1/4 inches or smaller.

CALL NUMBER
LC-USF34- 027684-D

REPRODUCTION NUMBER
LC-USF34-027684-D DLC (b&w film neg.)

SPECIAL TERMS OF USE
No known restrictions. For information, see U.S. Farm Security Administration/Office of War Information Black & White Photographs (http://www.loc.gov/rr/print/res/071_fsab.html)

PART OF
Farm Security Administration - Office of War Information Photograph Collection

REPOSITORY
Library of Congress Prints and Photographs Division Washington, DC 20540 USA http://hdl.loc.gov/loc.pnp/pp.print

DIGITAL ID
(intermediary roll film) fsa 8b18043 http://hdl.loc.gov/loc.pnp/fsa.8b18043

Source: Library of Congress, Prints & Photographs Division, FSA/OWI Collection, LC-USF34-027684-D; American Memory, "America from the Great Depression to World War II: Photographs from the FSA-OWI, 1935–1945." http://memory.loc.gov/ammem/fsowhome.html.

Figure 2.13. Functionality: Results of Indexed/Hyperlinked Subject Terms

Results 1-20 of 443 for Indians Montana

Page 1 of 23

Display: List View   Gallery View   Go to page: 1 2 3 4 5   Previous | Next

Item Titles	Collection Titles
1. U.S. Serial Set, Number 4015, 56th Congress, 1st Session, Pages 926 and 927	Century of Lawmaking
2. U.S. Serial Set, Number 4015, 56th Congress, 1st Session, Pages 924 and 925	Century of Lawmaking
3. Irene Rock, an Assinaboine [sic] schoolgirl at Fort Belknap	Photographs from the Detroit Publishing Company, 1880-1920
4. Custer's last stand	History of the American West
5. Custer's last stand	History of the American West
6. Cheyenne Indian houses. Tonque River Reservation, Montana	FSA/OWI
7. Custer's last charge	History of the American West
8. Custer's last fight	History of the American West
9. Cheyenne Indian and son. Tonque River Reservation, Montana	FSA/OWI
10. Cauthorn, Benjamin Ross. Trip to Montana by wagon train, 1865 April 14-November 9	Trails to Utah and the Pacific
11. Custer's last battle, "boots and saddles"	History of the American West
12. Great big Chickapoo chief; Burlesque Indian-coon song. 1904	Historic American Sheet Music
13. Battle of the Big Horn	History of the American West
14. Sunrise on Custer Battle field, the Custer scouts are Indians who were with Custer the morning of the fight	History of the American West

Source: Library of Congress, American Memory, "America from the Great Depression to World War II: Photographs from the FSA-OWI, 1935-1945." http://memory.loc.gov/ammem/fsowhome.html.

and aggregating by other metadata service providers. Metadata designers and creators usually choose to meet the immediate needs of their local collections and intended users first and foremost, but awareness of the need to take into account both local and shared element meanings can help to create good quality metadata that serves both local and shared resource discovery purposes at the same time. This important topic will be revisited in Chapters 3, 4, 9, and 10.

2.1.3. Describing Digital versus Original Resources

When creating metadata for a collection of digitized resources, you also need to keep in mind whether your metadata record is describing or representing the original analog/physical resource, the digitized resource, or some combination of both. Most metadata schemes and best practice guides today recommend creating separate descriptions (metadata

	Table 2.3. Customized Local versus Standard Dublin Core Elements	
Local Element Name	**Dublin Core Element Name**	**Value**
Title/Name of Bridge	**Title**	Manchester Street Bridge, Sauk County, Wisconsin
Date of Construction	**Date** Created	1896
Architect or Firm	**Creator**	Lassig Bridge and Iron Works
Type of Bridge	**Subject**	Truss bridges
Bridge Dimensions	**Format** Extent	128.9 ft. long; 13.7 ft. deck width
County	**Coverage** Spatial	Sauk County
Resource Type	**Type**	Still Image
Photographer	**Creator**	Kramer, Paul Jacob
Date of Photograph	**Date** Created	1955
Original Photograph Size	**Format** Extent	35 mm
Original Photograph Medium	**Format** Medium	Black & white slide
Original Photograph ID Number	**Identifier**	171, 33b-765
Original Photograph Collection	**Relation** IsPartOf	Paul J. Kramer Archival Photograph Collection
Original Photograph Repository	**Contributor**	Hagenville University Archives
Digital Collection	**Relation** IsPartOf	Bridges of Wisconsin
Digital Image Copyright	**Rights**	Copyright © 2009 Hagenville University
Digital Image Publisher	**Publisher**	Hagenville University
Digital File Format	**Format**	image/jpeg
Digital File Number	**Identifier**	WB0078736
Date Digitized	**Date** Created	2008-12-15

records) for the original analog object and the surrogate digital object, but in actual practice this is rarely followed in full.

2.1.3.1. The One-to-One Principle

The Dublin Core Metadata Initiative and several other metadata communities recommend following the so-called One-to-One (1:1) Principle—that is, one metadata description or record should describe or represent one and only one resource. For purposes of this chapter, the original analog object is considered to be one resource and the digital object another resource. This distinction is fully adequate for most metadata implementers. It should be briefly noted here that the concept of *resource* has a more particular meaning within the Semantic Web context, and the One-to-One Principle applies most clearly and fully in that context, to be covered in Chapter 11.

If you look again at the metadata elements and values in Table 2.3, you see that they include a mixture of information about the original resource, in this case a 35 mm black and white slide, and about the digital resource, in this case a JPEG image. For various reasons, to be discussed ahead, this is by far the most commonplace method of creating metadata records in digital collection databases today, despite the fact that it does not maintain the One-to-One Principle. In the example in Table 2.3, the metadata designer has devised local element names that explicitly distinguish between metadata values that apply to the original versus the digital resource.

2.1.3.2. Content versus Carrier

To better understand the issues entailed in the original versus digital resource distinction, it can be helpful to distinguish between the intellectual or artistic **content** of a resource and its physical or digital **carriers**. This distinction will also be helpful in understanding the difference between certain metadata elements such as Type and Format, to be covered in Chapter 4. The intellectual *content* of a textual document can, for example, be carried in multiple *carriers or manifestations* at the same time, without altering the intellectual content itself. The text of a document might exist in printed book form as ink on paper bound into a cover, as a Word document file, as a PDF file, and as an HTML text file all at the same time. The intellectual content is identical among each carrier or manifestation. This distinction, taken from the library cataloging tradition and the FRBR (Functional Requirements for Bibliographic Records) abstract model (International Federation of Library Associations and Institutions, 2009), can be quite useful for thinking about metadata for digital collections.

In the case of the image being represented by the metadata record in Table 2.3, you can distinguish between the intellectual/artistic content of what is depicted in the image, regardless of carrier, on the one hand, and the physical or analog photograph as one carrier or manifestation of that content, and the digital JPEG image file as another carrier or manifestation of the identical content, on the other hand. When you make this distinction, you can separate out those elements that apply to each aspect. In this particular example, the metadata scheme designer has already done this to a large extent in devising the set of local elements and their names. Table 2.4 illustrates a separation of metadata elements (or statements) that apply to each aspect.

These distinctions are useful for a better understanding of resource description, for a more informed approach to local metadata scheme design, and for exploring some possible alternative methods of realizing the One-to-One Principle, whether in whole or in part.

The *pure* One-to-One Principle presumes that an institution will create

Table 2.4. Content versus Carrier

Content:	
Title / Name of Bridge	Manchester Street Bridge, Sauk County, Wisconsin
Date of Construction	1896
Architect or Firm	Lassig Bridge and Iron Works
Type of Bridge	Truss bridges
Bridge Dimensions	128.9 ft. long; 13.7 ft. deck width
County	Sauk County
Resource Type	Still Image
Photographer	Kramer, Paul Jacob
Date of Photograph	1955

Original Carrier/Manifestation:	
Original Photograph Size	35 mm
Original Photograph Medium	Black & white slide
Original Photograph ID Number	171, 33b-765
Original Photograph Collection	Paul J. Kramer Archival Photograph Collection
Original Photograph Repository	Hagenville University Archives

Digital Carrier/Manifestation:	
Digital Collection	Bridges of Wisconsin
Digital Image Copyright	Copyright © 2009 Hagenville University
Digital Image Publisher	Hagenville University
Digital File Format	Image/jpeg
Digital File Number	WB0078736
Date Digitized	2008-12-15

separate database records for each logically distinct resource, link the records to each other in the database, and have some method of making that linkage obvious to users of the database interface, either though explicitly labeled links or by actually displaying the records together. Table 2.5 illustrates one method of realizing the One-to-One Principle by having two separate metadata records in a database.

Note how the unique ID numbers for the original and digital have been used to link the two records together. The assumption is that each will appear as a hyperlink in the user interface, allowing the user to select to view the other record. In this example, the decision was made to include the bulk of the metadata applicable to the intellectual artistic content in the database record for the original resource and not in the record for the digital resource. This is a scenario commonly given in examples of realizing the One-to-One Principle in database structures. It may, however, seem quite questionable, since the metadata about the intellectual/ artistic content applies equally to both the original and digital manifestations. One value of this method is not having to give the *content* information in more than one record within the database.

Table 2.5. One-to-One Principle: Separate Linked Records for Original and Digital Resources	
Record 1: Separate Record for Original Photograph:	
Title / Name of Bridge	Manchester Street Bridge, Sauk County, Wisconsin
Date of Construction	1896
Architect or Firm	Lassig Bridge and Iron Works
Type of Bridge	Truss bridges
Bridge Dimensions	128.9 ft. long; 13.7 ft. deck width
County	Sauk County
Resource Type	Still Image
Photographer	Kramer, Paul Jacob
Date of Photograph	1955
Size	35 mm
Medium	Black & white slide
ID Number	**171, 33b-765**
Collection	Paul J. Kramer Archival Photograph Collection
Repository	Hagenville University Archives
Has Digitized Format	**WB0078736**
Record 2: Separate Record for Digital Image:	
Title	Manchester Street Bridge, Sauk County, Wisconsin
Collection	Bridges of Wisconsin
Copyright	Copyright © 2009 Hagenville University
Publisher	Hagenville University
File Format	Image/jpeg
ID Number	**WB0078736**
Date Digitized	2008-12-15
Digitized Format Of	**171, 33b-765**

Another option would be to repeat that *content* information in both records. This is the typical approach in current library catalogs, where separate records are created for each manifestation of a resource, with the full bibliographic information given in each record.

It is worth noting here that the VRA Core standard makes a critical distinction between metadata records for a *Work*, meaning the original work of art held by a museum, and an *Image*, meaning a photograph or digital image surrogate representation of that work. They assume a database system in which these separate records are linked to one another. This will be explored in Chapter 8.

2.1.3.3. Problems with the One-to-One Principle in Practice

The most obvious problem with any of these scenarios is that most of those creating digital collections in medium to smaller-sized institutions, and even in many larger academic and research institutions, are creating a database of metadata records only for their digital resources, and the metadata records are often directly associated with the digital objects themselves in the user display. These implementers do not intend to catalog or represent the original resource per se. Many are using out-of-the-box digital content management systems, such as CONTENTdm, that link the digital image, text, or other type of digital file to a single metadata record. Such software packages do not usually have effective ways of linking the records in user-understandable ways in the public interface. Furthermore, the goal of most implementers is to have the online collection interface give users access to only the digital objects in the digital collection. It is not intended to be a catalog of the analog objects themselves, which may or may not have been individually cataloged in a separate database. This is often true as well for those designing their own local databases and interfaces using local programming expertise. This means that, in practice, most implementers must mix elements that describe the original object with those that describe the digital object in the same metadata record. This is a practical necessity.

2.1.3.4. Practical Options for Maintaining One-to-One

One way to deal with this issue is to use locally-defined elements that clearly distinguish between the two aspects when necessary, as is the case in the first column of Local Element Names in Table 2.3. Institutions that design a single Dublin Core based scheme instead of collection-specific schemes will often add separate local *Date Original* and *Date Digital* elements, both of which would be mapped to the Dublin Core *Date* element. Similarly, they might have a *Format Original* element that contains physical description information about an original photograph, painting, or sculpture and a *Format Digital* element that contains the digital image file type. In making these decisions, implementers will want to keep in mind which pieces of information their end users will find the most useful for finding and identifying each digital resource and not include more than is really useful.

There are, however, additional options for at least partially realizing the One-to-One Principle in a Dublin Core based environment. One is to put all of the information about the original object in a free-text form in a DC *Source* or *Relation IsFormatOf* element. Table 2.6 illustrates one of several possible ways of doing this.

Although this is not how the creators of the Dublin Core Metadata Element Set envisioned the *Source* element being used, it does provide a practical way of realizing the One-to-One principle using a single database record. The author of this book has rarely seen this done in practice, but it is nonetheless an option. The major

Table 2.6. One-to-One Principle: Single Record Using Free-Text Source Element for Information about the Original Resource

Element	Value
Title / Name of Bridge	Manchester Street Bridge, Sauk County, Wisconsin
Date of Construction	1896
Architect or Firm	Lassig Bridge and Iron Works
Type of Bridge	Truss bridges
Bridge Dimensions	128.9 ft. long; 13.7 ft. deck width
County	Sauk County
Resource Type	Still Image
Collection	Bridges of Wisconsin
Copyright	Copyright © 2009 Hagenville University
Publisher	Hagenville University
File Format	Image/jpeg
ID Number	WB0078736
Date Digitized	2008-12-15
Original Item [mapped to DC Source]	35 mm black & white slide, by Paul Jacob Kramer, 1955. Item no. 171, 33b-765 in the Paul J. Kramer Archival Photograph Collection, Hagenville University Archives.

downside of this method is that metadata values such as the date and creator of the photograph are not searchable, browsable, or indexable as dates and names in the database.

Another option is to simply reverse the logic and have the values for the original object in the body of the record and those for the digital object given in free text form in a DC *Relation* element. An advantage of this approach is that attributes of the original object are much more often of interest to users than those of the digital object, and they are more frequently of value for machine processing for searching, browsing, and indexing.

Yet another option is to keep all of the information about both the digital and original resource in separate elements for reasons of the fullest possible labeling, searching, and indexing, but to also have a free-text *Source*, *Relation*, or *Description* element that clarifies for users which dates, creators, and format characteristics apply to which manifestation. Although this may seem pointless within the immediate closed-system digital collection environment, this option takes on a much greater value when considering how the metadata will fare when taken out of its original environment, after having been harvested and aggregated with metadata from many other collections using simple, generic metadata element names. This *Source* or *Relation* element could be suppressed from public view and used only in metadata exposed for harvesting. Table 2.7 demonstrates the results of this last option after the local metadata has been harvested as simple Dublin Core.

Miller (2010) suggests a possible *compromise* option of putting into separate elements only those values applicable to the original manifestation that are considered necessary for user resource discovery and to intentionally use a *Source* element to explain any ambiguities that arise from having multiple dates, names, identifiers, and the like in the main body of the record.

The obvious downside in all of these scenarios is that a lot of information is duplicated in the metadata record, taking more time on the part of metadata creators and being potentially confusing or annoying to end users. These options are offered here for those who are strongly concerned with maintaining the One-to-One Principle and/or for those concerned with enhancing the meaning of their metadata used outside of its original context.

Table 2.7. Local Metadata after Harvesting as Simple Dublin Core: Value of *Source* Element for Clarifying Various Dates, Creator Roles, and Identifier Numbers in Body of Metadata

Element	Value
Title	Manchester Street Bridge, Sauk County, Wisconsin
Creator	Lassig Bridge and Iron Works
Creator	Kramer, Paul Jacob
Contributor	Hagenville University Archives
Coverage	Sauk County
Date	1896
Date	1955
Date	2008-12-15
Format	128.9 ft. long; 13.7 ft. deck width
Format	35 mm.
Format	Black & white slide
Format	Image/jpeg
Identifier	171, 33b-765
Identifier	WB0078736
Publisher	Hagenville University
Relation	Paul J. Kramer Archival Photograph Collection
Relation	Bridges of Wisconsin
Rights	Copyright © 2009 Hagenville University
Source	Digitized image of original 35 mm black & white slide of Manchester Street Bridge in Baraboo, Sauk County, Wisconsin, view to the north, taken by Paul Jacob Kramer in the Winter of 1955: item no. 171, 33b-765 in the Paul J. Kramer Archival Photograph Collection, Hagenville University Archives. Digital jpeg image WB0078736 created on Dec. 15, 2008.
Subject	Truss bridges
Type	Still Image

2.1.4. Descriptive versus Administrative Metadata

Chapter 1 noted the distinction between descriptive and administrative metadata and made the point that the same piece of metadata may sometimes serve both functions. In some cases, implementers include information in their descriptive metadata records that could be judged to serve a primarily administrative purpose. That is, it might be important for collection administration and preservation purposes, but be of little interest to end users. For example, the elements *Digital File Format, Digital File Number,* and *Date Digitized* in Table 2.8 could fall into this category. Some descriptive metadata schemes also include technical metadata, such as scanner settings, image resolution, and the like, as an element in their descriptive metadata scheme. See the *Digitization Specifications* element in Table 2.8 for an example.

One option is to simply not include this information as part of the descriptive metadata and to maintain it separately. In many cases, however, institutions and consortia need to keep this information directly associated with the descriptive metadata and with the linked digital object, either because they do not maintain separate administrative metadata, or, if they do, because there is a risk that this information may become disassociated from its digital file. A consortium may need this information, and the only practical way is to keep it with the descriptive metadata. Implementers do have the option, however, of keeping these metadata fields for staff view only, and not indexing or displaying them in the public interface. They may also block these fields from being harvested by metadata aggregators. This helps resolve some of the *original versus digital* metadata issues described in the previous section. In the local database, for example, it eliminates dates of digitization from search results. It is even more useful in an aggregated metadata environment.

2.1.5. The Need for Research

Creating metadata for unique digital objects, especially non-textual objects, can present special challenges that are not the case for published and textual items. Unlike most texts, which more or less identify their own subject content, images may come with little or no identifying information. The resource description process for digital image collections often entails doing research to identify

Table 2.8. Descriptive versus Administrative Metadata	
Element	**Value**
Title / Name of Bridge	Manchester Street Bridge, Sauk County, Wisconsin
Date of Construction	1896
Architect or Firm	Lassig Bridge and Iron Works
Type of Bridge	Truss bridges
Bridge Dimensions	128.9 ft. long; 13.7 ft. deck width
County	Sauk County
Resource Type	Still Image
Photographer	Kramer, Paul Jacob
Date of Photograph	1955
Original Photograph Size	35 mm.
Original Photograph Medium	Black & white slide
Original Photograph ID Number	171, 33b-765
Original Photograph Collection	Paul J. Kramer Archival Photograph Collection
Original Photograph Repository	Hagenville University Archives
Digital Collection	Bridges of Wisconsin
Digital Image Copyright	Copyright © 2009 Hagenville University
Digital Image Publisher	Hagenville University
Digital File Format	Image/jpeg
Digital File Number	WB0078736
Date Digitized	2008-12-15
Digitization Specifications	Scanned with Epson 1640XL flatbed scanner at 600 dpi. Edited with Adobe Photoshop.

Figure 2.14. The Need for Research

Source: From the Archives Department and Digital Collections, University of Wisconsin–Milwaukee Libraries. Image reproduced with permission.

the persons, places, and things depicted in the images. Take, for example, the image in Figure 2.14.

The metadata creator will ask the same questions at the time of cataloging that users would be expected to ask about this image, which might include the following:

- What is the name of the street?
- What year or time period is it?
- What kind of event is taking place?
- What is the name of the church in the background?
- What is the make and model of the automobile?
- Are there any identifiable business buildings in addition to private residences?

Table 2.9 shows metadata that was actually created for this image based on a combination of photographer's notes and original research.

When working with images, the cataloger is fortunate if the image comes with a written caption, title, or other accompanying textual material, or if some knowledgeable person has previously created a small local

Table 2.9. The Results of Research (Selected Elements)	
Title	Bremen Street
Description	Parade on Bremen Street with automobile looking south from Hadley to Clarke. Frank Burczyk Saloon at 1100 Bremen in foreground. St. Casimir's Church in background.
Date of Construction	1904
Neighborhood	Near North Side--Milwaukee
	Riverwest--Milwaukee
Address	1100 Bremen ST (pre-1930); 2778 N Bremen ST
Subject	Residential streets--Wisconsin--Milwaukee
	Parades and processions--Wisconsin--Milwaukee
	Automobiles--Wisconsin--Milwaukee
	Religious facilities--Wisconsin--Milwaukee
	Churches--Wisconsin--Milwaukee
	Bars--Wisconsin--Milwaukee
Alternate Terms	Polish Catholic churches--Wisconsin--Milwaukee
Business/Place	Frank Burczyk Saloon--Wisconsin--Milwaukee
	St. Casimir's Church--Wisconsin--Milwaukee

Source: From the Archives Department and Digital Collections, University of Wisconsin–Milwaukee Libraries. Reproduced with permission.

database or a written record of fairly reliable information for each image in a collection. If not, the cataloger will still be lucky if he or she at least has some notes about some or most of the images, such as a photographer's notes. These may be quite haphazard and may amount to only scribbling on the back of a photograph. Such notes may or may not be a good basis for constructing supplied titles for images in a collection, as well as descriptions and subject terms. A *supplied title* is a title invented by a cataloger for items that lack a title assigned by the creator or publisher of the item. Furthermore, any of these sources of information may be partial, incomplete, or sometimes even conflicting, misleading, or inaccurate.

Metadata projects do the best they can with the time, staff, and budget they have in terms of how much time and effort they can expend on doing research. Metadata creators often utilize various authoritative print and online reference sources. For images of local cities, for example, catalogers will often consult local city directories, phone books, census records, and historical atlases. It is not uncommon to find that street names, buildings, companies, and the like that are depicted in local photographs have changed names over time. These reference sources can help with making those connections. Such research helps with creating the content of name, subject, place, and time period metadata elements and composing descriptions, and they may also inform the formulation of supplied titles for images lacking formal titles. Web search engines such as Google and online sources such as Wikipedia can also serve as valuable and easily used research tools, especially with some healthy caution about authoritativeness of sources.

Many experts today see rich potential for end-user contributions to metadata, which can complement that created by in-house project staff. Digital image collections could potentially benefit from software that allows knowledgeable users to comment on an image and identify a person or place that the cataloger was not able to find or had inadvertently misidentified. Another option is to allow users to add their own tags via social or folksonomic tagging. Such information would need to be verified, of course. Best practice may be to keep the user-contributed comments, tags, and information separate from the staff-created metadata and clearly identify it as such. But staff may review and use user input to correct or enrich the professionally created metadata when warranted.

2.2. Introduction to the Dublin Core Metadata Element Set

This section of the chapter turns now to look at the first of the three standard metadata schemes or element sets covered in this book: the Dublin Core Metadata Element Set. The primary, official source for documentation of, and information about, Dublin Core is the Dublin Core Metadata Initiative website (http://www.dublincore.org/). The site is actively maintained and undergoes frequent revision as Dublin Core continues to evolve. It is useful to read through the "DCMI Frequently Asked Questions (FAQ)" at http://dublincore.org/resources/faq/.

The **Dublin Core Metadata Initiative (DCMI)** is the body that develops and oversees all aspects of the Dublin Core (DC) metadata scheme. Long before it had this name, a group of invited representatives from diverse information communities from around the world met in Dublin, Ohio (home of OCLC), in March 1995 to discuss the possibility of developing an international consensus on a simple resource description format. After much discussion, they reached consensus on a set of 12 or 13, soon expanded to 15, *core* descriptive metadata elements, known as the **Dublin Core Metadata Element Set (DCMES)**. The name "Dublin" is due to its origin at that 1995 workshop in Dublin, Ohio. It is known as Dublin "core" because its elements are broad and generic, usable for describing a wide range of resources. Those original 15 elements have been established as a formal ISO and ANSI/NISO standards (ISO 15836-2003; ANSI/NISO Z39.85-2007). After a time, the Dublin Core community developed various extensions, known as qualifiers, that could be added to the 15 core elements to further refine their meaning or define controlled vocabularies and other standardized schemes to be used with them. The original 15 elements without qualifiers are commonly known as **Simple** (or **unqualified**) **Dublin Core**, in contrast with **Qualified Dublin Core**, which makes use of these additional qualifiers.

The Dublin Core metadata elements and terms are officially documented on the web in the following two namespaces within the DCMI website. One way of understanding the meaning of the term "namespace" is as an identifier of a virtual space in which the names of terms are officially defined. The URLs for each of the following represents such a namespace:

- **Dublin Core Metadata Element Set, Version 1.1**: http:// dublincore.org/documents/dces/. This webpage documents the original 15 Dublin Core elements, which are also official ISO and NISO standards: ISO Standard 15836-2003 (February 2003): http://www.niso.org/international/SC4/n515.pdf and NISO Standard Z39.85-2007 (May 2007): http://www.niso .org/standards/resources/Z39-85-2007.pdf.

- **DCMI Metadata Terms**: http://dublincore.org/documents/ dcmi-terms/. This webpage includes the full range of current Dublin Core terms, including elements (properties), refinements (subproperties), vocabulary and syntax encoding scheme codes, and more.

2.2.1. Simple (Unqualified) Dublin Core

Table 2.10 lists each Dublin Core element in alphabetical order, along with its official DCMI definition and comment.

Table 2.10. The Dublin Core Metadata Element Set		
Element	**Definition**	**Comment**
contributor	An entity responsible for making contributions to the resource.	Examples of a Contributor include a person, an organization, or a service. Typically, the name of a Contributor should be used to indicate the entity.
coverage	The spatial or temporal topic of the resource, the spatial applicability of the resource, or the jurisdiction under which the resource is relevant.	Spatial topic and spatial applicability may be a named place or a location specified by its geographic coordinates. Temporal topic may be a named period, date, or date range. A jurisdiction may be a named administrative entity or a geographic place to which the resource applies. Recommended best practice is to use a controlled vocabulary such as the Thesaurus of Geographic Names [TGN]. Where appropriate, named places or time periods can be used in preference to numeric identifiers such as sets of coordinates or date ranges.
creator	An entity primarily responsible for making the resource.	Examples of a Creator include a person, an organization, or a service. Typically, the name of a Creator should be used to indicate the entity.
date	A point or period of time associated with an event in the lifecycle of the resource.	Date may be used to express temporal information at any level of granularity. Recommended best practice is to use an encoding scheme, such as the W3CDTF profile of ISO 8601 [W3CDTF].
description	An account of the resource.	Description may include but is not limited to: an abstract, a table of contents, a graphical representation, or a free-text account of the resource.
format	The file format, physical medium, or dimensions of the resource.	Examples of dimensions include size and duration. Recommended best practice is to use a controlled vocabulary such as the list of Internet Media Types [MIME].
identifier	An unambiguous reference to the resource within a given context.	Recommended best practice is to identify the resource by means of a string conforming to a formal identification system.
language	A language of the resource.	Recommended best practice is to use a controlled vocabulary such as RFC 4646 [RFC4646].
publisher	An entity responsible for making the resource available.	Examples of a Publisher include a person, an organization, or a service. Typically, the name of a Publisher should be used to indicate the entity.
relation	A related resource.	Recommended best practice is to identify the related resource by means of a string conforming to a formal identification system.
rights	Information about rights held in and over the resource.	Typically, rights information includes a statement about various property rights associated with the resource, including intellectual property rights.
source	The resource from which the described resource is derived.	The described resource may be derived from the related resource in whole or in part. Recommended best practice is to identify the related resource by means of a string conforming to a formal identification system.
subject	The topic of the resource.	Typically, the topic will be represented using keywords, key phrases, or classification codes. Recommended best practice is to use a controlled vocabulary. To describe the spatial or temporal topic of the resource, use the Coverage element.
title	A name given to the resource.	Typically, a Title will be a name by which the resource is formally known.
type	The nature or genre of the resource.	Recommended best practice is to use a controlled vocabulary such as the DCMI Type Vocabulary [DCMITYPE]. To describe the file format, physical medium, or dimensions of the resource, use the Format element.

Source: Dublin Core Metadata Element Set, Version 1.1:, http://dublincore.org/documents/dces/. Copyright 2010-10-11 Dublin Core Metadata Initiative. All rights reserved. http://www.dublincore.org/about/copyright/. Status: Recommendation.

The 15 elements are often listed in various orders and sometimes grouped in different ways. Table 2.11 illustrates one commonly used grouping. This grouping distinguishes those elements that pertain to the content of a resource, the intellectual property of a resource, and a particular instantiation of a resource. The distinction between content and instantiation is more or less the same as the distinction made previously in this chapter between *content* and *carrier*.

Table 2.11. DCMES Grouping Example 1

Content	Intellectual Property	Instantiation
Title	Creator	Date
Description	Publisher	Format
Type	Rights	Identifier
Subject	Contributor	Language
Source		
Relation		
Coverage		

Source: Composite based on Dublin Core Metadata Element Set, Version 1.1, 2010-10-11, http://dublincore.org/documents/dces/.

Table 2.12 offers another, complementary way of grouping the DC elements. While this grouping should not be taken too literally or have too much importance attached to it, it has been found useful in practice for teaching and learning the meaning of the individual elements and applying them in practice. This is the order in which the Dublin Core elements will be covered in Chapters 3 and 4.

Dublin Core was designed to be extremely simple, flexible, and extensible. Beyond the official definitions and comments on the elements, which include recommendations for the use of controlled vocabularies for some of the elements, the DCMI makes no specifications as to requirement or repeatability of DC elements. All Dublin Core elements are both optional and repeatable and may be used in any order. The goal is to make the basic element set as open, general, simple, and flexible as possible for a wide variety of applications in a wide variety of communities. It is expected that individual institutions and communities will create their own specifications for implementing Dublin Core locally, such as specifying required versus optional elements, element repeatability, the

Table 2.12. DCMES Grouping Example 2

Resource Identification	Responsibility	Content Type and Carrier	Subject Content	Relationships
Title	Creator	Type	Subject	Relation
Identifier	Contributor	Format	Coverage	Source
Date	Publisher		Description	
Language	Rights			

Source: Composite based on Dublin Core Metadata Element Set, Version 1.1, October 11, 2010. http://dublincore.org/documents/dces/.

order of the elements, and so forth, and that they will document these decisions in a local *application profile* or other type of usage document.

A distinction can be made between the original 15 Dublin Core elements and their original set of element refinements, on the one hand, and other elements and refinements added at a later time, on the other hand. The newer elements and refinements were added after roughly July 2000. At one time, the earlier group of elements and refinements had an official status of *Recommended*, while the later group had a status of *Conforming* (see, for example, the August 28, 2008, version of *DCMI Metadata Terms* at http://dublincore.org/documents/2006/08/28/dcmi-terms/). While this distinction is no longer made within the DCMI documentation, large numbers of implementations and digital content management systems do not include the newer group of elements and refinements. This later group includes such elements as *Audience, License, Provenance, Rights Holder, Instructional Method, Accrual Method, Accrual Periodicity*, and *Accrual Policy*. For the reasons just stated, this book does not cover the use of these newer Dublin Core elements and element refinements.

Table 2.13 shows an example of a simple, labeled set of Dublin Core metadata (NISO, 2004: 3). The element name is on the left, and the value of that element is on the right. Dublin Core is an element set with no prescribed data encoding format standard. There are any number of ways that this metadata content can be encoded for machine readability and use by an information search and retrieval system. The metadata may be encoded in proprietary database software, such as Microsoft Access, or in an open access standard such as XML. CONTENTdm encodes Dublin Core in XML behind the scenes.

Table 2.13. Simple Dublin Core Record Example

Element	Value
Title	Metadata Demystified
Creator	Brand, Amy
Creator	Daly, Frank
Creator	Meyers, Barbara
Subject	Metadata
Description	Presents an overview of metadata conventions in publishing.
Publisher	NISO Press
Publisher	The Sheridan Press
Date	2003-07
Type	Text
Format	application/pdf
Identifier	http://www.niso.org/standards/resources/Metadata_Demystified.pdf
Language	en

Source: Excerpt from *Understanding Metadata*. Copyright National Information Standards Organization (NISO). Used with permission.

2.2.2. Qualified Dublin Core

Large numbers of people implementing Dublin Core in cultural heritage settings soon discovered that the 15 simple elements were not rich enough for more nuanced resource description. The DC *Date* element provides a good example. It is defined as "a point or period of time associated with an event in the lifecycle of the resource" (Dublin Core Metadata Initiative, 2011). This could be any kind of date, such as the date the resource was created, published, updated, copyrighted, and so on. Simple Dublin Core has no way to specify which kind of date it is. The Dublin Core community, therefore, developed a set of **qualifiers** that can be added to the core elements to enrich the DC metadata scheme. *Qualified Dublin Core* (QDC) is a richer application of the Dublin Core metadata scheme than *simple* or *unqualified* Dublin Core. The terminology for qualifiers has developed over time, and the DCMI itself no longer uses this term. It is still common in practice, however, to speak of two kinds of Dublin Core qualifiers: element refinements and element encoding schemes.

Element refinements allow refinement and clarification of an element's content without changing the meaning of the base element that they qualify. They make the meaning of an element narrower or more specific. The qualified element shares the meaning of the unqualified element, but with a more restricted scope. Taking the DC *Date* element as an example, qualified Dublin Core includes the refinements *Created*, *Issued*, *Modified*, and others. To take another example, the meaning of the DC *Coverage* element may be more precisely specified as being either *Spatial* or *Temporal*, that is, the content of the element is a geographic area or place versus a date, date range, or time period. In the newer language of the DCMI, elements are called *properties*, and element refinements are called *subproperties*. This terminology shift is acknowledged here, but this book will nonetheless more frequently use the more common terms *element* and *refinement*.

Element encoding schemes constitute the other type of qualifier. The term "encoding" here is perhaps unfortunate because it sounds a lot like a type of machine-readable encoding standard, such as XML. But in this context, an *encoding scheme* refers to either a controlled vocabulary scheme or a standardized syntax encoding scheme. Dublin Core encoding scheme qualifiers serve as pointers to schemes, mostly external to the DCMI, that aid in the interpretation of an element's value. They allow an element's value to be identified as part of an existing controlled vocabulary, formal notation, or set of parsing rules. For example, the Dublin Core *Subject* element may contain any kind of subject term, ranging from uncontrolled keywords to terms taken from an established list, authority file, classification scheme, thesaurus, or subject heading list, such as the *Library of Congress Subject Headings* (LCSH), *Medical Subject Headings* (MeSH), or the *Dewey Decimal Classification* (DDC), among others. These types of **vocabulary encoding schemes** are designated in Qualified Dublin Core by standardized abbreviations, such as LCSH, MeSH, and DDC, respectively. Vocabulary encoding schemes also include simple lists, such as the *DCMI Type Vocabulary* (DCMIType) for the DC *Type* element and *Internet Media Types* (IMT) for the DC *Format* element. **Syntax encoding schemes** may include specific ways of formatting data, such as the World Wide Web Consortium's Date-Time Format (W3C-DTF) for formatting dates. These schemes will be covered in Chapters 3 and 4 in the sections on the Dublin Core elements to which they pertain and in Chapter 5 on Controlled Vocabularies.

Table 2.14 depicts which Dublin Core qualifiers go with which elements (slightly adapted from Dublin Core Metadata Initiative, 2005). Notice that not all elements have qualifiers. This table contains only the earlier set of DC elements and qualifiers established before roughly the year 2001, as discussed in section 2.1.1. These are the elements and qualifiers that are more widely adopted and implemented in many digital collection management systems, while the elements and qualifiers added after these are not as widely implemented.

Table 2.14. Dublin Core Qualifiers

DCMES Element	Element Refinement(s)	Element Encoding Scheme(s)
Title	Alternative	-
Identifier	-	URI
Date	Created Valid Available Issued Modified	DCMI Period W3C-DTF
Language	-	ISO 639-2 ISO 639-3 RFC 1766 RFC 4646
Type	-	DCMI Type Vocabulary
Format	-	IMT
	Extent	-
	Medium	-
Subject	-	LCSH MeSH DDC LCC UDC
Description	Table Of Contents Abstract	-
Coverage	Spatial	DCMI Point ISO 3166 DCMI Box TGN
	Temporal	DCMI Period W3C-DTF
Relation	Is Version Of Has Version Is Replaced By Replaces Is Required By Requires Is Part Of Has Part Is Referenced By References Is Format Of Has Format	URI
Source	-	URI
Rights	-	-
Creator	-	-
Publisher	-	-
Contributor	-	-

Source: Adapted from Dublin Core Metadata Initiative, "Using Dublin Core," http://dublincore.org/documents/usageguide/qualifiers.shtml.

The element refinement names are inherent to the Dublin Core element scheme per se, while encoding schemes refer to external vocabularies or syntax standards. Four of these, however, are maintained by the DCMI: DCMIType, DCMIPeriod, DCMIPoint, and DCMIBox. It is possible in practice to use other vocabulary schemes besides those listed in Table 2.14, such as AAT and TGM for subjects and the Library of Congress/NACO *Name Authority File* (NAF or LCNAF) or the Getty *Union List of Artist Names* (ULAN) for names.

Table 2.15 illustrates one useful way of representing qualified Dublin Core for a digital resource, following the model of using collection-specific local element names mapped to Dublin Core. The end user would see only the local element name and its value. The DC element mapping and designations of refinements and encoding schemes reside behind the scenes, unless configured to display to end users in some user-friendly fashion.

2.2.3. Creation and Use of Dublin Core Metadata

Like any scheme, Dublin Core has both strengths and weaknesses. In practice, many implementers have found unqualified Dublin Core *too* simple for fully effective description of digital cultural heritage resources. Even Qualified Dublin Core does not always have the processing power that some implementers need in order to accomplish the search, browse, navigation, and identification functions they desire to implement for their users. It can be useful in this regard to contrast the original intent of Dublin Core with the ways in which it is actually being used today. The original developers of Dublin Core wanted to develop a set of core metadata elements that any webpage creator could understand and use to embed in webpages. They wanted to develop an element set that was simple enough to be used by people who were not information professionals. The focus was on creating metadata descriptions for *document-like objects* (DLOs) on the web: that is, webpages, documents, and other resources with document-like characteristics. Their hope was that the web could begin to be populated with a good deal of descriptive metadata embedded in web resources, using a common set of core elements richer than simple HTML meta tags, and that Internet search engines would make use of these for richer and more effective information retrieval across the web.

Table 2.15. Qualified Dublin Core Representation Example

Local Element Name	DC Element	Refinement	Scheme	Value
Date of Creation	Date	Created	W3CDTF	1696-09-28
Dimensions	Format	Extent		3.5 x 5.3 meters
Type of Art Work	Subject		TGM	Landscape paintings
Place Depicted	Coverage	Spatial	TGN	Flanders

For various reasons, this originally envisioned use of Dublin Core has not happened. The first and major reason is that most of the major Internet search engines do not use embedded metadata at all, or, if they do, they use it only to a very small extent. Alta Vista was a search engine that used to make more expensive use of the embedded HTML *Keywords* and *Description* metadata elements, but it has largely abandoned this. This is primarily because of what can be boiled down to the practice of *meta tag spamming*. In an ideal world, metadata creators would create metadata that genuinely represents the content of their resources. But human nature being what it is, especially where commercial profit is to be made, a significant number of meta tag creators intentionally misuse the tags to insert inaccurate terms and repeat terms as many times as possible in order to bring their sites up in the top ten hits in search engine results. The result has been that a significant number of metadata creators, outside of trusted communities such as libraries, archives, and museums, cannot be trusted to create accurate metadata or not to misuse it for higher search engine rankings. Therefore, most of the major Internet search engines now disregard metadata embedded in webpage headers, either ignoring it altogether or making use of it only minimally and very selectively.

A second reason that Dublin Core has not been implemented as originally envisioned has been that large numbers of web resource creators are not interested in creating descriptive metadata for their resources, even using a relatively simple standard such as Dublin Core. And when they are interested, they often do a poor job of it, using elements incorrectly and supplying incomplete or unintentionally inaccurate values. Some still hope that this situation may change some day.

But the fact that the original vision for the Dublin Core metadata element set was not realized does not mean that it has been unsuccessful in other areas. Quite to the contrary, Dublin Core has been highly successful and is probably the most widely used single metadata element set in the world today. Large numbers of cultural heritage organizations, especially libraries, currently use Dublin Core as their base metadata element set in a wide variety of digital collections. In these contexts, DC is being used primarily by information professionals rather than by so-called lay metadata creators. As has been mentioned several times, many libraries and other institutions implement Dublin Core using digital collection management software such as Greenstone, Insight + LUNA, and especially CONTENTdm, and the like.

Dublin Core has also been used by several domain-specific resource description communities as the basis for their own richer metadata element sets. For example, IEEE's Learning Object Metadata standard uses Dublin Core as its starting point and has added many additional elements specific to the resource description needs of the educational community.

Dublin Core has been used in many other subdomains of the public web—that is, trusted and controlled environments such as within individual websites' internal search engines, corporate intranets, subject portal and gateway sites, and some database-driven websites. Dublin Core has also been used in subject-specific database-driven website portals or gateways, especially in Australia and the Scandinavian countries. Dublin Core is used in Adobe Acrobat PDF files, RSS feeds, and some e-commerce and web applications. In these applications, DC has been widely successful, but not quite in the ways originally envisioned.

Perhaps one of the most important and long-term uses of simple, unqualified Dublin Core is as a lowest-common-denominator *mapping* or *switching* language. Metadata from richer schemes such as MODS, EAD, MARC, or even Qualified Dublin Core can be mapped into simple Dublin Core for sharing and exchange among systems that can *read* Dublin Core, but that cannot process all of these other more complex schemes. The *Open Archives Initiative Protocol for Metadata Harvesting* (OAI-PMH), probably the most commonly used method of harvesting cultural heritage metadata as of this writing, requires that all participants provide a set of simple Dublin Core metadata for every digital resource, even when they also have and/or provide metadata in other, more complex formats. Thomas Baker and Pete Johnston have written about Dublin Core as a useful kind of *pidgin* language (Baker, 2000; Johnston, 2006). A *pidgin* is an amalgam of basic words from different languages that allows people speaking different native languages to communicate with one another using an extremely simplified, limited, shared vocabulary and syntax for purposes such as basic commercial transactions, without having to know the full richness of each other's native languages. In the metadata context, Dublin Core can serve this kind of function. These points having been made, however, a majority of digital cultural heritage metadata is currently created using some form of Dublin Core as its base metadata element set.

2.2.4. The Dublin Core Elements in Practice

Chapters 3 and 4 will explore the use of each of the 15 Dublin Core elements in practice, including the element refinements for each, and commonly used encoding schemes. Special emphasis is given to those elements that are the most frequently misunderstood, confused, or misused in common practice. This includes especially the meaning of, difference between, and correct use of the following pairs of elements:

- *Type* and *Format*
- *Relation* and *Source*
- *Date* and *Coverage Temporal*

The DC elements are covered in Chapters 3 and 4 following separate sections on general types of properties or elements used for digital resource description common to many schemes, not just Dublin Core. These sets of subsections are intended to be taken together: that is, points about resource description made in the Chapter 3 section on Titles, for example, are not repeated in the subsection on the Dublin Core *Title* element. The two are intended to be read together to give a fuller picture of how to deal with titles in general and specifically in Dublin Core. Examples used in the sections on Dublin Core are largely repeated in Chapter 7 on MODS, in order to provide a basis for comparing and contrasting the relative structure, complexity, and functional capabilities of the two schemes.

2.3. Summary

This chapter has given an overview of some of the most fundamental aspects of creating metadata for digital objects, also known as resource description, and therefore also of designing a local or consortial metadata scheme or application profile. First, it is important to understand what is meant by terms and phrases such as *resource, object, description, record, resource description, cataloging, indexing,* and *metadata creation.* A *resource* is any object or collection of objects that is of interest to you or your users and that can be described in some way. The basic unit of metadata is a *statement* about a resource, consisting of the combination of a *property* (attribute, element, or field) name and its *value* or content, often known as a *property-value pair.* A collection of such statements constitutes a *record* or *description.* Each record describes or represents a specific resource and often serves as a surrogate for that resource. As the processes of metadata scheme design and of resource description begin, metadata designers and creators encounter issues such as *granularity* of description, element *repeatability,* and the ways in which different metadata elements play different *functions* for users and how this affects the kind of data that needs to be entered into those particular elements. One of the most basic and intractable challenges in metadata for digital collections is the common practice of mixing statements about a digitized resource and its analog original in the same record. The One-to-One Principle in its pure form is not usually maintained in practice. Understanding the distinction between intellectual/artistic *content* and different *carriers* or *manifestations* of the same content provides a helpful framework for dealing with the *One-to-One* issues, as well as the differences between elements such as Dublin Core *Type* and *Format.* Some metadata may be treated as *administrative* rather than *descriptive* metadata. Resource description of unique unpublished resources, especially images, frequently requires *research* in order to understand what the resource is about or what it is depicting.

This chapter also provided a general introduction to the *Dublin Core Metadata Element Set* (DCMES). While not originally devised for digital collections, it is the element set most widely used for digital collection resource description today. The element set is maintained by the *Dublin Core Metadata Initiative* (DCMI). The *DCMI Metadata Terms* namespace includes the original 15 core elements, as well as element refinements specific to some of the elements, vocabulary and syntax encoding scheme designators, the *DCMI Type Vocabulary*, and a number of newer elements and qualifiers added after the original set. The 15 original core elements (along with their qualifiers) remain the most widely implemented, and some software systems can accommodate only these. The DCMI expects that institutions, consortia, and other application communities will create their own Dublin Core *application profiles*, making their own specifications as to requirements, cardinality, order of elements, and the like for applying Dublin Core for their own local needs. Many institutions use digital content management system software that allows them to devise nonstandard local element names and map them to Dublin Core for interoperability and metadata sharing. Most frequently, institutions use the *OAI Protocol for Metadata Harvesting* (OAI-PMH), and, most often, the harvesting institutions use only the simple, unqualified Dublin Core version of the metadata.

▶ **Companion Website**

See this book's companion website at **http://www.neal-schuman.com/metadata-digital-collections/** for Chapter 2 review questions, suggestions for exercises, and other resources.

References

Baker, Thomas. 2000. "A Grammar of Dublin Core." *D-Lib Magazine* 6, no.10 (October). http://mirrored.ukoln.ac.uk/lis-journals/dlib/dlib/dlib/october00/baker/10baker.html.

Dublin Core Metadata Initiative. 2005. "Using Dublin Core." Dublin Core Metadata Initiative. November 7. http://www.dublincore.org/documents/usageguide/qualifiers.shtml.

Dublin Core Metadata Initiative. 2011. "Dublin Core Metadata Element Set, Version 1.1." Last modified January 10. http://www.dublincore.org/documents/dces/.

International Federation of Library Associations and Institutions. 2009. "Functional Requirements for Bibliographic Records." Last modified February. http://www.ifla.org/files/cataloguing/frbr/frbr_2008.pdf.

Johnston, Pete. 2006. "Metadata Sharing and XML." In *Good Practice Guide for Developers of Cultural Heritage Web Services*. Bath, UK: UKOLN. http://www.ukoln.ac.uk/interop-focus/gpg/Metadata/.

Miller, Steven J. 2010. "The One-to-One Principle: Challenges in Current Practice." In *Proceedings of the International Conference on Dublin Core and Metadata Applications*, edited by Diane I. Hillmann and Michael Lauruhn, 150–164. http://dcpapers.dublincore.org/ojs/pubs/article/view/1043.

NISO (National Information Standards Organization). 2004. *Understanding Metadata*. Bethesda, MD: NISO Press. www.niso.org/publications/press/UnderstandingMetadata.pdf.

Sutton, Stuart. 2007. "Tutorial 1: Basic Semantics." Presentation at DC-2007: International Conference on Dublin Core and Metadata Applications, Singapore, August 27–31. http://dublincore.org/resources/training/dc-2007/T1-BasicSemantics.pdf.

Zeng, Marcia Lei, and Jian Qin. 2008. *Metadata*. New York: Neal-Schuman.

Resource Identification and Responsibility Elements

Chapters 3 and 4 continue the topics of *resource description* and the *Dublin Core Metadata Element Set* started in Chapter 2. Chapters 3 and 4 explore the most common kinds of information needed to describe and provide access to digital resources, digging into nitty-gritty challenges faced by metadata designers and creators when attempting to provide good quality descriptive metadata. These two chapters first examine these topics apart from any single standardized metadata scheme, because all metadata designers and creators face these issues regardless of the particular schemes they are using. The focus in these sections is on information of common interest to users of digital collections, types of functionality commonly desired in digital collection retrieval systems, and common challenges and issues that arise in resource description practice. This examination also allows readers to think about different levels of functionality that they might want to offer users of their collections, and how different levels of detail in different metadata schemes, such as Dublin Core versus MODS, could either enable or interfere with that functionality. Each of these general sections includes a table listing elements from the DC, MODS, and VRA Core schemes that are relevant to that section.

Immediately following the section on each general type of element, a subsequent section details how this applies using the Dublin Core element set. These Dublin Core sections include the official definition and comment for each element, along with any applicable element refinements and encoding schemes from the official documentation. These sections also include several examples of the application of Dublin Core for recording kinds of information common in digital collections, often showing several variants and sometimes including further explanations.

This book is written with the understanding that a majority of readers currently use, or will be most likely to use, Dublin Core as their base metadata element set. Instead of devoting a separate chapter to general resource description issues and another chapter to the Dublin Core scheme, the two have been presented together throughout Chapters 3 and 4. This is intended to be useful to readers because a great deal of the information covered in the general sections applies to the concrete application of Dublin Core in practice, as well as to other element sets. Rather than having to consult two separate chapters on how to deal with, for example, Dates or Subjects when using Dublin Core, the reader can consult two immediately adjacent sections within a single chapter.

Why, then, is this content covered in two Chapters (3 and 4) instead of only one chapter? First of all, this avoids having one extremely lengthy chapter in the book. Second, it facilitates the use of the book for educational purposes, in introducing students to certain groups of elements before others. Instructors might wish to use these two chapters for two different course units. Third, the general element types and the corresponding Dublin Core elements covered in Chapter 4 are those that people often find to be the more challenging. It can be useful to get your feet wet with the relatively straightforward elements first, before tackling the complex ones.

3.1. Basic Resource Identification Elements

This section of Chapter 3 deals with resource description elements and practices that identify some of the most basic and immediate digital resource characteristics and that do not fall into one of the other element groupings used in Chapters 3 and 4.

3.1.1. Titles

Although virtually every metadata scheme has a *Title* element among its most basic set, deciding on the content of that element is not always so easy. Sometimes it is relatively straightforward, as when a published text has a single and clearly presented title on a title page. But textual and published resources that come with written titles sometimes bear several different titles or have more than one version of the same title. You may need to make a decision as to which to select for your primary title element and which to include as alternative titles. How do different metadata schemes address this issue and encode and label different kinds of titles for users?

Initial articles in a title, such as *The, A, An, Le, La, Les, Der, Die, Das,* and so on, can present problems for searching, indexing, and sorting. Many Dublin Core best practice documents recommend omitting them or inserting the article at the end of the title string. Some metadata schemes, such as MODS, have a method of explicitly handling initial articles for computer indexing without omitting them or changing their order. This is a good example of how a more complex scheme like MODS is built to address the needs of both searching/indexing and display in the way that it encodes title information. Chapter 7 will illustrate this.

Local photographs of people, places, and things are usually unpublished and more often than not do not come with a formally assigned title. The metadata creator then needs to supply one. This is commonly called a *supplied title*, sometimes contrasted with a *transcribed title*, which is transcribed from the resource itself. While in the Anglo-American library cataloging tradition, cataloger supplied titles are put in brackets because they are not transcribed from the resource itself, virtually all digital collection metadata best practice guides instruct *not* to use brackets. The brackets convention comes from a different resource description environment than metadata for digital collections and from cataloging rules intended primarily for published items that bear titles. Brackets can also interfere with retrieval and indexing of titles. In creating supplied titles for digital collections, you should take into account how titles sort and display in your local system. In many if not most digital collection systems, the user display resulting from almost any kind of search is a group of resources arranged alphabetically by title. Figure 3.1 gives an example from CONTENTdm.

Figure 3.1. Example of a Typical Title Display

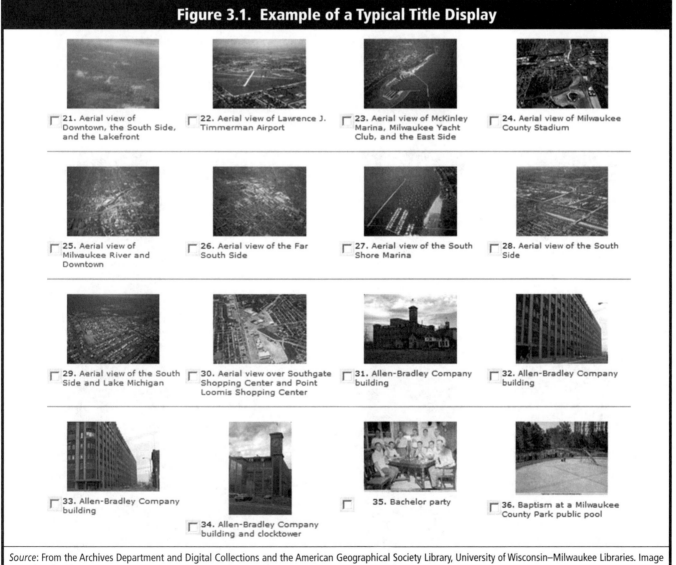

21. Aerial view of Downtown, the South Side, and the Lakefront

22. Aerial view of Lawrence J. Timmerman Airport

23. Aerial view of McKinley Marina, Milwaukee Yacht Club, and the East Side

24. Aerial view of Milwaukee County Stadium

25. Aerial view of Milwaukee River and Downtown

26. Aerial view of the Far South Side

27. Aerial view of the South Shore Marina

28. Aerial view of the South Side

29. Aerial view of the South Side and Lake Michigan

30. Aerial view over Southgate Shopping Center and Point Loomis Shopping Center

31. Allen-Bradley Company building

32. Allen-Bradley Company building

33. Allen-Bradley Company building

34. Allen-Bradley Company building and clocktower

35. Bachelor party

36. Baptism at a Milwaukee County Park public pool

Source: From the Archives Department and Digital Collections and the American Geographical Society Library, University of Wisconsin–Milwaukee Libraries. Image reproduced with permission.

When supplying a title, you have the freedom to decide on a system or consistent way to record titles for a particular collection so that they sort in a meaningful order. It is also a good general rule to make the titles as distinctive and informative as possible. Having 400 images with the title *Aerial view* or *Covered bridge*, for example, may not be good user-centered design. You also need to keep in mind what the metadata will look like when separated from the image it describes—after harvesting and aggregating, for example.

Figure 3.2 shows an image of a scene from Dresden, Germany, including the Semperoper opera house in the far left background, the Augustus Bridge over the Elbe River, passenger cruise boats, and more.

You might construct a title for this image differently if the theme of the digital collection is Rivers of the World, European Opera Houses, or Cities of Europe. In what order would you want them to sort for users? How might this affect your choice of the first word in the title? It is good to plan a general system for assigning titles for a given collection. Some title alternatives for this image might include the following, depending on the nature of the collection and the order desired for sorting hundreds or thousands of titles for a given collection:

- Dresden, Germany: View of Elbe River, Augustus Bridge, and Semperoper
- Germany—Saxony—Dresden: Augustus Bridge

Figure 3.2. Digital Image: Many Possible Supplied Titles

- Augustus Bridge, Dresden, Germany
- Augustusbrücke (Dresden)
- Germany, Dresden, Semperoper opera house
- Semperoper (Dresden, Germany)
- Elbe River, Dresden, Germany
- Many other possible variants

Notice that these titles are more descriptive, less likely to be duplicative, and arranged in an order more useful for alphabetical browsing than are the following:

- Dresden
- Elbe River
- Bridge in Germany
- Bridge in Dresden
- Augustus Bridge

Information objects may come with more than one title or variants on the same title. This may be the case, for example, with digitized books and other published textual resources. You may want to provide access to some or all of these in your metadata. Different standardized metadata schemes have ways of handling different forms of title. Even when supplying a title for a digital image, for example, there may be more than one form you wish to use for searching and indexing purposes.

Some implementers may be dealing with digitized journal articles or other resources that have volume and issue numbering or part names, or with resources in foreign languages for which they wish to include a title translated or transliterated into their own language or script, or various other issues related to titles. Some schemes, such as MODS, have developed ways of explicitly labeling and encoding these types of information, and implementers who need this functionality may wish to adopt such schemes instead of simpler schemes such as Dublin Core.

Table 3.1 provides a list of title elements from each of the four standard metadata element sets covered in this book. This type of table is given at the end of each section on general element types in this chapter and the following chapter, preceding the section on the relevant Dublin Core element. These tables are included for reference purposes and will be of use to those already familiar with these schemes and for readers who have completed subsequent chapters and come back to this chapter for reconsideration and review. These tables are summary overviews and do not include every possible attribute when they are not specifically relevant to the particular element covered in any given table.

3.1.2. Dublin Core *Title*

The Dublin Core *Title* element is fairly straightforward. Its content is usually free, unconstrained text that is either transcribed from the resource itself or supplied by the metadata creator when the resource

Dublin Core		
Title	*Qualifier:*	Alternative

MODS		
<titleInfo>	*Attributes:*	type (abbreviated, translated, alternative, uniform)
<title>		authority
<subTitle>		displayLabel
<partNumber>		
<partName>		

VRA 3.0		
Title	*Qualifiers:*	Variant
		Translation
		Series
		Larger Entity

VRA 4.0		
<title>	*Attributes:*	type (WORK title type: brandName, cited, creator, descriptive, former, inscribed, owner, popular, repository, translated, other IMAGE title type: generalView, partialView)
		pref
		source

Table 3.1. Title Elements in DC, MODS, and VRA

Source: This and all subsequent tables showing parallel elements from DC, MODS, and VRA have been compiled and adapted from the following sources:

- "DCMI Metadata Terms": http://dublincore.org/documents/dcmi-terms/. Copyright 2010-10-11 Dublin Core Metadata Initiative. All Rights Reserved. http://www.dublincore.org/about/copyright/. Status: Recommendation.
- "MODS User Guidelines (Version 3)": http://www.loc.gov/standards/mods/userguide/. Network Development & MARC Standards Office, Library of Congress.
- "VRA Core 3.0": www.vraweb.org/projects/vracore3/categories.html. Data Standards Committee, Visual Resources Association.
- "VRA Core Schemas and Documentation": http://www.loc.gov/standards/vracore/schemas.html. Network Development & MARC Standards Office, Library of Congress, and Data Standards Committee, Visual Resources Association.

itself bears no formal name. The Dublin Core Title element (or property) has one refinement qualifier (or sub-property): *Alternative*.

DC *Title*

- "A name given to the resource."
- "Typically, a Title will be a name by which the resource is formally known."

Refinement:

- **Alternative**
  - "An alternative name for the resource."
  - "The distinction between titles and alternative titles is application-specific."

Encoding Schemes: none

The following examples illustrate the application of the Dublin Core *Title* element and the *Alternative* refinement for various common situations.

Title Example 1: Simple title transcribed from title page of a digitized book:

Title: Plants of Upper Michigan

Title Example 2: Variant form of title transcribed from cover of same digitized book:

Title Alternative: Upper Michigan Plant Book

Title Example 3: Supplied title for digital still image, with supplied alternative title:

Title: Cologne Cathedral, Germany
Title Alternative: Kölner Dom, Germany

Title Example 4: Title with an initial article: three alternatives for recording in metadata:

Title: The Life and Times of Isabella Rios
Title: Life and Times of Isabella Rios, The
Title: Life and Times of Isabella Rios

Title Example 5: Title with subtitle:

Title: Plants of Upper Michigan: Descriptions and Drawings

Title Example 6: Alternative method of capitalization:

Title: The life and times of Isabella Rios: based on diaries and oral narratives as told to her daughter Maria Rios Campos

Title Example 7: Title with part name and number:

Title: Oregon Land Maps, Multnomah County, No. 12

In looking at these examples through Chapters 3 and 4, always keep in mind that *none* of the Dublin Core elements or refinements is required. Their use is a local application decision. If choosing to use Qualified Dublin Core, there is no obligation to use *all* of the available qualifiers. An institution may choose to use only certain qualifiers for certain elements as deemed useful for the institution or for a specific collection. It is, however, very important that the elements and refinements be used correctly, following the DCMI definitions and comments, when they are selected for use. Keep in mind that any or all of the refinement and scheme qualifiers given in these examples can be omitted, and the simple DC element and its value will still stand as an example of a correct use of that element.

The preceding examples are illustrative and not in any way definitive. Decisions about capitalization of titles are entirely a local implementation decision. Many implementers coming from the library cataloging tradition choose to capitalize only the first word of titles and any proper names included within the title.

It is up to local implementers to decide whether the *Alternative* refinement is useful for their application context. This element refinement allows implementers the option of selecting one title as the main or primary title and designating others as alternative. Some implementers may wish to use the value in the unqualified *Title* element as the only title form for alphabetical indexing and browsing, and make the titles designated as *Alternative* show only in the individual metadata record displays. Other implementers may not find a need to use the *Alternative* refinement at all for resources with variant forms of title. These points hold in general for the application of *all* DC refinements and will not be repeated in every section on DC elements in this and the following chapter.

3.1.3. Identifiers

Virtually all standard metadata schemes include some kind of identifier or ID element, often more than one or in more than one place in the scheme. An *identifier*, in metadata parlance, is a string of characters that uniquely identifies a resource.

The *uniqueness* of an identifier can be either global or local. Standard identifiers should be globally unique, while local identifiers may be unique only within the local institutional or consortial context. A digitized book might have an ISBN. Locally digitized resources should each have some kind of unique local ID number for easy and unambiguous identification. Each digital object should have a digital ID, which may be identical to its digital file name. Digital project coordinators need to give some thought to the file naming system they devise for each collection. Chapter 11 explores the conversion of local identifiers into truly unique, global identifiers, in the form of URLs, for use in a Semantic Web context.

It is important when creating a metadata record for a resource to be sure that the value of the identifier element is pointing the user to the resource being described in that record. This applies especially when the identifier is a URL. For example, if the record represents a specific item within a larger collection, the URL or other identifier must be specifically for that item, and not for the collection of which it is a part or for some other item in the collection. (A *Relation* or *Related Item* type of element presents a different situation and will be covered in Chapter 4.)

Table 3.2 provides a list of identifier elements from each of the standard metadata element sets covered in this book.

3.1.4. Dublin Core *Identifier*

The Dublin Core *Identifier* element is used to record a wide variety of types of identifiers, as shown in the sidebar on this page. Identifiers are by their nature constrained character strings that conform to some system, whether widely established and internationally standardized, such as an ISBN, or locally established, such as a local accession number or digital file name. The syntax encoding scheme qualifier *URI* may be used when the content of the element is a URL or other type of URI.

DC *Identifier*

- "An unambiguous reference to the resource within a given context."

- "Recommended best practice is to identify the resource by means of a string conforming to a formal identification system."

Identifiers

Standard identifiers include the following, among others:

- Uniform Resource Identifier (URI)
  - Uniform Resource Locator (URL): a specific type of URI
- Digital Object Identifier (DOI)
- International Standard Book Number (ISBN)
- International Standard Serial Number (ISSN)

Nonstandard identifiers may include the following types:

- Local database and system numbers
- Local accession and ID numbers

Table 3.2. Identifier Elements in DC, MODS, and VRA		
Dublin Core		
Identifier		
MODS		
<identifier>	*Attributes:*	type (doi, hdl, isbn, ismn, isrc, issn, issue number, istc, lccn, local, matrix number, music plate, music publisher, sici, upc, uri, videorecording identifier)
		displayLabel
		invalid
<location> <url>		
VRA 3.0		
ID Number	*Qualifiers:*	Current Repository
		Former Repository
		Current Accession
		Former Accession
VRA 4.0		
<location> <refid>	*Attributes:*	type (accession, barcode, shelfList, other)
<textref> <refid>	*Attributes:*	type (citation, openURL, ISBN, ISSN, URI, vendor, other)
Source: See Table 3.1.		

Syntax Encoding Scheme:

- **URI** (syntax encoding scheme)
  - "The set of identifiers constructed according to the generic syntax for Uniform Resource Identifiers as specified by the Internet Engineering Task Force."
  - "See: http://www.ietf.org/rfc/rfc3986.txt"

The following handful of DC examples provides concrete illustrations of common types of identifiers for digital resources that may be used with Dublin Core.

Identifier Example 1: ISBN:
    Identifier: 1234567890

Identifier Example 2: Music publisher number:
    Identifier: Z.Y. 22-0485 Obar Music Publishers

Identifier Example 3: Local accession number:
    Identifier: ABC-475985

Identifier Example 4: Digital file name:
    Identifier: TR_0003891

Identifier Example 5: URI for webpage displaying digital resource and its metadata:
    Identifier *URI*: http://www.xyz.edu/diglib/12345-678.html

3.1.5. Dates

Dates are another critical type of information about resources, and virtually every metadata scheme includes one or more kinds of date elements. Dates serve both an identification function, such as identifying the date on which a resource was published or created, and a retrieval function, because users commonly want to browse or limit their searches by date or date range.

Although at first glance they may seem among the more simple and straightforward pieces of metadata for a resource, dates can present some especially challenging problems for resource description, primarily in terms of their use for information retrieval by users. For one thing, human-readable dates are not usually unambiguously machine readable. A single date may be expressed in any number of different formats: for example, with names of months fully spelled out; with days, months, and years given in various orders; using various kinds of punctuation; with the year given fully or only the final two digits; with a zero preceding any single digit; and so on. The most common way to deal with this problem is to use a single consistent international date/time format, most commonly the YYYY-MM-DD format. For the date used in the example in the sidebar, this translates to: 2001-09-11. This is a method of restricting or controlling the value of an element.

When working with a resource, especially an unpublished local item, you do not always have a known or certain date. Sometimes you do not have any date at all. In some cases, you might be able to make an educated guess as to a probable range within which a photograph was taken, for example. Different communities have developed different conventions for dealing with unknown, approximate, and probable dates. Sometimes the dates are known, but they include a range of dates rather than a single date. Examples include the following:

- 1920? [questionable but probable year]
- circa 1920 [approximate year]
- 1920–1930? [questionable/probable date range]
- circa 1920–1930 [approximate date range]
- 1920–1930 [known/certain date range]
- 1920/1930 [known/certain date range]

You may also be dealing with known time periods that include a range of dates or that are widely known by a name such as Medieval, Renaissance, Restoration, Ming Dynasty, Nineteenth Century, and so on.

These examples all present issues for consistent information retrieval. Different systems handle dates in different ways. Not all systems will process question marks, hyphens, dashes, or the words *circa* or *approximately*. If the Date field contains the value *1920-1930* and a user limits a search by date to *1925*, will the system retrieve the item? These are questions to take up with the IT department, a systems person, or, probably more commonly, to find out yourself by experimenting with your digital collection software. Metadata schemes such as MODS have ways to explicitly encode the beginning and ending dates of a date range,

---

Computer Processing of Dates

All of the following are legitimate ways to record the same date, but a single computer system will not be able to interpret them all correctly.

- September 11, 2001
- Sept. 11, 2001
- 11 September, 2001
- 11 Sept., 2001
- de septiembre el 11
- il 11 settembre
- septembre 11
- 9/11/01
- 9/11/2001
- 09/11/01
- 09/11/2001
- 2001/09/11
- 2001-09-11
- 09-11-01
- 11/09/01
- 11/09/2001
- 11/9/01
- 11/9/2001
- 9.11.01
- 2001.11.09
- 2001.09.11

---

and ways of designating a date as approximate, inferred, or questionable. For metadata schemes that do not have this capability, such as Dublin Core, using a single hyphen without spaces is the most common format for representing a date range, for example: *1843-1878.* For unknown dates, most best practices recommend leaving the value blank rather than using a value such as *unknown, n.d., n/a,* or the like. This can clutter the database and date indexes with meaningless values for processing, as well as for harvesting by external aggregators and service providers. The University of Washington Libraries Metadata Implementation Group offers the following general advice about dates:

> Ideally you want to avoid distorting your data formatting as a workaround for software limitations. Software packages like CON-TENTdm could change through further development, or you could at some point want to migrate your data to a completely new software package. On the other hand, the search and display capabilities of the software package that your users will use for access is a reality you may need to take into account. There are no easy answers here. (University of Washington Libraries, "Date Field," http://www.lib.washington.edu/msd/mig/advice/datefield .html.)

Tables 3.3 through 3.5 illustrate different ways in which users might encounter date information for limiting their searches. In Table 3.3, the system has been configured to gather all of the dates from a given date range into a single search limit option presented to the user. For more recent time periods, these are presented as decades, and for older time periods, they are presented as centuries. This kind of decision would be based on the number of resources from these time periods in the collection. Table 3.4 depicts offering search limits by single date as a browse list from which the user selects. The decision to offer this kind of list might be questionable, since it may consist of nothing but an incredibly long list of years. Allowing the user to enter a specific year or gathering the years into decades as in Table 3.3 might be better options. Table 3.5 depicts one possible result that a user might experience when different conventions have been used for recording dates in a metadata *Date* element. Notice that dates that logically belong together appear in different places in the list. Computers read, sort, and process data literally unless a program is written or the system configured to specially handle characters such as question marks, hyphens, and introductory terms such as "circa."

Best practice is to use a widely adopted and documented standardized format, to consult with system administrators or those who know your local (and perhaps consortial) software, and most importantly to be consistent with whatever format you choose. Often your metadata can be processed or manipulated by computer when harvesting or when migrating from one system to another, especially if it has been recorded following a consistent pattern.

Another common challenge with dates is that various kinds of dates might apply to a single resource. Published resources sometimes contain various publication, copyright, and printing dates. Decisions need to be made about which date or dates to include for resource identification, without cluttering the record with multiple dates of little interest to end users.

Table 3.3. Date Range Search Limit Example

Limit Search by: Date Range
1700-1799
1800-1850
1850-1900
1900-1920
1920-1940
1940-1949
1950-1959
1960-1969
[etc.]

Table 3.4. Individual Date Search Limit Example

Limit Search by: Date
1900
1901
1902
1903
1904
1905
1906
1907
1908
1909
1910
[etc.]

Table 3.5. Example of Potential Problems with Indexing Uncertain Dates and Ranges

Limit Search by: Date
1900
1901
1901?
1902
1903
1904?
1904
1905
[etc.]
1900-1905?
1901-1903
1975-1980?
ca. 1900
ca. 1901
ca. 1904
ca. 1970

Some metadata schemes include elements or other designators that explicitly label the type of date, such as published or created, while others do not.

For digital images, the date of digitization, the date the photograph was taken, and dates applicable to what is depicted in the resource might all be judged important to include in the record. As discussed in Chapter 2, this can present problems in terms of distinguishing dates that apply to the original versus the digital object. Strictly speaking, the metadata record is representing the digital object, but you will often want or need to include information specific to the original object as well. The date of creation of an original photograph, the date of publication of an original book, or the date of creation of an object depicted in a digital image will be more important to end users than the date the digital file was created. To include these dates in a single metadata record violates a strict *One-to-One Principle*, as discussed in Chapter 2, but this is a better pragmatic choice if you want users to be able to search and sort objects in a collection by those dates that are intellectually meaningful to them.

It is debatable whether the date of digitization is meaningful to include in the descriptive metadata presented to public end users. It may better be left as administrative metadata and omitted from the descriptive metadata. There may, however, be various reasons why a project wants to include it in the descriptive metadata. Using local element names that make these distinctions, as one can do in CONTENTdm, is one solution in the immediate local closed-system context. After harvesting and aggregating as Simple Dublin Core, however, these distinctions are lost, and the result is multiple *Date* elements in a single record. In most systems it is also possible to omit these administrative dates from search and browse functionality, from public display if desired, and from exposure for harvesting.

It is unfortunately not uncommon that some metadata creators confuse the type of date information that is appropriate for use in the DC *Date* element with that for use in the DC *Coverage Temporal* element. Date information about the resource itself, such as when it was made, created, published, produced, and the like, goes into the DC *Date* element. The DC *Coverage* element, in contrast, is for *subject* content information: that is, when the resource is *about* or *depicts* a particular time period or event that can be represented by a single date or a range of dates. These are quite different uses of date information and should not be confused. The result is metadata that is incorrect and confusing to end users and that is not interoperable in a wider metadata sharing context.

Table 3.6 provides a list of date elements from each of the standard metadata element sets covered in this book.

3.1.6. Dublin Core *Date*

The Dublin Core *Date* element in its simple form can be used to record virtually any kind of date associated with a resource. The issues surrounding recording of date information in metadata and of machine processing of dates, discussed above, certainly apply when using the DC *Date* element. "DCMI Metadata Terms" includes five refinements and two encoding schemes for the *Date* element.

Table 3.6. Date Elements in DC, MODS, and VRA			
Dublin Core			
Date	*Qualifiers:*	Created	
		Valid	
		Available	
		Issued	
		Modified	
MODS			
<originInfo>			
<dateIssued>	*Attributes:*	encoding	
<dateCreated>		point (start, end)	
<dateCaptured>		keyDate	
<dateOther>		qualifier (approximate, inferred, questionable)	
VRA 3.0			
Date	*Qualifiers:*	Creation	
		Design	
		Beginning	
		Completion	
		Alteration	
		Restoration	
VRA 4.0			
<date>	*Attributes:*	type (alteration, broadcast, bulk, commission, creation, design, destruction, discovery, exhibition, inclusive, performance, publication, restoration, view, other)	
	Subelements:	earliestDate	
		latestDate	
Source: See Table 3.1.			

DC *Date*

- "A point or period of time associated with an event in the life-cycle of the resource."
- "Date may be used to express temporal information at any level of granularity. Recommended best practice is to use an encoding scheme, such as the W3CDTF profile of ISO 8601."

Refinements:

- **Created**
  - "Date of creation of the resource."
- **Issued**
  - "Date of formal issuance (e.g., publication) of the resource."
- **Available**
  - "Date (often a range) that the resource became or will become available."

- **Valid**
  - "Date (often a range) of validity of a resource."
- **Modified**
  - "Date on which the resource was changed."

Vocabulary Encoding Schemes:

- **W3CDTF**: W3C Date and Time Formats
  - "The set of dates and times constructed according to the W3C Date and Time Formats Specification."
  - "See: http://www.w3.org/TR/NOTE-datetime."
- **Period**: DCMI Period Encoding Scheme
  - "The set of time intervals defined by their limits according to the DCMI Period Encoding Scheme."
  - "See: http://dublincore.org/documents/dcmi-period/."

The following DC examples show several date situations that arise fairly commonly in digital collections, the use of the DC *Issued* and *Created* refinements, and the *W3CDTF* syntax encoding scheme.

Date Example 1: Known/certain date of publication of a book:
Date Issued *W3CDTF*: 1954

Date Example 2: Known date of creation of a photograph (year and month known, day not known:
Date Issued *W3CDTF*: 1966-03

Date Example 3: Known date of recording of an oral history interview (year, month, and day):
Date Created *W3CDTF*: 2002-11-27

Date Example 4: Date of digitization of a map:
Date Created *W3CDTF*: 2007-07-18

Date Example 5: Copyright date of a published music score:
Date: c1938

Date Example 6: Beginning and ending date of publication of a scholarly journal:
Date Issued: 1898-1935

Date Example 7: Approximate, uncertain, or questionable date of creation or publication (alternative possibilities):
Date Created: ca.1948
Date Created: 1948?

Date Example 8: Uncertain date, but within a certain date range of creation or publication:
Date Created: 1942-1944

Date Example 9: Uncertain/questionable date range of creation or publication (alternative possibilities):
Date Created: ca.1940-1949
Date Created: 1940-1949?

Dublin Core offers five element refinement qualifiers for the *Date* element. Of these refinements, *DateCreated* is most frequently applicable to unpublished objects and *DateIssued* to published objects. There are an additional three refinements added after the set of five refinements included in this chapter, but they are not yet widely implemented. These newer refinements include *DateAccepted*, *DateCopyrighted*, and *DateSubmitted*. Sometimes metadata designers have the impression that, because a qualifier exists, it ought to be used, or that it is commonly to be used in all application contexts. But this is not the case. For further guidance on the meaning of the various *Date* refinement qualifiers, see *Dublin Core—Dublin Core Qualifiers* (Dublin Core Metadata Initiative, 2005a). Recall again all of the examples given above and throughout Chapters 3 and 4 apply to both Simple and Qualified Dublin Core. If not using some or all of the qualifiers, simply omit them from the examples above.

The **W3CDTF** encoding scheme (http://www.w3.org/TR/NOTE-datetime) is commonly used in metadata for digital collections. This scheme presents a single, unambiguous way to record dates for which the year, month, and/or day is known. The format is YYYY-MM-DD, as shown in Date Examples 1–4. While this scheme works well for single dates when known or certain, it does not have a way to indicate approximate or questionable dates, or date ranges, as illustrated in Date Examples 6–9. The **DCMI Period** encoding scheme (http://www.dublincore.org/documents/dcmi-period/) is able to encode date ranges, but it must be implemented in an XML structure and is therefore not commonly used in metadata for most digital collections, especially if using a content management system such as CONTENTdm. Example 5 shows one optional method of indicating a copyright date by placing a lowercase *c* before the date, a method common in the library cataloging tradition.

Date Examples 7 and 8 show alternative ways to indicate an uncertain or questionable date. In the instance of Date Example 7, the metadata creator can estimate that the resource was probably, but not certainly, created or published in 1948, or that it was created or published sometime around 1948. Some metadata schemes, such as MODS, make a distinction between *approximate* dates, such as *ca. 1948*, and questionable dates, such as *1948?*. There may be cases in which the metadata creator knows with certainty that a resource was created or published in a certain decade or between a certain number of years, and he or she may give the date as a range, such as *1940-1949*, or *1942-1944*, and the like, as illustrated in Date Example 8. Date Example 9 illustrates a case in which the metadata creator can ascertain that a resource was probably, but not certainly, created or published during a given decade or other time range. There are yet other options for indicating approximate and questionable dates, such as *between 1942 and 1944*, *approximately 1948*, and so forth. The critical thing is to be consistent in using a single method of denoting such dates. The primary issue is one of machine processing of dates, as covered earlier in this chapter.

Practitioners commonly experience the challenge of wanting or needing to record multiple types of dates in a single metadata record. This is frequently especially true for dates relating to both a digital resource and the original analog resource from which it was digitized. Different kinds of dates may be distinguished from one another using distinctive, nonstandard local element names mapped to Dublin Core, and sometimes partially through the use of the DC *Date* refinements. But when harvested as Simple Dublin Core for metadata sharing and aggregation, these distinctions are lost. This issue was addressed in Chapter 2, and various options presented there for handling multiple dates. It will also be revisited in Chapter 9 on metadata harvesting and aggregating.

A not uncommon area of confusion can be dates used in the DC *Date* element and in the DC *Coverage Temporal* element. Dates in the *Date* element apply to the creation, publication, or other aspects of the resource itself as a work or a physical or digital manifestation. Dates in the *Coverage* element apply to the *subject content* of the resource, that is, when the resource is significantly *about* a particular date or time period, or an image *depicts* a person, place, or thing on a particular date or in a particular time period, and that temporal aspect is judged of significance for users' identification and retrieval needs in relation to the resource. This is a very important distinction to understand in order to use Dublin Core correctly and to give users accurate and good quality date information for resource identification, searching, browsing, and navigation.

3.1.7. Languages

Identification of the language of a resource is a common and important aspect of resource description. Users of digital collections frequently want to search for resources in specific languages or combinations of languages, or to limit their searches by language. Various metadata schemes and content standards often distinguish between textual and nontextual resources with regard to language. *Textual resources*, including books, pamphlets, printed music with lyrics, and some maps, as well as sung or spoken audio recordings that are presented in one or more languages, should be always assigned one or more *Language* elements. *Nontextual resources*, such as still and moving images without text, purely musical audio recordings, music scores without words, and so on, can simply omit a *Language* element. As with *Dates* and virtually all other metadata elements, most best practice guides recommend against using what are sometimes called *garbage* values such as *none* or *n/a* for *not applicable*, and recommend leaving elements or fields blank in such cases, with no data value.

Because *Language* elements are commonly used for searching, search limits, browsing, indexing, and gathering, it is important to use standardized or controlled forms of names for languages in either a verbal or coded form. Most schemes recommend or mandate the use of codes or terms taken from an internationally-established and controlled list of languages. The English names for languages are rarely the same as those that speakers of the language themselves use, such as *French* versus *Français* or *German* versus *Deutsch*. Using an internationally established code can eliminate this problem. The common working assumption is that such codes can be used for machine processing behind the scenes and that verbal forms can be generated for display in the language used for the metadata. Even though many systems cannot at present do this, such codes are still commonly used.

Table 3.7 provides a list of language elements from each of the standard metadata element sets covered in this book.

3.1.8. Dublin Core *Language*

The Dublin Core *Language* element is quite straightforward. Common practice is to use it only for resources with linguistic content, such as texts, images or maps with significant text, music scores with textual lyrics, and recorded sound and moving images with spoken or sung words. The language element is normally omitted for nonlinguistic resources such as images without significant text and recordings of purely instrumental music.

DC *Language*

- "A language of the resource."
- "Recommended best practice is to use a controlled vocabulary such as RFC 4646."

Refinements: none

Syntax Encoding Schemes:

- **ISO639-2**
  - "The three-letter alphabetic codes listed in ISO639-2 for the representation of names of languages."
  - "See: http://lcweb.loc.gov/standards/iso639-2/langhome.html."
- **ISO639-3**
  - "The set of three-letter codes listed in ISO 639-3 for the representation of names of languages."
  - "See: http://www.sil.org/iso639-3/."
- **RFC1766**
  - "The set of tags, constructed according to RFC 1766, for the identification of languages."
  - "See: http://www.ietf.org/rfc/rfc1766.txt."
- **RFC4646**
  - "The set of tags constructed according to RFC 4646 for the identification of languages."
  - "RFC 4646 obsoletes RFC 3066."
  - "See: http://www.ietf.org/rfc/rfc4646.txt."

While general best practice is to use a separate *Language* element for each instance of a language within the same resource, some systems, such as CONTENTdm, allow or may even require multiple language values in a single element or field, separated by a semicolon, space, or other designated piece of punctuation that signals the system to index the following character string as a separate value rather than as a contin-

Table 3.7. Language Elements in DC, MODS, and VRA

Dublin Core		
Language		

MODS		
	Attributes:	usage
<language>		objectPart
<languageTerm>	Attributes:	type (text, code)
		authority

VRA 3.0		
[none]		

VRA 4.0		
[none]		

Source: See Table 3.1.

uation of the preceding value. The following examples are divided into two main types, showing some alternative options for each.

Language Example 1: Digital text or sound recording in English (two alternatives):

Language *ISO 639-2*: eng
Language: English

Language Example 2: Digital text or sound recording in both English and French:

Option 1 (two separate elements using an internationally established controlled form):

Language *ISO 639-2*: eng
Language *ISO 639-2*: fre

Option 2 (two separate elements using English names of languages):

Language: English
Language: English

Option 3 (one element containing two separate values, separated by system-specific punctuation):

Language *ISO 639-2*: eng; fre
Or:
Language: English; French

The DCMI recommends as best practice using a controlled vocabulary, usually a coded form of language name, for the reasons discussed in the previous section. You may optionally give both a text and a coded form in the same record, although in Dublin Core practice this is rarely done.

3.1.9. Resource Attributes Not Readily Accommodated in Dublin Core

Some implementers of digital collections have a desire, and often a need, to include certain types of information about their resources for which no Dublin Core element exists. Common examples include *Audience*, *Edition*, *Place of Publication*, *Location*, and *Note*, be it a general, all-purpose note element or one or more specific types of note elements. Other elements could include lists of credits, cast, performers, and a host of other possibilities. It must be emphasized that "DCMI Metadata Terms" does include an *Audience* element, but it is not one of the original 15 elements, is not widely implemented, is not often included in many Dublin Core-based digital content management systems, and is not commonly added by implementers. Dublin Core has no element for separately recording an edition statement. If given in a metadata record, it could be included within the DC *Title* element along with the title to which it applies. *Location* refers to the location in which a resource resides: for example, the library, archive, or museum holding an original painting, sculpture, rare book, letter, personal diary, and the like. Museums and other institutions describing works of art and architecture frequently desire or need to separately record, label, and machine process information such as artistic technique, style, and period, among other elements. The following examples illustrate four types of information that have no corresponding Dublin Core elements. If used in most current applications of Dublin Core, they need to be shoehorned into one of the 15 original core elements.

Non–Dublin Core Element Examples

Audience Example 1: Digitized children's book:
   Audience: juvenile

Audience Example 2: Digitized oral reading of short story targeted for adolescents:
   Audience: adolescent

Editions Examples: Different editions of published books (two unrelated examples):
   Edition: 2nd ed.
   Edition: Third edition

Note Examples: Various types of notes:
   Note: Performers: Henry Strozier (Ebenezer Scrooge), Eugene J. Anthony (Nutley), Penelope Reed (Emily Claxton), Tom Blair (Fred), Dennis Kennedy (Topper), Lynn Mansbach (Fred's Wife).
   Note: Based on the play "The Underground" by Charles Wentwood, originally produced in London in 1917.

Location Example 1: Repository holding original diary:
   Location: Hagenville University Archives

Location Example 2: Physical location of painting:
   Location: National Gallery of Art (Washington, District of Columbia, United States)

Many implementers have chosen to use the DC *Description* element for any kind of information that does not fit into one of the other DC elements, in addition to its primary scope as covered in Chapter 4. Although this is beyond the original intended meaning of that element and is technically incorrect, it is probably the least offensive choice in such cases. If choosing to use the *Description* element in this way, any of the examples above could substitute the DC element name *Description* for the more specific, non-DC element name used there.

Another type of information included in many metadata schemes, but not in Dublin Core, is *metadata about the metadata*, sometimes called *meta-metadata*. Such information often includes elements such as the date of metadata creation, date of last metadata update, metadata record identifier, metadata creator or source (a person or organization), and metadata standard(s) used. Such information can be very helpful to some users of metadata records, especially other metadata professionals, consortia, harvesting and aggregating service providers, and sometimes also end users, in determining the quality, currency, and authoritativeness of the metadata. The MODS scheme includes this kind of information in a *RecordInfo* element and various subelements. Some schemes, such as the *Content Standard for Digital Geospatial Metadata*, also include the contact information of the person and/or institution that created the metadata.

Table 3.8 provides some selected examples of elements, subelements, and attributes in the MODS and VRA element sets that do not have any clear Dublin Core equivalents.

3.2. Name, Responsibility, and Intellectual Property Elements

3.2.1. Names and Roles of Agents Responsible for Resources

Individual persons, groups of persons, and organizations (also known as *corporate bodies*) may bear many different types of responsibility for analog and digital objects, such as author, editor, illustrator, commentator, photographer, painter, sculptor, architect, curator, donor, interpreter, and more. Some metadata schemes distinguish between primary and secondary levels of responsibility, as is evident in the Dublin Core *Creator* versus *Contributor* elements. Making these distinctions in practice can be difficult and sometimes seem rather arbitrary. Where do you draw the line? Some have asked whether it is even a meaningful distinction to make. Other metadata schemes, such as MODS, allow the inclusion of a *Role* subelement that specifically labels the type of responsibility that the named person or body bears in relation to the resource being described, such as photographer, artist, architect, editor, or illustrator. MODS uses these role designations with a single *Name* element, instead of having separate creator and contributor elements. VRA likewise has a single *Agent* element and uses role designators to convey the specific type of responsibility that a person or body bears in relation to the resource represented in the metadata.

Metadata creators often face other issues as well when recording names of persons and bodies responsible for resources. For example, they sometimes need to make decisions about how many names to include in a metadata record when there are many persons and/or bodies associated with a resource. How detailed do you want to be in including names for people or groups who play only minor or peripheral roles in relation to the content? You may need to make practical decisions about names likely to be of interest and value to users, including all names important for identification and retrieval.

Another critical issue is how to format names, because names of persons and bodies are often used for indexing, gathering, hyperlinking, navigation, and browsing in addition to identification. Issues of controlled versus uncontrolled forms of names arise. These are discussed further in the following section on the Dublin Core *Creator* and *Contributor* elements. Some implementers may wish to process parts of names separately for various purposes, such as first names, last or family names, dates of birth and death, and other aspects of names. Some

Table 3.8. Selected Elements, Subelements, and Attributes in MODS and VRA Not Readily Accommodated in DC

MODS		
<originInfo>		
<place>		
<placeTerm>	*Attributes:*	type (text, code)
		authority
<edition>		
<frequency>		
<targetAudience>	*Attributes:*	authority
<note>	*Attributes:*	type
<location>		
<physicalLocation>	*Attributes:*	authority
<recordInfo>		
[various subelements]		
VRA 3.0		
Technique		
Location	*Qualifiers:*	Current Site; Former Site; Creation Site, Discovery Site; Current Repository; Former Repository
Style/Period	*Qualifiers:*	Style; Period; Group; School; Dynasty; Movement
Culture		
VRA 4.0		
<culturalContext>		
<inscription>		
<author>		
<inscription>		
<text>	*Attributes:*	type (signature, mark, caption, date, text, translation, other)
<location>	*Attributes:*	type (creation, discovery, exhibition, formerOwner, formerRepository, formerSite, installation, intended, other, owner, performance, publication, repository, site)
<name>		
<refid>		
<stateEdition>	*Attributes:*	type (state, edition, or impression)
		num (state number or edition number)
		count (number of known states , known editions, or number of impressions in an edition)
<name>		
<description>		
<stylePeriod>		
<technique>		
<worktype>		

Source: See Table 3.1.

implementers want to be able to display names in natural language order and format within metadata records, and perhaps also in some indexes and browse selections, but to be able to process, gather, and create alphabetical indexes of names ordered by last name first. Some schemes such as MODS allow for this, while others such as Dublin Core do not.

Table 3.9 provides a list of name elements from each of the standard metadata element sets covered in this book.

Table 3.9. Name Elements in DC, MODS, and VRA

Dublin Core		
Creator		
Contributor		
MODS		
<name>	*Attributes:*	type (personal, corporate, conference)
		authority
<namePart>	*Attributes:*	type (date, family, given, termsOfAddress)
<displayForm>		
<affiliation>		
<description>		
<role>		
<roleTerm>	*Attributes:*	type (text, code)
		authority
VRA 3.0		
Creator	*Qualifiers:*	Role
		Attribution
		Personal name
		Corporate name
VRA 4.0		
<agent>		
<name>	*Attributes:*	type (personal, corporate, family, other)
<dates>	*Attributes:*	type (life, activity, other)
<earliestDate>		
<latestDate>		
<role>		
<culture>		
<attribution>		

Source: See Table 3.1.

3.2.2. Dublin Core *Creator* and *Contributor*

Dublin Core has two separate elements for the names of persons and corporate bodies that bear some kind of responsibility for the resource represented by the metadata record.

DC *Creator*

- "An entity primarily responsible for making the resource."
- "Examples of a Creator include a person, an organization, or a service. Typically, the name of a Creator should be used to indicate the entity."

Refinements: none

Encoding Schemes: none

DC *Contributor*

- "An entity responsible for making contributions to the resource."
- "Examples of a Contributor include a person, an organization, or a service. Typically, the name of a Contributor should be used to indicate the entity."

Refinements: none

Encoding Schemes: none

With Dublin Core, the metadata creator needs to make decisions about which persons and bodies bear primary responsibility for making the resource and which make secondary contributions to the resource. There may be a vague similarity between the concept of main and added entries in the library cataloging tradition, although any such similarity is far from exact. In general, primary responsibility is often construed to include such cases as the author or authors of a book or article, the photographer who took a photograph, the composer of a piece of music, or the painter of a painting. Secondary responsibility is often construed to encompass such cases as the illustrator of a book, when the illustrations are minor or secondary; the translator of a book written by someone else; or the editor of a book of collected essays. The lines are far from clear, and the metadata creator needs to make his or her best judgment. Developing a set of local guidelines and examples is also helpful. Ultimately it is rarely critical whether a name is entered in a *Creator* versus a *Contributor* element if the content of both elements are indexed and searchable together as names.

Some metadata schemes explicitly distinguish between *personal*, *family*, *corporate*, and *conference* names by having a means to label them as such within the metadata element coding. Dublin Core does not have this capacity. This would be of value if there were ever a need to separately process these types of names, such as generating separate personal and corporate body name indexes, or allowing users to limit their searches to one particular type of name.

Following the general spirit of the *Anglo-American Cataloguing Rules*, a corporate body would be designated as *Creator* only if the resource is substantially *about* the corporate body itself, such as the history of an organization, or a set of policies and procedures for an organization. This is mentioned here simply as a possible source for guidance, but Dublin Core is completely separate from any set of content guidelines or cataloging rules.

It is tremendously useful to be able to designate the specific role that a person or body plays in relation to the resource. Some schemes, such as MODS and VRA, have a single *Name* or *Agent* element, and they make use of *Role* terms to designate the precise role that the person or body plays in relation to the resource, such as Author, Editor, Illustrator, Translator, Photographer, Painter, Sculptor, and so on. This can eliminate the need to make the distinction between primary and secondary responsibility. Each user can make his or her own judgment as to the relative importance of the person or body based on the role. The "DCMI Metadata Terms" namespace does not include a *Role* refinement. A 2005 DCMI document titled "MARC Relator Terms and Dublin Core" (http://dublincore.org/usage/documents/relators/) deals with the use of role terms taken from the MARC Code List for Relators (http://www.loc.gov/marc/relators/), with further documentation in "Using Dublin Core - Appendix, Roles" (Dublin Core Metadata Initiative, 2005b). But this possibility has not been widely adopted in practice or implemented in most digital resource content management systems such as CONTENTdm, and the examples are given only in XML and RDF formats.

Practitioners still have the option of including role terms in *Creator* and *Contributor* elements, as illustrated as variant options in the Name Examples that follow. There are a few quite reputable implementers, application profiles, and best practice guides that *do* recommend this usage, although most do not. The problem with this practice is that it usually breaks the text-matching link among names using controlled forms. In the examples, the controlled form of Melville's name concludes with his death date, and the addition of the term "author" adds characters to the text string that break the exact match used to create a hyperlink. This reduces interoperability. Implementers who do choose to follow this practice almost all recommend using an established controlled list of role terms, most frequently the MARC Code List for Relators, or a selected subset of terms from such a list. Keep in mind that, although this list was originally developed for use in MARC records, it stands on its own as a controlled vocabulary that can be used by any community of practice in any metadata scheme, just as the DCMI Type Vocabulary is not restricted to used only in Dublin Core records.

Practitioners may also face issues with having multiple *Creators* in the same record, for example, the architect who created the building depicted in the image, the photographer who created the original analog photograph, and the digitizer who created the digital image from the photograph. This relates to the *One-to-One Principle* that is addressed in Chapter 2.

Names may be given in an uncontrolled or a controlled form taken from an authority file such as the Library of Congress/NACO *Name Authority File* (NAF) or the Getty *Union List of Artist Names* (ULAN), both mentioned and cited in Chapter 5, or a locally established list of names. Names may be given in *natural language* form, in *direct order* with first name first and last name last, or *inverted* to give the last name first for generating indexes arranged alphabetically by last name. Controlled forms usually use this inverted order, but a locally created authority file would not necessarily have to follow this practice, as long as a single form of name is established and used consistently. Controlled forms of name are preferred when the name is to be used for collocating, browsing, hyperlinking, and navigation. Systems normally create hyperlinks among all names that have exactly identical character strings, so a form of name that has any slight variation will not link to others.

Best practice is to use forms of names from a standardized and widely used authority file whenever applicable. It will often be the case, however, that local names will not be established in national authority files. Consistency in form of entry of names is then the best practice to follow, with inclusion of as much information as the metadata creator has available. a widely common best practice is to prefer the form of name in the Library of Congress *Name Authority File*, and if the name is not listed there, to give the name in this format: Last name, First name, Middle initial with period, year of birth and/or death if known, separated by a hyphen, insofar as any of these elements can be determined.

The following examples are not presented as in any way definitive. They represent a range of practice, not all of them best practices, including the option of using uncontrolled, *natural language* forms of personal names, given in *direct order*. They also include instances of using controlled forms of names, with last name given first, and other elements added, and taken whenever possible from an authority file such as the NAF or ULAN. This is the best practice common to most implementers and application profiles. Controlled forms of name may come from a locally established list of names or an authority file. The noncontrolled forms in the examples below are included for contrast and because there are a minority of implementers who use them. Note again that while some reputable implementers add role terms, most do not.

Name Example 1: Book author (several alternatives for recording a personal name):
   Creator: Herman Melville
   Creator: Melville, Herman
   Creator: Melville, Herman, 1819-1891
   Creator: Melville, Herman, 1819-1891, author

Name Example 2: Book illustrator (illustrations in an edition of Melville's Moby Dick, considered secondary or supplementary to the text):
   Contributor: Moser, Barry
   Contributor: Moser, Barry, illustrator

Name Example 3: Book translator (the third option, from the NAF, is general best practice):
   Contributor: Richard Hakluyt
   Contributor: Hakluyt, Richard
   Contributor: Hakluyt, Richard, 1552?-1616
   Contributor: Hakluyt, Richard, 1552?-1616, translator

Name Example 4: Photographer (two of several alternatives for recording a personal name):
   Creator: Paul Jacob Kramer
   Creator: Kramer, Paul Jacob

Name Example 5: Painter (two alternatives out of many):
   Creator: Cropsey, Jasper Francis, 1823-1900
   Creator: Jasper Francis Cropsey (American painter, 1823-1900)

Name Example 6: Corporate body name (used as either **Creator** or **Contributor** depending on the specific resource):
   Creator: United States. Court of Appeals (2nd Circuit)
   Contributor: United States. Court of Appeals (2nd Circuit)

Name Example 7: Conference name (for a resource consisting of content about a conference):
   Creator: Conference on War Work and Post-War Organization (1945 : Chicago, Ill.)

3.2.3. Publishers and Publication

Digital collections may consist of digitized versions of published or unpublished resources, or a combination of both. You may, for example, be creating metadata for a digitized book that was formally published in its original print format. You may want to include information on the original publisher in your metadata. This again touches on the original versus digital issue and the *One-to-One Principle*, since you may want to include both the online publisher of the digitized object and the publisher of the original analog object in your metadata.

Table 3.10. Publication Elements in DC, MODS, and VRA		
Dublin Core		
Publisher		
MODS		
<originInfo>		
<publisher>		
<place>		
<placeTerm>	*Attributes:*	type (text, code)
		authority
VRA 3.0		
[none]		
VRA 4.0		
[none]		
Source: See Table 3.1.		

Even unique, unpublished local resources such as photographs and slides, when digitized and made public on the Internet, may be considered to be *published* in the digitized form. To *publish* is to *make public* and available. The institution responsible for making a digital resource available online may therefore be considered to be the publisher of that digital resource. It may be worth noting that in *AACR2*, the library cataloging code, everything on the Internet is considered to be *published* for cataloging purposes.

Table 3.10 provides a list of publication elements from each of the standard metadata element sets covered in this book.

3.2.4. Dublin Core *Publisher*

DC *Publisher*

- "An entity responsible for making the resource available."
- "Examples of a Publisher include a person, an organization, or a service. Typically, the name of a Publisher should be used to indicate the entity."

Refinements: none

Encoding Schemes: none

The Dublin Core *Publisher* element can encompass the name of the publisher of an original resource—such as a digitized book, postcard, sound recording, map, or music score—that has an actual publisher, as well as the publisher of digital resource: that is, the institution making the digital resource available online. Dublin Core does not have a way to readily accommodate the place of publication, which is commonly given in citations for published works. The most common practice is to simply omit place of publication in Dublin Core records. The following examples illustrate the use of the DC *Publisher* element.

Publisher Example 1: Original book publisher name:
  Publisher: G. P. Putnam's Sons

Publisher Example 2: Original postcard publisher name:
  Publisher: Acmegraph Co.

Publisher Example 3: Institution making the digital collection publicly available on the Internet:
  Publisher: Hagenville University Digital Library
  Publisher: Greenfield Public Museum

Publisher Example 4: Postcard place of publication (publisher's location): inclusion in DC Publisher element not recommended as good practice:
  Publisher: Chicago, Illinois
  Publisher: Chicago, Illinois: Acmegraph Co.
  Publisher: Acmegraph Co. (Chicago, Illinois)
  Source: Original postcard publication: Chicago, Illinois: Acmegraph Co., 1955.

The first three options in Publisher Example 4 for handling place of publication, in cases where implementers consider it important to include this information, are quite awkward and are not recommended. The last option using the *Source* element is much better practice. Including the place of publication in the *Publisher* element goes beyond the intent of this element and adds extraneous information beyond the name of the publisher alone. It should also be mentioned that place of publication definitely does *not* go into a Dublin Core *Coverage Spatial* element. Some implementers use a local name for this element such as *Place*, and some metadata creators have put place of publication information in this element, which is quite incorrect.

3.2.5. Rights, Ownership, and Restrictions on Access

Rights management metadata ranges from the simple to the complex, depending on the nature of the resource and the complexity of ownership and access rights. Different metadata schemes include such information as copyright statements and other more complex statements of rights, restrictions on access, terms and conditions of use, and provenance. Many digital collections have separate webpages that state the general intellectual property rights for the resources in the collection as a whole and policies for use of those resources. See, for example, "Guidelines for Using Public Domain Text, Images, Audio, and Video Reproduced from Cornell Digital Library Collections" at http://cdl.library.cornell.edu/guidelines.html and Syracuse University Digital Library's "Rights and Permissions" and "Remote Access to Restricted Collections" sections at http://library.syr.edu/cdm4/about.php. It is possible for a *Rights* element to contain a URL that points to a separate rights page, instead of or in addition to a copyright statement. Including an actual copyright statement in the metadata record is a best practice, even if also including a link to a separate page.

Different institutions may, for example, allow their digital images to be reused as long as attribution is made to its original source and the original copyright statement is included. Some may allow free use for educational purposes but not for commercial purposes. Some may allow access to higher resolution versions of digital images for a fee, and the website may have automated ways of handling these transactions. All of this information needs to be conveyed to end users somehow, most frequently in the metadata.

Table 3.11 provides a list of rights elements from each of the standard metadata element sets covered in this book.

Table 3.11. Rights Elements in DC, MODS, and VRA

Dublin Core		
Rights		
MODS		
<accessCondition>	*Attributes:*	type (no controlled list of types)
		displayLabel
VRA 3.0		
Rights		
VRA 4.0		
<rights>	*Attributes:*	type (copyrighted, publicDomain, undetermined, other)
<rightsHolder>		
<text>		
Source: See Table 3.1.		

3.2.6. Dublin Core *Rights*

DC *Rights*

- "Information about rights held in and over the resource."
- "Typically, rights information includes a statement about various property rights associated with the resource, including intellectual property rights."

Refinements: none

Encoding Schemes: none

Here are three examples of different rights statements varying in content and degree of detail. (The text of Example 3 is taken from an example in the *MODS User Guidelines* [http://www.loc.gov/standards/mods/userguide/] but here used in a DC element.)

Rights Example 1: Simple copyright statement:
  Rights: Copyright (c)2010 Hagenville University

Rights Example 2: Restrictions on use statement:
  Rights: Copying allowed only for noncommercial use with acknowledgement of source.

Rights Example 3: More complex rights and access conditions statement:
  Rights: Transmission or reproduction of materials protected by copyright beyond that allowed by fair use requires the written permission of the copyright owners. In addition, the reproduction of some materials may be restricted by terms of gift of purchase agreements, donor restrictions, privacy and publicity rights, licensing and trademarks. Works not in the public domain cannot be commercially exploited without permission of the copyright owner. Responsibility for any use rests exclusively with the user.

It is also possible to include a URL that links to a separate webpage that contains detailed information about rights, restrictions on access, and use of digital content for the particular collection or for all digital collections within an institution. Examples include "Guidelines for Using Public Domain Text, Images, Audio, and Video Reproduced from Cornell University Library Collections" at http://cdl.library.cornell.edu/guidelines.html, and "Copyright and Other Restrictions That Apply to Publication/Distribution of Images: Assessing the Risk of Using a P&P Image" at http://www.loc.gov/rr/print/195_copr.html.

3.3. Summary

Metadata scheme designers and metadata creators need to meet the resource discovery needs of their users. This chapter looks at some of the types of metadata elements most frequently needed for resource identification and retrieval. Basic resource identification elements include titles, identifiers, dates, and language designations. Elements relating to responsibility and intellectual property include names, publishers, and rights. With a few exceptions, the standard metadata schemes of Dublin Core, MODS, and VRA Core each include their own versions of, and specifications for, each type of element covered in this chapter. A summary table for each of these three schemes is included for each general type of element. This chapter includes detailed coverage of the relevant Dublin Core elements, while the relevant MODS and VRA elements are covered in Chapters 7 and 8, respectively.

Each type of element can present its own specific challenges in resource description practice and in serving common user needs and functions. Titles, for example, are commonly used in alphabetical displays that result from user searches. Their format and the presence of initial articles will affect this for users. Identifiers unique in their local context may not be unique when metadata is shared in wider contexts. Dates that include months and days need to be formatted in a consistent and unambiguous way for consistent computer processing. Computer systems often have problems processing date ranges and approximate and questionable dates designated with question marks and terms such as "circa," yet these are important designators of the nature of date information. Names of persons, groups, and organizations (corporate bodies) are usually entered in a controlled form in order to create links that allow users to navigate and collocate together everything by or about a particular person or body.

Despite the simplicity, flexibility, and extensibility of the Dublin Core Metadata Element Set, the elements do have official definitions and comments that define their meaning and scope, and implementers need to understand these and use the elements as intended in order for their metadata to be of reasonably good quality and to be interoperable in the larger metadata sharing environment. A common source of confusion is the practical necessity of most implementers to mix elements that describe the digital resource with those that describe an original analog resource in a single Dublin Core record. This may be the case in the DC *Identifier*, *Date*, *Relation*, *Creator*, and *Contributor* elements. Dublin Core's simplicity makes it highly interoperable compared to more complex, hierarchical schemes such as MODS, but it also makes Dublin Core more difficult to use for handling all of the resource identification and retrieval needs of many digital collection implementers. This becomes all the more obvious when comparing Dublin Core with a scheme such as MODS, which is the topic of Chapter 7. Most of the examples used in this chapter will appear again in that chapter for purposes of comparison and contrast. Chapter 4 continues the approach of this chapter, dealing with some of the more complex and challenging types of resource description information and their corresponding Dublin Core elements.

> ▶ **Companion Website**
>
> See this book's companion website at **http://www.neal-schuman.com/ metadata-digital-collections** for Chapter 3 review questions, suggestions for exercises, and other resources.

References

Dublin Core Metadata Initiative. 2005a. "Using Dublin Core - Dublin Core Qualifiers." Dublin Core Metadata Initiative. Last modified November 7. http://dublincore.org/documents/usageguide/qualifiers.shtml.

Dublin Core Metadata Initiative. 2005b. "Using Dublin Core - Appendix, Roles." Dublin Core Metadata Initiative. Last modified December 7. http://dublincore.org/documents/2005/12/07/usageguide/appendix_roles .shtml.

Dublin Core Metadata Initiative. 2010. "DCMI Metadata Terms." Last modified October 11. http://dublincore.org/documents/dcmi-terms/.

Resource Content and Relationship Elements

This chapter continues where Chapter 3 left off, turning to more complex and challenging types of resource description information and to the corresponding Dublin Core elements. This chapter explores information and metadata elements having to do with the intellectual or artistic *content* of digital resources, including general *resource type* and *genre* of content as well as *subject* content, be it topical, geographic, temporal, or other kinds of subject matter. Subject analysis and representation are two of the most challenging aspects of resource description and cataloging, regardless of the metadata scheme being used. This chapter provides an overview of these topics, with a special focus on subject analysis and indexing of still images. In addition to covering general *content* types (resource type and genre), this chapter also deals with *carriers* of that content, commonly found in format or physical description elements. The chapter concludes with a section on *relationships* among information resources and on metadata elements used to refer the user to other resources related to the one being represented in the main body of a metadata record. An understanding of these resource description issues and of these Dublin Core elements is also critical for good local or consortial DC-based metadata scheme or application profile design.

4.1. Resource Content and Carrier Elements

4.1.1. Content Types and Genres

Users frequently want to browse and to restrict or limit their searches for digital resources by the type or genre of resource. Terms such as *type*, *resource type*, and *type of resource* are commonly used in metadata schemes to indicate the broad, general kind of content of a resource. Common designations at this broad, general level include such terms as *text, image, sound, still image, moving image, notated music, software,* and the like. At this broad level, the term used in a *resource type* element applies to the *intellectual or artistic content* of the resource regardless of its physical or digital *carriers*. Thus a text that is digitized as multiple image files remains textual content and retains a resource type element value of *Text*, even when the carrier or digital file format is *Image*. These types of terms go into the Dublin Core *Type* element and the MODS *TypeOfResource* element. The "DCMI Type Vocabulary" (http://www.dublincore.org/documents/dcmi-type-vocabulary/) provides a good example of a controlled list of resource type terms and is in fact strongly recommended, if not mandated, for use in most Dublin Core implementations.

In a collection that consists of only one type of resource, the value of including this element might be questioned. But when one thinks about this collection being cross-searched along with other collections containing various resource types and the metadata being harvested and aggregated by an outside agency, the value of this element becomes much more apparent. This is one of the most important ways by which users typically want to browse or to limit or refine their searches to particular types of content. Tables 4.1 and 4.2 illustrate this. If a resource type element has not been included in the metadata for a given collection, users' ability to limit searches by resource type when searching across collections of multiple types of resources has been taken away.

Some institutions want to allow users to browse and search by yet more specific designations for types of content than the very broad terms such as *text*, *image*, *sound*, and the like. Table 4.3 contains a random selection of diverse examples of more specific content type terms that various implementers might want to use. These terms are closer to what some metadata schemes consider *Genre* terms. The concept of *genre* in resource description practice is fuzzy, often encompassing aspects of content, media, carrier, form, and physical characteristics. In MODS, these kinds of terms go into the *genre* element, in contrast to the *TypeOfResource* element, which is reserved for more general, high-level terms used for basic content type designation, search limits, browse categories, and so forth. In Dublin Core, which is a much simpler scheme than MODS, these more specific content type and genre terms might need to go into a *Type* element.

Virtually all standard metadata schemes and best practice guides agree that resource type and genre terms should be taken from a controlled vocabulary. It is critical that the values entered into these elements be consistent if they are to function for search limits, browse categories, and hyperlinking. The vocabularies recommended or mandated for general, high-level resource type terms are the "DCMI Type Vocabulary" for Dublin Core and the "Values for <typeOfResource>" for MODS (http://www.loc.gov/standards/mods/userguide/typeofresource.html). Vocabularies commonly recommended for more specific resource type and genre terms are the *Art and Architecture Thesaurus* (AAT), the *Thesaurus for Graphic Materials* (TGM), and sometimes also the *Library of Congress Subject Headings* (LCSH) and the "MARC Genre Term List" (http://www.loc.gov/standards/valuelist/marcgt.html).

Table 4.1. Broad, Generic Type of Resource Search Limit Example

Limit Search by: Type of Resource
Moving Image
Physical Object
Still Image
Sound
Text

Table 4.2. Broad, Generic Type of Resource Browse Example

Browse by: Type of Resource			
TEXT	STILL IMAGE	SOUND	MOVING IMAGE

Table 4.3. More Specific Type of Resource or Genre Search Limit Example

Limit Search by: Type of Resource	
Adventure fiction	Paintings
Animations	Pamphlets
Books	Photographs
Book chapters	Plans
Children's literature	Poems
Daguerreotypes	Portraits
Diaries	Postcards
Drawings	Rock music
Engravings	Sculptures
Folktales	Sketches
Glass transparencies	Slides
Manuscripts	Technical reports
Movies	Television
Music scores	programs
Newspaper articles	Videos

Chapter 5 will give an overview of these and other common vocabularies. The Library of Congress maintains a useful list of controlled "Genre/ Form Code and Term Source Codes" (http://www.loc.gov/standards/sourcelist/genre-form.html). These are not in any way restricted to being used within MARC catalog records. It is also not uncommon for implementers to devise their own local controlled lists of terms, whether taking terms from one or more existing vocabularies, creating their own original lists, or some combination of the two.

Table 4.4 provides a list of type and genre elements from each of the standard metadata element sets covered in this book.

4.1.2. Dublin Core *Type*

DC *Type*

- "The nature or genre of the resource."
- "Recommended best practice is to use a controlled vocabulary such as the DCMI Type Vocabulary. To describe the file format, physical medium, or dimensions of the resource, use the Format element."

Refinements: none

Vocabulary Encoding Scheme:

- **DCMIType**: DCMI Type Vocabulary
  - "The set of classes specified by the DCMI Type Vocabulary, used to categorize the nature or genre of the resource."
  - "See: http://dublincore.org/documents/dcmi-type-vocabulary/."

The Dublin Core *Type* element is intended to provide a high-level designation of the content of the resource. For example, a resource may consist of text, sound, still image, moving image, or cartographic content. The *Type* element is especially useful for machine processing: that is, as a basis for users to be able to browse or limit searches to general resource types. With any element intended for these types of functions, the values must be drawn from a controlled list of terms if they are to successfully provide those functions. The most common such vocabulary used by Dublin Core practitioners is the "DCMI Type Vocabulary" (http://www.dublincore.org/documents/dcmi-type-vocabulary/). This vocabulary consists of 12 terms: *Collection, Dataset, Event, Image, Interactive Resource, Moving Image, Physical Object, Service, Software, Sound, Still Image,* and *Text.* It should be noted that the term *Image* in this vocabulary

Table 4.4. Type and Genre Elements in DC, MODS, and VRA

Dublin Core		
Type		
MODS		
<typeOfResource>	*Attributes:*	collection
		manuscript
<genre>	*Attributes:*	type
		authority
VRA 3.0		
Record Type		
Type		
VRA 4.0		
<work>, <collection>, or <image>		
<worktype>		

Source: This and all subsequent tables showing parallel elements from DC, MODS, and VRA have been compiled and adapted from the following sources:

- "DCMI Metadata Terms": http://dublincore.org/documents/dcmi-terms/. Copyright October 11, 2010, Dublin Core Metadata Initiative. All Rights Reserved. http://www.dublincore.org/about/copyright/. Status: Recommendation.
- "MODS User Guidelines (Version 3)": http://www.loc.gov/standards/mods/userguide/. Network Development & MARC Standards Office, Library of Congress.
- "VRA Core 3.0": www.vraweb.org/projects/vracore3/categories.html. Data Standards Committee, Visual Resources Association.
- "VRA Core Schemas and Documentation": http://www.loc.gov/standards/vracore/schemas.html. Network Development & MARC Standards Office, Library of Congress, and Data Standards Committee, Visual Resources Association.

Dublin Core Examples and Presentation Conventions Used in This Chapter
See Chapter 3, p. 65, for source information.

predates the later addition of the terms *Still Image* and *Moving Image*, and that it was retained in the vocabulary. General best practice is to use the more specific terms to allow users greater precision in narrowing their searches. But older DC records that used the term *Image* still have a valid DCMI Type Vocabulary term. Some best practice guides recommend or mandate the use of both the general term *Image* and the more specific term *Still Image* or *Moving Image*, when applicable, in order to ensure maximum consistency in user functionality and interoperability in diverse metadata environments. It should also be noted that the term *Physical Object* is intended for metadata records representing actual physical objects themselves, such as objects in a museum, and *not* digital images or other surrogate representations of those objects. Digital images of physical objects should be assigned a DC *Type* element value of *Image* and/or *Still Image*.

As discussed in the previous section, some implementers want to have more specific designations than the kinds of very broad, high-level terms used in the DCMI Type Vocabulary. They might want their users to be able to browse, search, or limit searches to more specific subtypes or genres of texts, still images, and so on. It is equally valuable to draw these terms from a controlled vocabulary. The most common controlled vocabularies for more specific type and genre terms were listed in the previous section. It is also common for implementers to devise their own local controlled lists of terms, whether taking terms from one or more existing vocabularies, creating their own original lists, or some combination of the two.

Suggested best practice for Dublin Core implementers wishing to use more specific type or genre terms than those contained in the DCMI Type Vocabulary is to include in their metadata both a broad DCMI Type Vocabulary term *and* a more specific type or genre term. The terms may be given in separate DC *Type* elements within a metadata record or in a single *Type* element with the values separated by a semicolon (in systems that use multiple values in a single field). This is, for example, the recommendation in the "Mountain West Digital Library Dublin Core Application Profile" (http://mwdl.org/public/mwdl/MWDL_DC_Profile_Version_1.1.pdf). This practice maintains the significant value and functionality resulting from use of the DCMI Type Vocabulary terms in addition to allowing use of more specific terms.

The following small selection of examples shows both uses of the DC Type element. Examples 1–5 illustrate the use of high-level DCMI Type designators, while examples 6–9 illustrate just a handful of the many possible more specific content or genre designators.

Type Example 1: Digitized photograph:
   Type *DCMIType*: Still image

Type Example 2: Text digitized as PDF or HTML document:
   Type *DCMIType*: Text

Type Example 3: Text digitized as set of image files (each page a separate image file):
   Type *DCMIType*: Text

Type Example 4: Digitized audio recording of an oral history interview:
Type *DCMIType*: Sound

Type Example 5: Digitized video recording of an oral history interview:
Type *DCMIType*: Moving image

Type Example 6: Digitized yearbook (text content):
Type: yearbooks

Type Example 7: Digitized novel (text content):
Type: novels

Type Example 8: Digitized slide (still image content):
Type: slides

Type Example 9: Digitized technical drawing (still image content):
Type: technical drawings

Type Example 10: Digitized oral history interview (text, sound, or moving image content):
Type: interviews

There is a strong argument to be made in favor of mandating a *Type* element in all DC records and using the DCMI Type Vocabulary terms, even when all the resources in a particular collection are of the same type and even if also using more specific subtype terms. These terms have value for users searching across multiple collections consisting of various resource types even within the same local institution, allowing them to limit their searches. These terms have the same value for users outside of the local context when searching repositories of harvested and aggregated metadata records. Most digital content management system software allows the metadata designer to set up a template that automatically provides an element and its value when they will be the same for all resources in that collection. That means that this needs to be done only once at the template creation stage, and metadata creators do not need to fill in the *Type* field in every new record they create.

A common source of confusion is the difference between the DC *Type* and *Format* elements. The DCMI definition of the *Type* element includes this distinction. The *Type* element designates the general type of *content* of the resource, regardless of the physical or digital carrier of that content. The *Format* element designates specifics about the physical or digital *carrier* of the content, such as digital file format, physical medium, dimensions or size of a physical object, digital file size, and duration or playing time of a digital or physical sound or moving image file. The DCMI does not make this equation of *Type* and *Format* with *content* and *carrier*, respectively, and in truth the correspondence is not exact, but it most often does apply and provides a useful basis for understanding the difference between these two elements and applying them correctly. The *Type* should remain constant regardless of the *Format*. There may be multiple *Formats* of the same *Type* of content. For example, a *Text* may be provided in print, HTML, PDF, and image formats. Printed books are often digitized by making a digital image of each page of the book, as well as its cover. The *Type* remains *Text*, while the

Format becomes *JPEG image* or *TIFF image* or some other specific digital image file format. For library catalogers, it is often helpful to consider DC *Type* as roughly equivalent to the Leader character Position 06, *Type of record* (the *Type* fixed field element in OCLC), while DC *Format* is roughly equivalent to the MARC 300 field (*Physical Description*). While the value in the DC *Type* element is used primarily for machine processing for browsing, searching, and navigation, and therefore requires a consistent controlled vocabulary value, the values in DC *Format* elements are much less often so-used by implementers and therefore usually contain free, uncontrolled text. The exception is when using DC *Format* to designate the digital file type, in which case a controlled vocabulary *is* normally used.

4.1.3. Formats and Physical Description

In contrast to type of resource, which usually indicates the generic characteristics of the intellectual or artistic content of a resource, most standard schemes also include one or more elements used to record more specific format characteristics, such as the specific physical material, medium, or media of which the resource is made; specific physical size, dimensions, or measurements; specific length, duration, or playing time (for sound and moving image resources); or specific digital file format and file size. For the most part, these all have to do with the type and characteristics of the *carrier* of the intellectual/artistic content of a resource. Sometimes the distinction between content and carrier is not quite so smooth, and sometimes the same types of terms used in a *type* or *genre* element might also be used in a *format* element, when the term indicates specific type of physical or digital resource. Examples of common kinds of information recorded in these elements include the following: color slide; black and white photograph; 35 mm; 35 mm color slide; 17 minutes; image/gif; audio/mp3; 32343 bytes.

The Dublin Core *Format* element covers all of these aspects, as does the MODS *PhysicalDescription* element. In VRA, these characteristics are recorded in separate elements for *Measurements*, *Material*, and *Technique*. Each of these standard schemes includes methods of further designating these characteristics, as outlined in Table 4.5 and illustrated for Dublin Core in this chapter, MODS in Chapters 7, and VRA in Chapter 8.

4.1.4. Dublin Core *Format*

The Dublin Core *Format* element encompasses a fairly wide variety of information about the physical and/or digital characteristics of a resource. In contrast to the *Type* element, which for the most part designates the type of content regardless of carrier, as discussed, the *Format* element usually designates or describes specific details about the carrier. See the discussion on the difference between DC *Type* and *Format* in the preceding section.

Table 4.5. Format and Physical Description Elements in DC, MODS, and VRA

Dublin Core		
Format	*Qualifiers:*	Extent
		Medium

MODS		
\<physicalDescription\>		
\<form\>	*Attributes:*	type (material, technique)
		authority
\<reformattingQuality\>	*Values:*	(access, preservation, replacement)
\<internetMediaType\>		
\<extent\>		
\<digitalOrigin\>	*Values:*	(born digital, reformatted digital, digitized microfilm, digitized other analog)
\<note\>	*Attributes:*	type (no controlled list of types)
		displayLabel

VRA 3.0		
Measurements	*Qualifiers:*	Dimensions
		Format
		Resolution
Material	*Qualifiers:*	Medium
		Support
Technique		

VRA 4.0		
\<material\>	*Attribute:*	type (medium, support, other)
\<measurements\>	*Attributes:*	type (area, base, bit-depth, circumference, count, depth, diameter, distanceBetween, duration, fileSize, height, length, resolution, runningTime, scale, size, target, weight, width, other)
		unit
\<technique\>		

Source: See Table 4.4.

DC *Format*

- "The file format, physical medium, or dimensions of the resource."
- "Examples of dimensions include size and duration. Recommended best practice is to use a controlled vocabulary such as the list of Internet Media Types."

Refinements:

- **Medium**
  - "The material or physical carrier of the resource."
- **Extent**
  - "The size or duration of the resource."

Vocabulary Encoding Scheme:
- **IMT**: Internet Media Types (MIME)
  - "The set of media types specified by the Internet Assigned Numbers Authority."
  - "See: http://www.iana.org/assignments/media-types/."

The following examples illustrate some common uses of the DC *Format* element for digital collections.

Format Example 1: Digital file format of digitized photograph:
Format *IMT*: image/jpeg

Format Example 2: Digital file format of textual transcription of oral history interview:
Format *IMT*: text/html

Format Example 3: Digital file format of digital sound recording of oral history interview:
Format *IMT*: audio/mp3

Format Example 4: Digital file size of digital audio file:
Format Extent: 2.18 MB

Format Example 5: Physical medium of original postcard (digitized as JPEG image file):
Format Medium: color lithograph

Format Example 6: Physical medium of original tapestry (photographed and digitized as TIFF image file):
Format Medium: wool and silk with gold and silver threads

Format Example 7: Digital audio file duration/playing time:
Format Extent: 2 min., 23 sec.

Format Example 8: Physical dimensions of original photograph (digitized as JPEG image file):
Format Extent: 3 x 7 in.

Format Example 9: Physical dimensions of original slide (digitized as JPEG image file):
Format Extent: 35 mm

Format Example 10: Physical height of original book (digitized as set of JPEG image files):
Format Extent: 27 cm

Format Example 11: Analog audio cassette duration/playing time (digitized as MP3 audio file):
Format Extent: 4 min., 12 sec.

Format Example 12: Physical characteristics of an original slide, given in a single *Format* element:
Format: 35 mm color slide

These examples show the correct use of the DC element refinements. Notice that when the *Format* element is used to give the digital file type, none of the refinement qualifiers applies. The DCMI also recommends the use of the *Internet Media Type* (IMT or MIME) vocabulary when the *Format* element contains the digital file format. Like the use of all controlled vocabularies, this increases functionality and interoperability. Format Examples 1–3 use these terms and illustrate the correct syntax.

Format Examples 5–6 show the use of the *Medium* refinement, which can apply only to physical format characteristics and not to digital file characteristics. Example 5 provides an instance in which the medium can be very similar to, and may often overlap with, the kind of terms that may sometimes be given in a *Type* element when using it for a more specific subtype or genre term. There is no absolute dividing line, and some implementers choose to take terms from a controlled vocabulary for use in the *Format* element to designate the medium. The same vocabularies listed previously in this chapter for more specific type and genre terms are also commonly used for Format terms in such cases. That having been said, it is more common to use *Type* for broad resource type designations taken from a controlled list and to use *Format* for specific details given in a less controlled or free-text form.

Format Examples 7–11 show the wide range of uses of the *Extent* refinement. It can apply to characteristics of either a digital or an analog resource. It encompasses both size and duration. This includes digital file size, physical size or dimensions of an analog object, and playing time of an analog or digital sound or moving image resource. In example 12, the physical characteristics, including both medium and extent, have been given in a single field. This is perfectly acceptable and is in fact quite common. But in such a case, a refinement is not used because neither *Medium* nor *Extent* applies to the entirety of the value given for the element.

It is important to keep in mind once again that all DC refinements are optional and that local implementers decide whether or not to use them, and, if they do use them, they also decide whether to designate each of them as required, recommended, optional, and the like.

Take special care not to confuse the Dublin Core *Format* and *Type* elements. Practitioners and students frequently find it difficult to distinguish between these two elements. Part of the confusion may stem simply from the names of the elements, which do not automatically convey for most people what each is intended to cover. This is a good case in point of why it is imperative to read Dublin Core element definitions and comments and to look at examples from usage guides in order to understand the meaning and intent of elements and not attempt to simply guess based on the element name alone.

Another common source of confusion for people new to Dublin Core is the frequent use of the *Format* element to include characteristics of both the digital resource and an original analog resource from which it was digitized. See the discussion of the *One-to-One Principle* in Chapter 2 for a better understanding of why this is usually a practical necessity. This means the inclusion of multiple *Format* elements in Dublin Core, some of them recording characteristics of the physical resource and some of them recording characteristics of the digital resource. Table 4.6 shows

Table 4.6. Format Elements for Both Original and Digital Manifestations in a Single Record

Record for 35 mm color slide digitized as GIF digital image file (selected elements)

DC Element	Refinement	Scheme	Value
Title			Women suffragists demonstrating for the right to vote, March 1913
Type		DCMI Type	Still Image
Format	Medium		Color photograph
Format	Extent		8 x 5 inches
Format		IMT	image/gif
Format	Extent		30175 bytes

Record for printed book with all pages digitized as set of JPEG image files (selected elements)

DC Element	Refinement	Scheme	Value
Title			Travel accounts of the Explorer P.J. Martins, The
Type		DCMI Type	Text
Format	Extent		157 p. ; 22 cm.
Format		IMT	image/jpeg

Record for 35 mm film reel digitized as QuickTime video file (selected elements)

DC Element	Refinement	Scheme	Value
Title			Civil rights marchers in Alabama, March 9, 1965
Type			Moving Image
Format	Medium		film
Format	Extent		35 mm.
Format	Extent		3 min., 37 sec.
Format		IMT	video/quicktime
Format			3879 bytes

three examples of the mixture of *Format* elements for the original and digital objects in a single record, including correct use of the *Medium* and *Extent* qualifiers for both original and digital characteristics. While some Dublin Core implementers chose to use the DC *Format* element only for the digital resource and not for its analog original, as reflected in their application profiles or best practice guides, this is not as common as including values for both the digital and the original resource in the same record.

4.2. Subject Content Elements

Some users may come to an online digital collection to do a *known item* search. That is, they are searching for a specific digital object that they already know about, or they are searching for everything by a specific photographer, artist, or publisher, or in a specific collection, of which they are already aware. In cases where a user knows exactly the item she wants, a highly targeted known-item search on title, name, standard identifier, or the like, will yield quick and immediate results. Many more users, however, come to explore a collection to find out what it contains and to discover what they don't already know about its contents. They will do *exploratory* searching or browsing. The most common and useful type of exploratory searching or browsing is by *subject*. Large numbers of users will search or browse a collection by subject terms.

Virtually all metadata schemes include either a general subject element or several specific types of subject elements to convey the subject content of a resource. Textual descriptions, abstracts, and tables of contents provide additional ways of conveying subject content in greater detail, and they contain text that can be rich for general keyword searching. Subject terms may be uncontrolled, but almost all metadata schemes and implementations strongly recommend if not mandate the use of terms from one or more controlled vocabularies in order to serve the functions of controlled browsing, hyperlinking, collocating, and faceted and other methods of navigation.

4.2.1. Subjects

Before turning to description, abstract, and table of contents element types, this section explores elements and resource description issues related to the analysis of the subject content of resources and the selection of individual terms to represent that subject content, terms that may be used not only to identify subject content, but also to allow users to search, browse, and gather together resources *about* the same concepts, topics, persons, places, events, and objects.

4.2.1.1. Subject Analysis, Representation, and Retrieval

Metadata creators commonly need to analyze the subject content of resources and represent that content by means of words that can be used for retrieval by searching, browsing, and navigation. Subject analysis and representation are among the most challenging and the most important of metadata creation or cataloging activities. Subject analysis and representation are inherently mired in the subjectivity and ambiguity of human thought processes; personal, cultural, social, linguistic, and subject knowledge limitations and potential biases, whether conscious or unconscious, and the ambiguity of human language itself. Yet searching by subject is one of the most frequent and important ways that users seek information.

A subject *term* may consist of a single word or a compound term made up of two or more words. In some cases a series of terms are assembled together as a *pre-coordinated* subject *string* composed of a primary term followed by one or more *subdivisions*. Subject terms may be controlled or uncontrolled. Subject content may also be represented by composing an abstract or summary description of the subject content of the resource or by a table of contents.

General keyword searching in most online collection databases executes a query matching the user's search term(s) or phrase(s) against all of the words in all of the metadata records in the database, regardless of specific metadata element or field. Some systems may also allow for keyword searching of the full text of textual resources that have been digitized in a format capable of being searched by words. Even in such cases of full-text keyword searching, there are still great advantages in having human beings analyze the subject content of the text and select key terms that they judge represent the primary subject content of the resource. For non-textual resources, such as still and moving images, maps, and sound files, the only option for representing their subject content and making it searchable or browsable by subject is for the metadata creator to enter subject terms into the metadata record representing each resource.

Subject terms may be controlled or uncontrolled. Uncontrolled terms are key terms that the metadata creator assigns to a resource from her or his own head that are not taken from a controlled vocabulary and do not necessarily have consistency as to form of term or deal with synonymy (different words that are used for the same concept) or ambiguity (a single word with different meanings). Controlled subject vocabularies usually deal with these two aspects of natural human language and provide greater consistency and structure in resource discovery based on subject content. Chapter 5 deals with the topic of controlled vocabularies, which include simple lists of controlled terms, synonym rings, authority files, classification schemes or taxonomies, thesauri, and subject heading lists. Almost all metadata schemes and best practice guidelines strongly recommend the use of one or more controlled vocabularies for subject terms.

Controlled subject vocabularies commonly used in many cultural heritage digital collections include the Library of Congress *Thesaurus for Graphic Materials* (LCTGM or TGM), *Library of Congress Subject Headings* (LSCH), the Getty *Art and Architecture Thesaurus* (AAT), and the Getty *Thesaurus of Geographic Names* (TGN). See Chapter 5 for more information on these and other types of vocabularies.

Another critical aspect of subject analysis and representation in actual practice, and one not often mentioned in textbooks, is the need to establish limits on the amount of time that you can afford to spend analyzing the subject content of resources, especially if this entails significant research. Practical considerations of project deadlines, staffing levels, cataloger expertise, and budget most definitely come into play in real-world metadata creation. Metadata project coordinators will usually need to do their best to attempt to strike a healthy balance between thorough, accurate, and good quality subject indexing, on the one hand, and practical limits of time, staff, budget, and deadlines, on the other hand.

4.2.1.2. Analyzing and Identifying Subject Content

Creating subject metadata is inherently a two-step process, even when the two steps merge together for experienced catalogers who have gained familiarity with one or more subject vocabularies. The first step or aspect is to examine the information resource, analyze its subject content, and decide which aspects to represent in the metadata record. The second step or aspect is to formulate specific terms or descriptions that represent that subject content, usually working with a given controlled vocabulary to select the terms that best correspond to your analysis. In vocabularies that allow for the use of subdivisions, this also means building pre-coordinated strings of terms, following the parameters established for the particular controlled vocabulary.

The methods of analyzing subject content differ to some extent depending on the specific type of resource you are dealing with. Analyzing the subject content of texts, still images, moving images, maps, spoken word sound recordings, and musical sound recordings, for example, can entail different methods and thought processes.

When analyzing **texts**, you have words to work with: words expressing concepts; personal, place, event, and object names; and so forth. While professional indexers of journal articles may read the entire article before determining subject terms, catalogers of books do not normally read the entire book before doing so. They rely heavily on titles, abstracts, summaries, tables of contents, chapter headings and subheadings, indexes, and the like. Creators of metadata for digital texts will do the same, when applicable. Digitized personal letters and diaries, and similar kinds of resources, however, will not often include these aids to subject analysis.

Recorded sound and moving images present different challenges for subject analysis. Catalogers usually rely as much as possible on accompanying material that includes summaries of the content or lists of contents including subjects covered and names of interviewees, interviewers, narrators, song titles, performers, actors, directors, and so forth. But it may also be necessary to listen to or view the actual recorded content, especially when there is little or no accompanying information, or the reliability and accuracy of that information is open to question.

Still images, such as digitized photographs, slides, etchings, images of paintings, sculptures, and other artworks present their own special challenges, some similar to those for recorded sound and moving images, others different. Because such a large number of digital collections consist of digitized images, the topic of subject analysis and indexing of images is given more detailed treatment in an upcoming section of this chapter. It should be noted that the construction of *supplied titles* for digitized images, as discussed in Chapter 3, involves subject analysis and representation of images, and entails the same processes as covered in this chapter. Supplied titles of digital still images usually reflect the subject content of what is depicted in the image, to a greater or lesser extent. The words of titles are searchable by keyword, but this is quite different from the inclusion of subject terms specifically designated as subject terms for user searching and browsing, and it is especially different from the use of terms from a controlled vocabulary for gathering and hyperlinking of subject terms.

4.2.1.3. Aboutness, Ofness, Isness, and Facets

One method of doing subject analysis and identifying what a resource is about is to ask the questions *Who? What? When? Where? Why?* Who created the resource, what kind of resource is it, when was it created, and why was it created? Who is the target audience of the resource, not only from the viewpoint of the creator, but also from the viewpoint of your digital collection and your intended or anticipated primary end users? Asking these questions can help with making decisions about determining and assigning subject terms, including issues of *exhaustivity* (number of subject terms to include) and *specificity* (general versus specific subject terms to include), as discussed later in this chapter. Taylor and Joudrey (2009: 314–327) and Baca et al. (2006: 207–234) are a couple of sources that provide some guidance of the process of subject analysis and determining aboutness.

A central question to ask about most resources is "What is this resource **about**?" In the cataloging tradition this is aptly called *aboutness*. The same questions of *Who? What? When? Where?* and *Why?* apply here also. Is the resource *about* a particular person or corporate body, a group or class of persons or bodies, a particular time period or historical event, a particular place or geographic area, a particular object or a group or class of such objects, one or more topics or concepts? The *What?* question can also apply to the resource itself: that is, what kind of resource is it? What is its type, genre, or form? Is it a diary, a letter, an oral history interview, a painting, a sculpture?

Texts, spoken word sound recordings, moving image recordings, scientific data sets, and many cartographic resources lend themselves to the *aboutness* approach to subject analysis and representation. The answers to the questions of what the resource is *about* often include one or more abstract concepts, in addition to the other types of subjects mentioned previously. Still images, on the other hand, are not always *about* something, but they are usually **of** something, except for purely abstract, nonrepresentational works of art and the like. They may depict specific persons, places, objects, events, or instances of these, without being strictly *about* them in the conceptual sense. Sara Shatford Layne has made the distinction between *ofness* and *aboutness* in the subject indexing of images (Layne, 1994). This distinction has also been made in the Library of Congress *Thesaurus for Graphic Materials* (http://www.loc.gov/rr/print/tgm1/), Introduction, Section II, "Indexing Images: Some Principles," which provides an excellent, concise, and readable introduction to this topic. Alexander and Meehleib (2001: 195–207) serves as another highly recommended resource for practical guidelines and principles for subject analysis and indexing of images.

Aboutness and *ofness* can be further contrasted with *isness*. This is not a commonly used term, but it is nonetheless useful for referring to what a resource **is** rather than what it is *about* or *of*. For example, a diary or a daguerreotype *is* a diary or a daguerreotype but is not *about* diaries or daguerreotypes. The idea of *isness* also tends to apply to many purely instrumental musical sound recordings without a specific conceptual or representational theme. The subject terms usually designate what the music *is*: that is, the musical genre, form, types and numbers of instruments, and so forth. Examples include terms such as *folk music*, *orchestral music*, *string quartets*, and *piano sonatas*.

Any given resource will typically have several different kinds or types of subject content at the same time. That is, a resource may be about or depict topics, concepts, persons, places, objects, time periods, events, or general classes of any of these, in various combinations. These and other aspects of subject content are sometimes called **facets**. Facets are distinct aspects or characteristics of subject content common to large numbers of resources in a given collection. Analyzing and recording subject terms for such *facets* provides the basis for one very useful method of information retrieval often called *faceted navigation, faceted browsing,* or *faceted search. Faceted classification* in traditional library and information science is usually restricted to subject content alone and is developed systematically and rigorously. But a broader, looser use of the concept of faceted classification for browsing and navigation in online retrieval interfaces is extremely useful. Figure 1.6 from Chapter 1 (p. 11) provides a representative example of this approach. A good example of faceted navigation in practice, as of this writing, is in the University of North Texas Digital Library (http://digital.library.unt.edu/help/guide/facets/).

Only by entering different types of subject terms into different specified types of subject elements or fields, or having some method of specifically designated the facet to which each belongs in the metadata, can computer systems process the data to allow for this user functionality. Some metadata element sets include different elements or subelements for different aspects, facets, or types of subject terms. Dublin Core, for example, uses the *Coverage* element and the *Spatial* and *Temporal* element refinements for the geographical/spatial and temporal subject content of a resource, and it uses a general *Subject* element for all other types of subject content. The Dublin Core *Type* and sometimes also the *Format* element can also be used for the *isness* aspect of resource description. The MODS scheme goes much further by including separate subject elements for topical, geographic, and temporal subjects, and for names of persons, corporate bodies, and titles of works used as subjects.

4.2.1.4. Exhaustivity: Number of Subject Terms

Metadata designers and creators inevitably need to make decisions about how exhaustive to be in analyzing and representing concepts and other aspects of subject content. How many concepts should be represented by terms in the metadata? How many subject terms should be included in a metadata record in order to adequately represent the subject content and provide good access points for users searching the collection? This aspect of subject indexing is known as **exhaustivity**. The more exhaustive or detailed the subject analysis, the greater the number of subject terms included in the metadata record. Exhaustivity also has to do with the degree or extent to which a resource is about a given topic, concept, or person.

Say, for example, that a digitized text is primarily about the abolition of slavery in the United States in the first half of the nineteenth century and only peripherally about the living conditions and the spiritual beliefs of African American slaves at that time. The inclusion of subject terms representing each of these concepts has implications for the user retrieval experience and the relevance of their search results. If a resource is primarily or centrally about the topic, the likelihood is greater that it will be relevant to a user who searches or browses on that term. Conversely, if a resource deals with a topic only tangentially, there is a greater chance that larger number of users will find the resource irrelevant to their needs, insofar as they are looking for resources primarily about the topic of interest to them. But users wanting to do an exhaustive search, finding every resource in a collection that treats a given topic even to a very small extent or percentage of the larger whole, will benefit from indexing subject content at a higher level of exhaustivity. These scenarios tie into the traditional measures of *relevance* used in information science called *precision* and *recall*. The treatment of these measures lies beyond the scope of this book, but they are mentioned here for those familiar with them or for those who might be interested in learning about them from other sources. These same issues of exhaustivity apply to persons, places, and things depicted in a still image. Which are central to the image and which are relatively peripheral? Obviously there is a good deal of subjectivity in making judgments about what is primary or central and what is secondary or peripheral, and to what degree, but this does not nullify the value of the process and the results for end users' information retrieval options. Metadata creators need to make their best judgment calls, and project managers and documentation should offer some guidance. The key is to find the best balance for your anticipated users, insofar as that is possible.

As with all aspects of subject analysis and indexing, the more that a collection is aimed at a specific audience or user group, the more such judgments can be easier to make. Take, for example, a collection of historical texts intended primarily for professional historians and scholars versus the general public, or a collection of medical images intended primarily for practicing physicians versus laypeople.

4.2.1.5. Specificity: Specific versus General Subject Terms

Somewhat related to the concept of exhaustivity, but distinct from it in many ways, is the concept of **specificity**. Regardless of the number of concepts represented and the number of subject terms used (exhaustivity), any of those concepts and terms may be relatively more *general* or more *specific* in nature. Specificity is related to the concept of hierarchy. The broader the term, the higher it is in a hierarchy. What is true of a broader term is also true of each narrower term within the hierarchy. The following illustrates a hierarchy of terms that could be used to represent subject content: Animals > Dogs > Terriers > Airedale Terriers. The most specific term in this example is *Airedale Terriers*. It would be the most specific term to use for a text primarily or exclusively about that particular breed or an image that depicts one or more Airedale terriers. For a text about, or image of, several different kinds of terriers, the subject term *Terriers* would be the most specific. In a text dealing with dogs, in general, or a wide range of dog breeds, the term *Dogs* would be the most appropriate. In some cases, implementers may want to index a text, image, or other kind of resource under one or more narrower, more specific terms and a broader, more general term at the same time, to allow users to retrieve the resource when searching on either type of term.

4.2.1.6. Subject Analysis and Indexing of Images

Because such a large number of digital collections consist of still images, this section of the chapter is dedicated specifically to the analysis and indexing of these resources. A fair amount of the content of this section has been adapted from Alexander and Meehleib (2001). Analyzing the subject content of any information resource can be a challenge. But analyzing the subject content of images presents some special challenges. What is depicted in an image? How much, and what aspects, specifically, should you try to represent with subject terms? What, for example, do you do with an image that includes:

- numerous people of different ages, genders, and occupations, performing different types of activities?
- various types of buildings, streets, rivers, lakes, landscapes, and cityscapes, some known and some unknown?
- street signs, advertisements, billboards, and other components that include text?

These are just a few of many possible questions, to which there are no absolute answers. A great deal depends on the individual digital project, the subject matter of the particular collection, and what aspects of the images you consider most important to bring out for your users, not to mention the amount of time, staff, and expertise you have to work with.

People creating subject metadata for images often encounter images that have little or no accompanying textual documentation and that must be analyzed visually. The indexer, cataloger, or metadata creator must decide which aspects of the image are important to index in order to provide good access for users. The first thing to do is to determine the major focus of the image. This is the subject analysis aspect. Second, formulate those subject concepts into concrete terms. These may be uncontrolled subject terms or *keywords*, on the one hand, or they may be terms selected from an established controlled vocabulary, on the other hand. Or a project may include both. If the image has a title or accompanying notes, this may assist in determining the major focus. If not, the cataloger must rely solely on visual elements.

What should metadata creators do with visually less prominent aspects of an image? Should they attempt to represent every item and object in the image, even if only partially shown? Take, for example, the image in Figure 3.2 in the previous chapter (p. 62). This is a digital image of a scene from Dresden, Germany, including the Semperoper opera house in the far left background, the Augustus Bridge over the Elbe River, passenger cruise boats, and much more. Which things depicted in the image would you choose to represent with subject terms in the metadata? Should you include a subject term for Automobiles or Cars? Streetlamps? Fences? Clouds? Trees? They all appear in the image, but are they major enough to represent with subject metadata? To answer this question, ask: What will be the results for users searching for images of automobiles, streetlamps, or fences? Will they be happy to retrieve this image among a result set of hundreds of other images? How prominent should an object be to be indexed by a subject term?

Decisions must be made as to detail of indexing and the inclusion of primary versus secondary aspects of what is depicted in an image. This will vary from one collection to another. If the collection has a special topical focus, then a more detailed level of indexing for any object relevant to that subject may be useful. If not, it may be unnecessary and even counterproductive to represent every item depicted in every image when not a primary focus of the image. For example, referencing again the image in Figure 3.2 (p. 62), if the topic of the collection were opera or music, then you would want to include Semperoper and perhaps other opera-specific subject terms. If it were about boats or transportation, this would also influence your choice and level of detail in subject terminology. If your collection was about cities of the world, this might also change the subject terms you include in your indexing. Practical considerations of staff time, budget, and expertise also come into play in making these decisions. Subject expertise can be a great help.

Many metadata creators face the need for often time-consuming research in order to identify what is depicted in an image. Creating supplied titles already entails some degree of subject analysis, since the title normally also expresses subject content. Metadata creators sometimes need to do somewhat extensive research, such as consulting past and present city directories, visiting actual locations, interviewing current and former residents, and so forth, to gather information for identifying what is depicted in a particular image, such as Figure 3.2 discussed above. Opening up the possibility of user tagging, or at least allowing users to submit comments or suggestions, can also be tremendously helpful, because there may be end users who can identify the content of an image from their own knowledge and experience.

Sara Shatford Layne has made the distinction between *ofness* and *aboutness* in the subject indexing of images (Layne, 1994). This distinction has also been made in the Introduction to the Library of Congress *Thesaurus for Graphic Materials* (http://www.loc.gov/rr/print/tgm1/) and in Alexander and Meehleib (2001). Images can be both *of* and *about* something. This is sometimes referred to as the difference between the signifier and what is signified. For example, an allegorical image may be of a man and a lion but be about pride (Layne, 1994). A photograph may be of a person crying but about sorrow. In the context of images, *ofness* is more likely to be concrete and objective, while *aboutness* is more likely to be abstract and subjective.

Certain types of visual resources, such as political cartoons, often use people and objects to symbolically represent something else. That which is represented should be brought out in the subject metadata. Take, for example, the 1942 political cartoon by Dr. Seuss in Figure 4.1. It is *of* a man playing a pipe organ and Uncle Sam tapping him on the shoulder. There is also text depicted in the image. The cartoon uses musical harmony and black and white keys to symbolically represent racial harmony and the use of both black and white labor in the war industry of the time. This is what the cartoon is *about* rather than what it is *of*.

Figure 4.1. Political Cartoon Example of *Ofness* versus *Aboutness*

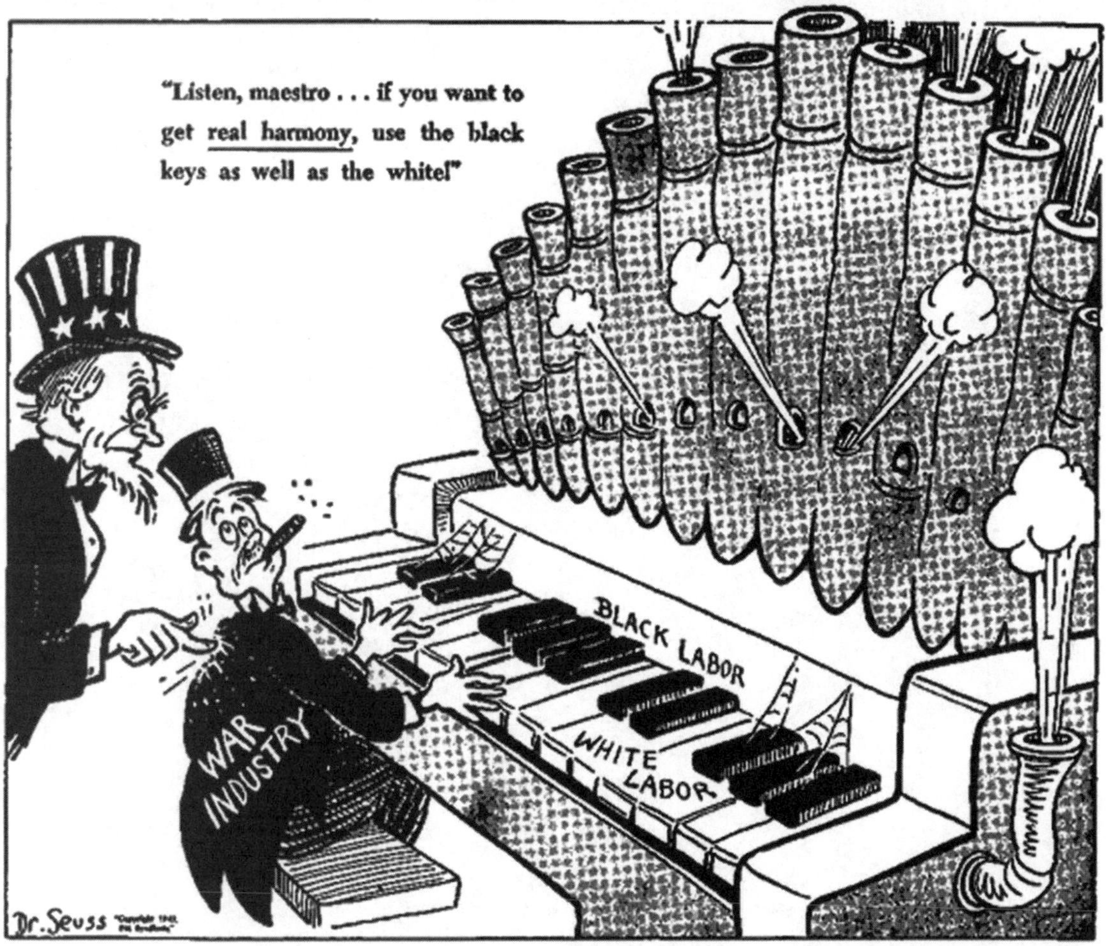
"Listen, maestro . . . if you want to get real harmony, use the black keys as well as the white!"
BLACK LABOR
WHITE LABOR
WAR INDUSTRY
Dr. Seuss

Source: Dr. Seuss Collection, Mandeville Special Collections Library, University of California, San Diego.

Metadata creators do need, however, to avoid projecting their own subjective interpretations onto an image and into its metadata. Take for example the image in Figure 4.2.

> Although it is important to index for context, catalogers should avoid projecting any subjectivity into an image and corresponding catalog record. One of P&P's most famous images "Migrant Mother"...taken by Dorothea Lange in 1936, is captioned "Destitute peapickers in California, a 32 year old mother of seven children." The cataloger chose the subject terms, "Migrant agricultural laborers," "Mothers & children," and "Poor persons." Although it might have been tempting to index for other concepts, such as "Worry," "Distress," and "Social classes," the cataloger could not verify the feelings of the mother, nor the intent of the photographer, therefore, these terms were not applied. (Alexander and Meehleib, 2001: 199)

Unless you can objectively verify such aspects as the feelings of the person depicted or the intent of the artist or photographer, it is definitely

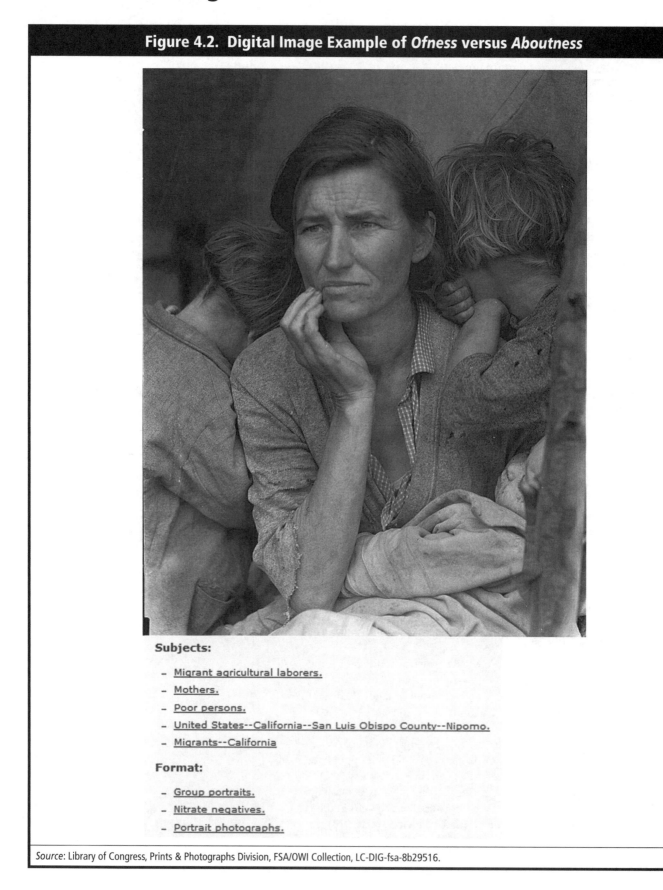

Figure 4.2. Digital Image Example of *Ofness* versus *Aboutness*

Subjects:

- Migrant agricultural laborers.
- Mothers.
- Poor persons.
- United States--California--San Luis Obispo County--Nipomo.
- Migrants--California

Format:

- Group portraits.
- Nitrate negatives.
- Portrait photographs.

Source: Library of Congress, Prints & Photographs Division, FSA/OWI Collection, LC-DIG-fsa-8b29516.

preferable not to apply terms that are your own personal interpretation. A good rule of thumb is to apply only accurate, *verifiable* subject terms for indicating the *aboutness* of an image.

Images may also be an example of a particular kind of image. An image may *be* an etching as opposed to being *about* etchings. The image in Figure 4.2 is a portrait and a photographic print. Some call this the *object* characteristics as opposed to *subject* characteristics of an image. This may also be called this *isness*, what an image *is*, as opposed to what it is *of* or *about*. For a digitized photograph of an etching or a woodcut, your subject terms might include *Etchings* and *Woodcuts*, respectively, since the original resources depicted in the digital images are examples of these things, and users might want images of resources that are wood-cuts. This is especially valuable for searching and gathering/grouping in a collection that includes images of many different physical types. This aspect of *isness* might be covered in a Dublin Core *Format* element instead of a *Subject* element or possibly a *Type* element if choosing to use this for more specific type and genre terms. In MODS, it would be appropriate to cover it in a *Genre* or a *PhysicalDescription Form* element.

A general principle of traditional library cataloging subject analysis and representation is to use the most specific term possible from a given controlled vocabulary. This is one applied aspect of the concept of *specificity*. If an image is of a suspension bridge, and the vocabulary has a term for that, use the term for *Suspension Bridges* specifically rather than for *Bridges* generically. To include both terms in the same record is sometimes called *double indexing*. As with any rule, however, there are exceptions, and different metadata projects may have different polices on this depending on the size of the collection and the anticipated users. In some cases you may want to index an image under both the broader and the more specific term if it serves the information retrieval needs of your users, perhaps also taking into account cross-collection and aggre-gated metadata searching.

Besides cases such as the one just described, there are also instances in which the most specific term is a proper name. In these cases, a generic subject term is usually best also used. For example, an image of the *Brooklyn Bridge* would have the name of the bridge as its most specific subject term because it is an image of that specific bridge. But it is a good idea to also include a subject term for *Bridges* and/or *Suspension Bridges*, so that a researcher interested in the topic of bridges or suspension bridges would not have to know and enter the name of every specific suspension bridge in the collection in order to retrieve relevant images.

Table 4.7 provides a list of subject elements from each of the standard metadata element sets covered in this book.

4.2.2. Dublin Core *Subject*

DC *Subject*
- "The topic of the resource."
- "Typically, the subject will be represented using keywords, key phrases, or classification codes. Recommended best practice is

Table 4.7. Subject Elements in DC, MODS, and VRA

Dublin Core		
Subject		
Coverage	*Qualifiers:*	Spatial
		Temporal

MODS		
<subject>	*Attributes:*	authority
<topic>		
<geographic>		
<temporal>	*Attributes:*	encoding ; point ; keyDate
<titleInfo>		
<name>		
<genre>		
<hierarchicalGeographic>	*Subelements:*	<continent> ; <country> ; <province> ; <region> ; <state> ; <territory> ; <county> ; <city> ; <citySection> ; <island> ; <area> ; <extraterrestrialArea>
<cartographics>	*Subelements:*	<coordinates> ; <scale> ; <projection>
<geographicCode>	*Attribute:*	authority
<occupation>		
<classification>	*Attributes:*	authority
		edition
		displayLabel

VRA 3.0		
Subject		
Style/Period	*Qualifiers:*	Style
		Period
		Group
		School
		Dynasty
		Movement

VRA 4.0		
<subject>		
<term>	*Attributes:*	type (corporateName, familyName, otherName, personalName, scientificName, builtworkPlace, geographicPlace, otherPlace, conceptTopic, descriptiveTopic, iconographicTopic, otherTopic)
<stylePeriod>		

Source: See Table 4.4.

to use a controlled vocabulary. To describe the spatial or temporal topic of the resource, use the Coverage element."

Refinements: none

Vocabulary Encoding Schemes:

- **LCSH**
  - "The set of labeled concepts specified by the Library of Congress Subject Headings."
- **MeSH**
  - "The set of labeled concepts specified by the Medical Subject Headings."
  - "See: http://www.nlm.nih .gov/mesh/meshhome.html"
  - "See: http://wwwcf.nlm.nih.gov/class/"
- **DDC**
  - "The set of conceptual resources specified by the Dewey Decimal Classification."
  - "See: http://www.oclc.org/dewey/"
- **LCC**
  - "The set of conceptual resources specified by the Library of Congress Classification."
  - "See: http://lcweb.loc.gov/catdir/cpso/lcco/lcco.html"
- **NLM**
  - "The set of conceptual resources specified by the National Library of Medicine Classification."
- **UDC**
  - "The set of conceptual resources specified by the Universal Decimal Classification."
  - "See: http://www.udcc.org/"

The DC *Subject* element is very broad and can contain any types of terms or phrases that represent the subject content of the resource. These terms are the result of the process of subject analysis, discussed in the previous section of this chapter. They may range from uncontrolled subject terms or *keywords* invented by the metadata creator to terms selected from one or more controlled vocabularies, such as an established term list, authority file, taxonomy, classification scheme, or thesaurus. The *Subject* element may include single terms or phrases or pre-coordinated subject strings such as those common in *Library of Congress Subject Headings* or the *Thesaurus for Graphic Materials*, for example: *Bridges—Wisconsin—Janesville*. The DC *Subject* element also encompasses classification codes, which represent the subject content of a resource by means of numerical or alphanumerical notations designating a subject class of which the resource is a member.

DC *Subject* does not have a way to distinguish among topical, personal, form, or other types of subject terms, except for geographic areas and time periods as subjects. These types of subject terms go into the DC *Coverage Spatial* and DC *Coverage Temporal* elements, respectively. All other types of subject terms go into DC *Subject*.

DCMI recommends use of controlled vocabularies. This allows for better quality user browsing, fielded searching, hyperlinking, collocating, and navigating. Most implementations use primarily or exclusively terms taken from a controlled vocabulary. The "DCMI Metadata Terms" namespace includes the six vocabulary encoding schemes listed with the DC *Subject* element definitions at the beginning of this Section (4.2.2), but users are not restricted to these alone. Other commonly used schemes for digital images include the Library of Congress *Thesaurus for Graphic Materials* (TGM or LCTGM) and the Getty *Art and Architecture Thesaurus* (AAT), but any number of other vocabulary schemes may be used as well. Some implementers recommend the use of separate local subject elements or fields for terms from different vocabularies, including the designation for the vocabulary as part of the element or field label, for example: *Subject-AAT* and *Subject-LCSH*, both mapping to DC *Subject*.

Uncontrolled, free-text keywords may be used instead of, or preferably in addition to, controlled terms, in one or more DC *Subject* elements in order to increase subject retrieval. This is, however, a much less common practice than to use controlled vocabulary terms exclusively. Subject terms may be entered into separate *Subject* elements or into a single *Subject* element in systems that allow for that and have a machine-readable demarcator for separate subject terms, such as the semicolon space. If uncontrolled terms are to be used purely for free text keyword searching and not for controlled linking, collocation, browsing, and such, it is usually not problematic to enter them all into a single Subject element. In any case, implementers should test how their local system processes multiple values in a single field.

The following examples show the use of Dublin Core *Subject* elements using a variety of vocabularies and illustrating the use of pre-coordinated subject strings as well as individual terms.

Topical Subject Examples (resource is about this topic, class of persons, named object, and the like, or an image depicts it in some way):
    Subject *AAT*: drawbridges
    Subject *TGM*: Drawbridges
    Subject *TGM*: Drawbridges--Illinois--Chicago
    Subject *TGM*: Farmers
    Subject *TGM*: Farmers--Georgia
    Subject *LCSH*: Farmers--Southern States--Political activity--History
    Subject *LCSH*: Civil rights movements
    Subject *LCSH*: African Americans--Civil rights
    Subject *TGM*: Steamboats
    Subject *LCSH*: Titanic (Steamship)

Name Subject Examples (the first uncontrolled, the second controlled):
    Subject: Herman Melville
    Subject *LCNAF*: Melville, Herman, 1819-1891

Title as Subject Example (a critical analysis of Moby Dick):
    Subject: Moby Dick, or the Whale

Genre/Form Subject Example (usually used only as subdivision in schemes such as MODS):

Subject *TGM*: Etchings

Classification Number Example (a method of classifying resource content into subject categories):

Subject *DDC*: 943.085
Subject *LCC*: D639.J4

Uncontrolled Subject Example: String of uncontrolled, free-text keywords (used instead of, or preferably in addition to, controlled terms, to increase subject retrieval):

Subject: boats, ships, sailboats, transportation, water transportation, vessels, sailing vessels, harbors, oceans, seas

4.2.3. Dublin Core *Coverage*

DC *Coverage*

- "The spatial or temporal topic of the resource, the spatial applicability of the resource, or the jurisdiction under which the resource is relevant."
- "Spatial topic and spatial applicability may be a named place or a location specified by its geographic coordinates. Temporal topic may be a named period, date, or date range. A jurisdiction may be a named administrative entity or a geographic place to which the resource applies. Recommended best practice is to use a controlled vocabulary such as the Thesaurus of Geographic Names. Where appropriate, named places or time periods can be used in preference to numeric identifiers such as sets of coordinates or date ranges."

Refinements:

- **Spatial**
  - "Spatial characteristics of the resource."
- **Temporal**
  - "Temporal characteristics of the resource."

Vocabulary Encoding Scheme:

- **TGN**
  - "The set of places specified by the Getty Thesaurus of Geographic Names."
  - "See: http://www.getty.edu/research/tools/vocabulary/tgn/index.html."

Syntax Encoding Schemes:

- **ISO3166**
  - "The set of codes listed in ISO 3166-1 for the representation of names of countries."
  - "See: http://www.iso.org/iso/en/prods-services/iso3166 ma/02iso-3166-code-lists/list-en1.html."

- **Point**
  - "The set of points in space defined by their geographic coordinates according to the DCMI Point Encoding Scheme."
  - "See: http://dublincore.org/documents/dcmi-point/."

- **Box**
  - "The set of regions in space defined by their geographic coordinates according to the DCMI Box Encoding Scheme."
  - "See: http://dublincore.org/documents/dcmi-box/."

Use the DC *Coverage* element for subject coverage when the intellectual or artistic content of the resource is substantially *about* a particular place or time period or when an image depicts a particular place or time period, and when place or time period are likely to be important aspects by which users will want to search, browse, and retrieve sets of related digital resources about the same place and/or time period. The refinements may be used to distinguish *Spatial* from *Temporal* coverage. A *Spatial Coverage* element may contain a named place or a location specified by its geographic coordinates. A *Temporal Coverage* element may contain a named time period, a date, or a date range.

A common misunderstanding and misuse of the Dublin Core *Coverage Spatial* and *Temporal* element is for place and date of publication, creation, or other aspects relating to the resource itself, rather than to its subject content. *Coverage* deals with what a resource is *about* rather than when and where it was made. A book about the attack on Pearl Harbor published in 2005 in New York would have: *Date Issued*: 2005; *Coverage Temporal*: 1941-12-07; *Coverage Spatial*: Pearl Harbor (Hawaii).

Recommended best practice for place names is to use a controlled vocabulary such as the *Thesaurus of Geographic Names* (TGN). This thesaurus is widely used in the United States and is available in searchable format online at http://www.getty.edu/research/tools/vocabulary/tgn/index.html. It is well worth exploring a little to get a sense of its scope. It is also valuable to read about its purpose, scope, and structure in "About the TGN" at http://www.getty.edu/research/conducting_research/vocabularies/tgn/about.html.

ISO 3166 is an international list of two- and three-character codes for all of the countries of the world: http://userpage.chemie.fu-berlin.de/diverse/doc/ISO_3166.html. Codes are often more easily machine-processable than natural language terms, and they also have the advantage of being international and not specific to any one human language. Such codes would be used behind the scenes and not displayed directly to end users, or an English-language place name could be generated from the code by the software for user display, if desired and possible.

DCMI Point and *DCMI Box* are ways to specify one particular geographic point or a larger geographic area based on geographic coordinates in a machine-readable format. These are not widely implemented. Geospatial *coordinates* offer much greater precision for locating specific points and areas in space. Geospatial data processing software applications can allow users to zoom in and out with great precision. Google Maps uses coordinates, and Wikipedia includes geographic coordinates when applicable. See, for example, the Wikipedia entry for Ponte Sant'Angelo: the coordinates 41°54'06"N, 12°27'59.25"E appear in the upper right corner. In order for a computer to process these coordinates, they need to be entered according to a specific scheme useable by a particular software application. There are several schemes for coordinates, no one of which is especially widely used in this author's experience.

The following examples illustrate a range of uses of the Dublin Core *Coverage* element.

Spatial Subject Coverage Examples (resource is about, covers, or takes place in this geographic area, or image depicts something in that place):

Coverage Spatial *TGN*: Argentina
Coverage Spatial *ISO3166*: ARG
Coverage Spatial: Chicago, Illinois
Coverage Spatial *LCSH*: Chicago (Ill.)
Coverage Spatial: Vancouver, British Columbia, Canada
Coverage Spatial *DCMI Box*: name=Western Australia; northlimit=-13.5; southlimit=-35.5; westlimit=112.5; eastlimit=129

Temporal Subject Coverage Examples (resource is about, covers, or takes place in this time period, or image depicts something during that time period):

Coverage Temporal: 1914-1918
Coverage Temporal: Nineteenth century
Coverage Temporal *LCSH*: 19th century

4.2.4. Descriptions, Abstracts, and Tables of Contents

Many times the nature or content of a resource is not adequately conveyed by its title, subject terms, or the content of the other metadata elements in a record. Virtually all metadata schemes include some kind of description element that allows you to compose a free-text, concise, objective, and accurate summary or description of the object. The metadata creator may compose the description or take part or all of it from the object itself or from accompanying information such as a photographer's notes or log. The richer the description—especially if it contains information not immediately evident by looking at an image itself, for example—the more useful it is for the user in identifying the content of that image. For sound and moving image objects, a description is sometimes all the more useful because it provides users with information about the subject content of the resource without them having to view or listen to the resource itself, helping them to decide whether or not it is relevant to their interests and worth their while to play.

In addition to identification of the content of the object, a narrative description also assists with subject retrieval. It provides additional natural language subject vocabulary for uncontrolled keyword searching within a database. In aggregated metadata repositories, in which the metadata is harvested without its digital object, a good description may also help users evaluate whether or not to select and access the original source file that they cannot initially see.

Figure 4.3 offers an example of a digital image and of a metadata record containing a free text *Description* of that image that further explains what is depicted.

Some metadata schemes include an *Abstract* and/or a *TableOfContents* element or include these as ways of refining a Description element. An *Abstract* may be used for a the formal kind of summary written by the author or publisher of an article or research paper, or it may be used for any general type of description. *TableOfContents* will apply to digital texts that contain such tables, but can also apply to other types of digital files for which the contents may be listed, such as a digital sound file containing separate sections that can be clearly identified.

Figure 4.3. Description Element Example

Title:	Airplane accident at Four Mile Bridge
Photographer:	Gruver, Lowell "Bud"
Date:	ca. 1940
Place/Time:	20th Century / Rock County (Wisconsin)
Description:	1940s photo of the rescue of a pilot who tried to fly under the Four Mile Bridge. This photo shows people lined up on the bridge looking at an airplane wing sticking out of the water below. Rescuers approach in a rowboat.
TGM Subjects:	Bridges--Wisconsin--Janesville
Subjects:	Aircraft accidents--Wisconsin--Janesville

Source: Janesville's Past, University of Wisconsin Digital Collections. Photo by Lowell "Bud" Gruver, owned by Hedberg Public Library, Janesville, Wisconsin. http://digicoll.library.wisc.edu/WI/subcollections/JanesvillesPastAbout.html.

Table 4.8 provides a list of description, abstract, and table of contents elements from each of the standard metadata element sets covered in this book.

4.2.5. Dublin Core *Description*

The Dublin Core *Description* element is intended to encompass a wide range of information that is descriptive of a resource, including those discussed in the preceding section. This DC element normally contains free text rather than controlled values.

DC *Description*

- "An account of the resource."

- "Description may include but is not limited to: an abstract, a table of contents, a graphical representation, or a free-text account of the resource."

Refinements:

- **Abstract**
  - "A summary of the resource."

- **TableOfContents**
  - "A list of subunits of the resource."

Table 4.8. Description Elements in DC, MODS, and VRA

Dublin Core		
Description	*Qualifiers:*	Abstract
		Table Of Contents
MODS		
\<abstract\>	*Attributes:*	type (no controlled list of types)
\<tableOfContents\>	*Attributes:*	type (no controlled list of types)
VRA 3.0		
Description		
VRA 4.0		
description		

Source: See Table 4.4.

The following examples provide three concrete instances of the application of this element and its two refinements. The definition of the *Abstract* refinement is broad enough to encompass most summary style descriptions as well as abstracts formally so-named. It is up to local implementers to decide how widely to use this refinement and its value. Normally refinements have value insofar as they are used to machine process or label and display the content of elements differently.

Description Example 1: Description of digital image:
Description: Southeast side of the Cologne Cathedral viewed from outside the Hauptbahnhof (train station), Köln, Germany, October, 1952.

Description Example 2: Abstract of digitized research article:
Description Abstract: This paper explores reasons why large numbers of practitioners do not adhere to the DCMI One-to-One Principle; discusses why it is problematic; explores how the principle itself would benefit from greater clarity; presents some practical options for maintaining the principle in current systems, with advantages and disadvantages of each; and suggests a possible compromise option. The paper focuses on the widespread application context of small to medium-sized cultural heritage institutions digitizing unique local resources, creating metadata using digital collection software packages such as CONTENTdm, and exposing only simple Dublin Core metadata for OAI harvesting and aggregating.

A Taxonomy of Resource Relationships

An abbreviated summary of principal types of bibliographic relationships, slightly adapted from Tillett (1991, 2001).

- **Equivalence Relationships**
  - Exist between exact copies of the same resource, or between an original resource and a reproduction of it, as long as the intellectual content and authorship are preserved.
  - Included here are copies, issues, facsimiles, photocopies, microforms, digitized versions of texts and images, and other similar reproductions.
- **Derivative (or Horizontal) Relationships**
  - Exist between a resource and a modification based on that same resource, including variations, versions, editions, revisions, translations, adaptations, paraphrases, etc.
- **Descriptive Relationships**
  - Exist between a resource and a description, criticism, evaluation, or review of that resource, including annotated editions, casebooks, commentaries, critiques, etc.
- **Whole-Part (or Vertical) Relationships**
  - Exist between a component part of a resource and its whole, including a selection from an anthology, collection, or series, or a digital object that is part of a digital collection.
- **Accompanying Relationships**
  - Exist between a resource and the resource it accompanies, such that the two resources augment each other equally or one resource augments the other principle or predominant resource, including supplements, concordances, indexes, catalogs, etc.
- **Sequential (or Chronological) Relationships**
  - Exist between resources that continue or precede one another, including successive titles in a serial, sequels of a monograph, parts of a series, etc.
- **Shared Characteristic Relationships**
  - Exist between a resource and other resources that are not otherwise related but coincidentally have a common author, title, subject, or other characteristic used as an access point.

Description Example 3: Table of contents of digitized rare book:
> **Description TableOfContents**: Chapter 1: Introduction. Chapter 2: Chamber Music. Chapter 3: Orchestral Music. Chapter 4: Operas. Chapter 5: Incidental Pieces.

The DC *Description* element is often used in practice for two different purposes. One is for giving a free text summary or other indication of the subject content of the resource, as covered above, which is the primary if not exclusive original intent for this element. The second purpose is to use *Description* as a kind of catch-all element for including any kind of information that does not fit well into one of the other DC elements. For implementers adopting this usage, the kinds of information covered in Section 3.1.9 in the previous chapter on "Attributes Not Readily Accommodated in Dublin Core" could be put into a DC *Description* element. This practice uses the element in a way not originally intended, and it is perhaps technically incorrect. But it is sometimes the only practical option when implementers judge certain pieces of information important for their users and the Dublin Core Metadata Element Set does not include an element that readily encompasses that information.

4.3. Resource Relationship Elements

4.3.1. Relationships among Different Resources

Information resources often have various kinds of relationships with other information resources. In many cases it is useful to express one or more of these relationships in the metadata record for a given resource. In this case, the value of the metadata element is a reference to some other resource than the one being described in the rest of the metadata record, but to which it is related in some way. Within the library community, Barbara Tillett (1991, 2001) has developed a useful and highly influential typology of bibliographic relationships.

Although any of these types may apply to digital resources in digital collections, two are of special note in being especially common. *Whole-part*: the relationship between an individual resource at the *item level* and the larger digital or physical collection of which it is a part at the *collection level*. Item and collection level metadata are discussed in Chapter 2. *Equivalence*: the relationship between a digital resource and the original analog/physical resource from which it was derived through the process of digitization.

The distinction made between *content* versus *carrier*, also covered in Chapter 2, is helpful in understanding the *equivalence* and *derivative* relationships. Has there been a change in the actual intellectual or artistic content of the resource, or is there simply a different physical or digital carrier that conveys the same identical information to the user? In the current library community, the Functional Requirements for Bibliographic Records (FRBR) conceptual model includes these kinds of relationships at a more complex level (International Federation of

Library Associations and Institutions, 2009). But for most digital collection applications, a distinction between the intellectual/artistic content of a resource and various manifestations of that resource is sufficient. Such manifestations are in an *equivalence* relationship with each other, because they have the identical or equivalent content regardless being conveyed by different carriers. The other distinction, encompassed within this, is between different versions of a resource that entail changes in the intellectual/artistic content. A resource that contains a modification of the content of another resource is in a *derivate* relationship with that resource. It is very important to understand that the use of the term *derived* in the Dublin Core *Source* element definition is not being used in the same way as the term *derivative* in Tillett's taxonomy. The Dublin Core *Source* element seems to be intended to express an *equivalence* relationship in terms of this taxonomy. The next section on DC *Source* will go into this further.

What kinds of values should be used in relationship elements in metadata records? Ideally in most schemes the value will be either a unique identifier or a character string that is capable of creating a dynamic link to the related resource itself or to another metadata record in the database representing that related resource. A URL or other type of URI is ideal when applicable, and has the added advantage of being maximally useful in a Semantic Web context. A controlled text string may also be able to create a link within a database by exact character string matching. An identifier or the title of the related resource may be able to serve this purpose. Even if not creating an actual hyperlink, it still serves as a reference to that resource.

An alternative is to give a brief free text description of the related resource, including aspects such as its title, creators, dates, format or physical description, publication information, non-standard local identifier, and the like. This type of free text description of the related resource is one way of dealing with the *One-to-One Principle*, as discussed in Chapter 2. It can be used in a Dublin Core *Source* element, for example. The MODS *RelatedItem* element potentially provides an elegant and sophisticated way to adhere to this principle when creating a single record, because it allows in effect a complete metadata description, with all aspects given in separate, machine-processable subelements, inside of the container *RelatedItem* element. In practice, however, this may not be very usable by current retrieval systems, and some best practice guides recommend against it. Chapter 7 on MODS discusses this and includes an example.

Table 4.9 provides a list of relationship elements from each of the standard metadata element sets covered in this book.

4.3.2. Dublin Core *Relation* and *Source*

These two Dublin Core elements are intended to contain values that refer to a different information resource than the one being described in, or represented by, the metadata record as a whole. In this sense these two elements are very different from all of the other DC elements.

Table 4.9. Relationship Elements in DC, MODS, and VRA

Dublin Core

Relation	Qualifiers:	Is Version Of
		Has Version
		Is Replaced By
		Replaces
		Is Required By
		Requires
		Is Part Of
		Has Part
		Is Referenced By
		References
		Is Format Of
		Has Format
		Conforms To
Source		

MODS

<relatedItem>	Attributes:	type (preceding, succeeding, original, host, constituent, series, otherVersion, otherFormat, isReferencedBy, references, reviewOf)
	Subelements:	*[all of the MODS elements]*

VRA 3.0

Relation	Qualifiers:	Identity
		Type

VRA 4.0

<relation>	Attributes:	type (relatedTo, partOf, largerContextFor, formerlyPartOf, formerlyLargerContextFor, componentOf, componentIs, partnerInSetWith, preparatoryFor, basedOn, studyFor, studyIs, cartoonFor, cartoonIs, modelFor, modelIs, planFor, planIs, counterProofFor, counterProofIs, printingPlateFor, printingPlateIs, reliefFor, impressionIs, prototypeFor, prototypeIs, designedFor, contextIs, mateOf, pendantOf, exhibitedAt, venueFor, copyAfter, copyIs, depicts, depictedIn, derivedFrom, sourceFor, facsimileOf, facsimileIs, replicaOf, replicaIs, versionOf, versionIs, imageOf, imageIs)
		relids

Source: See Table 4.4.

While all of the other elements contain characteristics of the resource that the record as a whole is about, these two elements contain information about another resource to which it is related in some way. These elements let the user know that the object described in this metadata record is related in some way to another digital or analog object or collection of objects, which may or may not be described in its own metadata record. While the DC *Relation* element can encompass a wide variety of types of relationships, some of them evident from its various refinement qualifiers, the DC *Source* element basically encompasses only one very specific type of relationship. These elements are two of the most frequently misunderstood and misapplied Dublin Core elements, especially *Source*.

DC *Relation*

- "A related resource."
- "Recommended best practice is to identify the related resource by means of a string conforming to a formal identification system."

Refinements:

- *IsVersionOf*
  - "A related resource of which the described resource is a version, edition, or adaptation."
  - "Changes in version imply substantive changes in content rather than differences in format."

- *HasVersion*
  - "A related resource that is a version, edition, or adaptation of the described resource."

- *IsFormatOf*
  - "A related resource that is substantially the same as the described resource, but in another format."

- *HasFormat*
  - "A related resource that is substantially the same as the pre-existing described resource, but in another format."

- *IsPartOf*
  - "A related resource in which the described resource is physically or logically included."

- *HasPart*
  - "A related resource that is included either physically or logically in the described resource."

- *IsReferencedBy*
  - "A related resource that references, cites, or otherwise points to the described resource."

- *References*
  - "A related resource that is referenced, cited, or otherwise pointed to by the described resource."

- *IsReplacedBy*
  - "A related resource that supplants, displaces, or supersedes the described resource."

- *Replaces*
  - "A related resource that is supplanted, displaced, or superseded by the described resource."

- *IsRequiredBy*
  - "A related resource that requires the described resource to support its function, delivery, or coherence."

- *Requires*
  - "A related resource that is required by the described resource to support its function, delivery, or coherence."
- *ConformsTo*
  - "An established standard to which the described resource conforms."

Encoding Schemes: none

DC *Source*

- "A related resource from which the described resource is derived."
- "The described resource may be derived from the related resource in whole or in part. Recommended best practice is to identify the related resource by means of a string conforming to a formal identification system."

Refinements: none

Syntax Encoding Scheme:

- **URI**
  - "The set of identifiers constructed according to the generic syntax for Uniform Resource Identifiers as specified by the Internet Engineering Task Force."
  - "See: http://www.ietf.org/rfc/rfc3986.txt."

Vocabulary Encoding Schemes: none

The content of these elements may be either the name or an identifier, often a URI, of a related object or collection. The DCMI recommends a best practice of entering a value that consists of a character string or URI that formally identifies the related resource. This may be the title of the related resource, using the text string to create a link when it exactly matches the text string in a metadata record for the related resource, or a URI or other unique identifier such as an ISBN that points or links to the other resource.

In practice, while not exactly what was originally envisioned by the creators of the Dublin Core scheme, it is often valuable to use these elements for entering free-text descriptions of the related resource, giving detailed information about the related resource that should not go into the body of the metadata record. Such information may include the title, creator, dates, publication information, and various other identifying information about the other resource. This is one possible use of the *Source* element for giving information about the original analog object from which the digital object was created. Names of persons or corporate bodies are not intended to go in the *Relation* or *Source* elements according to their DCMI definitions and intents, but sometimes compromises must be made in practice.

In digital collections, one of the most common types of relationship is that of the digital or the original analog object to a collection of which it is a part. This is the whole-part relationship. If using Qualified Dublin Core, the *Relation* element refinement *IsPartOf* is used to express this relationship. While hardly exclusive, this is the most common usage of DC *Relation* in large numbers of digital collections today.

DC *Source* is probably the most ambiguous, misunderstood, and misused of the 15 core elements. In part this is probably attributable to the generality and vagueness of the element name itself and of its official definition and comment. Whereas the DC *Relation* element covers a variety of types of bibliographic relationships, as evidenced by its many element refinements, the DC *Source* element covers only one specific type of relationship. A primary source of confusion on the use of the *Source* element seems to come from different interpretations of the meaning of the term *derived* in the DCMI definition. Based on a variety of sources, it seems likely the DCMI does not use the term *derived* in the sense of Tillett's *derivative* relationship. Rather, they seem to use it to indicate an *equivalence* relationship, specifically an *IsFormatOf* relationship.

Jackson and colleagues state, "The source field should be used only for information identifying the original object from which a digital reproduction was created" (2008: 15). In harmony with this interpretation, the *Mountain West Digital Library Dublin Core Application Profile* (Mountain West Digital Library, 2010) gives the following instruction on how to use the *Source* element: "Use only when the resource is the result of digitization of non-digital originals." The "Best Practices for CONTENTdm and Other OAI-PMH Complaint Repositories" document (OCLC, 2010) similarly gives the following definition of their local *Source* element, mapped to DC *Source*: "Original object which the digital surrogate represents." If proceeding with this understanding of the DC *Source* element, it should not be used for the name of an original collection of objects of which the specific digital object represented by the current metadata record is a part. In this case, the current object is only one of many component parts of the collection. The DC *Source* element should definitely *not* be used for the names of persons who donated an original item, the names of institutions or repositories where the original item is housed, or the like. Instead, the *Source* element indicates a one-to-one relationship between two information resources, one being the analog original from which the digital reproduction was created. The DCMI definition of *Source* does include the terminology "in whole or in part." "In part" should be understood to apply to cases such as describing a digitized journal article and using the DC Source element for the name or identifier of the original journal from which the digitized article was taken, or for the book from which a scanned chapter was taken.

The following examples show several instances of the use of DC *Relation* and *Source*.

Relation Example 1: The digital map represented by the metadata record is a part of this digital collection:

Relation IsPartOf: Historic Maps of Delaware

Relation Example 2: The digital image represented by the metadata record is a part of this digital collection:

Relation IsPartOf: Paul J. Kramer Digital Images Collection

The Difference between the Dublin Core *Version* and *Format* Relationship Refinements

People often struggle with understanding the difference between these two Dublin Core *Relation* element refinements. Here is some further explanation.

DC *IsVersionOf*:

- Resource B is a version, edition, or adaptation of Resource A.
- Changes in version imply substantive changes in intellectual or artistic content rather than differences in format (media or carrier).
- This is a *derivative* relationship in Tillett's taxonomy.
- Library catalogers may think of it in terms of a different *edition* of a bibliographic resource.
- For those familiar with the FRBR model (International Association of Library Federations, 2009), this would apply to a different *expression* of a work.

DC *IsFormatOf*:

- Resource B has the identical intellectual/artistic content as Resource A, but it is presented in another format (media or carrier).
- Example: the same text in print, HTML, and PDF formats; the same image in printed photograph, JPEG, and GIF formats.
- This is an *equivalence* relationship in Tillett's taxonomy (1991, 2001).
- For those familiar with the FRBR model (International Association of Library Federations, 2009), this would apply to a different *manifestation* of the same expression of a work.

Relation Example 3: The digital image represented by the metadata record is a digitized format of an original analog 35 mm color slide that is part of this physical collection:

Relation IsPartOf: Paul J. Kramer Archival Photograph Collection

Relation Example 4: The digital text represented by the metadata record is an English translation by Richard Hakluyt of a French original by Jacques Cartier; it is therefore a version of the French document:

Title: Shorte and Briefe Narration of the Two Nauigations and Discoueries to the Northwest Partes called Newe Fraunce
Creator: Cartier, Jacques
Contributor: Hakluyt, Richard
Relation IsVersionOf: Bref récit et succincte narration de la navigation faite en MDXXXV et MDXXXVI / Jacques Cartier

Relation Example 5: The digital image represented by the metadata record is a digitized format of an original analog 35 mm color slide; it is therefore a different format (manifestation) of that analog object; the *Relation* element contains the identifier and additional information to uniquely identify the original item, which may be of interest to researchers wishing to visit the archives and view the original item itself:

Relation IsFormatOf: Item no. 171, 33b-765, Paul J. Kramer Archival Photograph Collection, Hagenville University Archives

Source Example 1: The digital image represented by the metadata record is derived from an original analog 35 mm color slide; that slide is therefore the *source* of the digital image (the *Source* element here contains the same information that can be contained in a *Relation.IsFormatOf* element):

Source: Item no. 171, 33b-765, Paul J. Kramer Archival Photograph Collection, Hagenville University Archives

Source Example 2: An expanded variation on Example 1, with a more complete description of the original object; this use of the *Source* element is one way to maintain the *One-to-One Principle* in single record systems, but with drawbacks, as outlined in Chapter 2:

Source: 35 mm black & white slide, by Paul Jacob Kramer, 1955. Item no. 171, 33b-765 in the Paul J. Kramer Archival Photograph Collection, Hagenville University Archives.

Source Example 3: The digital text represented by the metadata record is a TEI marked up format of a digital text available online in HTML at a specific URL:

Source *URI*: http://abc.xyz.edu/digitaltexts/12345.html

4.4. Dublin Core Full Record Examples

Tables 4.10 and 4.11 give two examples of complete Dublin Core records, the first of Simple (unqualified) Dublin Core, and the second of Qualified Dublin Core. The records were given previously as examples in Chapter 2 and are repeated here at the conclusion of Chapters 3 and 4, which have covered the use of Dublin Core elements in some detail. Readers should keep in mind that these examples are presented not as standards or best practices, but purely as two of many possible types of examples, illustrating only limited use of the full range of Dublin Core elements, refinements, and schemes. In practice the selection and use of DC elements and qualifiers varies tremendously among various institutions and often among different specific collections. Also recall that these are tabular representations of Dublin Core metadata and that the way the metadata is actually encoded and input in practice will differ from system to system. For examples from the CONTENTdm system software, see the examples in Chapter 10.

Table 4.12 illustrates a possible use of the DC *Source* element to assist in disambiguating the use of elements representing both the digital and the original resource in a single record.

Table 4.10. Simple Dublin Core Record Example

DC Element	Value
Title	Manchester Street Bridge, Sauk County, Wisconsin
Creator	Lassig Bridge and Iron Works
Creator	Kramer, Paul Jacob
Contributor	Hagenville University Archives
Coverage	Sauk County
Date	1896
Date	1955
Date	2008-12-15
Format	128.9 ft. long; 13.7 ft. deck width
Format	35 mm
Format	Black & white slide
Format	Image/jpeg
Identifier	171, 33b-765
Identifier	WB0078736
Publisher	Hagenville University
Relation	Paul J. Kramer Archival Photograph Collection
Relation	Bridges of Wisconsin
Rights	Copyright © 2009 Hagenville University
Subject	Truss bridges
Type	Still Image

Table 4.11. Qualified Dublin Core Record Example

DC Element	Refinement	Scheme	Value
Title			Manchester Street Bridge, Sauk County, Wisconsin
Date	Created	W3CDTF	1896
Creator			Lassig Bridge and Iron Works
Subject		TGM	Truss bridges
Format	Extent		128.9 ft. long; 13.7 ft. deck width
Coverage	Spatial	TGN	Sauk County
Type		DCMI Type	Still Image
Creator			Kramer, Paul Jacob
Date	Created	W3CDTF	1955
Format	Extent		35 mm.
Format	Medium		Black & white slide
Identifier			171, 33b-765
Relation	Is Part Of		Paul J. Kramer Archival Photograph Collection
Contributor			Hagenville University Archives
Relation	Is Part Of		Bridges of Wisconsin
Rights			Copyright © 2009 Hagenville University
Publisher			Hagenville University
Format		IMT	image/jpeg
Identifier			WB0078736
Date		W3CDTF	2008-12-15

Table 4.12. Simple Dublin Core Record Example Using Detailed Source Element	
DC Element	**Value**
Title	Manchester Street Bridge, Sauk County, Wisconsin
Creator	Lassig Bridge and Iron Works
Creator	Kramer, Paul Jacob
Contributor	Hagenville University Archives
Coverage	Sauk County
Date	1896
Date	1955
Date	2008-12-15
Format	128.9 ft. long; 13.7 ft. deck width
Format	35 mm
Format	Black & white slide
Format	Image/jpeg
Identifier	171, 33b-765
Identifier	WB0078736
Publisher	Hagenville University
Relation	Paul J. Kramer Archival Photograph Collection
Relation	Bridges of Wisconsin
Rights	Copyright © 2009 Hagenville University
Source	Digitized image of original 35 mm black & white slide of Manchester Street Bridge in Baraboo, Sauk County, Wisconsin, view to the north, taken by Paul Jacob Kramer in the Winter of 1955: item no. 171, 33b-765 in the Paul J. Kramer Archival Photograph Collection, Hagenville University Archives. Digital jpeg image WB0078736 created on Dec. 15, 2008.
Subject	Truss bridges
Type	Still Image

4.5. Mapping Local Elements to Dublin Core

Chapters 1 and 2 noted and illustrated that many metadata applications create their own, non-standard, collection-specific element names for use within the local closed-system database, and map them behind the scenes to Dublin Core elements for cross-collection searching, interoperability, and OAI harvesting. Table 4.13 takes the same example from Tables 4.10–4.12, but adds a set of local element names. This record example reflects a collection-specific model of metadata scheme design, which will be further detailed in Chapter 10.

4.6. Summary

This chapter has been a continuation of the previous chapter, covering some of the more complex and challenging resource description elements. Like Chapter 3, this chapter looked first at general types of metadata

Table 4.13. Local Collection-Specific Elements Mapped to Dublin Core

Local Element	Mapped to DC	Value
Title / Name of Bridge	Title	Manchester Street Bridge, Sauk County, Wisconsin
Date of Construction	Date Created	1896
Architect or Firm	Creator	Lassig Bridge and Iron Works
Type of Bridge	Subject	Truss bridges
Bridge Dimensions	Format Extent	128.9 ft. long; 13.7 ft. deck width
County	Coverage Spatial	Sauk County
Resource Type	Type	Still Image
Photographer	Creator	Kramer, Paul Jacob
Date of Photograph	Date Created	1955
Original Photograph Size	Format Extent	35 mm
Original Photograph Medium	Format Medium	Black & white slide
Original Photograph ID Number	Identifier	171, 33b-765
Original Photograph Collection	Relation IsPartOf	Paul J. Kramer Archival Photograph Collection
Original Photograph Repository	Contributor	Hagenville University Archives
Digital Collection	Relation IsPartOf	Bridges of Wisconsin
Digital Image Copyright	Rights	Copyright © 2009 Hagenville University
Digital Image Publisher	Publisher	Hagenville University
Digital File Format	Format	image/jpeg
Digital File Number	Identifier	WB0078736
Date Digitized	Date Created	2008-12-15

elements most frequently needed for resource identification and retrieval. Basic resource content and carrier elements include resource type and genre, format, and physical description. Subject content elements include various kinds of subject term elements, descriptions, abstracts, and tables of contents. Subject content elements make especially heavy use of controlled vocabularies. Finally, some elements are used to indicate relationships with other resources. With a few exceptions, the standard metadata schemes of Dublin Core, MODS, and VRA Core each includes its own version of, and specifications for, each type of element covered in this chapter. This chapter includes the relevant Dublin Core elements, while the relevant MODS and VRA elements are covered in subsequent chapters.

The most frequently misunderstood, confused, and misused Dublin Core elements are *Type*, *Format*, *Relation*, and *Source*. Misunderstanding the distinction between DC *Date* and *Coverage Temporal* is a close second. When using Dublin Core, another common source of confusion is the common practice of most implementers of mixing elements that describe the digital resource with those that describe an original analog resource in a single Dublin Core record. This is perhaps the most evident with the DC *Format* element. This chapter has addressed these common misunderstandings and has also dealt with the complex and challenging practice of subject analysis and representation, including a special focus on subjects for still images.

▶ **Companion Website**

See this book's companion website at **http://www.neal-schuman.com/ metadata-digital-collections** for Chapter 4 review questions, suggestions for exercises, and other resources.

Dublin Core's simplicity makes it highly interoperable compared to more complex, hierarchical schemes such as MODS, but it also makes Dublin Core less able to handle all of the resource description and retrieval functions needed by some digital collection implementers. This becomes all the more obvious when comparing Dublin Core with a scheme such as MODS, which is the topic of Chapter 7. Most of the examples used in this and the previous chapter will appear again in Chapter 7 for purposes of comparison and contrast. Chapter 5 turns to the topic of controlled vocabularies, which are fundamental to the functionality of so many of the metadata elements covered in Chapter 3 and especially in Chapter 4.

References

Alexander, Arden, and Tracy Meehleib. 2001. "The Thesaurus for Graphic Materials: Its History, Use, and Future." *Cataloging & Classification Quarterly* 31, no. 3/4: 189–212.

Baca, Murtha, Patricia Harpring, Elisa Lanzi, Linda McRae, and Ann Baird Whiteside, eds. 2006. *Cataloging Cultural Objects: A Guide to Describing Cultural Works and Their Images.* Chicago: American Library Association.

Dublin Core Metadata Initiative. 2010. "DCMI Metadata Terms." Last modified October 11. http://dublincore.org/documents/dcmi-terms/. Copyright 2010-10-11 Dublin Core Metadata Initiative. All Rights Reserved. http://www.dublincore.org/about/copyright/. Status: Recommendation.

International Federation of Library Associations and Institutions. 2009. "Functional Requirements for Bibliographic Records." Last modified February. http://www.ifla.org/files/cataloguing/frbr/frbr_2008.pdf.

Jackson, Amy S., Myung-Ja Han, Kurt Groetsch, Megan Mustafoff, and Timothy W. Cole. 2008. "Dublin Core Metadata Harvested Through OAI-PMH." *Journal of Library Metadata* 8, no. 1: 5–21.

Layne, Sara Shatford. 1994. "Some Issues in the Indexing of Images." *Journal of the American Society for Information Science* 45, no. 8: 583–588.

Mountain West Digital Library. 2010. "Mountain West Digital Library Dublin Core Application Profile." Version 1.1. Last modified June 7. http://mwdl .org/public/mwdl/MWDL_DC_Profile_Version_1.1.pdf.

OCLC. 2010. "Best Practices for CONTENTdm and Other OAI-PMH Complaint Repositories." October. http://www.oclc.org/uk/en/gateway/support/ best_practices.pdf.

Taylor, Arlene G., and Daniel N. Joudrey. 2009. *The Organization of Information.* 3rd ed. Westport, CT: Libraries Unlimited.

Tillett, Barbara B. 1991. "A Taxonomy of Bibliographic Relationships." *Library Resources & Technical Services* 35, no. 2 (April): 150–158.

———. 2001. "Bibliographic Relationships." In *Relationships in the Organization of Knowledge*, edited by Carol A. Bean, and Rebecca Green, 19–35. Information Science and Knowledge Management, vol. 2. Dordrecht: Kluwer Academic Publishers.

Controlled Vocabularies for Improved Resource Discovery

Integral to the process of resource description is the use of controlled vocabularies. A **controlled vocabulary**, in the broadest sense, is any standardized list of terms that have been selected for consistent use in describing or indexing information resources. Many controlled vocabularies also include synonym and ambiguity control, as well as semantic relationships and cross references among terms. Individuals and communities create controlled vocabularies to serve certain functions in an information organization and retrieval environment. "A controlled vocabulary is a way to insert an interpretive layer of semantics between the term entered by the user and the underlying database to better represent the original intention of the terms of the user" (Leise, Fast, and Steckel, 2002).

5.1. Improving Resource Discovery

Controlled vocabularies serve an important role in users' experience of discovering digital resources in online collections. Controlled vocabularies allow users to retrieve sets of meaningfully related resources rather than just single resources or sets of resources with no meaningful or semantic relationship to one another. Controlled vocabularies allow the grouping, gathering, and collocation of resources that share one or more significant characteristics, such as being of the same resource type, created by the same person, or about the same topic, place, or time period. Only when metadata creators enter consistent, standardized values into metadata fields can search and browse successfully function in this way for users.

The example in Figure 5.1 illustrates three different ways that users can browse an online database of digital collections, automatically narrowing their search to resources about the same subject, being of the same object or resource type, or related to the same place or geographic area. Each category likely corresponds with a specific metadata field, and each of the terms presented as choices under each category is a controlled vocabulary term used for that field. Under *Place*, for example, consistent

Figure 5.1. Controlled Vocabulary Term Browse

Digital Resources From Libraries, Museums, and Archives

Includes collections from model projects supported by IMLS that help preserve library resources, develop best practices for digitization, and digitize collections of national value.

Search For Items

[ ] Search

Advanced Search for Items

Browse Collections By:

Subject	Object	Place
Social Studies (333)	image (289)	United States (nation) (286)
Arts (132)	text (224)	Midwest U.S. (general region) (69)
Science (62)	physical object (91)	Southern U.S. (general region) (65)
Religion (27)	sound (55)	Europe (continent) (35)
Language Arts (26)	Interactive Resource (30)	Illinois (state) (34)
Vocational Education (16)	moving image (22)	Asia (continent) (25)
View all subjects...	View all objects...	View all places...

Source: Institute of Museum and Library Services (IMLS) Digital Collections and Content: http://imlsdcc.grainger.uiuc.edu/. Screen capture used with permission.

Table 5.1. Uncontrolled and Inconsistent Values for Resource Type

TypeOfResource:
book
books
digital images
digitized text
image
Image
image.
image/jpeg
images
JPEG image
photographic image
still image
text
text pamphlet
text scanned as PDF
Text.
texts

use of the controlled term *Southern U.S. (general region)* groups together every instance of a resource in the database that is about or depicts that geographic region.

Figure 5.1 is also a good illustration of the difference between the two basic methods of information seeking: searching and browsing. The figure includes options for both. With *search*, the burden is on the user to think up terms that will hopefully match terms in the metadata. With *browse*, categories and terms used in the metadata are presented to the user, from which he or she may make selections.

It is not uncommon, especially in aggregated repositories, to see inconsistent use of values in metadata fields. For example, Table 5.1 illustrates what the user encounters if different metadata creators have entered an inconsistent set of values into a *TypeOfResource* field. Notice differences not only in terminology but also in punctuation and capitalization. Computers are extremely literal and interpret each of these as a different term. This example has included only a few variants for still images and texts. The result is both user confusion and the inability of users to be able limit their retrieval sets to all textual or still image resources. This is why consistent use of controlled terms is important for effective information retrieval and resource discovery.

Figure 5.2 illustrates a digital collection of images from productions of a repertory theater. Browsing by the names of playwrights has been judged to be valuable for users of the collection, in addition to the titles of the plays.

Suppose that a user wants to find images of all productions by the playwright Pedro Calderon de la Barca. He or she can do so only if one

---

Figure 5.2. Personal Name Browse

Milwaukee Repertory Theater Photographic History

UW MILWAUKEE | Mark Avery Collection 1977–1994
From the Archives of the University of Wisconsin-Milwaukee Libraries

| Home | About | **Browse** | Advanced Search | Contact Us |

Browse the collection

Browse all items in the collection

Browse by Play Title

```
"Master Harold" ... and the boys
2 X 5 X 4
4 AM America
A Christmas Carol
A Flea in Her Ear
A Gershwin Serenade
```
[clear] [go]

Browse by Playwright (Author)

```
Abarbanel, Jonathan
Abe, Kobo
Albers, Kenneth
Ayckbourn, Alan
Baldwin, Nigel
Barca, Calderon de la
```
[clear] [go]

Source: From the Archives Department and Digital Collections, University of Wisconsin–Milwaukee Libraries. Image reproduced with permission.

---

form of the playwright's name has been selected and used consistently in the metadata. Table 5.2 illustrates various forms of name for this playwright that could be used. If any two or more of these were to be used in the metadata, it would result in a *split file*: that is, indexing the same person under more than one form of name, with the result that users will be unable to gather together all instances of images showing productions by this playwright. These forms would also be scattered alphabetically in an index of names or a dropdown list of names.

Controlled vocabularies help to deal with two problems inherent in "natural" human language: *ambiguity* and *synonymy* (NISO, 2005: 1, 12–14). **Ambiguity** refers to the fact that the same word or name can refer to different concepts, persons, places, or things. For example, the term *bank* can refer to a financial institution; a container; a mound, ridge, or slope; a group of objects arranged in a row; and so forth. Controlled vocabularies deal with this problem by employing some method of **disambiguation**: that is, a means of differentiating between the different terms. A qualifier is often added in parentheses: for example, *Banks (financial institutions), Banks (containers)*; *Mercury (planet), Mercury (metal), Mercury (Roman god)*. For names of people, birth and death dates are often added, and/or other qualifiers that distinguish one person with the same name from another.

Table 5.2. Variant Forms of a Playwright's Name

Barca, Calderon de la
Barca, Pedro Calderon de la
Calderon de la Barca
Calderon de la Barca, P. (Pedro)
Calderon, Pedro
De Calderon, Pedro
De la Barca, Calderon
De la Barca, Pedro Calderon
La Barca, Pedro Calderon de
Pedro Calderon de la Barca

Synonymy refers to the opposite problem in natural language: the fact that more than one word or phrase can represent the same concept, person, place, or thing. To take a simple but effective example, the terms *peanuts, earthnuts, ground nuts, goober peas, monkey nuts, pygmy nuts,* and *pig nuts* are all variant names for the same type of nut. These terms are in **equivalence relationships** with one another. Controlled vocabularies provide synonym control by identifying and explicitly linking these terms together for users. In most cases one of the terms is selected as the *preferred* term used in the metadata, and the other terms are used as cross references or links to that term. In traditional controlled vocabularies, the user would be directed to *See* or *Use* the preferred term. But in newer interfaces the user may be directly presented with the preferred term as an active hyperlink or may be directly taken to the results using the preferred term, with a message displayed informing him or her that this term, rather than the one he or she entered, is used in this database.

Many kinds of controlled vocabularies go beyond synonym control and ambiguity control to arrange terms in **hierarchical relationships** of broader and narrower terms. Hierarchies are one method of grouping large numbers of terms into categories that make them easier to navigate and can in fact be used for online browse navigation by users. The vast majority of e-commerce websites today use such hierarchies or taxonomies as the primary method of organizing their products into browsable categories and subcategories. In traditional controlled vocabularies, *Broader Term* and *Narrower Term* or *BT* and *NT* references would direct the user to also search on these types of terms, but in many online interfaces today, these hierarchical relationships can be presented as browsable hierarchies, and the broader and narrower terms presented as hyperlinks that the user can select to be taken to the relevant result set.

Although many digital collection software packages do not allow for hierarchical browsing, Figure 5.3 illustrates one way that a simple two-level hierarchy of terms has been created for browsing in a CONTENTdm environment. In this particular example, *Transportation Mode* is a broader term encompassing *Airplane, Animals, Boats,* and *Trains* as narrower terms in a simple, pragmatic form of hierarchy.

Some controlled vocabularies also indicate other kinds of relationships among concepts, persons, places, and things that are of likely interest to users. These types of semantic relationships that are neither equivalent synonyms nor hierarchical broader/narrower terms are put under the broad umbrella term of **associative relationships**. Traditionally these are indicated by *Related Term* or *RT* references, but in web-based environments they may be presented as hyperlinks and so forth, as stated for the other types of semantic relationships.

5.2. Types of Controlled Vocabularies

Controlled vocabularies come in many different shapes and sizes, ranging from very simple lists of a handful of terms to massive and complex thesauri and subject heading lists consisting of hundreds of thousands of terms

Controlled Vocabularies for Improved Resource Discovery

Figure 5.3. Simple Hierarchical Browse

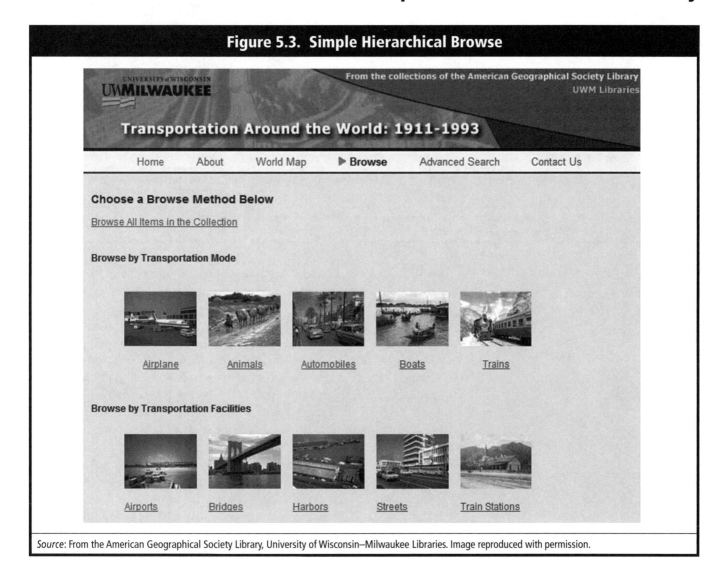

Source: From the American Geographical Society Library, University of Wisconsin–Milwaukee Libraries. Image reproduced with permission.

with various kinds of semantic relationships and linkages among those terms. Controlled vocabularies can range from those created locally for a single collection, a single institution, or a consortium of institutions, on the one hand, to those created by large agencies such as the Library of Congress and the Getty Research Institute, and used by institutions around the world, on the other hand.

Figure 5.4 presents a typology of four different kinds of controlled vocabularies arranged on a spectrum from the simple to the complex (NISO, 2005: 16–19). The four general types of controlled vocabularies are *lists*, *synonym rings*, *taxonomies*, and *thesauri*. Moving from left to right in the diagram, we see increasing structural complexity that ties into the three types of semantic relationships discussed above: *equivalence*, hierarchical, and *associative*. *Lists* do not include any of the semantic relationships. *Synonym rings* handle equivalence relationships by linking synonymous terms to one another. *Taxonomies* or *classification schemes* arrange terms into broader and narrower categories and thereby implement hierarchical relationships, usually in addition to equivalence relationships.

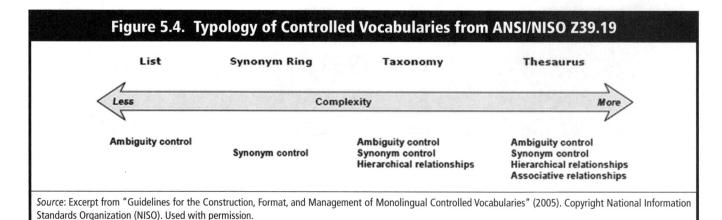

Figure 5.4. Typology of Controlled Vocabularies from ANSI/NISO Z39.19

Source: Excerpt from "Guidelines for the Construction, Format, and Management of Monolingual Controlled Vocabularies" (2005). Copyright National Information Standards Organization (NISO). Used with permission.

The full-fledged *thesaurus* includes both of those types of semantic relationships, but also includes associative relationships by creating links among related terms.

Ideally, system software can make use of these relationships to create dynamic links among terms. For example, the software could take users directly from non-preferred variant terms to the preferred term used for the same person, topical subject, and so forth. The software could allow users to browse up and down through broader and narrower levels of subject terms related to each other hierarchically in the underlying controlled vocabulary. The software could also display links to related terms not directly related either synonymously or hierarchically. Few if any current digital collection management system software packages are, however, capable of using semantic relationships for this type of dynamic user navigation. For that reason, the simple flat list is the most common form of controlled vocabulary in these contexts. But terms used in a simple flat list format are often taken from established taxonomies, thesauri, authority files, and subject heading lists and used without their semantic relationships.

5.2.1. Lists

A *list* consists of a controlled list of terms: that is, names for concepts, people, places, events, or objects that have been selected as the established forms to be used in metadata records. Lists can range in size from a small handful of terms to hundreds or thousands of terms. The "DCMI Type Vocabulary" (http://dublincore.org/documents/dcmi-type-vocabulary/) list of resource type terms, for example, consists of just 12 terms, while the "MARC Code List for Relators" (http://www.loc.gov/marc/relators/relaterm.html) consists of over 250 terms. Lists may include ambiguity control, by adding qualifiers to terms as needed to disambiguate them from otherwise identical terms, but they do not include full-fledged synonym control: that is, linking synonymous terms to one another. Commonly used established term lists for cultural heritage metadata include the "DCMI Type Vocabulary" for resource type terms, MIME Internet Media Type (IMT) (http://www.iana.org/

assignments/media-types/) terms for digital file formats, "MARC Code List for Relators" terms for roles of persons and corporate bodies, and ISO 639-2 and 639-3 "Codes for the Representation of Names of Languages" (http://www.loc.gov/standards/iso639-2/langhome.html and http://www.sil.org/iso639-3/, respectively).

The *list* is probably the most commonly used form of controlled vocabulary in a majority of cultural heritage digital collections. This is so, first, because a relatively larger number of metadata elements are better served by lists than by more complex vocabularies. That is, elements such as resource type, genre, format, language, and audience typically use flat lists as the source of terms. In some cases these terms are taken from a thesaurus that includes synonyms, hierarchies, and related terms, but they are implemented locally in the form of a simple list. Therefore, even when taxonomies, thesauri, and subject heading lists are used for the values in *Subject* fields, for example, they are brought into the software in the form of flat lists without the semantic relationships from the original vocabulary. Figure 5.5 illustrates the use of selected subject terms from the *Library of Congress Subject Headings* imported into a metadata editing screen in CONTENTdm in the form of a simple alphabetical list.

Figure 5.5. Controlled Subject Terms Used as Flat List in CONTENTdm

Field Name	Field Values
Title	Japan, toy store display
Part of Set	Enami glass lantern slide collection
Notes	
Date of Photograph	[ca. 1900-1920]
Photographer's Note	
Photographer	Enami, T., 1859-1929
Description	
Source of Descriptive Information	
Related Resources	
Subject TGM	Stores & shop; Daggers & swords; Toys; Balls (Sporting goods); Merchandise displays
Subject LC	
Continent	Asia
Subcontinent	
Country	Japan
Region	
State/Province	
City/Place	
Geographic Feature	
Type	Image

Controlled Vocabulary

Alexandria (Egypt)
Alley, Rewi, 1897-1987
American Geographical Society of New York
Aswan Dam (Egypt)
Ataturk, Kemal, 1881-1938
Babylon (Extinct city)
Badshahi Masjid
Baghmati River (Nepal and India)
Bamian (Afghanistan)
Bamiyan Region (Afghanistan)
Bang Khen (Bangkok, Thailand)
Bangkok (Thailand)
Bani Hasan Site (Egypt) 1860-1900
Bechard, Henri
Bedouins Egypt
Bhaktapur (Nepal)
Blue Mosque (Istanbul, Turkey)
Cairo (Egypt)
Cairo (Egypt) 1860-1890
Chamundeswari Temple (Mysore, India)
Chamundi Hill (India)
Changdokkung (Seoul, Korea)
Changsha (Hunan Sheng, China)
Cheops, Pyramid of (Egypt)
Chiang Dao (Thailand : Amphoe)
Chiang Kham (Phayao, Thailand)
Chiang Mai (Thailand)
Chiang Rai (Thailand)
Chiang Saen (Thailand)
Chiang, Ching-kuo, 1910-1988
Chinese New Year
Chongqing (China)
Citadel (Cairo, Egypt)
Cochin (India)
Coimbatore (India)
Coonoor (India)
Damascus (Syria)
Dandara (Egypt)
Dandara (Egypt) Antiquities
Darjeeling (India)
Deir el-Bahri Site (Egypt)
Dhaka (Bangladesh)
Djoser, King of Egypt
Evans, Charles, 1918-1995
Forman, Harrison, 1904-1978

Source: CONTENTdm screenshots are used with OCLC's permission. CONTENTdm® is a registered trademark of OCLC Online Computer Library Center, Inc.

Secondly, many current digital collection software packages do not have the capability of integrating more complex vocabularies into their navigation and display structures. They are not able to express semantic relationships and linkages among equivalent, hierarchical, and related terms. In this context, if an implementer judges it important to include some semantic relationships, he or she needs to add them manually into a simple flat list without dynamic linking. Table 5.3 shows two examples, one for a place name and the other for a personal name. In implementation, these terms would appear in long, alphabetically arranged indexes of place and personal names. This example illustrates only one of many ways that equivalence relationships could be indicated in a flat list of terms with regard to notation and punctuation. One could also choose to include only the *USE* references and omit the *USED FOR* references. The most important thing is that a user searching for resources about Burma, for example, would be directed to search using Myanmar instead.

In addition to nationally and internationally established lists of terms, many institutions create their own lists of terms. For example, many implementers need to develop lists of topical terms at a much more detailed level of coverage of the subject content of a collection than that found in established thesauri or subject heading lists. Many implementers will also develop local lists of names of persons and bodies not established in national authority files.

Table 5.3. Inclusion of Equivalence Relationships in Flat Lists

Burma (USE: Myanmar)
…
Myanmar (USED FOR: Burma)
…
Barca, Calderon de la (USED FOR: De la Barca, Calderon)
…
De la Barca, Calderon (USE: Barca, Calderon de la)

5.2.2. Synonym Rings

A synonym ring is a set of terms selected to be treated as equivalent for purposes of search engine retrieval within a website. They form a *ring* because none of the terms is selected as the preferred or authorized term. They are all equivalent to one another. For example, the following terms could be entered into search engine software as a synonym ring: *peanuts, earthnuts, ground nuts, goober peas, monkey nuts, pygmy nuts, pig nuts.* The following terms, although they are not true synonyms as are those in the previous example, could be *treated* as synonyms for purposes of information retrieval, if this were judged useful in a particular application context: *sports, athletics, competitions, sports teams.* When a user searches on any one of the terms in the ring, they retrieve results for metadata, documents, or webpages that contain any of these terms. This is equivalent to performing a Boolean *OR* search using all of the terms in the synonym ring, but it is hidden from the user at the time of search and becomes apparent only in the search results. Synonym rings are different from the other kinds of controlled vocabularies discussed here in that the terms are not used in metadata records but are entered into search engine software. Thus they lie outside of metadata per se, but mention of them is included here because they do fall on the controlled vocabulary spectrum.

5.2.3. Authority Files

An authority file is a file of records documenting the so-called "preferred," "established," or "authorized" forms of names, subject terms, and the like, to be used in metadata records. Although they do not appear in the taxonomy in Figure 5.4, authority files overlap with some of those types of vocabularies, depending on which types of semantic relationships they include. One typical type of authority record documents the authorized form of a person's name and often includes synonym control if the person has created works using more than one form of their name. Name authority files commonly used in cultural heritage metadata include the Library of Congress/NACO *Name Authority File* (NAF) and the Getty *Union List of Artist Names* (ULAN) (http://www.getty.edu/research/conducting_research/vocabularies/ulan/).

In this sense, authority files may lie more or less in between synonym rings and taxonomies on the spectrum illustrated in Figure 5.4. In a synonym ring, no term is selected as preferred, while in an authority file, one form has been so selected, and the variant forms of name for the same person, or the synonymous terms for the same concept, have been connected to it as cross-references. Figure 5.6 offers a sample record from the Library of Congress/NACO *Name Authority File*, accessed through the Library of Congress Authorities website (http://authorities.loc.gov/). Here the *Heading* is the form used in metadata records that will achieve the gathering and linking functions in the user interface, while the *Used For/See From* references are for the variant forms of the name that ideally take or point the user to the form used in the metadata. The term *authority file* in its broadest sense can actually encompass virtually any type of vocabulary. The Library of Congress Subject Authority File, for example, consists of online records for *Library of Congress Subject Headings*.

Figure 5.6. LC/NACO Name Authority Example

LIBRARY OF CONGRESS AUTHORITIES

| Help ⓘ | New Search | Search History | Headings List | Start Over |

◀ Previous   Next ▶

MARC Display | Labelled Display

LC Control Number: n 79040086
LC Class Number: PQ6280-PQ6319
HEADING: Calderón de la Barca, Pedro, 1600-1681
Used For/See From: Kal'deron de la Barka, Pedro, 1600-1681
La Barca, Pedro Calderón de, 1600-1681
Barca, Pedro Calderón de la, 1600-1681
De la Barca, Pedro Calderón, 1600-1681
Calderón, Pedro, 1600-1681
De Calderón, Pedro, 1600-1681
Calderón de la Barca, P. (Pedro), 1600-1681
Kalnteron de la Barka, 1600-1681

Source: Library of Congress Authorities: http://authorities.loc.gov/.

5.2.4. Taxonomies and Classification Schemes

In terms of the spectrum of vocabularies illustrated in Figure 5.4, taxonomies and classification schemes are essentially the same thing and fall into the third slot in the spectrum. A taxonomy or classification scheme can be viewed from one perspective as basically a list of established terms arranged into hierarchal categories of broader and narrower, or parent and child, terms. The term *taxonomy* can refer to a rigorous and formal classification scheme such as the Linnean taxonomy of living organisms; or to a relatively informal, loose hierarchical scheme used for organizing and navigating a website; or to many types of schemes in between. One value of taxonomies or classification schemes for digital collections is that they can be used for user browsing, allowing users to *drill down* from a small set of broad categories into increasingly more specific subcategories to retrieve sets of resources that have been tagged with the corresponding controlled vocabulary term at any level of specificity. As has been noted previously, however, most current digital collection software packages are not able to make use of hierarchical relationships for this type of browsing. Earlier in this chapter, Figure 5.3 illustrated one way of implementing a very simple two-level classification scheme for browsing in a CONTENTdm context.

The kinds of bibliographic classification schemes used in libraries, such as the *Dewey Decimal Classification* scheme (DDC) and the *Library of Congress Classification* scheme (LCC), use **notation** to designate each subject concept and the hierarchical level, among other things. Notation is a relatively short alphanumeric string that represents a subject concept: for example, the DDC notation 943.085 or the LCC notation D639.J4. Some digital collection metadata implementers make use of traditional library bibliographic classification numbers, especially for books or other resources that have been digitized from existing library resources and that have already been classified using one of the schemes. These notational schemes, especially Dewey Decimal and Universal Decimal classifications, have the advantage of consisting solely of numbers and therefore having greater potential for international classification, because they are not tied to any one language. But such notation is not essential to a classification scheme, and many schemes or taxonomies consist of terms without notation.

5.2.5. Thesauri

The full-fledged thesaurus falls into the fourth place on the spectrum of controlled vocabulary complexity, because it includes all three types of semantic relationships. Thesauri are usually focused on a particular subject area, be it broad or narrow, such as the Library of Congress *Thesaurus for Graphic Materials* (TGM) (http://www.loc.gov/rr/print/tgm1/), the Getty *Art and Architecture Thesaurus* (AAT) (http://www.getty.edu/research/conducting_research/vocabularies/aat/), and the Getty *Thesaurus of Geographic Names* (TGN) (http://www.getty.edu/research/conducting_research/vocabularies/tgn/), all three of which are commonly used in cultural heritage metadata. Figure 5.7 offers a record display for a term in the online *National Agricultural Thesaurus* that clearly shows all three kinds of semantic relationships. Each term in the record is hyperlinked to a reciprocal record for that term.

This network of relationships and cross references is called *syndetic structure* in traditional library cataloging parlance. It is a network or web of semantic relationships and links among terms representing concepts. When these terms are used in metadata for resources, and the links among terms are able to be fully implemented by database software, it presents users with these linkages not only among the terms themselves, but among all of the resources in the database represented by these terms. Some digital collections are able to fully incorporate a subject thesaurus and use this kind of network of linkages for user display and dynamic navigation. As has been mentioned, however, most current

Figure 5.7. National Agricultural Thesaurus Record Example

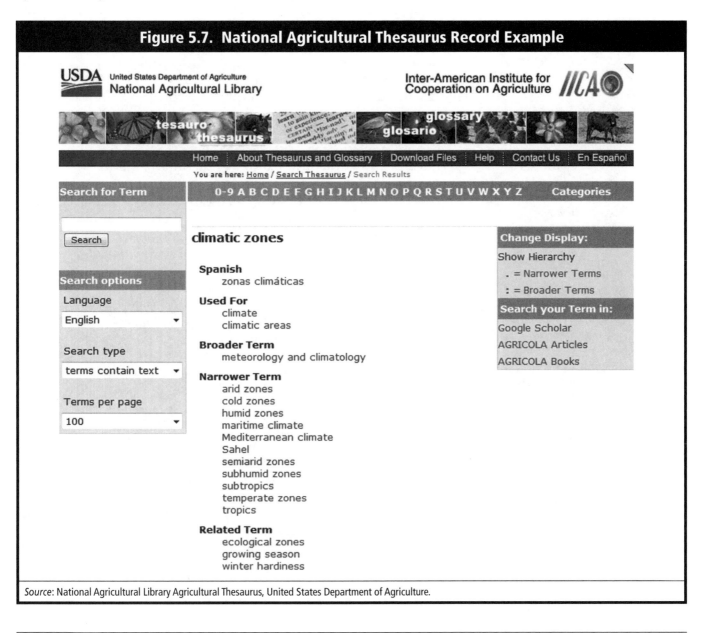

Source: National Agricultural Library Agricultural Thesaurus, United States Department of Agriculture.

digital collection management software systems cannot do this. But implementers still frequently use the thesauri just discussed as sources for authorized or preferred subject terms, implemented in the form of a flat list without the semantic relationships. Section 5.3 will say more about the TGM and AAT vocabularies and will include a comparative example from each.

5.2.6. Subject Heading Lists

Subject heading lists are lists of controlled subject terms that may also include any or all of the semantic relationships listed above. The best known and most widely used subject heading list is the massive *Library of Congress Subject Headings* (LCSH). LCSH does in fact include equivalence, hierarchical, and associative semantic relationships, just as any thesaurus does. Subject headings are, however, often distinguished from thesauri for several reasons, although the dividing lines are far from absolute. First, most thesauri cover a more specific or restricted subject domain, whereas subject heading lists such as LCSH cover the entire range of human knowledge, since it is intended for the collections of the Library of Congress, which potentially encompasses virtually any and every topic in any subject domain. Second, most thesauri consist of single-word terms, or restricted use of compound, multi-word terms, whereas subject heading lists tend to be more varied in this regard and more often include inverted terms, and other term forms generally avoided in thesauri. An example of an inverted term is *Poetry, Modern*, in contrast to *Modern Poetry*. Third, most thesauri do not allow for subdivisions to be added to terms, whereas subject heading lists such as LCSH regularly use subdivisions: that is, the addition of one or more terms that create pre-coordinated strings of subject terms. An example of a pre-coordinated LCSH string is *Poetry--Appreciation--United States--History--20th century*. Thesauri rely primarily on post-coordination rather than pre-coordination of terms. But distinctions between vocabularies called thesauri and subject headings definitely become blurred, especially when comparing TGM and LCSH, for example, both of which allow for subdivisions, except that TGM allows only for geographic subdivisions and has a narrower topical domain than LCSH.

5.3. Using Established Vocabularies

Almost all established metadata schemes such as Dublin Core, as well as local application profiles, strongly recommend the use of established controlled vocabularies for certain elements or fields. Delving into the details of each of these vocabularies lies beyond the scope of this book. But a comparison between a few aspects of two subject vocabularies here can be useful for getting a general sense of how different vocabularies are structured and applied.

This section explores a few comparative aspects of the Library of Congress *Thesaurus for Graphic Materials* and the Getty *Art and Architecture*

Controlled Vocabularies for Digital Collections Commonly Recommended for Use with DC, MODS, and VRA

Resource Types, Genre, Format, Material, Technique
- *Art and Architecture Thesaurus* (AAT)
- *Dublin Core Type Vocabulary* (DCT or DCMIType)
- MIME Internet Media Types (MIME or IMT)
- *Thesaurus for Graphic Materials* (TGM or LCTGM II)

Names and Roles
- Library of Congress/NACO *Name Authority File* (LCNAF or NAF)
- MARC Relator Terms and Codes (MARC Relator)
- *Union List of Artist Names* (ULAN)

Subjects (Topical, Geographic, Temporal, Form/Genre)
- *Art and Architecture Thesaurus* (AAT)
- *Getty Thesaurus of Geographic Names* (TGN)
- *Library of Congress Subject Headings* (LCSH)
- *Medical Subject Headings* (MeSH)
- *Thesaurus for Graphic Materials* (TGM or LCTGM)

Classification (Subject)
- *Dewey Decimal Classification* (DDC)
- *Library of Congress Classification* (LCC)
- *National Library of Medicine Classification* (NLM)
- *Universal Decimal Classification* (UDC)

Thesaurus. To begin with, it can be useful to look at examples of individual term records from each vocabulary. Figures 5.8 and 5.9 show records for the term *drawbridges* in TGM and AAT, respectively.

Notice some key differences, first of all, in how the terms are formatted in each vocabulary. Both terms are in the plural, which is the norm for any noun that names something that can be counted. TGM begins its terms with an uppercase letter, while AAT uses all lowercase. Both records include indications of semantic relationships, but in somewhat different ways. TGM indicates the **equivalence relationship** with the traditional *USED FOR* notation, while in AAT the first term under the heading *Terms* is designated as *preferred*, meaning that the other two are non-preferred equivalents. Notice also that AAT sometimes designates different preferred forms for different languages. *American English-P* indicates the preferred form of a term for those using American English. In this particular example, the American English preferred form happens to be identical to the main preferred form. TGM indicates **hierarchical relationships** using the headings *Broader Term(s)* and *Narrower Terms(s)*.

Figure 5.8. TGM Record for the Term *Drawbridges*

TGM
Thesaurus For
Graphic Materials

Related

- Browse neighboring items by call number.
Collection: Thesaurus For Graphic Materials

Drawbridges

Term: Drawbridges
[check for pictures with this index term]

Facet Note:

- --[country or state]--[city]

Scope Note:

- Search under SWING BRIDGES for bridges that move horizontally and under VERTICAL LIFT BRIDGES for bridges that move vertically.

Used For:

- Lift bridges
- Movable bridges

Broader Term(s):

- Bridges [check for pictures with this index term] [thesaurus term(s) only]

Reproduction Number: None
Notes:

- Former Usage Note: Formerly TGMI term.
- Former Control Number: lctgm003269
- Term Type Category: Subject (MARC 150/650)

Collections:

- Thesaurus For Graphic Materials

Bookmark This Record:
http://www.loc.gov/pictures/collection/tgm/item/tgm003275/

Source: Thesaurus for Graphic Materials, Prints & Photographs Division, Library of Congress. Online record: http://www.loc.gov/pictures/item/tgm003275/.

Figure 5.9. AAT Record for the Term *drawbridges*

Art & Architecture Thesaurus® Online
Full Record Display

🔍 New Search   ◄ Previous Page   ❓ Help

Click the 🔩 icon to view the hierarchy.

ID: 300007858   **Record Type:** concept

🔩   **drawbridges** (movable bridges, <bridges by form>, ... Built Environment (Hierarchy Name))

Note: Movable bridges in which one or more span sections can be pivoted upward by means of chains, cables, or other ropelike devices; if the sections are pivoted by counterweights, use "bascule bridges."

Terms:
    drawbridges (preferred,C,U,LC,American English-P,D,U,PN)
    drawbridge (C,U,American English,AD,U,SN)
    draw-bridges (C,U,British English,UF,U,N)

Facet/Hierarchy Code: V.RK

Hierarchical Position:
🔩   Objects Facet
🔩   .... Built Environment (Hierarchy Name) (G)
🔩   .... Single Built Works (Hierarchy Name) (G)
🔩   .... <single built works (Built Environment)> (G)
🔩   .... <single built works by specific type> (G)
🔩   .... <single built works by function> (G)
🔩   .... <transportation structures> (G)
🔩   .... <transportation structures by form> (G)
🔩   .... bridges (built works) (G)
🔩   .... <bridges by form> (G)
🔩   .... movable bridges (G)
🔩   .... drawbridges (G)

Related concepts:
    distinguished from .... **bascule bridges**
    .... (movable bridges, <bridges by form>, ... Built Environment (Hierarchy Name))
                                      [300007859]

In this particular case there is a broader term but no narrower terms. AAT indicates hierarchical relationships by means of the *Hierarchical Position* display. The triangular icons on the left can be clicked to open up a fuller display of the hierarchy at any level. In this particular TGM record there are no **associative relationships** for related terms, but AAT indicates such a relationship under the *Related concepts* heading. Both records include scope notes that define the use of the term. In TGM this is labeled *Scope Note*, while in AAT it is labeled simply *Note*.

Finally, it is very important to observe that TGM allows **subdivisions** and specifies the allowable form in each record. TGM covers its general subdivision practices in the *Introduction* to the vocabulary, Section III. The allowable format is given in the term record under the heading *Facet Note* as --[country or state]--[city]. This is the only type of subdivision that is allowed, and subdivision must come in this order. City is included if applicable, but if included, it must follow the name of the country or state. AAT, in contrast, does not use subdivisions in any form.

How does the use of established vocabularies work in practice in metadata for digital collections? When designing the metadata scheme for a collection, the designer will have decided which controlled vocabularies will be used for the values in specific fields. The metadata creators then need to use only terms from the selected vocabulary when entering metadata terms into that field. Tables 5.4 and 5.5 illustrate two possibilities of Dublin Core *Subject* metadata for a digital image of a drawbridge. The examples are based on the model of using collection-specific local fields and mapping them to Dublin Core. Note that the end user encounters only the element name and the value. The mapping to Dublin Core and the designation of the vocabulary appear only to the staff in the database software and/or in local documentation. In some cases, however, implementers choose to include the vocabulary name as part of their local field name: for example, *Subject*-TGM or *Subject*-AAT.

If the repository is using TGM as the controlled vocabulary for the *Type of Bridge/Subject* field, and the metadata designer has also decided to use subdivisions, the metadata would look like the illustration in Table 5.4. If AAT has been selected as the vocabulary for this element, the metadata would look like the illustration in Table 5.5. In either case, consistent use of the exact preferred term will serve the function of

Table 5.4. Subject Metadata Example Using Term from TGM

Element	Dublin Core	Vocabulary	Value
Type of Bridge	Subject	TGM	**Drawbridges--Wisconsin--Milwaukee**

Table 5.5. Subject Metadata Example Using Term from AAT

Element	Dublin Core	Vocabulary	Value
Type of Bridge	Subject	AAT	**drawbridges**

collocating or gathering together everything in the collection that is of or about drawbridges. The use of subdivisions with TGM further designates a specific geographic location that applies to a particular image of a drawbridge. Two primary purposes of using a controlled vocabulary are to achieve disambiguation and collocation. To achieve these two user-centered goals, it is critical that metadata creators use the terms exactly as they have been established, including singular versus plural, upper versus lower case, spacing, and punctuation.

If one delves into the AAT, one discovers that it takes a highly faceted approach in general. With regard to the terminology for bridges, for example, AAT designates terms for bridges by *form*, by *function*, and by *construction*. In Figure 5.9, for example, in the *Hierarchical Position* display, the facet <bridges by form> appears in angle brackets to indicate that the term *drawbridges* belongs to this facet. A particular type of bridge could have different terms for each of these three facets. A particular institution might decide to offer its users a greater degree of precision or granularity in its subject terms for a collection of digital images of bridges, and it might even go so far as to include three separate local elements for each aspect, as illustrated in Table 5.6. The point here is that different controlled vocabularies can allow different degrees of detail or precision. A decision to do subject analysis and representation at the level of detail and specificity illustrated in Table 5.6 would depend on an

Element	Dublin Core	Vocabulary	Value
Title	Title	---	Ponte Sant'Angelo, Rome
Type of Bridge by Form	Subject	AAT	**arch bridges**
Type of Bridge by Function	Subject	AAT	**road bridges**
Type of Bridge by Construction	Subject	AAT	**column bridges**

Table 5.6. More Detailed Subject Metadata Example Using Terms from AAT

analysis of the number and variety of items in the particular collection, on anticipated user retrieval needs, and on practical issues of time, budget, and staffing.

5.4. Creating Your Own Vocabularies

It is not uncommon in designing and creating metadata for digital collections that there is no established controlled vocabulary that meets local needs for a particular collection. This can be the case, for example, when dealing with names of local people, places, and corporate bodies that have not been established in national authority files. It can also be the case that a collection is focused on a very specific subject, and terms for that subject in existing established vocabularies are too few and too general to give the level of rich subject indexing desired for that collection. At that point, it is common to develop your own local controlled vocabularies for names, subject terms, and other terms as well. A collection on Great Lakes vessels, for example, might need to develop a controlled list of types of vessels used in Great Lakes shipping, sailing, transportation, and the like, as well as a controlled list of proper names of specific vessels. Some institutions develop their own list of more detailed *TypeOfResource* or *Genre* terms, as discussed in Chapter 4.

The process and level of detail in creating an original controlled vocabulary will vary depending on the type of vocabulary and the level of detail needed. For example, developing a list of personal names will not likely be as demanding as developing a list of subject terms. The process is usually approached from both a *top-down* and a *bottom-up* perspective. *Top-down* in this context means consulting existing controlled vocabularies and various other existing sources to glean potential terms and perhaps also ideas for hierarchical and other relationships among terms. *Bottom-up* means starting with the individual digital objects, analyzing their content and generating a list of potential terms from them. The process of generating a list of potential terms logically precedes decisions about preferred versus non-preferred terms, hierarchical levels, and the like.

Once a list of potential terms has been assembled, the next step in the process is to sift and winnow the list, refining the set of terms to be used. After that, or as part of that step, decisions must be made about the form of the terms, including use of singular versus plural forms, capitalization, single-word terms and multiple-word compound terms, and many other aspects of term format. This part of the process may also include identification of synonymous terms and selection of one of those terms as the preferred term. Many digital collection implementers will stop at this point and use a simple controlled list of names or terms. But some will want to go on to the next step of identifying equivalence relationships and implementing the cross references from non-preferred to preferred terms in some fashion in their collection interface. Figure 5.10 offers an example of a Subject term browse interface that identifies equivalence relationships by means of a *maps to* designation following the term. Searching or clicking on the term *Maladies*, for example, will automatically retrieve results in which the preferred term *Diseases* has been used in the Subject field in the metadata, while searching or selecting the term *Males* will retrieve results with the preferred subject term *Men* used in the metadata.

Figure 5.10. Subject Browse with Equivalence Relationships Implemented

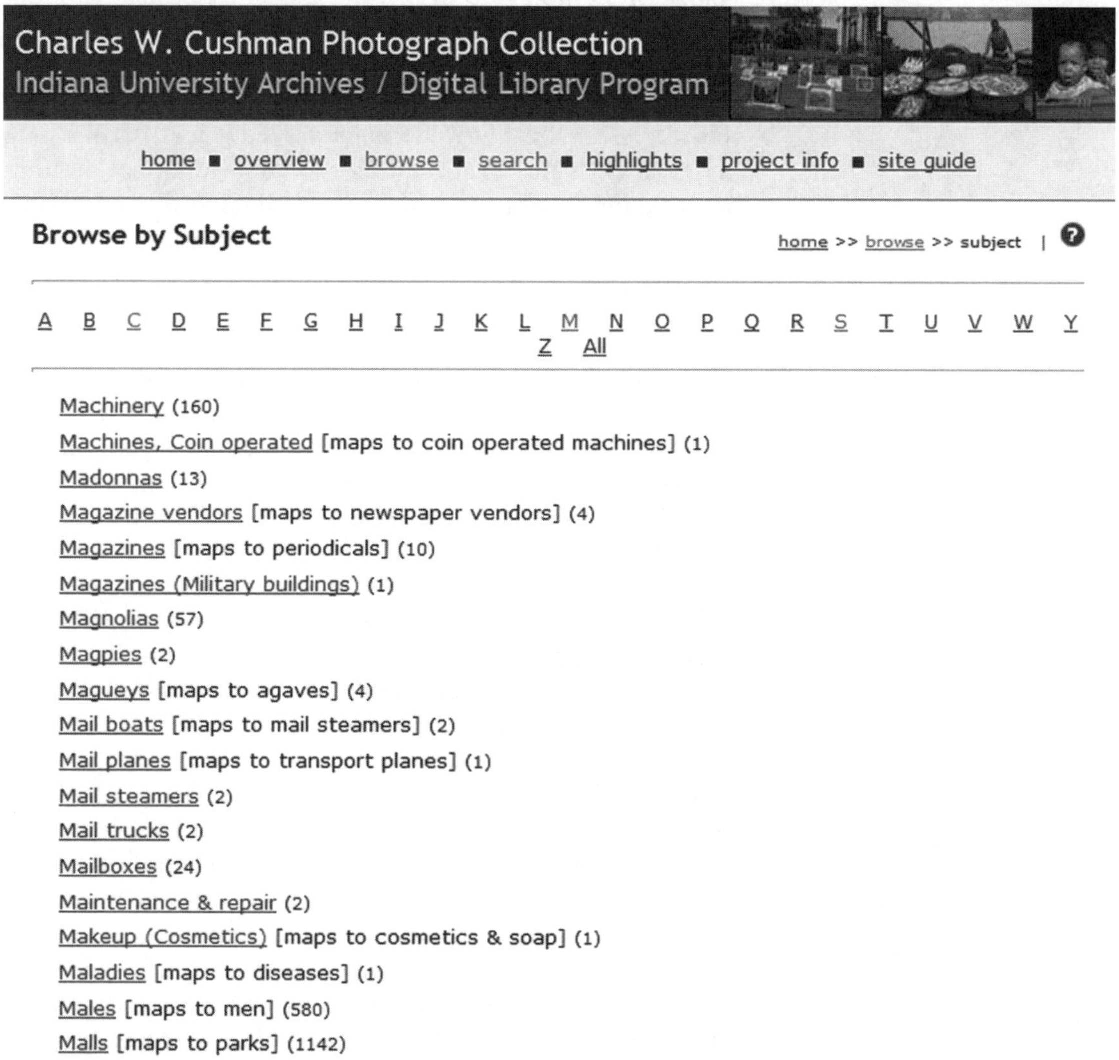

Charles W. Cushman Photograph Collection
Indiana University Archives / Digital Library Program

home ■ overview ■ browse ■ search ■ highlights ■ project info ■ site guide

Browse by Subject   home >> browse >> subject | ❓

A B C D E F G H I J K L M N O P Q R S T U V W Y
Z All

Machinery (160)

Machines, Coin operated [maps to coin operated machines] (1)

Madonnas (13)

Magazine vendors [maps to newspaper vendors] (4)

Magazines [maps to periodicals] (10)

Magazines (Military buildings) (1)

Magnolias (57)

Magpies (2)

Magueys [maps to agaves] (4)

Mail boats [maps to mail steamers] (2)

Mail planes [maps to transport planes] (1)

Mail steamers (2)

Mail trucks (2)

Mailboxes (24)

Maintenance & repair (2)

Makeup (Cosmetics) [maps to cosmetics & soap] (1)

Maladies [maps to diseases] (1)

Males [maps to men] (580)

Malls [maps to parks] (1142)

Source: Permission for reproduction granted by The Charles W. Cushman Collection, University Archives, Indiana University, Bloomington, IN.

The next step in traditional controlled vocabulary and thesaurus development is to identify hierarchal relationships and to begin arranging terms into hierarchical levels of broader and narrower terms, adding levels if needed to group similar terms together and to differentiate specific types, instances, or parts of broader terms. The final step is to identify useful associative relationships and add related terms.

The details of this process go beyond the scope of this book, but the ANSI/NISO Z39.19 Guidelines (NISO, 2005) provide an excellent guide for anyone creating a controlled vocabulary, even a flat list without semantic relationships. The Guidelines present the collective wisdom and experience of many experts over many years as to how to format terms, how to deal with acronyms, punctuation, compound terms, and a host of other issues inevitably encountered when creating a controlled vocabulary of one's own. They are intended more as helpful best practice recommendations and not as absolute rules. They take account of the fact that every application has its own unique context, content, and users. Vanda Broughton's *Essential Thesaurus Construction* (Broughton, 2006) provides an excellent step-by-step guide for controlled vocabulary construction, using an ongoing practical case study to concretely illustrate the process. Another resource that some might find helpful is Heather Hedden's *The Accidental Taxonomist* (Hedden, 2010). Although oriented more towards the creation of corporate taxonomies, it contains useful information that can be applied to the digital collection context as well.

5.5. Summary

Chapter 5 follows up on Chapters 3 and 4 by turning to the topic of controlled vocabularies, which are fundamental to the functionality of so many of the metadata elements covered in the previous two chapters. Controlled vocabularies serve an important role in user discovery of digital resources and in allowing users to retrieve not only sets of meaningfully related resources, but also individual resources or groups of resources lacking any meaningful semantic relation to each other. Controlled vocabularies address problems inherent in natural human language such as ambiguity and synonymy. They also link terms representing concepts, persons, places, and things that have various kinds of semantic relationships with one another, including equivalence, hierarchical, and associative relationships.

Controlled vocabularies come in many shapes and sizes, from the simple to the complex and from the formal to the informal. Common general types of controlled vocabularies include lists, synonym rings, authority files, taxonomies or classification schemes, thesauri, and subject heading lists. Each of these lies on a spectrum from the relatively more simple to the relatively more complex in terms of the kinds of semantic relationships each includes. Within each of these general types are many instances of specific controlled vocabularies created by different communities to serve different purposes. Different subject vocabularies, such as the *Thesaurus for Graphic Materials* and the *Art and Architecture*

Thesaurus, have their own approaches to formatting terms, indicating semantic relationships, and using or not using subdivisions to create pre-coordinated subject strings versus a post-coordinated approach to subject retrieval.

Most metadata implementers in the digital collection environment use various types of established vocabularies recommended for specific metadata elements. But it is not uncommon to find that established vocabularies do not always sufficiently serve local needs. Local institutions and consortia therefore sometimes create their own controlled vocabularies for names of persons, bodies, places, objects, events, and concepts. Knowledge of the principles of controlled vocabularies and semantic relationships can help local implementers to create more robust and reusable vocabularies.

▶ Companion Website

See this book's companion website at **http://www.neal-schuman.com/ metadata-digital-collections/** for Chapter 5 review questions, suggestions for exercises, links to online versions of several controlled vocabularies, and other resources.

References

Broughton, Vanda. 2006. *Essential Thesaurus Construction*. London: Facet.

Hedden, Heather. 2010. *The Accidental Taxonomist*. Medford, NJ: Information Today.

Leise, Fred, Karl Fast, and Mike Steckel. 2002. "What Is a Controlled Vocabulary?" Boxes and Arrows. Last modified April 7. http://www.boxesandarrows .com/view/creating_a_controlled_vocabulary.

NISO (National Information Standards Organization). 2005. *ANSI/NISO Z39.19-2005 - Guidelines for the Construction, Format, and Management of Monolingual Controlled Vocabularies*. Bethesda, MD: NISO Press.

XML-Encoded Metadata

6.1. XML Metadata Basics

This section of the chapter offers a very brief and highly simplified introduction to metadata encoding, specifically in XML. The intention is not to provide a comprehensive overview of XML and its background, but to present just enough practical information and examples to allow readers of this book to learn how to understand and work with XML-encoded metadata records in OAI-DC, MODS, and VRA 4.0. It is important to realize that this is only the tip of the iceberg of XML, but it is sufficient for the purposes just stated.

6.1.1. Introduction to Metadata Encoding and XML

In order for metadata to function in any computer-based system it needs to be encoded for machine readability and processing. When you create a document in Word, a spreadsheet in Excel, or a database in Access, these are encoded in Microsoft's proprietary encoding formats. The code is not free or open source. Most database and web interface software is *proprietary*. In contrast, XML is an *open-source*, nonproprietary encoding standard.

Library catalog data has been encoded in the **MARC** format since the 1960's. MARC stands for *MAchine-Readable Cataloging*. MARC is used for communicating and sharing bibliographic data among library systems and bibliographic utilities, such as OCLC and its WorldCat database. Generically, MARC is an encoding system composed of fields, most of them designated by three-character tags, and so on. Furrie (2009) offers an excellent, nontechnical introduction to MARC for those new to the scheme. Different countries have developed their own implementations of MARC, with specific tags designating different types of bibliographic information (metadata) in different countries. Within the past decade, US MARC and Canadian MARC merged to become MARC 21. The MARC Standards website (http://www.loc.gov/marc/) includes all of the official MARC documentation for the United States.

Today there are continuing movements for harmonization of MARC among many countries.

XML is an acronym that stands for *EXtensible Markup Language*. XML falls into the general category of a *markup language*. Actually, it is a metalanguage for creating specific markup languages. The mother language of this family of markup languages is **SGML**, *Standard Generalized Markup Language*, developed in the 1960s as an open-source, non-proprietary metalanguage for defining specific markup languages for specific types of documents. **HTML**, *Hypertext Markup Language*, the language of the current World Wide Web, is one specific type of SGML markup language. HTML is defined by an SGML *Document Type Definition* (DTD), which specifies its allowed tags. SGML is a vast and highly complex metalanguage. HTML is a very simple SGML language. HTML deals primarily with visual presentation rather than the structure and content of documents.

XML was developed in the 1990s as a more manageable subset of the much more vast SGML. But unlike HTML, XML deals with the content and structure of documents. Like SGML, XML is a metalanguage for defining specific markup languages. XML has been widely adopted in publishing, e-commerce, and other communities, including various cultural heritage metadata communities. XML functions in the metadata environment as a nonproprietary method of encoding metadata for machine processing, sharing, exchange, interoperability, and reuse. A majority of current metadata schemes include an expression in XML for purposes of encoding metadata content for computer processing and interchange among systems.

A specific XML language is defined either by a **DTD** (*Document Type Definition*) or by an **XML schema**. These are formal, machine-readable documents that define the allowable elements and other aspects of the specific XML language. Today, most of the major cultural heritage metadata schemes have been expressed as XML schemas. This is true of both the Metadata Object Description Schema (MODS) and the Visual Resources Core Categories (VRA), Version 4.0, which are examples of specific XML markup languages. The current MODS XML schema, for example, is available online at http://www.loc.gov/standards/mods/mods.xsd. This document will not make much sense to someone not already familiar with XML schema language, and it is not vital to be able to understand this type of document in order to work with MODS XML metadata records. This XML schema document is the formal, machine-readable file that defines all of the valid MODS elements and attributes.

6.1.2. XML Syntax: Elements and Attributes

XML uses tags to demarcate elements. **Tags** begin and end with angle brackets: <...>. Each **element** is marked by an opening and a closing tag, which are identical, except that the closing tag is preceded by a forward slash inside of the angle brackets. The following examples are generic and do not follow any particular metadata element set DTD or XML

Recommended Readings on XML

For more overview and background information on markup languages, SGML, and especially XML, the following articles are recommended:

- Johnston, Pete. 2006. "Metadata Sharing and XML." In *Good Practice Guide for Developers of Cultural Heritage Web Services*. Bath, UK: UKOLN. Last modified January. http://www.ukoln.ac.uk/interop-focus/gpg/Metadata/ (accessed November 3, 2010).
- Rhyno, Art. 2005. "Introduction to XML." In *Technology for the Rest of Us: A Primer on Computer Technologies for the Low-Tech Librarian*, edited by Nancy Courtney, 71–84. Westport, CT: Libraries Unlimited.
- Yott, Patrick. 2005. "Introduction to XML." In *Metadata: A Cataloger's Primer*, edited by Richard P. Smiraglia, 213–235. Binghamton, New York: Haworth Press.
- W3C Extensible Markup Language (XML) website (http://www.w3.org/XML/).

schema. Table 6.1 illustrates the way that a metadata element for a place name could be encoded in XML.

It is easy to see how XML tags and elements work well for encoding metadata elements. In a tabular database structure, this same metadata could appear as shown in Table 6.2.

XML also frequently makes use of **attributes**, which are pairs of names and values that occur inside of the start tag of an element to further refine its meaning. Table 6.3 gives an example of adding an XML attribute name and value for the *Place* element from the previous example. This attribute refines the meaning of the *Place* element by specifying a particular *type* of place. The name of the attribute is *Type*, and the value of the attribute is *city*. The attribute name must be followed by an equal sign, and the attribute value must be inside of quotation marks, all without any spaces.

Table 6.4 gives an example of an element with two attributes. Note that both attributes follow the same structure as illustrated in Table 6.3, and both occur inside of the start tag of the element to which they apply.

The generic example in Table 6.4, for example, could be expressed in a table format as illustrated in Table 6.5. This closely parallels the structure of qualified Dublin Core, in which the terminology for *element type* would be *element refinement* and for *element authority* would be *encoding scheme*.

Every XML file or document begins with a standard **XML declaration**, which declares what kind of file it is. The following is commonly used: <?xml version="1.0" encoding="utf-8"?>. It declares that this is an XML document, which version of XML it is, and what character set the file is encoded in. Following the XML declaration there must be a **root element**, demarcated with a start and end tag. The root element contains all of the other elements as child elements of the parent root element. In the example given below, the root element is named *metadata*.

```
<?xml version="1.0" encoding="utf-8"?>
<metadata>
    <place type="city" authority="TGN">Toronto</place>
</metadata>
```

The previous example includes line breaks and indentation. XML processors themselves do not recognize any whitespace except that which exists between start and end tags. In order to make XML documents more human-readable, however, spaces and line breaks are frequently inserted. Indentation is also frequently used to visually show

Table 6.1. Simple *Place* Element Example in XML Format

Start Tag	Element Value	End Tag
<place>	Toronto	</place>

Table 6.2. Simple *Place* Element Example in Tabular Database Format

Element Name	Element Value
place	Toronto

Table 6.3. Simple XML *Place* Element with an XML Attribute

Start Tag	Attribute Name and Value	Element Value	End Tag
<place	type="city">	Toronto	</place>

Table 6.4. Simple XML *Place* Element with Two XML Attributes

Start Tag	First Attribute Name and Value	Second Attribute Name and Value	Element Value	End Tag
<place	type="city"	authority="TGN">	Toronto	</place>

Table 6.5. Table Format Example of Element with Two Qualifiers

Element Name	Element Type	Element Authority	Element Value
place	city	TGN	Toronto

child elements nested within their parent elements. The example below presents a slightly more detailed example of nested parent and child elements, also called elements and subelements.

```
<?xml version="1.0" encoding="utf-8"?>
<metadata>
    <place type="city" authority="TGN">Toronto</place>
    <name type="personal" authority="NAF">
        <firstName>Margaret</firstName>
        <lastName>Atwood</lastName>
    </name>
</metadata>
```

In this example, the *name* element contains two child elements: *First Name* and *Last Name*. XML processors do not care whether spaces, line breaks, and indentations are there or not, but human eyes usually appreciate them!

6.1.3. Well-Formed versus Valid XML

Well-formed XML conforms to the generic rules for XML as a metalanguage. For example, well-formed XML must begin with an XML declaration and have a root element; all tags must be in angle brackets with a start and end tag; all child tags must be correctly nested within their parent tags; all attributes must be expressed inside of the opening tag with the attribute name, equals sign, and the attribute value surrounded by quotation marks, and so on.

Most current web browsers can detect whether or not an XML document (that is, a file with an .xml file extension) is *well-formed*. XML allows individuals and communities to create their own sets of tags to suit their own purposes and needs. But in order for XML documents to be usable and interchangeable, they must conform to some set of shared tags and other specifications. DTDs and XML schemas are used to define a particular XML language by declaring a set of elements and attributes and to some extent also their allowed values. The examples given in the previous section are made up and do not conform to any established DTD or schema. They are *well-formed* XML, but not *valid*, because there is no DTD or schema against which to validate them.

The MODS metadata scheme or element set has a formal MODS XML schema that defines all of the MODS elements and attributes. A **valid** MODS XML document is one that conforms to all of the specifications of the MODS XML schema. Certain types of XML editing or processing software can not only detect whether an XML document is generically well-formed but also validate that document against a DTD or schema. An XML document that conforms to a specific XML DTD or schema is said to be valid. Thus, a MODS document in XML can be valid or not valid in terms of whether or not it conforms to the specifications of the MODS XML schema. When creating a valid MODS metadata record, the creator cannot simply invent his or her own elements, subelements, and attributes. Only those established in the XML schema may be used. There is also human-readable documentation that defines and illustrates all of the valid MODS elements, subelements, and attributes, their correct order, and the like, as covered in Chapter 7.

6.1.4. XML Namespaces and Metadata Modularity

For purposes of this book, a **namespace** is considered to be a nameable location on the Internet that contains the official documentation of a metadata element set, preferably a formal XML Schema, if one exists. By including namespace declarations in an XML file, it is possible to use elements from more than one element set in a single XML document. Including namespace declarations in an XML file also allows metadata records from more than one scheme to be aggregated or cross-searched while identifying the scheme to which each element belongs. A namespace declaration in XML appears inside the root element tag and begins with *xmlns*, followed by the equals sign, followed by the URI for the namespace. It may also include an abbreviation, such as *dc* for Dublin Core, as follows: xmlns:dc="http://purl.org/dc/elements/1.1/. This declares the namespace on the Internet for the simple Dublin Core element set and also declares that the code *dc* will be used in the rest of the document as a prefix in individual tags to indicate that the source of the element is simple Dublin Core. The following is an example.

```
<?xml version="1.0" encoding="utf-8"?>
<metadata xmlns:dc="http://purl.org/dc/elements/1.1/>
    <dc:title>Metadata</dc:title>
    <dc:creator>Marcia Zeng</dc:creator>
    <dc:creator>Jian Qin</dc:creator>
    <dc:publisher>Neal-Schuman</dc:publisher>
</metadata>
```

Actually, a complete XML namespace declaration must include more information than the oversimplified example above, but this serves well enough to illustrate the basic idea. Namespaces are useful for various reasons. One value is that they help to disambiguate metadata elements from different schemes or element sets that have the same name. For example, a music-related element set, a railroad-related element set, and an electrical engineering-related element set might all have a *Conductor* element (based on an example given in Johnston, 2006). But the meaning and usage of this Conductor element would be quite different in each. By declaring the namespace and using a prefix, the three different conductor elements could be distinguished as follows:

```
<mus:conductor>
<rr:conductor>
<engr:conductor>
```

Turning to a real-world example, say for example that you wanted to use simple Dublin Core as your main element set, but you also wanted to include one or more VRA elements that cover aspects of a resource not covered by DC, such as artistic style or period. Duval et al. (2002) have called this mixing of elements from more than one element set *metadata modularity*. The following instance provides a simplified example for the sake of illustrating the basic idea. Notice the use of two namespaces in the XML declaration and two prefixes in the element tags to indicate which element set each element comes from.

```
<?xml version="1.0" encoding="utf-8"?>

<metadata
  xmlns:dc="http://purl.org/dc/elements/1.1/>
  xmlns:vra="http://www.loc.gov/standards/vracore/>

<dc:title>Starry Night</dc:title>
<dc:creator>Vincent van Gogh</dc:creator>
<vra:stylePeriod vocab=AAT">Post-Impressionist</vra:stylePeriod>

</metadata>
```

It is also possible to reference an actual XML schema if it is available on the web. An XML schema file is indicated by the *.xsd* file name extension, standing for XML schema Definition. The formal VRA XML schema file, for example, resides at http://www.loc.gov/standards/vracore/vra-strict .xsd. This URL with the .xsd file extension identifies the actual VRA XML schema file, itself written in XML, which formally defines all of the VRA elements, attributes, and so on. It is not necessary to be able to read and make sense of an XML schema in order to use it. There is also human-friendly documentation on VRA, which will be introduced in Chapter 8. The example below illustrates how an XML schema is referenced within an XML root tag.

```
<?xml version="1.0" encoding="UTF-8" ?>

<vra xmlns="http://www.loc.gov/standards/vracore/"
xmlns:xsi="http://www.w3.org/2001/XMLSchema-instance"
xsi:schemaLocation="http://www.loc.gov/standards/vracore/
http://www.loc.gov/standards/vracore/vra-strict.xsd">
```

In this example, the first line of the <vra> root tag includes a reference to the VRA namespace. The second line declares that this document should be validated against an XML Schema and uses the *xsi* prefix to reference the XML Schema Instance namespace. The third line uses the *SchemaLocation* attribute to specify the namespace where the XML Schema is located, and the fourth line contains a second value for the *SchemaLocation* attribute from the third line, this time specifying the location of the XML schema (.xsd) file itself. This same basic pattern can be seen in the two full XML records in Section 6.2 for OAI DC XML and MODS XML.

Section 6.3 at the end of this chapter includes an illustrative overview of each of the major aspects of XML covered in the sections above in a table called *Anatomy of an XML Metadata Record*.

6.1.5. Creating Metadata in XML

Depending on the specific institution, application context, and metadata scheme, metadata creators may work directly with XML code quite a lot, only partially, or not at all. Various software packages, free online tools, and sometimes locally created tools exist that can automatically generate some or all of the XML coding for metadata. Section 7.3.2 in Chapter 7 includes screen capture illustrations of two MODS XML creation tools as two good examples of such software. Many digital content management systems such as CONTENTdm encode metadata in XML entirely behind the scenes, and the metadata creator works with a user-friendly interface, as illustrated in Figure 1.8 from Chapter 1 (p. 21). One interesting free online tool that is worth experimenting with is the Dublin Core Generator at http://www.dublincoregenerator.com. When first learning an XML-based metadata scheme such as MODS, however, there is no substitute for typing out some XML code by hand before relying on automated tools. Once familiar with the scheme, such tools become invaluable in an actual metadata production environment.

6.2. XML Metadata Record Examples

This section of the chapter includes a few examples of XML-encoded metadata, including simple and qualified Dublin Core and MODS. It is possible to understand some of the basics of the XML structure of MODS without having yet studied the scheme. In each of these examples, selected parts of the XML coding are in bold font in order to draw special attention to them as illustrative of XML structures.

6.2.1. Dublin Core in XML

The following example shows simple Dublin Core as implemented in an Open Archives Initiative (OAI) XML syntax for communicating Dublin Core metadata. The OAI Protocol for Metadata Harvesting (OAI-PMH) will be discussed in Chapter 9, but it is used here because it is a relatively clear-cut and easy to read form of real-world XML encoding of Dublin Core Metadata. The following example is from the OAI-PMH 2.0 documentation (OAI, 2008).

```
<metadata>
  <oai_dc:dc
        xmlns:oai_dc="http://www.openarchives.org/OAI/2.0/
        oai_dc/"
        xmlns:dc="http://purl.org/dc/elements/1.1/"
        xmlns:xsi="http://www.w3.org/2001/XMLSchema-instance"
        xsi:schemaLocation="http://www.openarchives.org/OAI/
        2.0/oai_dc/
        http://www.openarchives.org/OAI/2.0/oai_dc.xsd">
    <dc:title>Using Structural Metadata to Localize Experience
    of Digital Content</dc:title>
    <dc:creator>Dushay, Naomi</dc:creator>
    <dc:subject>Digital Libraries</dc:subject>
    <dc:description>With the increasing technical
    sophistication of both information consumers and
    providers, there is increasing demand for more
    meaningful experiences of digital information. We
    present a framework that separates digital object
    experience, or rendering, from digital object storage
    and manipulation, so the rendering can be tailored to
    particular communities of users.</dc:description>
    <dc:description>Comment: 23 pages including 2 appendices,
    8 figures</dc:description>
```

```
<dc:date>2001-12-14</dc:date>
<dc:type>e-print</dc:type>
<dc:identifier>http://arXiv.org/abs/cs/
  0112017</dc:identifier>
  </oai_dc:dc>
</metadata>
```

Notice the use of the *dc:* prefix that refers to the namespace that formally documents the 15 basic Dublin Core elements. The OAI DC XML scheme is used only for the simple, unqualified Dublin Core elements. It is a simple *flat* scheme, without hierarchically nested subelements, in contrast to MODS XML.

The DCMI has offered various methods for expressing Qualified Dublin Core at various times in its history as it continues to evolve. The partial example below depicts one possible method, included here to demonstrate that even qualified DC can be expressed in a *flat*, rather than hierarchical, XML syntax. This is possible because the DC refinement names, such as *Alternative* and *IsPartOf*, are unique and have been established as terms on their own in the *DCMI Metadata Terms* namespace. They therefore do not need to be explicitly associated in the XML file with the element name that each refines. It is understood that the term *Alternative* refines the *Title* element, or is a subproperty of the *Title* property, and that the term *IsPartOf* refines the *Relation* element, or is a *subproperty* of the relation property.

```
<dcterms:title>Plants of Upper Michigan</dcterms:title>

<dcterms:alternative>Upper Michigan Plant Book</dcterms:
  alternative>

<dcterms:publisher>Hagenville University Library</dcterms:
  publisher>

<dcterms:isPartOf>Historic Biology Text Collection</dcterms:
  isPartOf>
```

Contrast this with the following hypothetical hierarchical example, which is not a method that the DCMI has recommended for expressing Qualified Dublin Core in XML.

```
<dc:title>
    <dc:alternative>Upper Michigan Plant Book</dc:alternative>
</dc:title>

<dc:relation>
    <dc:isPartOf>Historic Biology Text Collection</dc:isPartOf>
</dc:relation>
```

The following hypothetical example of a complete set of Qualified Dublin Core for a digital text uses a convention for expressing DC encoding schemes by means of a *scheme* attribute. This does not conform to any DCMI Dublin Core XML practice at the present time, but it works perfectly well for the sake of this hypothetical example. Prefixes of *dc:* or *dcterms:* are not used because no namespaces outside of the document are being referenced in this particular example.

```
<title>The life and times of Isabella Rios: based on diaries
  and oral narratives as told to her daughter Maria Rios
  Campos</title>
```

```
<creator>Campos, Maria Rios, 1923-</creator>

<contributor>Alvarez, Alejandro</contributor>

<isVersionOf>La vida y la época de Isabella Rios: basado en
 los diarios y narraciones orales como dijo a su hija Maria
 Rios Campos</isVersionOf>
<source>45097833</source>

<type scheme="DCMIType">Text</type>

<type>biography</type>

<publisher>Palm Press</publisher>

<issued>1960</issued>

<description>2nd ed.</description>

<extent>137 pages; 21 cm.</extent>

<description>A narrative of the life of Los Angeles native
 Isabella Rios, focusing especially on her experiences as a
 Hispanic American woman living in 1920s and 1930s Los
 Angeles and her work as an extra on the sets of film
 productions at the Paramount and Warner Bros. motion
 picture studios.</description>

<description>One of three known surviving copies. Donated to
 the Hagenville University Libraries by Marco Campos, son of
 Maria Rios Campos, in 1995.</description>

<contributor>Hagenville University Libraries Special
 Collections</contributor>

<subject>Rios, Isabella, 1899-1976</subject>

<subject scheme="LCSH">Hispanic American women--California--
 Los Angeles--Biography</subject>

<spatial scheme="TGN">North and Central America</spatial>

<spatial scheme="TGN">United States</spatial>

<spatial scheme="TGN">California</spatial>

<spatial scheme="TGN">Los Angeles</spatial>

<temporal>1899-1976</temporal>

<temporal>Nineteen twenties</temporal>

<temporal>Nineteen thirties</temporal>

<subject scheme="DDC">920.7208968</subject>

<format scheme="IMT">image/jpeg</format>

<identifier>UDL-HAOC-005739<identifier>

<created scheme="W3CDTF">2007-01-04</created>

<rights> Use of this public-domain resource is
 unrestricted.</rights>

<publisher>Hagenville University Digital Library</publisher>

<isPartOf>Hispanic Americans of California</isPartOf>

<isPartOf scheme="URI>http://www.hdl.edu/HAOC/</isPartOf>
```

6.2.2. MODS XML

Although the next chapter provides an introduction to the MODS metadata element set, an example of a simple MODS record is useful here to

illustrate its use of XML elements, attributes, and nested subelements. Even without yet knowing the MODS scheme, the basic XML structure should be comprehensible after having read this chapter. The following example is from the *MODS User Guidelines*, MODS Full Record Examples (http://www.loc.gov/standards/mods/userguide/examples.html).

Notice the nesting of subelements within parent elements, some of them two levels deep. For example, the *RoleTerm* element is a child or subelement of the parent *Role* element, which is itself a child or

---

Complete MODS Record Example

```xml
<?xml version="1.0" encoding="UTF-8"?>
<modsCollection xmlns:xlink="http://www.w3.org/
  1999/xlink" xmlns:xsi="http://www.w3.org/2001/
  XMLSchema-instance" xmlns="http://www.loc.gov/
  mods/v3" xsi:schemaLocation="http://www.loc
  .gov/mods/v3 http://www.loc.gov/standards/
  mods/v3/mods-3-3.xsd">
<mods version="3.3">
<titleInfo>
    <title>At Gettysburg, or, What a Girl Saw
      and Heard of the Battle: A True
      Narrative</title>
</titleInfo>
<name type="personal">
    <namePart>Alleman, Tillie Pierce [1848-
      1914]</namePart>
    <role>
        <roleTerm type="code" authority=
          "marcrelator">aut</roleTerm>
        <roleTerm type="text" authority=
          "marcrelator">Author</roleTerm>
    <role>
</name>
<typeOfResource>text</typeOfResource>
<originInfo>
    <place>
        <placeTerm type="text">New
          York</placeTerm>
    </place>
    <publisher>W. Lake Borland</publisher>
    <dateIssued keyDate="yes"
      encoding="w3cdtf">1889</date Issued>
</originInfo>
<language>
    <languageTerm authority="iso639-2b">
      eng</languageTerm>
    <languageTerm type="text">
      English</languageTerm>
</language>
```

```xml
<physicalDescription>
    <internetMediaType>text/html</internet
      MediaType>
    <digitalOrigin>reformatted
      digital</digitalOrigin>
</physicalDescription>
<subject authority="lcsh">
    <topic>Gettysburg, Battle of, Gettysburg, Pa.,
      1863</topic>
</subject>
<subject authority="lcsh">
    <topic>Gettysburg (Pa.) -- History -- Civil
      War, 1861-1865</topic>
</subject>
<subject authority="lcsh">
    <topic>United States -- History -- Civil
      War, 1861-1865 -- Campaigns</topic>
</subject>
<classification authority="lcc">E475.53
  .A42</classification>
<relatedItem type="host">
    <titleInfo type="uniform" authority=
      "dlfaqcoll">
        <title>A Celebration of Women Writers:
          Americana</title>
    </titleInfo>
</relatedItem>
<location>
    <url usage="primary display" access="object
      in context"> http://digital.library.upenn.edu/
      women/alleman/gettysburg/gettysburg.html
    </url>
</location>
<accessCondition>Personal, noncommercial use of
  this item is permitted in the United States of
  America. Please see http://digital.library
  .upenn.edu/women/for other rights and
  restrictions that may apply to this resource.
</accessCondition>
```

(Continued)

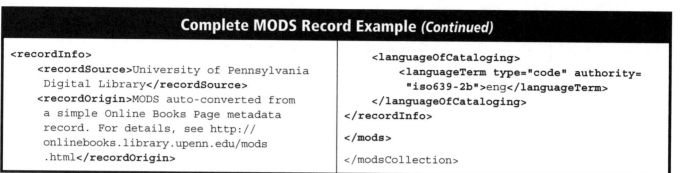

Complete MODS Record Example *(Continued)*

```
<recordInfo>
   <recordSource>University of Pennsylvania
   Digital Library</recordSource>
   <recordOrigin>MODS auto-converted from
   a simple Online Books Page metadata
   record. For details, see http://
   onlinebooks.library.upenn.edu/mods
   .html</recordOrigin>

   <languageOfCataloging>
      <languageTerm type="code" authority=
      "iso639-2b">eng</languageTerm>
   </languageOfCataloging>
</recordInfo>

</mods>

</modsCollection>
```

subelement of the parent *Name* element. Notice also the frequent use of *Type* and *Authority* attributes within the opening tags of several elements. The allowable attributes and attribute values have been formally declared in the MODS XML schema, as have the allowable nested element-subelement structures. The next chapter will delve more deeply into the structure and meaning of the MODS elements and attributes.

6.3. Anatomy of an XML Metadata Record

To conclude this chapter, the following example is a small portion of a MODS XML record.

```
<?xml version="1.0" encoding="UTF-8"?>

<mods xmlns="http://www.loc.gov/mods/v3"
xmlns:xsi="http://www.w3.org/2001/XMLSchema-instance"
xsi:schemaLocation="http://www.loc.gov/mods/v3
http://www.loc.gov/standards/mods/v3/mods-3-2.xsd">

<titleInfo>
    <title>General view of Balaklava, the hospital on the
    right</title>
</titleInfo>

<name type="personal" authority="naf">
    <namePart>Fenton, Roger</namePart>
    <namePart type="date">1819-1869</namePart>
    <role>
        <roleTerm authority="marcrelator"
        type="text">creator</roleTerm>
    </role>
    <role>
        <roleTerm authority="marcrelator"
        type="text">photographer</roleTerm>
    </role>
</name>

</mods>
```

Table 6.6 labels each part of the record, providing a recap of most of the aspects of XML covered in this chapter. It also coincidentally serves as a gentle introduction to some aspects of the MODS scheme, presented in detail in the next chapter.

Table 6.6. Anatomy of an XML Metadata Record

XML declaration: declares that this is an XML file, defines the XML version (1.0) and the encoding used (UTF-8 character set)	`<?xml version="1.0" encoding="UTF-8"?>`
MODS root element start tag: parent element of all of the child elements in the file	`<mods`
XML namespace attribute: inside of the root element tag: gives the namespace for the MODS element set	`xmlns="http://www.loc.gov/mods/v3"`
XSI namespace attribute: tells XML parsers or processing software that this document should be validated against an XML Schema, which is generically documented in the XML Schema Instance (XSI) namespace stated here	`xmlns:xsi="http://www.w3.org/2001/XMLSchema-instance"`
Schema location attribute: contains two values, the first states the general namespace where the MODS XML Schema resides and the second states the specific location of the .xsd Schema file itself. The closing angle bracket closes the MODS root element start tag.	`xsi:schemaLocation="http://www.loc.gov/mods/v3` `http://www.loc.gov/standards/mods/v3/mods-3-2.xsd">`
MODS *titleInfo* element start tag: parent of the nested *title* subelement	`<titleInfo>`
Hierarchically nested ***title*** subelement, including start and end tags and the element value	`<title>General view of Balaklava, the hospital on the right</title>`
MODS *titleInfo* element end tag	`</titleInfo>`
MODS *name* element start tag, with two element attributes. The ***type*** attribute specifies the type of name applicable to the element value. The ***authority*** attribute specifies the authority file from which the element value is taken, in this case the LC/NACO Name Authority File (*naf*)	`<name type="personal" authority="naf">`
First ***namePart*** subelement: contains a value consisting of the main part of a personal name, given in the form established in the *naf*	`<namePart>Fenton, Roger</namePart>`
Second ***namePart*** subelement: contains a value consisting of the birth and death dates of the person, completing the form of name established in the *naf*	`<namePart type="date">1819-1869</namePart>`
MODS ***role*** subelement start tag: contains one child subelement	`<role>`
The ***roleTerm*** subelement: a child of its parent *role* element. Includes an ***authority*** and ***type*** attribute, establishing that its value is a *textual* term taken from the *marcrelator* controlled term list.	`<roleTerm authority="marcrelator" type="text">photographer</roleTerm>`
End tag for the first *role* subelement	`</role>`
Start tag for the second *role* subelement	`<role>`
This ***roleTerm*** subelement contains a value from the same term list, but in this instance a *code* rather than a textual term	`<roleTerm authority="marcrelator" type="code">pht</roleTerm>`
End tag for the second *role* subelement	`</role>`
MODS *name* element end tag. Note the hierarchical nesting of start and end tags within the name element.	`</name>`
MODS root element end tag	`</mods>`

6.4. Summary

Chapter 6 provides a very brief and highly simplified introduction to metadata encoding in Extensible Markup Language (XML). The purpose of the chapter is to give an introductory basis for learning how to read and work with XML-encoded metadata records in OAI-DC, MODS, and VRA 4.0.

In order for metadata to function in any computer-based system, it needs to be encoded for machine-readability and processing. XML is an open-source, nonproprietary encoding standard. XML is a member of the Standard Generalized Markup Language (SGML) family of markup languages. Like SGML, it is a metalanguage for defining more specific XML languages. A specific XML language is defined either by a DTD (Document Type Definition) or by an XML schema. These are formal, machine-readable documents that define the allowable elements and other aspects of the specific XML language. Today, most of the major cultural heritage metadata schemes have been expressed as XML schemas. This is true of both MODS and VRA 4.0, which are examples of specific XML markup languages.

Chapter 6 goes on to give an overview of the basic building blocks of XML syntax: elements, attributes, and hierarchically-nested sub-elements. Well-formed XML conforms to the generic rules for XML as a metalanguage. A valid XML document, in contrast, is one that is well-formed but that also conforms to the specifications of particular XML DTD or XML schema, such as the MODS XML schema. Certain types of XML editing or processing software can not only detect whether an XML document is generically well-formed, but also validate that document against a DTD or schema. A namespace is a nameable location on the Internet that contains the official documentation of a metadata element set, which may or may not be a formal DTD or XML schema. Associating individual elements in an XML record with a specific namespace allows disambiguation of those elements, distinguishing elements from multiple sets when included in a single XML document and when aggregating and cross-searching metadata records created from different element sets.

The chapter concludes with examples of a simple Dublin Core metadata record encoded in the OAI DC XML syntax and a Metadata Object Description Schema (MODS) metadata record encoded in the MODS XML syntax.

> ► **Companion Website**
>
> See this book's companion website at **http://www.neal-schuman.com/ metadata-digital-collections** for Chapter 6 review questions, suggestions for exercises, and other resources.

References

Duval, Erik, Wayne Hodgins, Stuart Sutton, and Stuart L. Weibel. 2002. "Metadata Principles and Practicalities." *D-Lib Magazine* 8, no. 4 (April). http://www.dlib.org/dlib/april02/weibel/04weibel.html.

Furrie, Betty, and Follett Software Company. 2009. *Understanding MARC Bibliographic: Machine-Readable Cataloging*. Washington, DC: Library of Congress. http://www.loc.gov/marc/umb/.

Johnston, Pete. 2006. "Metadata Sharing and XML." In *Good Practice Guide for Developers of Cultural Heritage Web Services*. Bath, UK: UKOLN. Last modified January. http://www.ukoln.ac.uk/interop-focus/gpg/Metadata/.

OAI (Open Archives Initiative). 2008. *OAI-PMH (The Open Archives Initiative Protocol for Metadata Harvesting)* Protocol Version 2.0 of 2002-06-14. Document Version 2008-12-07T20:42:00Z. http://www.openarchives .org/OAI/2.0/openarchivesprotocol.htm.

MODS: The Metadata Object Description Schema

This chapter gives an overview of the Metadata Object Description Schema (MODS) element set. Like Dublin Core, MODS is a general metadata scheme intended for description of a wide range of resources, rather than for a specific type of object or in a specific discipline or subject domain. A number of digital libraries that formerly used Dublin Core as their base scheme have moved, and continue to move, to MODS, because of its capacity for richer resource description and because their peer institutions have moved to it. Learning about MODS is valuable for anyone who wants to understand metadata for digital collections, even those who do not or will not use it in practice. To be well-informed about metadata and to be able to critically assess the characteristics and relative strengths and weaknesses of Dublin Core for digital resource description, some level of familiarity with another metadata scheme is needed. A study of MODS serves this purpose, besides being worthwhile in and of itself. It has the additional advantage of providing a good example of a richer XML-based scheme that uses attributes and hierarchically-nested subelements. This kind of scheme is the most common type in the current cultural heritage metadata world. Knowing how to read a MODS record and how to create a MODS record from scratch provides an excellent foundation for learning other XML-based metadata schemes, such as the Visual Resources Core Categories (VRA) version 4.0, covered in the next chapter; Encoded Archival Description (EAD), not covered in this book; and many others.

Having some familiarly with MODS in addition to Dublin Core also allows you to intelligently compare and contrast the characteristics of two different metadata schemes. It allows you to make a more informed assessment of the relative advantages and disadvantages of both schemes for resource description and for general interoperability. It also allows you to learn about mapping from one metadata element set to another, and to experience firsthand the challenges and issues entailed in this process, whether it is done by a human being or by an automated computer process. For all of these reasons, an introductory study of MODS is useful for anyone working with descriptive metadata for digital collections.

This chapter does not attempt to give a complete picture of the entire MODS scheme. It uses selected elements and attributes to illustrate how MODS works in general and how it compares to Dublin Core. This chapter does not provide complete documentation for MODS. Readers of this book are strongly encouraged to look at the *MODS User Guidelines* (http://www.loc.gov/standards/mods/userguide/). Implementers of MODS will need to read this documentation carefully and consult it regularly. Instructors and students using this book are strongly encouraged to work with the *User Guidelines* for getting some hands-on practice with creating MODS records.

7.1. Introduction and Overview

MODS originated as an abbreviated XML version of the *MARC 21 Format for Bibliographic Data*. MARC is an acronym for *Machine Readable Cataloging* and is the encoding standard used for library catalog data. MODS has a high level of compatibility with MARC and includes a subset of MARC fields, but often grouped differently than in MARC 21. MODS can be used to carry selected data from existing MARC 21 records, but it can also be used for creating original resource description records. The Library of Congress developed and maintains the MODS standard. Unlike MARC, MODS uses language-based tags rather than numeric ones, and it does not assume the use of any specific cataloging code, such as the *Anglo-American Cataloguing Rules* (AACR2) or *Resource Description and Access* (RDA). As an element set, MODS is richer than Dublin Core but simpler than the full MARC bibliographic format. MODS was born in the XML environment, created explicitly as an XML schema. MODS records and documentation express MODS elements in the MODS XML encoding syntax. The MARC background of MODS is evident is some of the elements and attributes and in some of the controlled vocabularies and codes provided within the MODS scheme documentation. In some cases, these are present for the purpose of mapping or converting records from MARC 21 to MODS. Digital collection implementers do not need to know or use all of these MARC-based schemes in order to use MODS as their metadata element set, although a few of them can prove to be very useful and are not any more difficult to learn than those used with Qualified Dublin Core.

7.1.1. MODS Implementation Projects

Compared to institutions using Dublin Core as their base scheme, a proportionally much smaller but gradually growing number of digital libraries today have selected MODS as the base metadata scheme for their digital collections. This is especially true among larger academic and research libraries in the United States. Three examples are mentioned here. The MODS Implementation Registry (http://www.loc.gov/standards/mods/registry.php) provides a fuller, but by no means exhaustive, list of some of the institutions currently using MODS.

The **Center for Digital Initiatives, Brown University Library** (http://dl.lib.brown.edu/) uses MODS as the standard metadata format for its digital repository. Brown maps metadata from other standards, such as MARC, DC, VRA, EAD, various project databases, and other legacy data, into MODS as the common denominator.

The **Texas Digital Library (TDL)** (http://www.tdl.org/repositories/) includes a repository of electronic theses and dissertations (ETDs). The TDL Metadata Working Group has developed a MODS Application Profile for Electronic Theses and Dissertations (http://www.tdl.org/wp-content/uploads/2009/04/etd_mods_profile.pdf) as well as a set of Guidelines (http://www.tdl.org/wp-content/uploads/2009/04/tdl-descriptive-metadata-guidelines-for-etd-v1.pdf).

The **Digital Library Federation (DLF) Aquifer Initiative** (http://www.diglib.org/aquifer/) has established the goal of enabling distributed content to be used effectively by libraries and scholars for teaching, learning, and research. The Metadata Working Group of the DLF Aquifer Initiative developed a set of implementation guidelines for MODS (DLF Aquifer Metadata Working Group, 2009). This document provides guidance in using the MODS element set to describe "digital cultural heritage and humanities-based scholarly resources that are to be shared within the Aquifer Initiative and beyond." They are intended to provide a best practice for "rich, shareable metadata that is coherent and consistent." These guidelines, developed to serve Aquifer participants, can be useful to anyone using MODS, and they have in fact now been incorporated into the official *MODS User Guidelines* hosted by the Library of Congress.

7.1.2. MODS Documentation

All of the authoritative documentation for MODS can be found on the official MODS website at http://www.loc.gov/standards/mods/. The current working version of MODS is version 3.4 as of this writing. The MODS v.3.4 XML schema is located at http://www.loc.gov/standards/mods/v3/mods-3-4.xsd. It is strongly recommended that readers of this book look over the range of documentation and information included in the whole MODS website, with a special focus on the "Guidance for MODS record creation" section. This chapter focuses on the *MODS User Guidelines, Version 3* (http://www.loc.gov/standards/mods/userguide/). These Guidelines provide human-readable documentation and guidance for use of all of the MODS elements and attributes. Readers of this book are especially strongly encouraged to read the "Introduction and Implementation" and "General Application" sections of the User Guidelines. When working with MODS records, the core section of the User Guidelines is the "MODS Elements and Attributes" section. It includes links to the complete documentation for every element in the scheme. There is also a handy "Outline of Elements and Attributes in MODS Version 3.4" at http://www.loc.gov/standards/mods/mods-outline.html. Like any living metadata scheme, MODS goes through occasional major changes from one version to another and more frequent minor changes. Readers should therefore be aware that information in this chapter may not reflect changes to the *MODS User Guidelines* made after this writing. This holds true for all metadata and controlled vocabulary schemes.

7.1.3. MODS XML Structure

Unlike Dublin Core, but like a growing number of metadata schemes, MODS was designed specifically as an XML-encoded element set. This section provides an overview of some especially noteworthy aspects of MODS in XML. First of all, all MODS documents are created according to the MODS XML Schema and validated against it to ensure that they are valid MODS documents. The XML schema gives MODS all of the advantages of XML for data interchange and reuse. A MODS document normally contains a schema declaration that indicates the MODS namespace and the current MODS XML Schema .xsd file. The previous chapter included an example and explanation of this, and the example of a complete MODS record in Section 7.3.1 of this chapter also illustrates this.

7.1.3.1. Container Elements and Subelements

MODS makes use of nested, hierarchical, parent-child elements to bundle together related information, as in the following <originInfo> and <subject> illustrations. MODS often uses **container** (or *wrapper*) elements, such as <titleInfo> and <originInfo>, as parent elements whose purpose is purely to contain, wrap, or bind together their child elements, also called subelements. These *container elements* contain no metadata values themselves. The metadata values can be entered only in their subelements. While roughly half of the MODS top-level elements are container elements, other top-level elements such as <typeOfResource> and <accessCondition> are *not* container elements. They directly contain metadata values without any subelements. The following are examples of two top-level container elements with nested subelements, and one non-container top-level element.

```
<originInfo>
    <place>
        <placeTerm>Washington, D.C.</placeTerm>
    </place>
    <publisher>Library of Congress</publisher>
    <dateIssued>1998</dateIssued>
</originInfo>

<typeOfResource>still image</typeOfResource>

<subject>
    <geographic>United States</geographic>
    <topic>Politics and government</topic>
    <temporal>20th century</temporal>
</subject>
```

Note that some subelements have their own subelements, as in the case of <place> in the preceding example, which has a <placeTerm> subelement. MODS <place> is itself a container subelement, with actual place names allowable only in its child <placeTerm> element. Recall also from the previous chapter on XML that line breaks and indentations are typically used to make the XML easier for humans to read, but that XML itself is indifferent to these, and XML processors ignore them.

7.1.3.2. Element Attributes

MODS also makes use of XML attributes to refine the meaning or scope of an element, to designate an authority or encoding scheme used for an element value, and for other similar purposes. Recall that attributes are included within an element's start tag. They follow the *attributename="attributevalue"* pattern, as in the example <placeTerm **type="text"**>. The source of controlled vocabularies are usually designated in MODS by the use of an *authority* attribute, such as <subject **authority="lcsh"**>. This indicates that the content of that MODS subject element is taken from the *Library of Congress Subject Headings*. A single element may include more than one attribute within the start tag, but it may contain only those that have been established in the MODS XML Schema. The examples below include several uses of attributes within MODS elements, indicated by bold font.

```
<originInfo>
   <place>
      <placeTerm authority="marccountry"
       type="code">dcu</placeTerm>
      <placeTerm type="text">Washington, D.C</placeTerm>
   </place>
   <publisher>Library of Congress</publisher>
   <dateIssued>1977-2002</dateIssued>
   <dateIssued encoding="marc" point="start">
    1977</dateIssued>
   <dateIssued encoding="marc" point="end">
    2002</dateIssued>
</originInfo>

<language authority="iso639-2b">eng</language>

<subject authority="lcsh">
   <geographic>United States</geographic>
   <topic>Politics and government</topic>
   <temporal>20th century</temporal>
</subject>
```

In the first example above, notice the use of both a coded and a textual form for place of origin (publication), and the ability to explicitly encode beginning and ending dates in a date range by using the *point* attribute with values of *start* and *end*. In the third example, the Library of Congress subject heading with two subdivisions, *United States--Politics and Government--20th Century*, has each segment broken into a separate subelement designating the type of heading or subdivision that it is. They are placed within a single <subject> element because they are all part of a single subject string consisting of a heading and two subdivisions. MARC 21 does the same thing using its own tagging system: for example, *651 _1 $a United States $x Politics and government $y 20th century*, an instance of three subfields within a single subject field.

While most attributes are specific to individual elements, MODS does include a few attributes to be used throughout the MODS schema, specifically language and related attributes, date attributes, and linking attributes (http://www.loc.gov/standards/mods/v3/mods-userguide-generalapp.html#list). If elements are incorrectly nested, or if attributes are incorrectly applied, the MODS record will not validate against the MODS XML Schema.

7.1.4. Flexibility in MODS Level of Detail and Granularity

MODS gives implementers a great deal of freedom to be as simple or as detailed as they wish in the use of many MODS subelements, attributes, and vocabularies. As with Dublin Core, MODS itself mandates almost nothing, and implementers create their own local application profiles, or use a shared, consortial profile, documenting their local MODS application decisions. Like Dublin Core, this includes such aspects as which MODS elements are required versus optional, which elements are repeatable, and the order in which they are used in XML records and/or displayed locally.

MODS records can therefore range from the very simple, at the same level of detail as a Simple Dublin Core record, to the complex, with much greater detail than Qualified Dublin Core, depending on local resource description needs. MODS gives implementers a greater range of options for breaking metadata into smaller, separately tagged chunks. The important thing for any implementer to keep in mind is what you want your metadata to *do*. MODS allows you, for example, to tag a person's given name and family name in separate subelements. This would be useful if you want to machine process these pieces of information separately. If not, you do not need to make your MODS metadata that finely granular.

The Digital Library Federation's Aquifer Project has published some MODS Guidelines Levels of Adoption, included here in a sidebar. This document outlines five levels of adoption of the MODS guidelines, ranging from the loosest to the strictest, for institutions contributing records to the shared Aquifer repository. The focus is on the usability of aggregated MODS records for end users. For each level, specific MODS elements are listed. Even for non-Aquifer participants, looking at these levels can be useful for getting a sense of the range of possibilities in using MODS and for understanding that an institution does not have to use every available subelement and attribute in order to implement MODS.

7.2. MODS Elements: An Overview with Examples

MODS has 20 top-level elements as of this writing. Some are very simple, while others are more complex and are able to carry and encode a much richer set of distinctions and specificity than Dublin Core, even Qualified

---

MODS Requirements

- **Order of Elements**
  - "The order of elements in the MODS schema does not assume display order. A style sheet is used to control display order of MODS records."

- **Element Repeatability**
  - "All MODS top-level elements are repeatable except <recordInfo>."

- **Mandatory Elements**
  - "No element is mandatory in a MODS record, however, every MODS record requires at least one element. Applications may wish to develop profiles specifying mandatory elements as needed."
  - "The DLF/Aquifer guidelines specify a profile for sharable metadata in the DLF/Aquifer Summary of Requirements and Recommendations table that indicates required, recommended and optional elements."

(Library of Congress, 2010.)

Dublin Core. Recall that some of the top-level MODS elements contain actual metadata values, while others are container elements which themselves contain only subelements; these subelements contain the metadata values, as explained and illustrated in section 7.1. Table 7.1 lists the top-level MODS elements and their immediate subelements. No second-level subelements or any of the element attributes are included in this summary overview table. Top-level elements without any subelements have the characters --- in the second column of the table.

The following sections of this chapter constitute a brief introduction to each of the 20 top-level MODS elements, with examples of each. Most of the illustrative examples are the same as those used in the Chapters 3 and 4 sections on Dublin Core, but expressed here in the MODS

Table 7.1. MODS Top-Level Elements and Subelements

Top-Level Element	Subelements (first level only)
titleInfo	title | subTitle | partNumber | partName | nonSort
name	namePart | displayForm | affiliation | role | description
typeOfResource	---
genre	---
originInfo	place | publisher | dateIssued | dateCreated | dateCaptured | dateValid | dateModified | copyrightDate | dateOther | edition | frequency
language	languageTerm | scriptTerm
physicalDescription	form | reformattingQuality | internetMediaType | extent | digitalOrigin | note
abstract	---
tableOfContents	---
targetAudience	---
note	---
subject	topic | geographic | temporal | titleInfo | name | geographicCode | genre | hierarchicalGeographic | cartographics | occupation
classification	---
relatedItem	titleInfo | name | typeOfResource | genre | originInfo | language | physicalDescription | abstract | tableOfContents | targetAudience | note | subject | classification | relatedItem | identifier | location | accessCondition | part | extension | recordInfo
identifier	---
location	physicalLocation | shelfLocator | url | holdingSimple | holdingExternal
accessCondition	---
part	detail | extent | date | text
extension	---
recordInfo	recordContentSource | recordCreationDate | recordChangeDate | recordOrigin | languageOfCataloging | descriptionStandard

Source: Adapted from "Outline of Elements and Attributes in MODS Version 3.4," http://www.loc.gov/standards/mods/mods-outline.html. Network Development & MARC Standards Office, Library of Congress.

DLF Aquifer MODS Guidelines Levels of Adoption

1. **Minimum for participation:** Allows users to cite the resource.
   - The minimum for participation level defines the information necessary for the most basic indexing of records.

2. **Minimum for doing anything useful:** Allows users to perform basic searches and filtering.
   - This second level of adoption represents a minimum that will allow an institution's resources to be incorporated meaningfully into an aggregation.

3. **Allows more advanced functionality:** Allows users to browse and group search results.
   - The third level of adoption allows the more advanced discovery features expected of an aggregation of records from the high caliber of institution that participates in the Aquifer initiative.

4. **Adopt all required guidelines (and some recommended):** Allows users to perform more precise searches.
   - The fourth level of adoption, like the third, represents more advanced functionality than that found in traditional aggregations. Meeting this fourth level would allow the introduction of very precise searching capabilities across a wide variety of resources.

5. **Completely adopt all recommendations:** Allows users to effectively evaluate resources.
   - The fifth and highest level of adoption includes information a user would review to make a final evaluation as to whether the resource is relevant to his or her needs. Often this information is only present on the contributing institution's site, but its inclusion in shared records helps enhance the user's experience for the aggregation.

(Abbreviated from DLF Aquifer *MODS Guidelines Levels of Adoption*, 2009, added by Jenn Riley, lasted edited by Tom Habing, June 30, http://wiki.dlib.indiana.edu/confluence/display/DLFAquifer/MODS+Guidelines+Levels+of+Adoption. Network Development & MARC Standards Office, Library of Congress.)

scheme. This allows comparison between DC and MODS, and shows how MODS can address many of the resource description problems that DC is not able to handle. Section 7.3.4 provides side-by-side Qualified Dublin Core and MODS records for the same digital resource for further comparison of the two schemes and their functional capabilities.

The following information and examples cover only a selected subset of all of the possible subelements and attributes in MODS. Each section begins with a table taken directly from the *MODS User Guidelines* that lists the name of the top-level element, its definition, its attributes at the top level, and its subelements, if applicable. These sections do not include definitions or lists of attributes for any of the subelements, nor do they list valid attribute values. It is necessary to consult the *MODS User Guidelines*: "MODS Elements and Attributes" to get the full information. It would be impossible to replicate it all in this book. The purpose of this chapter is to gain an introductory exposure to the MODS scheme, not to cover it exhaustively, and especially to see the power of MODS for rich digital resource description compared to Dublin Core. Two common MODS element attributes of special interest in the following examples are *Type* and *Authority*. These are valid for only some elements, and the values for each differ from one element to another.

7.2.1. *TitleInfo*

MODS <titleInfo>

- "A word, phrase, character, or group of characters, normally appearing in a resource, that names it or the work contained in it."

Attributes:

- type; authority; displayLabel; xlink; ID; lang; xml:lang; script; transliteration

Subelements:

- <title> <subTitle> <partNumber> <partName> <nonSort>

The following examples illustrate some of the many possible combinations of subelements and attributes that may be used with the <titleInfo> container element. Remember that each of the subelements and attributes has its own definition in the *MODS User Guidelines*, and that most of these are not reproduced here. For the most part, these are the same examples used for the Dublin Core Title element in Chapter 3 and can be compared and contrasted with them.

Title Example 1: Simple title transcribed from title page of a digitized book:

```
<titleInfo>
    <title>Plants of Upper Michigan</title>
</titleInfo>
```

Notice that the metadata value for title must be entered into the <title> subelement wrapped inside of the <titleInfo> container element.

MODS Definitions

The source for this and all subsequent MODS element definitions and lists of attributes and subelements in this chapter: *MODS User Guidelines* (Version 3), last updated October 2010, http://www.loc.gov/standards/mods/userguide/. Network Development & MARC Standards Office, Library of Congress.

Title Example 2: Variant form of title transcribed from cover of same digitized book:

```
<titleInfo>
    <title type="alternative">Upper Michigan Plant
    Book</title>
</titleInfo>
```

Notice that MODS, like Qualified Dublin Core, has a method for indicating an alternative form of title.

Title Example 3: Supplied title for digital still image, with supplied alternative title:

```
<titleInfo supplied="yes">
    <title>Cologne Cathedral, Germany</title>
</titleInfo>
<titleInfo supplied="yes">
    <title type="alternative">Kölner Dom, Germany</title>
</titleInfo>
```

Notice that each title must be entered in a separate <titleInfo> container element. MODS includes a *Supplied* attribute for indicating that a title is supplied by the metadata creator. This may be meaningful to other metadata creators, but may be of little or no meaning to the majority of end users and, if so, would simply not be used.

Title Example 4: Title with an initial article:

```
<titleInfo>
    <nonSort>The</nonSort>
    <title>Life and Times of Isabella Rios</title>
</titleInfo>
```

Unlike Dublin Core, MODS has a method for explicitly coding an initial article so that the title may be displayed with the article, but the article can be ignored for indexing purposes. There is no need to omit the initial article or to put it at the end of the title following a comma.

Title Example 5: Title with subtitle:

```
<titleInfo>
    <title>Plants of Upper Michigan</title>
    <subTitle>Descriptions and Drawings</subTitle>
</titleInfo>
```

Unlike Dublin Core, MODS can separately code title and subtitle. This can allow, among other potential uses, generating a user display of any desired punctuation between the title and subtitle values, or displaying them in separately labeled lines.

Title Example 6: Alternative method of capitalization:

```
<titleInfo>
    <nonSort>The</nonSort>
    <title>life and times of Isabella Rios</title>
    <subTitle>based on diaries and oral narratives as told
    to her daughter Maria Rios Campos</subTitle>
</titleInfo>
```

Title Example 7: Title with part name and number:

```
<titleInfo>
    <title>Oregon Land Maps</title>
    <partName>Multnomah County</partName>
    <partNumber>No. 12</partNumber>
</titleInfo>
```

MODS allows explicit coding of part names and numbers, allowing various kinds of computer processing, such as sorting, indexing, and displaying, that may be valuable to users. This allows the ability to separately index and sort parts of the same series of resources by name and/or number.

7.2.2. *Name*

MODS <name>

- "The name of a person, organization, or event (conference, meeting, etc.) associated in some way with the resource."

Attributes:

- type; authority; xlink; ID; lang; xml:lang; script; transliteration

Subelements:

- <namePart> <displayForm> <affiliation> <role> <description>

The MODS <name> element is capable of expressing various specific pieces of information about a person, corporate body, or conference that can be useful for processing, identification, and information retrieval. The following examples illustrate several options among many for expressing the name of the author Herman Melville.

Name Example 1, Alternatives A through E: Book author (several among many possible alternatives for recording a personal name):

Name Example 1, Alternative A:

```
<name>
    <namePart>Herman Melville</namePart>
</name>
```

The example above is the simplest possible form of a personal name in MODS.

Name Example 1, Alternative B:

```
<name type="personal">
    <namePart>Melville, Herman</namePart>
    <displayForm>Herman Melville</displayForm>
    <role>
        <roleTerm type="text">creator</roleTerm>
    </role>
</name>
```

In the Alternative B example, an inverted form of the author's name is used for indexing, and the natural language form is designated for display. The name is specifically tagged as a *personal* rather than a corporate or conference name using the *Type* attribute. This allows these three types of name to be separately searched and indexed if desired. The role of this person is indicated using the <role> <roleTerm> subelements. In this example, the generic role term *creator* has been used.

Name Example 1, Alternative C:

```
<name authority="naf" type="personal">
    <namePart>Melville, Herman, 1819-1891</namePart>
    <role>
        <roleTerm type="text" authority="marcrelator">
        author</roleTerm>
    </role>
    <role>
        <roleTerm type="code" authority="marcrelator">
        aut</roleTerm>
    </role>
</name>
```

In the Alternative C example, a controlled form of the person's name has been used, and its source has been designated with the code *naf*, which stands for the Library of Congress/NACO *Name Authority File*. A more specific role term also been given, indicating to users that the role of this person in relation to the resource described in the metadata record is specifically that of *author*. Either a textual or a coded role term may be used, or both may be used as in this example. The text and coded form of the role terms come from the *marcrelator* controlled list, which is indicated by the *Authority* attribute within each <roleTerm> element.

Name Example 1, Alternative D:

```
<name type="personal" authority="naf">
    <namePart>Melville, Herman</namePart>
    <namePart type="date">1819-1891</namePart>
</name>
```

MODS can also encode the dates associated with a person's name separately from the name itself, which may be useful for processing and displaying the name without the dates, but still including the dates for the controlled form of the name used for collocation and other indexing purposes.

Name Example 1, Alternative E:

```
<name type="personal">
    <namePart type="given">Herman</namePart>
    <namePart type="family">Melville</namePart>
    <role>
        <roleTerm type="text" authority="marcrelator">
        author</roleTerm>
        <roleTerm type="code" authority="marcrelator">
        aut</roleTerm>
    </role>
</name>
```

MODS can also separately tag the given name and the family name, allowing even more processing power, if so desired and useful for an implementing institution. This might include, for example, indexing by family name, but displaying the given name first within the user display of the metadata.

Name Example 2: Book illustrator (illustrations in an edition of Melville's *Moby Dick*, considered secondary or supplementary to the text):

```
<name authority="naf" type="personal">
    <namePart>Moser, Barry</namePart>
    <role>
        <roleTerm type="text" authority="marcrelator">
        illustrator</roleTerm>
        <roleTerm type="code" authority="marcrelator">
        ill</roleTerm>
    </role>
</name>
```

This example shows the name of the illustrator of a particular edition of Moby Dick. In Dublin Core, metadata creators need to make judgments about which names to designate as *Creator* versus *Contributor*. In MODS, there is only a single <name> element for all names, and the <role> subelement may be used to indicate the specific type of responsibility that person has in relation to the resource.

Name Example 3: Book translator:

```
<name authority="naf" type="personal">
    <namePart>Hakluyt, Richard, 1552?-1616</namePart>
    <role>
        <roleTerm type="text" authority="marcrelator">
        translator</roleTerm>
        <roleTerm type="code" authority="marcrelator">
        trl</roleTerm>
    </role>
</name>
```

Name Example 4: Photographer:

```
<name type="personal">
    <namePart>Kramer, Paul Jacob</namePart>
    <role>
        <roleTerm type="code" authority="marcrelator">
        pht</roleTerm>
        <roleTerm type="text" authority="marcrelator">
        photographer</roleTerm>
    </role>
</name>
```

In a metadata record containing several names, or containing information about both the original and a digital version of a resource, using role terms takes away the ambiguity and potential confusion for users by explicitly labeling the role of that person in relation to the resource. Take, for example, an image of a work of architecture designed by one person, constructed by another person or body, photographed by yet another person, and so forth. This is not possible in most common implementations of Dublin Core.

Name Example 5: Painter:

```
<name type="personal">
    <namePart>Cropsey, Jasper Francis, 1823-1900</namePart>
    <description>American painter, 19th c.</description>
    <role>
```

```
    <roleTerm type="code" authority="marcrelator">
     art</roleTerm>
    <roleTerm type="text" authority="marcrelator">
     artist</roleTerm>
   </role>
 </name>
```

Many museums include information such as that given in the <description> subelement in this example. This can be used for display, but kept out of the form of name used for indexing and linking.

Name Example 6: Corporate body name:

```
<name type="corporate" authority="naf">
   <namePart>United States</namePart>
   <namePart>Court of Appeals (2nd Circuit)</namePart>
</name>
```

MODS can explicitly tag a corporate body name as such, enabling a labeled display and separate searching limits and/or indexes of personal, corporate body, and conference names. In the LC/NACO *Name Authority File*, and following AACR2 practice, if a corporate body name consists of a unit and subunit, the larger unit is given first, followed by the subunit. In MODS these can be put into separate <namePart> subelements, contained within a single <name> container element, as in Name Example 6, indicating that they form parts of a single name. A style sheet will determine how they are assembled and displayed to users.

Name Example 7: Conference name (for a resource consisting of content about a conference):

```
<name type="conference" authority="naf">
   <namePart>Conference on War Work and Post-War
    Organization (1945 : Chicago, Ill.)</namePart>
</name>
```

Finally, MODS can also explicitly designate a name as being that of a conference. This may be especially helpful when mapping from MARC to MODS, since personal, corporate, and conference names are separately tagged in MARC records.

7.2.3. *TypeOfResource*

MODS <typeOfResource>

- "A term that specifies the characteristics and general type of content of the resource."

Attributes:

- collection; manuscript

Subelements:

- None

The MODS <typeOfResource> element is quite similar to the Dublin Core *Type* element, except that it is not used for more specific type and genre terms, which are sometimes used in DC *Type*. MODS <typeOfResource>

is intended for terms designating content at a very general, high level. "This element includes a high-level type that categorizes the material in a general way using an enumerated list of values. More specific typing is done in the <genre> element" (Library of Congress, 2010). The scope is narrower than DC *Type* because the MODS scheme includes a separate <genre> element intended to contain more specific terms than those used in <typeOfResource>.

MODS has its own enumerated list of controlled values for the <typeOfResource> element that are similar to those in the DCMI Type Vocabulary. In some cases they are identical, except that the MODS terms are given entirely in lowercase. The list contains the following values (documented and defined at http://www.loc.gov/standards/mods/userguide/typeofresource.html): *text, cartographic, notated music, sound recording, sound recording-musical, sound recording-nonmusical, still image, moving image, three dimensional object, software, multimedia, mixed material.*

The following examples parallel those used in the section on Dublin Core *Type* in Chapter 4 and illustrate the use of the MODS <typeOfResource> element and the MODS controlled vocabulary for this element.

Type of Resource Example 1: Digitized photograph:

```
<typeOfResource>still image</typeOfResource>
```

Type of Resource Example 2: Text digitized as PDF or HTML document:

```
<typeOfResource>text</typeOfResource>
```

Type of Resource Example 3: Text digitized as set of image files (each page a separate image file):

```
<typeOfResource>text</typeOfResource>
```

Type of Resource Example 4: Digitized audio recording of an oral history interview:

```
<typeOfResource>sound recording-nonmusical</typeOfResource>
```

Type of Resource Example 5: Digitized video recording of an oral history interview:

```
<typeOfResource>moving image</typeOfResource>
```

7.2.4. *Genre*

MODS <genre>

- "A term or terms that designate a category characterizing a particular style, form, or content, such as artistic, musical, literary composition, etc."

Attributes:

- type; authority; lang; xml:lang; script; transliteration

Subelements:

- None

The MODS <genre> element

> contains terms that give more specificity for the form of an object
> than the broad terms used in <typeOfResource>. The terms may
> be from a controlled list with a designation of the authoritative list
> used in the authority attribute, or it may be an uncontrolled term.
> If no authority is specified, it is assumed that the term is uncon-
> trolled. For an example genre list, see MARC Genre Term List.
> The <genre> element should be used to characterize the content
> of the resource rather than the resource itself which would be
> <form> (Library of Congress, 2010).

The *MODS User Guidelines* include the following *Genre* examples.

```
<genre authority="rbgenr">Hymnals-Germany<genre>

<genre authority="marcgt">folktale</genre>

<genre authority="aat" type="style">baroque</genre>
<genre authority="aat" type="culture"> Netherlandish</genre>
```

For a digital image of a Civil War era daguerreotype portrait:

```
<genre authority="aat">daguerreotypes</genre>
<genre authority="aat">portraits</genre>
```

For a children's adventure story:

```
<genre authority="gsafd">adventure fiction</genre>
<genre authority="lcsh">Children's literature</genre>
```

For the most part, MODS <genre> includes terms that indicate more
specifically the type of content of the resource, rather than the format of
the resource. Terms designating the physical format of the original item
should go into the MODS <physicalDescription><form> element. There
may still be some ambiguity in clearly distinguishing *Genre* from *Form*.
The concept of *genre* in resource description practice can be rather fuzzy,
often encompassing aspects of content, media, carrier, form, and physical
characteristics. The Library of Congress "Genre/ Form Code and Term
Source Codes" webpage (http://www.loc.gov/standards/sourcelist/
genre-form.html) makes this point. The previous example of the digital
image of a daguerreotype is a good example. The digital image depicts not
only the content depicted in the daguerreotype, but also the daguerreotype
itself, as a physical object of interest to users as such, and so may be
regarded as a genre term. Genre terms can be extremely useful for user
browsing, search limits, and the like. Allowing for both a high-level
TypeOfResource term and one or more specific *genre* terms in the same
record enhances identification and retrieval functionality for users. In Dublin
Core, both types of terms need to be entered into DC *Type* elements.

7.2.5. *OriginInfo*

MODS <originInfo>

- "Information about the origin of the resource, including place
  of origin or publication, publisher/originator, and dates associated with the resource."

Attributes:

- lang; xml:lang; script; transliteration

Subelements:

- <place> <publisher> <dateIssued> <dateCreated> <dateCaptured> <dateValid> <dateModified> <copyrightDate> <dateOther> <edition> <issuance> <frequency>

The MODS <originInfo> container element groups together various types of information about the origin of a resource, including publisher, place of publication, edition, various types of dates, such as publication, creation, and copyright, as well as other information indicated by the list of subelements above. The following examples parallel those used in Chapter 4, and demonstrate how MODS deals with various kinds of publication information and dates.

Origin Info Example 1: Book publisher name:

```
<originInfo>
    <publisher>G. P. Putnam's Sons</publisher>
</originInfo>
```

This example shows the use of simple publisher name without including place of publication.

Origin Info Example 2: Postcard publisher name and place of publication:

```
<originInfo>
    <place>
        <placeTerm type="text">Chicago</placeTerm>
    </place>
    <publisher>Acmegraph Company</publisher>
</originInfo>
```

This example illustrates how MODS can include the place of publication along with the publisher name. A <placeTerm> element may contain either a textual or a coded form of place name.

Origin Info Example 3: Known/certain date of publication of a book:

```
<originInfo>
    <dateIssued>1954</dateIssued>
</originInfo>
```

This example shows the simplest form of a date element in MODS, in this case, a <dateIssued>. Like the Dublin Core refinement, the term *issued* is also used in MODS for dates of publication.

Origin Info Example 4: Known date of creation of a photograph (year and month known, day not known):

```
<originInfo>
    <dateCreated encoding="w3cdtf">1966-03</dateCreated>
</originInfo>
```

MODS has several specific types of date subelements. This example illustrates use of the <dateCreated> subelement. In this example, the encoding scheme of *w3cdtf* has also been added. This MODS example expresses the same kinds of information that Qualified Dublin Core can express.

Origin Info Example 5: Known date of recording of an oral history interview (year, month, and day):

```
<originInfo>
    <dateCreated encoding="w3cdtf" keyDate="yes">2002-11-27
    </dateCreated>
</originInfo>
```

This example illustrates the use of the *KeyDate* attribute in MODS. The only allowable value for this attribute is *yes*, and this attribute and value are included only when one date in the MODS record is to be distinguished from one or more others in the same record. This attribute can be used to instruct a system to use this date for indexing, search limits, and the like, and to ignore other dates in the record for certain purposes.

Origin Info Example 6: Date of digitization of a map:

```
<originInfo>
    <dateCaptured encoding="w3cdtf">2007-07-18</dateCaptured>
</originInfo>
```

The MODS <dateCaptured> element is defined as "The date on which the resource was digitized or a subsequent snapshot was taken." Thus MODS has a separate element for the *date of digitization*. In Qualified Dublin Core, this could only be designated as a *Date Created*. Implementers will still want to decide whether this information is better considered as administrate or technical metadata and not included in the descriptive metadata record. The same may be true of the MODS <dateValid> and <dateModified> elements.

Origin Info Example 7: Copyright date of a published music score

```
<originInfo>
    <copyrightDate>1938</copyrightDate>
</originInfo>
```

MODS can explicitly designate a copyright date and distinguish it from other kinds of dates, such as date issued. Although *DCMI Metadata Terms* includes a *Date Copyrighted* refinement, it is a relatively later DC addition and not as widely implemented in practice.

Origin Info Example 8: Beginning and ending date of publication of a scholarly journal

```
<originInfo>
    <dateIssued encoding="iso8601" point="start">
    1898</dateIssued>
    <dateIssued encoding="iso8601" point="end">
    1935</dateIssued>
</originInfo>
```

MODS includes a method of dealing with *date ranges* by explicitly coding both the *start* and *end* dates of a time period, as illustrated in this example. This has the potential to allow for more precise machine processing of dates within a date range. For example, it could *display* the dates as *1898–1935*, but *index* every year within that range for searching and browsing purposes.

Origin Info Example 9: Approximate, uncertain, or questionable date of creation or publication (alternative possibilities)

```
<originInfo>
    <dateCreated qualifier="approximate">1948</dateCreated>
</originInfo>

<originInfo>
    <dateCreated qualifier="questionable">1948
      </dateCreated>
</originInfo>
```

The MODS scheme includes a *Qualifier* attribute for date elements that allows any date to be qualified as *approximate*, *questionable*, or *inferred*. These are defined in the *MODS User Guidelines* as follows:

- *approximate*—This value is used to identify a date that may not be exact, but is approximated, such as "ca. 1972".

- *inferred*—This value is used to identify a date that has not been transcribed directly from a resource, such as "[not before 1852]".

- *questionable*—This value is used to identify a questionable date for a resource, such as "1972?"

The *inferred* qualifier is especially useful when using a content standard such as AACR2, which makes a strong distinction between information transcribed from a resource versus information taken from an external source, but it is perhaps less important in other resource description contexts.

Origin Info Example 10: Uncertain date, but within a certain date range of creation or publication:

```
<originInfo>
    <dateCreated qualifier="approximate" point="start">
     1942</dateCreated>
    <dateCreated qualifier="approximate" point="end">
     1944</dateCreated>
</originInfo>
```

The *Qualifier* attribute may also be used with date ranges, as in the previous example.

Origin Info Example 11: Edition:

```
<originInfo>
    <edition>2nd ed.</edition>
</originInfo>
```

Recall that Dublin Core does not include an element that readily accommodates edition information. Such information is perhaps best entered as part of the title in a DC *Title* element, or put into a DC *Description* element, although this is not a comfortable fit given the defined meaning of that element.

Origin Info Example 12: More complete <originInfo> element for the seventh edition of a book published by Putnam in 1954 and digitized on July 18, 2007:

```
<originInfo>
    <place>
        <placeTerm type="code" authority="marccountry">
         nyu</placeTerm>
        <placeTerm type="text">New York</placeTerm>
    </place>
    <publisher>G. P. Putnam's Sons</publisher>
    <dateIssued encoding="w3cdtf" keyDate="yes">
     1954</dateIssued>
    <dateCaptured encoding="w3cdtf">2007-07-18</dateCaptured>
    <edition>7th ed.</edition>
</originInfo>
```

This example gives an instance of a complete <originInfo> element. It illustrates the use of both a <dateIssued> and <dateCaptured> in the same <originInfo> container element. Being able to explicitly tag a date as <dateCaptured>, which is the date of digitization, allows implementers to include this date in the descriptive metadata but omit it from indexing, display, and other functions, if desired.

7.2.6. *Language*

MODS <language>

- "A designation of the language in which the content of a resource is expressed."

Attributes:

- objectPart

Subelements:

- <languageTerm>

The MODS <language> container element uses the <languageTerm> subelement to express the language of the resource in either a textual or coded form, or both. If using a coded form, the authority attribute is used to indicate the source of the code.

Language Example 1: Digital text or sound recording in English:

```
<language>
    <languageTerm type="text">English</languageTerm>
    <languageTerm type="code" authority="iso639-2b">
     eng</languageTerm>
</language>
```

In this example, both a textual and a coded form have been given in a single <language> element, because they are both ways of expressing the name of a single language. Either the textual or the coded form alone could also be used. Coded forms are international, are not restricted to English forms of names, and are more easily processed by computers. The ideal is to use the code for processing and to generate an English-language term for user display.

Language Example 2: Digital text or sound recording in both English and French:

```
<language>
    <languageTerm type="text">English</languageTerm>
    <languageTerm type="code" authority="iso639-2b">
     eng</languageTerm>
</language>
<language>
    <languageTerm type="text">French</languageTerm>
    <languageTerm type="code" authority="iso639-2b">
     fre</languageTerm>
</language>
```

Each language must be given in a separate <language> element in the metadata record for this resource.

7.2.7. *PhysicalDescription*

MODS <physicalDescription>

- "Describes the physical attributes of the information resource."

Attributes:

- lang; xml:lang; script; transliteration

Subelements:

- <form> <reformattingQuality> <internetMediaType> <extent> <digitalOrigin> <note>

The MODS <physicalDescription> element is roughly parallel to the Dublin Core *Format* element. This element may contain information about either a digital resource, the analog original from which it has been digitized, or both. The MODS <form> and <extent> subelements are roughly equivalent to the DC *Medium* and *Extent* refinements, respectively. MODS includes a separate subelement for Internet Media Type. The MODS <digitalOrigin> subelement specifically indicates that the resource represented in the body of the record is a digital resource, and information about its source.

Physical Description Example 1: A digitized photograph:

```
<physicalDescription>
    <form>photograph</form>
    <extent>3 x 7 in.</extent>
    <internetMediaType>image/jpeg</internetMediaType>
    <digitalOrigin>reformatted digital</digitalOrigin>
</physicalDescription>
```

Physical Description Example 2: A digitized photograph:

```
<physicalDescription>
    <form authority="marcsmd">photoprint</form>
    <form authority="marcform">electronic</form>
    <reformattingQuality>access</reformattingQuality>
    <internetMediaType>image/jpeg</internetMediaType>
    <extent>1 photograph</extent>
    <digitalOrigin>reformatted digital</digitalOrigin>
</physicalDescription>
```

Example 2 offers another of many alternatives for representing a digitized photograph in MODS. This example has been taken directly from the *MODS User Guidelines*. It illustrates the use of a controlled vocabulary for the value in the <form> subelement. This allows browsing and limiting by format in addition to type of resource and genre. In this instance a form subelement has been used for both the original analog and the digital resource. The <extent> subelement contains a free-text description of the number and type of items. This maps to and from a MARC 300 subfield $a, for those knowledgeable about MARC.

Physical Description Example 3: A text digitized as a set of images and also encoded in XML:

```
<physicalDescription>
    <form authority="marcform">electronic</form>
    <form authority="marcform">print</form>
    <internetMediaType>image/jpeg</internetMediaType>
    <internetMediaType>text/xml</internetMediaType>
    <extent>177 p.</extent>
    <digitalOrigin>reformatted digital</digitalOrigin>
</physicalDescription>
```

This example is for a diary that has been scanned as image files and for which a text transcription has been made. It has also been taken directly from the *MODS User Guidelines*. It illustrates a case in which the same text has been digitized as a set of JPEG image files and has also been electronically marked up as an XML-encoded text.

Physical Description Example 4: A digitized sound recording:

```
<physicalDescription>
    <form authority="marcsmd">sound cassette</form>
    <internetMediaType>audio/mp3</internetMediaType>
    <extent>4 min., 12 sec.</extent>
    <extent>2.18 MB</extent>
    <digitalOrigin>reformatted digital</digitalOrigin>
</physicalDescription>
```

This example includes giving both the duration of the sound recording and the digital file size in <extent> subelements.

7.2.8. *Abstract*

**MODS **

- "A summary of the content of the resource."

Attributes:

- type; displayLabel; xlink; lang; xml:lang; script; transliteration

Subelements:

- None

The MODS element can be used for any kind of free-text summary or description of the content of a resource, including a formal abstract. Recall that this kind of element is often a good source of keywords for user searches in addition to identifying the content of the resource.

Abstract Example 1: Description of digital image:

```
<abstract>Southeast side of the Cologne Cathedral viewed
from outside the Hauptbahnhof (train station), Köln,
Germany, October, 1952.</abstract>
```

Abstract Example 2: Abstract of digitized research article:

```
<abstract>This paper explores reasons why large numbers
of practitioners do not adhere to the DCMI One-to-One
Principle; discusses why it is problematic; explores how
the principle itself would benefit from greater clarity;
presents some practical options for maintaining the
principle in current systems, with advantages and
disadvantages of each; and suggests a possible compromise
option. The paper focuses on the widespread application
context of small to medium-sized cultural heritage
institutions digitizing unique local resources, creating
metadata using digital collection software packages such
as CONTENTdm, and exposing only simple Dublin Core
metadata for OAI harvesting and aggregating.</abstract>
```

7.2.9. TableOfContents

MODS <tableOfContents>

- "A description of the contents of a resource."

Attributes:

- type; displayLabel; xlink; lang; xml:lang; script; transliteration

Subelements:

- None

Table of Contents Example 1: Table of contents of digitized rare book:

```
<tableOfContents>Chapter 1: Introduction. Chapter 2: Chamber
Music. Chapter 3: Orchestral Music. Chapter 4: Operas.
Chapter 5: Incidental Pieces.</tableOfContents>
```

Table of Contents Example 2: Table of contents of digitized book:

```
<tableOfContents displayLabel="Chapters included in
book">Bluegrass odyssey -- Hills of Tennessee -- Sassafrass
-- Muddy river -- Take your shoes off Moses -- Don't let
Smokey Mountain smoke get in your eyes -- Farewell party --
Faded love -- Super sonic bluegrass -- Old love letters --
Will the circle be unbroken</tableOfContents>
```

This second example has been taken from the *MODS User Guidelines* and illustrates the use of the optional *displayLabel* attribute, and a method of formatting contents notes used in the *Anglo-American Cataloguing Rules*.

7.2.10. TargetAudience

MODS <targetAudience>

- "A description of the intellectual level of the audience for which the resource is intended."

Attributes:

- authority; lang; script; transliteration

Subelements:

- None

The MODS <targetAudience> element may be used "whenever there is a specific audience for a resource (for example, a text marked up specifically for historians)" (Library of Congress, 2010). Perhaps the most common use is when the resource is targeted especially for children, adolescents, or non-adult students within a certain grade range. The optional authority attribute may be used if taking the value from a controlled list.

Audience Example 1: Digitized children's book:

```
<targetAudience authority="marctarget">
  juvenile<targetAudience>
```

Audience Example 2: Digitized oral reading of short story targeted for adolescents:

```
<targetAudience authority="marctarget">
  adolescent<targetAudience>
```

7.2.11. *Note*

MODS <note>

- "General textual information relating to a resource."

Attributes:

- type; displayLabel; xlink; ID; lang; xml:lang; script; transliteration

Subelements:

- None

The MODS <note> element provides the opportunity to record information considered important for users of the resource but that does not go into any other more specific MODS elements. The following offer two of an almost unlimited possible number of examples.

Note Example 1: Historical background information about a book based on a play:

```
<note>Based on the play "The Underground" by Charles
Wentwood, originally produced in London in 1917.</note>
```

Note Example 2: Actors in a stage play depicted in a digital image and the roles each plays:

```
<note type="performers">Henry Strozier (Ebenezer Scrooge),
Eugene J. Anthony (Nutley), Penelope Reed (Emily Claxton),
Tom Blair (Fred), Dennis Kennedy (Topper), Lynn Mansbach
(Fred's Wife)</note>
```

The *type* attribute may be used to indicate the specific type of note, with values drawn from the MODS <note> Types controlled list, available in the *User Guidelines*.

7.2.12. *Subject*

MODS <subject>

- "A term or phrase representing the primary topic(s) on which a work is focused."

Attributes:

- authority; xlink; ID; lang; xml:lang; script; transliteration

Subelements:

- <topic> <geographic> <temporal> <titleInfo> <name> <genre> <hierarchicalGeographic> <cartographics> <geographicCode> <occupation>

The MODS <subject> container element includes several subelements for designating particular types of subject content of a resource. The <topic> subelement is the default subject subelement for subject terms that are not appropriate for any of the other MODS subject subelements, or when the specific type of subject string is unknown. The source of controlled subject terms is designated using the *authority* attribute. The following examples illustrate the use of some of these subelements.

Topical Subject Examples (the resource is *about* this topic, class of persons, named object, and the like, or an image *depicts* it in some way):

```
<subject authority="aat">
    <topic>drawbridges</topic>
</subject>

<subject authority="lctgm">
    <topic>Drawbridges</topic>
</subject>

<subject authority="lctgm">
    <topic>Drawbridges—Illinois—Chicago</topic>
</subject>

<subject authority="lctgm">
    <topic>Drawbridges</topic>
    <geographic>Illinois</geographic>
    <geographic>Chicago</geographic>
</subject>

<subject authority="lcsh">
    <topic>Jazz</topic>
    <geographic>Louisiana</geographic>
    <geographic>New Orleans</geographic>
    <temporal>1921-1930</temporal>
</subject>
```

Notice that a single precoordinated subject string composed of heading and subdivisions may be included in a single <topic> element, or the string may be broken into its components parts, each going into separate subelements within a single <subject> container element. This indicates that this is one subject heading, and that the subelement should be processed in that order. A display may be generated by means of a style sheet that could add the dashes or display the subject string in any other way desired by the implementing institution. But separating them into distinctively coded subelements also allows for various types of machine processing, such as including the main heading and subdivisions as values in faceted browsing by topic, place, time period, form, and so on. It is very important to understand that only one subject heading may be placed within a single <subject> element. If there is more than one subelement within a <subject> container element, this indicates a main heading with subdivisions that together form a single logical whole. If subject terms are not part of a pre-coordinated subject string, they must be placed in separate <subject> container elements.

Personal name subject example (the resource is about Melville):

```
<subject>
    <name type="personal" authority="naf">
        <namePart>Melville, Herman</namePart>
        <namePart type="date">1819-1891</namePart>
    </name>
</subject>
```

Locally-established subject term example:

```
<subject authority="local">
    <topic>water transportation</topic>
</subject>
```

Temporal subject examples (resource is about, covers, or takes place in this time period, or image depicts something during that time period):

```
<subject authority="lcsh">
    <temporal>19th century</temporal>
</subject>

<subject>
    <temporal encoding="w3cdtf" point="start">
    1914</temporal>
    <temporal encoding="w3cdtf" point="end"> 1918</temporal>
</subject>
```

The first example uses a textual name for a time period taken from the *Library of Congress Subject Headings*. The second example uses a date range, which can be explicitly encoded in MODS with the *start* and *end* date of the range. Recall that in Dublin Core, temporal subject information is expressed in a *Coverage Temporal* element.

Spatial subject example (resource is about, covers, or takes place in this geographic area, or image depicts something in that place):

```
<subject authority="tgn">
    <geographic>Argentina</geographic>
    <geographicCode authority="iso3166"> ar</geographicCode>
</subject>
```

This example includes both a textual term, taken from the *Thesaurus for Geographic Names*, and a code, taken from the *ISO 3166* international standard. Recall that in Dublin Core, geographic subject information is expressed in a *Coverage Spatial* element.

The MODS <hierarchicalGeographic> subject subelement provides another way to express geographical subject terms in MODS, when applicable. The *User Guidelines* provides this definition of this element: "A geographic name given in a hierarchical form relating to the resource." It includes the subelements <continent>, <country>, <province>, <region>, <state>, <territory>, <county>, <city>, <citySection>, <island>, <area>, and <extraterrestrialArea>. The *MODS User Guidelines* contain the following guidelines for use of this element:

> <hierarchicalGeographic> is a container element for the hierarchical form of place name, which is both readable by humans and parsable by machines. This form can be applied to the degree of specificity that is known or relevant and used to generate browsable hierarchies even when values are specified to different levels. Explicit inclusion of the complete hierarchy is of potential benefit for automated consultation of a gazetteer to derive map coordinates or to support a map-based interface for searching by country or state. The authority attribute is specified at the main <subject> level. (Library of Congress, 2010)

The *User Guidelines* include the following two examples, among others.

```
<subject>
    <hierarchicalGeographic>
        <country>Canada</country>
        <province>British Columbia</province>
        <city>Vancouver</city>
    </hierarchicalGeographic>
</subject>

<subject authority="tgn">
    <hierarchicalGeographic>
        <country>United States</country>
        <state>Mississippi</state>
        <county>Harrison</county>
        <city>Biloxi</city>
    </hierarchicalGeographic>
</subject>
```

If expressing a single geographic term, or more than one geographic term that are not part of hierarchical levels intended to be processed for hierarchical browsing and other uses explained in the extract from the *MODS User Guidelines* above, one or more individual <subject> <geographic> elements should be used instead of <subject> <hierarchicalGeographic>.

7.2.13. *Classification*

MODS <classification>

- "A designation applied to a resource that indicates the subject by applying a formal system of coding and organizing resources according to subject areas."

Attributes:

- authority; edition; displayLabel; lang; xml:lang; script; transliteration

Subelements:

- None

MODS, having originally been based on MARC, and serving especially digital libraries, has a separate top-level *<classification>* element. The following are two examples, the first from the *Dewey Decimal Classification* (DDC) scheme and the second from the *Library of Congress Classification* (LCC) scheme. Recall that in Dublin Core, classification numbers are expressed in the DC *Subject* element.

Classification number examples

```
<classification authority="ddc" edition="11">
 943.085</classification>
<classification authority="lcc">D639.J4</classification>
```

7.2.14. *RelatedItem*

MODS <relatedItem>

- "Information that identifies other resources related to the one being described."

Attributes:

- type; xlink:href; displayLabel; ID

Subelements:

- All MODS elements can appear as subelements.

Like the Dublin Core *Relation* and *Source* elements, the MODS <relatedItem> element provides information about a different resource related to the one described or represented in the main body of the metadata record. Unlike Dublin Core, however, the MODS <relatedItem> element may contain much more detailed information about the related resource. Every one of the MODS top-level elements, subelements, and attributes can be used as subelements within the <relatedItem> container element. The specific type of relationship of the related item is designated by the value in the *Type* attribute, which includes these values: *preceding, succeeding, original, host, collection, constituent, series, otherVersion, otherFormat,* and *isReferencedBy.*

Related Item Example 1: The digital image represented by the metadata record is a part of this digital collection:

```
<relatedItem type="host">
    <titleInfo>
        <title>Paul J. Kramer Digital Images
        Collection</title>
    </titleInfo>
</relatedItem>
```

Notice that the type attribute value is *host* and that the title of the collection is given in a <titleInfo> <title> element. The same thing would be done for the name of a physical collection when the digital image represented by the metadata record is a digitized format of an original analog 35 mm color slide that is part of this physical collection.

Related Item Example 2: The digital text represented by the metadata record is an English translation by Richard Hakluyt of a French original by Jacques Cartier; it is therefore a version of the French document:

```
<titleInfo>
    <title> Shorte and Briefe Narration of the Two
    Nauigations and Discoueries to the Northwest Partes
    called Newe Fraunce</title>
</titleInfo>
<name type="personal">
    <namePart>Cartier, Jacques</namePart>
        <role>
            <roleTerm type="text">author</roleTerm>
        </role>
    </namePart>
</name>
<name type="personal">
    <namePart>Hakluyt, Richard</namePart>
        <role>
            <roleTerm type="text">translator</roleTerm>
    </namePart>
</name>
<relatedItem displayLabel="Translation of" type=
 "otherVersion">
    <titleInfo>
        <title> Bref récit et succincte narration de la
            navigation faite en MDXXXV et MDXXXVI</title>
    </titleInfo>
</relatedItem>
```

In this example, the title and names of the author and translator have been included in the main body of the record preceding the <relatedItem> element in order to give it context. Notice the use of the *displayLabel* attribute value of *Translation of* and the type value of *otherVersion*.

Related Item Example 3: The digital image represented by the metadata record is a digitized format of an original analog 35 mm black & white slide, by Paul Jacob Kramer, 1955; item no. 171, 33b-765 in the Paul J. Kramer Archival Photograph Collection; located in the Hagenville University Archives:

```
<relatedItem type="original">
    <name type="personal">
        <namePart>Kramer, Paul Jacob</namePart>
        <role>
            <roleTerm authority="marcrelator"
            type="text">photographer</roleTerm>
        </role>
    </name>
    <originInfo>
        <dateCreated encoding="w3cdtf"> 1955</dateCreated>
    </originInfo>
    <physicalDescription>
        <extent>35mm. black & white slide</extent>
     </physicalDescription>
    <relatedItem type="host">
        <titleInfo>
            <title>Paul J. Kramer Archival Photograph
            Collection</title>
```

```
        </titleInfo>
      </relatedItem>
      <identifier>171, 33b-765</identifier>
      <location>Hagenville University Archives</location>
   </relatedItem>
```

In this example, all of the information related to the analog original resource is given inside of a <relatedItem> element in a MODS record for the digital resource. Notice the use of the *type* value *original*. All of the information given in the <relatedItem> element could then be omitted from the main body of the record, so that the main body contains only the information about the digital manifestation and its intellectual/artistic content, and the information about the original manifestation is given in a <relatedItem> element. Because MODS separately tags each piece of information within the <relatedItem> element, there is the potential for these to be separately processed for searching, browsing, display, and so forth.

This use of <relatedItem> therefore has the potential, at least theoretically, to provide an elegant method of realizing the **One-to-One Principle** in MODS, because it could avoid the defects that come from embedding this information in a single long text string, as when giving all of this information in a DC *Source* element. In practice, however the DLF/Aquifer community of practice has found this to be impractical at the present time within an aggregated metadata context. The *MODS User Guidelines* include some information from the DLF/Aquifer Guidelines. Those Guidelines recommend that the MODS <relatedItem> element be used only to describe a host item, series, or other version and that "information about the original from which a digital surrogate or reproduction was made should be included in the main record" (Library of Congress, 2010). The DLF/Aquifer community made a pragmatic decision of taking a "hybrid approach" of mixing values representing the digital and original resources in the main body of a single MODS record (Riley et al., 2008).

7.2.15. *Identifier*

MODS <identifier>

- "Contains a unique standard number or code that distinctively identifies a resource."

Attributes:

- type; displayLabel; invalid; lang; xml:lang; script; transliteration

Subelements:

- None

The MODS <identifier> element may use the *type* attribute to indicate the specific type of identifier contained in the element. Values are best taken from the "Standard Identifier Source Codes" at http://www.loc.gov/standards/sourcelist/standard-identifier.html.

Identifier Example 1: ISBN:

```
<identifier type="isbn">1234567890</identifier>
```

Identifier Example 2: Music publisher number:

```
<identifier type="music-publisher"> Z.Y. 22-0485 Obar Music
Publishers</identifier>
```

Identifier Example 3: Local accession number:

```
<identifier type="local">ABC-475985</identifier>
```

Identifier Example 4: Digital file name:

```
<identifier type="local">TR_0003891</identifier>
```

Identifier Example 5: URI for webpage displaying digital resource and its metadata:

```
<identifier type="uri">http://www.xyz.edu/diglib/ 12345-
678.html</identifier>
```

7.2.16. *Location*

MODS <location>

- "Identifies the institution or repository holding the resource, or the electronic location in the form of a URL where it is available."

Attributes:

- None

Subelements:

- <physicalLocation> <shelfLocator> <url> <holdingSimple> <holdingExternal>

Whereas Dublin Core does not have a clear method of designating the location of an analog or digital item, the MODS scheme does, as illustrated in the following two examples. The MODS <location> element includes several subelements and may be used to express varied and detailed kinds of information. The examples below illustrate only one type of usage of the element.

Location Example 1: Repository holding original diary:

```
<location>
    <physicalLocation>Hagenville University
    Archives</physicalLocation>
</location>
```

Location Example 2: Physical location of painting

```
<location>
    <physicalLocation>National Gallery of Art (Washington,
    District of Columbia, United States)</physicalLocation>
</location>
```

7.2.17. *AccessCondition*

MODS <accessCondition>

- "Information about restrictions imposed on access to a resource."

Attributes:

- type; displayLabel; xlink; lang; xml-lang; script; transliteration

Subelements:

- None

The MODS <accessCondition> element is quite similar to the Dublin Core *Rights* element in terms of the kind of content it is intended to include, but it also has *type* and *displayLabel* attributes that can express a little more information about that content.

Access Condition Example 1: Simple copyright statement

```
<accessCondition>Copyright (c)2010 Hagenville
University</accessCondition>
```

Access Condition Example 2: Restrictions on use statement

```
<accessCondition type="use and reproduction">Copying allowed
only for noncommercial use with acknowledgement of
source</accessCondition>
```

Access Condition Example 3: More complex rights and access conditions statement

```
<accessCondition type="use and reproduction" displayLabel=
"Restricted">Transmission or reproduction of materials
protected by copyright beyond that allowed by fair use
requires the written permission of the copyright owners. In
addition, the reproduction of some materials may be restricted
by terms of gift of purchase agreements, donor restrictions,
privacy and publicity rights, licensing and trademarks. Works
not in the public domain cannot be commercially exploited
without permission of the copyright owner. Responsibility for
any use rests exclusively with the user.</accessCondition>
```

7.2.18. *Part*

MODS <part>

- "The designation of physical parts of a resource in a detailed form."

Attributes:

- type; order; ID

Subelements:

- <detail> <extent> <date> <text>

The MODS <part> element has no counterpart in Dublin Core. The following example is taken from the *MODS User Guidelines*.

```
<titleInfo>
    <title>Dana</title>
    <subTitle>an Irish magazine of independent
     thought</subTitle>
    <partNumber>Vol. 1, no. 4</partNumber>
</titleInfo>
<part>
```

```
        <detail>
            <title>Wayfarers (Poem)</title>
        </detail>
        <extent unit="pages">
            <start>97</start>
            <end>98</end>
        </extent>
    </part>
```

7.2.19. *Extension*

MODS <extension>

- "Provides additional information not covered by MODS."

Attributes:

- None

Subelements:

- None

The *MODS User Guidelines* provide the following information on guidelines for use: "<extension> may be used for elements that are local to the creator of the data. In addition, it may be used to extend MODS for various purposes when another XML schema may handle the type of information. Depending on the nature of the added information, <extension> may be a container element."

The User Guidelines also include the following example taken from a MODS application profile and XML schema for an electronic thesis or dissertation (ETD):

```
<extension xmlns:etd="http://www.ntltd.org/standards/
  metadata/etdms/1.0/etdms.xsd">
    <etd:degree>
        <etd:name>Doctor of Philosophy</etd:name>
        <etd:level>Doctoral</etd:level>
        <etd:discipline>Educational Administration</etd:
          discipline>
    </etd:degree>
</extension>
```

For those familiar with MARC, the MODS <extension> element has a certain similarity to MARC 9XX fields.

7.2.20. *RecordInfo*

MODS <recordInfo>

- "Information about the metadata record."

Attributes:

- lang; xml:lang; script; transliteration

Subelements:

- <recordContentSource> <recordCreationDate> <recordChangeDate> <recordIdentifier> <recordOrigin> <languageOfCataloging> <descriptionStandard>

Finally, the MODS <recordInfo> element provides a way to include information about the MODS metadata record itself, sometimes called *meta-metadata* because it is metadata *about* the metadata. Such information may include the date of metadata creation, date of last metadata update, metadata record identifier, metadata creator or source, metadata standard(s) used, and language of the metadata, which can be different from the language of the resource being described. Such information can be very helpful to users of the metadata record, especially other metadata professionals, consortia, harvesting and aggregating service providers, and sometimes also end users, in determining the quality and authoritativeness of the metadata, its currency, and the like. The following *recordInfo* example has been invented for purposes of illustration.

```
<recordInfo>
    <recordCreationDate encoding="w3cdtf">2009-07-
    07</recordCreationDate>
    <recordChangeDate encoding="w3cdtf">2002-11-
    11</recordChangeDate>
    <recordOrigin>MODS record originally created by
    Hagenville Digital Library staff to conform to the MODS
    User Guidelines, Version 3.</recordOrigin>
    <languageOfCataloging>
        <languageTerm authority="iso639-2b">
        eng</languageTerm>
    </languageOfCataloging>
</recordInfo>
```

7.3. MODS Records

7.3.1. Complete MODS Record Example

The example on pages 196–197 is a complete MODS XML record for a digitized photograph in the Library of Congress Prints and Photographs Division, LC-USZC4-9198. The record itself is from the *Digital Library Federation/Aquifer Implementation Guidelines for Shareable MODS Records* (DLF Aquifer Metadata Working Group, 2009), for which the Library of Congress Network Development & MARC Standards Office now has intellectual responsibility. This version of the record may have a few instances of content and encoding that have been altered from the original to conform to the DLF/Aquifer Guidelines.

Recall that MODS records may be displayed in any number of different ways, including all or selected pieces of information. The original version of the MODS record above is displayed to public users on the Library of Congress website at http://www.loc.gov/pictures/collection/ftncnw/item/2001698800/. Figure 7.1 (p. 198) shows this display.

7.3.2. Creating MODS XML Records

Implementers who use the MODS metadata scheme for their digital projects will rarely if ever type out all of the MODS XML coding by

Complete MODS Record Example

```
<mods xmlns="http://www.loc.gov/mods/v3" xmlns:
 xsi="http://www.w3.org/2001/XMLSchema-instance"
 xsi:schemaLocation="http://www.loc.gov/mods/v3
 http://www.loc.gov/standards/mods/v3/mods-3-
 2.xsd">

<titleInfo>
    <title>General view of Balaklava, the
     hospital on the right</title>
</titleInfo>

<name type="personal" authority="naf">
    <namePart>Fenton, Roger</namePart>
    <namePart type="date">1819-1869</namePart>
    <role>
        <roleTerm authority="marcrelator"
         type="text"> creator</roleTerm>
    </role>
    <role>
        <roleTerm authority="marcrelator"
         type="text"> photographer</roleTerm>
    </role>
</name>

<typeOfResource>still image</typeOfResource>

<genre authority="gmgpc">Salted paper prints-
 1850-1860.</genre>

<originInfo>
    <place>
        <placeTerm type="code" authority=
         "marccountry">enk</placeTerm>
        <placeTerm type="text">
         England</placeTerm>
    </place>
    <dateIssued encoding="w3cdtf" keyDate="yes"
     qualifier="inferred">1855</dateIssued>
</originInfo>

<physicalDescription>
    <extent>1 photographic print : salted paper
     ; 30 x 36 cm.</extent>
    <note>The entire content of the original
     has been digitized.</note>
    <internetMediaType>image/jpeg</internet
     MediaType>
    <internetMediaType>image/tiff</internet
     MediaType>
    <digitalOrigin>reformatted
     digital</digitalOrigin>
</physicalDescription>

<abstract>Includes buildings in the foreground,
 a view of the harbor, and military tents
 scattered on the hills to the left in the
 background.</abstract>

<note>Title transcribed from verso.</note>

<note>Roger Fenton, photographer of the Crimean
 War: His photographs and his letters from the
 Crimea, with an essay on his life and work /
 Helmut and Alison Gernsheim. London : Secker
 and Warburg, 1954, no. 21.</note>

<subject authority="lcsh">
    <geographic>Ukraine</geographic>
    <geographicCode authority="marcgac">
     e-un---</geographicCode>
</subject>

<subject authority="lcsh">
    <topic>Crimean War, 1853-1856</topic>
</subject>

<subject authority="lctgm">
    <topic>Cities and towns</topic>
    <geographic>Ukraine</geographic>
    <geographic>Balaklava</geographic>
    <temporal>1850-1860</temporal>
</subject>

<subject>
    <geographic>Balaklava (Ukraine)</geographic>
    <temporal>1850-1860</temporal>
</subject>

<classification authority="lcc">PH - Fenton (R.),
 no. 81</classification>

<relatedItem type="host">
    <titleInfo>
        <title>Roger Fenton Crimean War
         photograph collection</title>
    </titleInfo>
    <name>
        <namePart>Fenton, Roger, 1819-
         1869.</namePart>
    </name>
    <identifier type="lccn">
     2001696100</identifier>
    <note>Purchase; Frances M. Fenton;
     1944.</note>
    <accessCondition type="restrictionOnAccess">
     Restricted access: Materials extremely
     fragile; Served by appointment
     only.</accessCondition>
</relatedItem>

<identifier type="lccn">2001698800</identifier>

<identifier type="stock number">LC-USZC4-9198
 DLC</identifier>

<identifier type="stock number">LC-USZ62-2370
 DLC</identifier>
```

(Continued)

Complete MODS Record Example (*Continued*)

```
<identifier type="hdl" displayLabel="color
 film copy transparency">hdl:loc.pnp/cph.
 3g09198</identifier>
<identifier type="hdl" displayLabel=
 "b and w film copy neg.">hdl:loc.pnp/cph
 .3a06070</identifier>
<location>
    <url usage="primary display" access="object
    in context">http://hdl.loc.gov/loc.pnp/
    cph.3g09198</url>
</location>
<location>
    <physicalLocation>Library of Congress Prints
    and Photographs Division Washington, D.C.
    20540 USA</physicalLocation>
</location>
<accessCondition type="useAndReproduction">
 No known restrictions on
 publication.</accessCondition>
```

```
<recordInfo>
    <recordContentSource authority="marcorg">
    DLC</recordContentSource>
    <recordCreationDate encoding="w3cdtf">2001-
    07-25</recordCreationDate>
    <recordChangeDate encoding="w3cdtf">2002-
    11-11</recordChangeDate>
    <recordIdentifier source="DLC">
    2001698800</recordIdentifier>
    <recordOrigin>Derived from a MARC record
    using the Library of Congress stylesheet
    then edited to conform to the DLF
    Implementation Guidelines for Shareable
    MODS Records.</recordOrigin>
    <languageOfCataloging>
        <languageTerm authority="iso639-2b">
        eng</languageTerm>
    </languageOfCataloging>
</recordInfo>
</mods>
```

hand. Metadata creators will normally use some kind of software interface for creating MODS XML records. This may range from an XML editor to other kinds of user-friendly interfaces which will do some or all of the XML coding for the metadata creator, including proper nesting of subelements and coding of attributes. When using XML editing software, the MODS XML Schema is declared in each new MODS document, and the software fills in a great deal of the coding by referencing the schema. In the case of graphical input interfaces, the metadata designer or project coordinator will select which MODS elements, subelements, attributes, and encoding schemes to use, and they will develop policies on how to enter the metadata. This may be based entirely on local implementation decisions and application profiles or on consortial guidelines, in whole or in part, such as those of the DLF/Aquifer Initiative. These choices will then be presented to the metadata creators in a template to be filled in, often including drop-down menu choices for certain attributes and schemes.

For initial learning purposes, however, typing out a full MODS XML record by hand can provide an excellent way to get a deeper feel for the element set and its XML structures, and to be able to scan and *read* a MODS XML record. This is often a useful skill for a metadata specialist to have, and it is sometimes needed to find problems in the code or to work on mapping to and from MODS and other element sets.

Some MODS implementers work directly with the native MODS XML using XML editing software. Two of the best-known XML editors are oXygen (http://www.oxygenxml.com/) and Altova's XMLSpy (http://www.altova.com/xmlspy.html). Both are very powerful and provide the ability to do much more than only create and edit XML

Figure 7.1. Public Display of MODS Record

General view of Balaklava, the hospital on the right

About This Item | Obtaining Copies | Access to Original

Title: General view of Balaklava, the hospital on the right
Creator(s): Fenton, Roger, 1819-1869, photographer
Date Created/Published: [1855]
Medium: 1 photographic print : salted paper ; 30 x 36 cm.
Summary: Includes buildings in the foreground, a view of the harbor, and military tents scattered on the hills to the left in the background.
Part of: Fenton, Roger, 1819-1869. Roger Fenton Crimean War photograph collection
Reproduction Number: LC-USZC4-9198 (color film copy transparency) LC-USZ62-2370 (b&w film copy neg.)
Rights Advisory: No known restrictions on publication.
Access Advisory: Restricted access: Materials extremely fragile; Served by appointment only.
Call Number: PH - Fenton (R.), no. 81 (A size) [P&P]
Repository: Library of Congress Prints and Photographs Division Washington, D.C. 20540 USA
Notes:

- Title transcribed from verso.
- Purchase;
  Frances M. Fenton;
  1944.
- Forms part of: Roger Fenton Crimean War photograph collection.
- Roger Fenton, photographer of the Crimean War: His photographs and his letters from the Crimea, with an essay on his life and work / Helmut and Alison Gernsheim. London : Secker & Warburg, 1954, no. 21.

Subjects:

- Crimean War, 1853-1856.
- Cities & towns--Ukraine--Balaklava--1850-1860.
- Balaklava (Ukraine)--1850-1860.

Format:

- Salted paper prints--1850-1860.

Collections:

- Fenton Crimean War Photographs

Bookmark This Record:
http://www.loc.gov/pictures/item/2001698800

View the MARC Record for this item.

Rights assessment is your responsibility.

Source: Library of Congress, Fenton Crimean War Photographs: http://www.loc.gov/pictures/collection/ftncnw/item/2001698800/.

files. The following examples are screen captures from the oXygen XML Editor software. In the actual software, some color coding is used to visually distinguish attributes, for example, from elements and subelements. Figure 7.2 shows the top portion of an oXygen XML Editor window with a MODS metadata record open in the central pane.

Figure 7.2. oXygen XML Editor Example

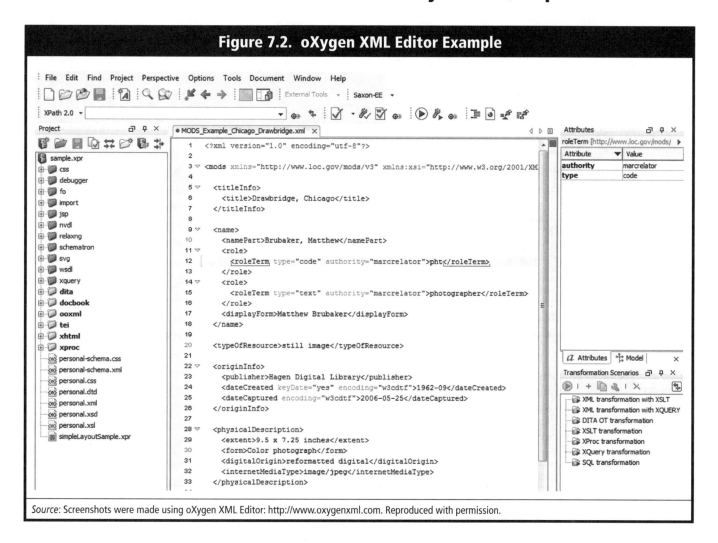

Source: Screenshots were made using oXygen XML Editor: http://www.oxygenxml.com. Reproduced with permission.

Figure 7.3 depicts an instance in which the metadata creator has typed an opening angle bracket inside of the <name> element. Because the XML document references the MODS XML Schema, the software is able to display the available <name> subelements in a dropdown list. The metadata creator can simply double click on any one of these, and the software will automatically fill in the opening and closing tags. For users who know MARC, the equivalent MARC tags are also displayed.

Figure 7.4 shows a similar example, but in this case the metadata creator has simply entered a space following the opening <roleTerm> tag, before the closing angle bracket. The available attributes for that element are displayed. In this instance the *authority* attribute is highlighted, and some information about the use of that attribute and the authorized sources are also displayed. Double clicking on the *authority* attribute from the drop down list will automatically insert it, along with as much of the XML coding as is possible before the metadata creator needs to make her or his next decision.

Figure 7.5 shows an alternative *grid* display available in oXygen. In this display, the XML tagging is absent and the metadata creator deals only with the names of the various MODS elements and attributes,

Figure 7.3. oXygen XML Editor <name> Subelement Example

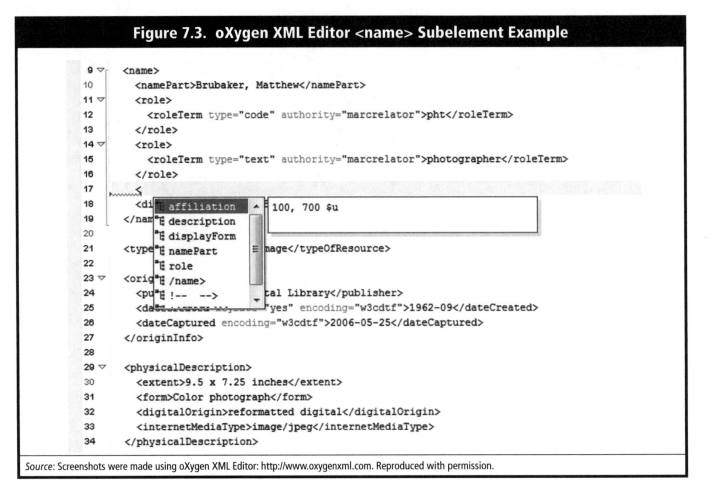

```
 9 ▽   <name>
10       <namePart>Brubaker, Matthew</namePart>
11 ▽     <role>
12         <roleTerm type="code" authority="marcrelator">pht</roleTerm>
13       </role>
14 ▽     <role>
15         <roleTerm type="text" authority="marcrelator">photographer</roleTerm>
16       </role>
17       ⌇
18       <di▯  affiliation      ▲  100, 700 $u
19     </nam ▯ description
20          ▯ displayForm
21     <type▯ namePart       ≣ nage</typeOfResource>
22          ▯ role
23 ▽   <orig▯ /name>
24       <pu▯ !-- -->           al Library</publisher>
25       <da▯              'yes" encoding="w3cdtf">1962-09</dateCreated>
26       <dateCaptured encoding="w3cdtf">2006-05-25</dateCaptured>
27     </originInfo>
28
29 ▽   <physicalDescription>
30       <extent>9.5 x 7.25 inches</extent>
31       <form>Color photograph</form>
32       <digitalOrigin>reformatted digital</digitalOrigin>
33       <internetMediaType>image/jpeg</internetMediaType>
34     </physicalDescription>
```

Source: Screenshots were made using oXygen XML Editor: http://www.oxygenxml.com. Reproduced with permission.

which are displayed in a way that graphically shows hierarchical nesting. In this example, the metadata creator has prompted to add a new subelement under the <name> element, and he or she can double click to add that subelement.

Some institutions have developed their own graphical user interfaces for creating MODS records, in which the metadata creator does not work at all with the underlying XML code. Instead, the coding is all done by the software behind the scenes. One such example is the University of Alberta MODS Editor Prototype (http://chelsea.library .ualberta.ca/cocoon210/modseditor/index.html). Figure 7.6 offers an example of the *mods:titleInfo* input screen. Notice that the metadata creator simply types the values into the boxes for the various subelements and may select any applicable Type attributes from the drop-down list.

Figure 7.7 shows an example of the *mods:originInfo* input screen, and Figure 7.8 shows an example of the *mods:Subject* element input screen. Notice in each case the various options available to the metadata creator to add new instances and to select from various drop-down menus.

For examples of other MODS creation tools, see "Tools for MODS" at http://www.loc.gov/standards/mods/tools_for_mods.php.

Figure 7.4. oXygen XML Editor <roleTerm> Attribute Example

```
9  ▽   <name>
10       <namePart>Brubaker, Matthew</namePart>
11 ▽     <role>
12         <roleTerm type="code" authority="marcrelator">pht</roleTerm>
13       </role>
14 ▽     <role>
15         <roleTerm type="text" authority="marcrelator">photographer</roleTerm>
16       </role>
17 ▽     <role>
18         <roleTerm ></roleTerm>
19       </role>
20                    ┌ authority    The value of this attribute is from list
21       <displayForm>a type        at
22     </name>                      http://www.loc.gov/marc/sourcecode/relato
23                                  r/relatorsource.html. If the value is
24     <typeOfResource>still image</type "marcrelator" the content is from list at
25                                  http://www.loc.gov/marc/sourcecode/relato
26 ▽   <originInfo>                 r/relatorlist.html
27       <publisher>Hagen Digital Library</publisher>
28       <dateCreated keyDate="yes" encoding="w3cdtf">1962-09</dateCreated>
29       <dateCaptured encoding="w3cdtf">2006-05-25</dateCaptured>
30     </originInfo>
31
32 ▽   <physicalDescription>
33       <extent>9.5 x 7.25 inches</extent>
34       <form>Color photograph</form>
35       <digitalOrigin>reformatted digital</digitalOrigin>
36       <internetMediaType>image/jpeg</internetMediaType>
37     </physicalDescription>
```

Source: Screenshots were made using oXygen XML Editor: http://www.oxygenxml.com. Reproduced with permission.

7.3.3. Displaying and Transforming MODS XML Records

One of the core characteristics of XML is that content is separated from presentation. While HTML is primarily about displaying content on a webpage, XML is about structuring the meaning of the content. Most web browsers today will display an XML file in its native format, but this is not meant for end-user display and use. XML makes use of style sheets to render the content of an XML file for user display. Publishers, for example, may mark up their books, catalogs, technical manuals, and other documents in XML, following a DTD or schema, and then use different **style sheets** to render the same XML document in a variety of different ways. For example, publishers may use one style sheet to output the content of an XML file as a PDF file, another style sheet to output the same XML file as a webpage, and another style sheet to output that same XML file to a handheld device.

Most XML users make use of two kinds of style sheets, **Cascading Style Sheets (CSS)**, which allow great control over the formatting and visual display of both HTML and XML documents, and **XML Style**

Figure 7.5. oXygen XML Editor Grid View Example

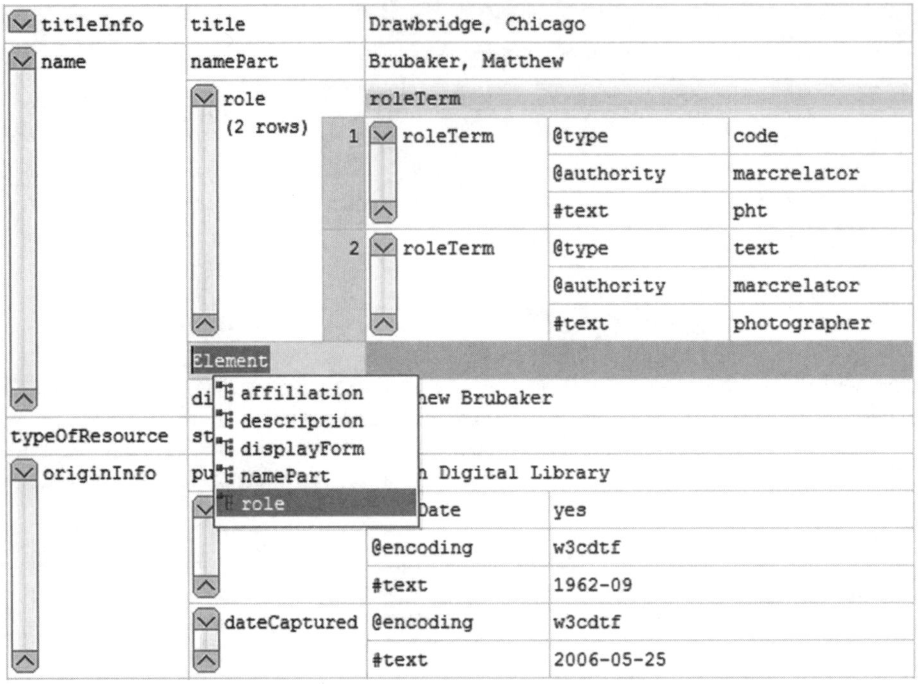

titleInfo	title	Drawbridge, Chicago		
name	namePart	Brubaker, Matthew		
	role (2 rows)	roleTerm		
		1 roleTerm	@type	code
			@authority	marcrelator
			#text	pht
		2 roleTerm	@type	text
			@authority	marcrelator
			#text	photographer
	Element			
	di affiliation	hew Brubaker		
	description			
	displayForm			
typeOfResource	st namePart	n Digital Library		
originInfo	pu role			
		Date	yes	
		@encoding	w3cdtf	
		#text	1962-09	
	dateCaptured	@encoding	w3cdtf	
		#text	2006-05-25	

Source: Screenshots were made using oXygen XML Editor: http://www.oxygenxml.com. Reproduced with permission.

Figure 7.6. University of Alberta MODS Editor <titleInfo> Example

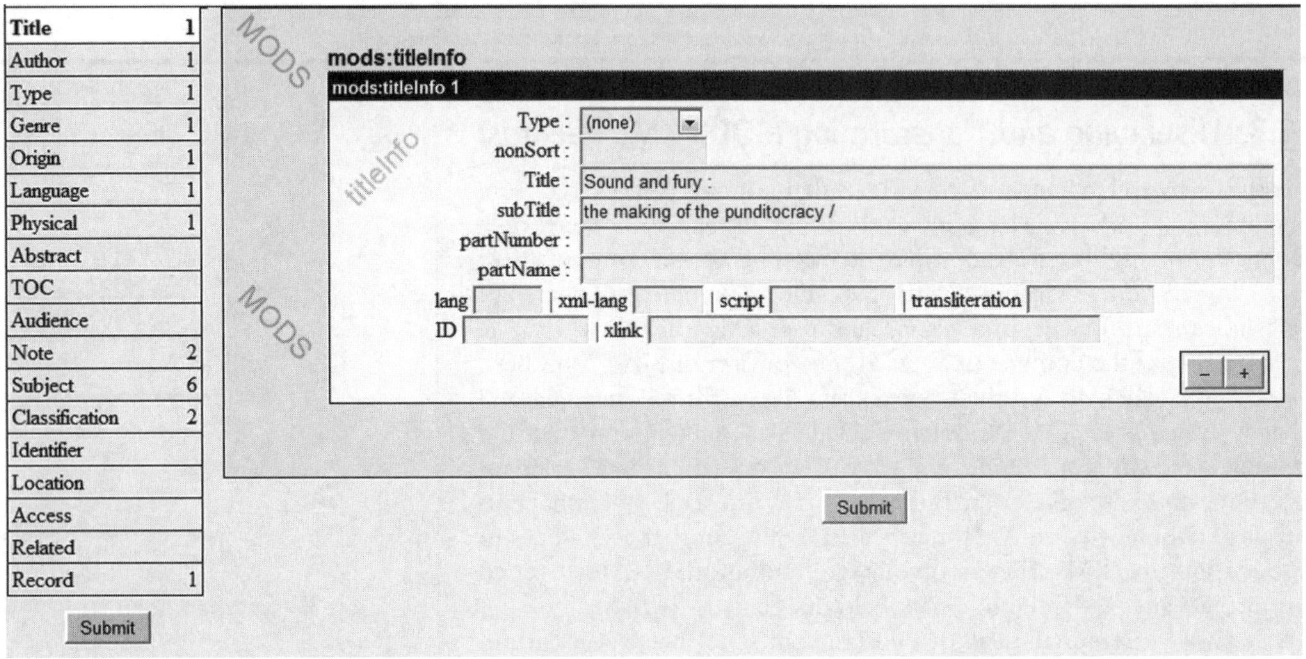

Title	1
Author	1
Type	1
Genre	1
Origin	1
Language	1
Physical	1
Abstract	
TOC	
Audience	
Note	2
Subject	6
Classification	2
Identifier	
Location	
Access	
Related	
Record	1

Submit

mods:titleInfo

mods:titleInfo 1

Type : (none)
nonSort :
Title : Sound and fury :
subTitle : the making of the punditocracy /
partNumber :
partName :
lang | xml-lang | script | transliteration
ID | xlink

– | +

Submit

Source: Peter Binkley, University of Alberta Libraries. Reproduced with permission.

Figure 7.7. University of Alberta MODS Editor <originInfo> Example

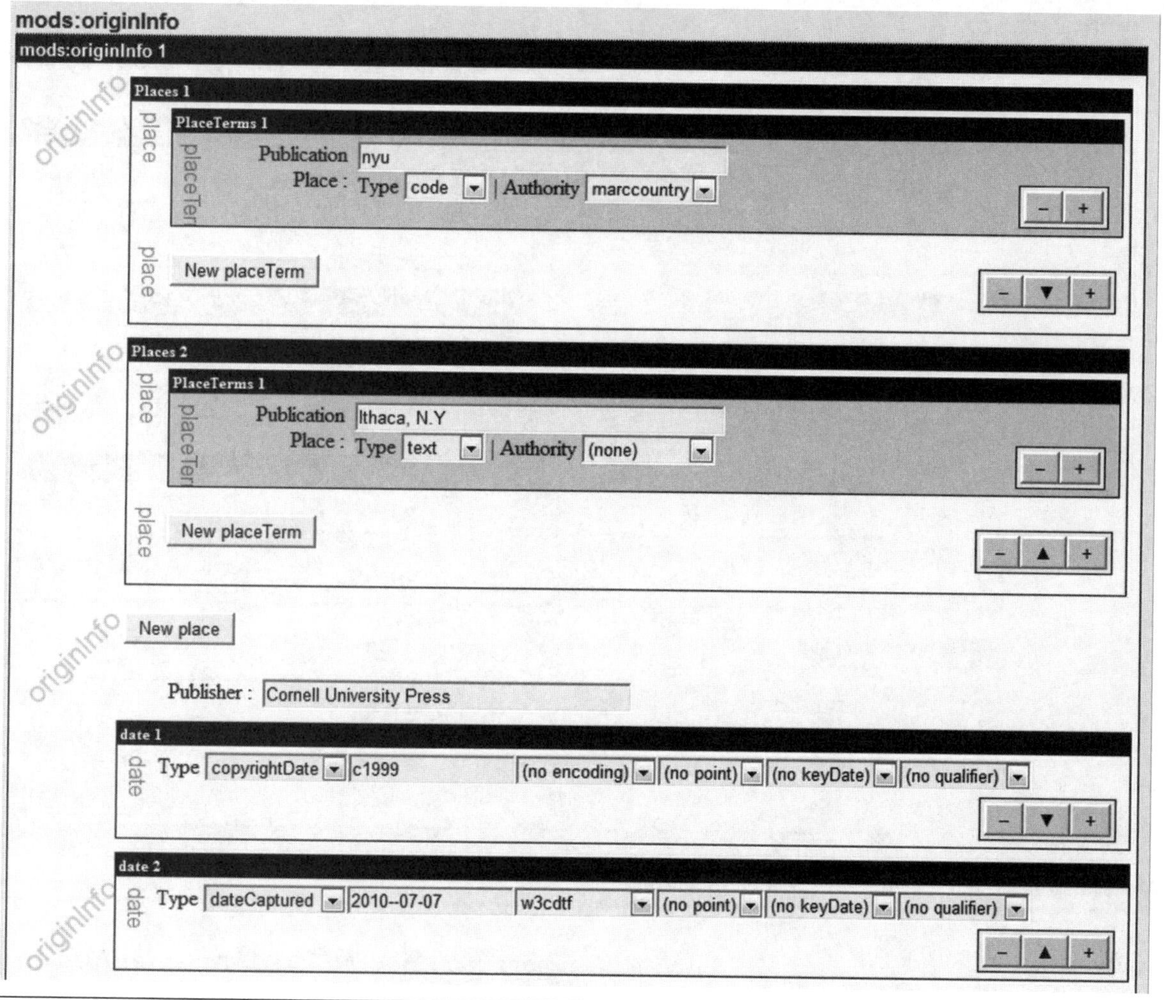

Sheet Language Transformations (XSLT), which actually transforms XML documents into other document formats, such as PDF, RTF (rich text format), HTML, and XHTML. XSLT and CSS are frequently used together for XML document transformation and display.

A project that uses MODS will need the requisite technical infrastructure to create, display, query, and retrieve results from MODS XML documents/records. What users see displayed on their computer screens will more often than not be the result of applying an XSLT style sheet, perhaps along with CSS, to a MODS XML file. Authoring XML style sheets is a special skill, which a metadata staff member may learn if needed. XSLT style sheets may also be used for transforming one type of metadata record into another, including *mapping* elements from one scheme to another, such as Dublin Core to MODS, MARC to MODS, MODS to Dublin Core, and so on. The MODS website includes several of these style sheets (see http://www.loc.gov/standards/mods/under "MODS Style sheets").

Figure 7.8. University of Alberta MODS Editor<subject> Example

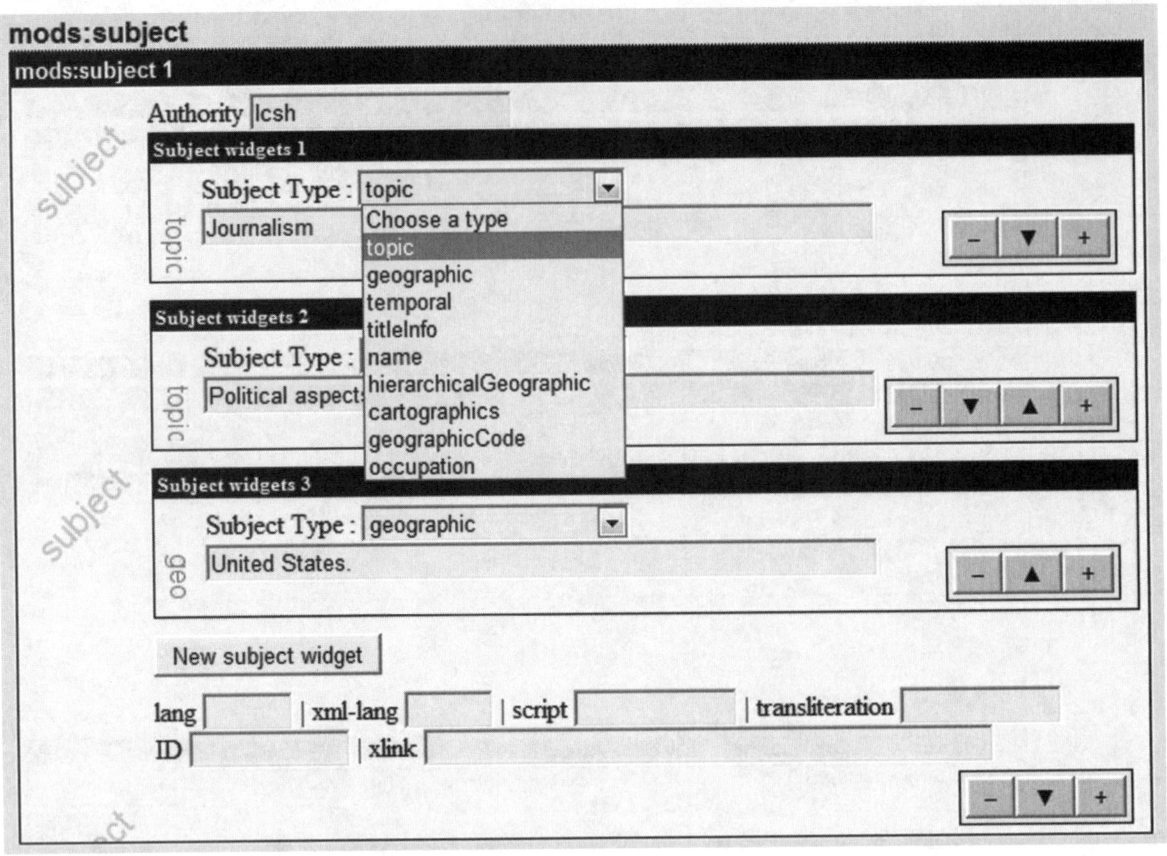

Source: Peter Binkley, University of Alberta Libraries. Reproduced with permission.

Here is a snippet from the *MODS User Guidelines*: "An 'XSLT stylesheet' (Extensible Stylesheet Language Transformation) may be written to transform the MODS data in some way for output. Examples include using a stylesheet to place the record into a template with easy-to-understand element names in XML; using a stylesheet to formulate a display that looks like a catalog card; using a stylesheet to transform coded data into textual form" (Library of Congress, 2010: "Introduction and Implementation").

7.3.4. Qualified Dublin Core and MODS Record Comparison

Having now covered MODS record structures, creation, and display, it can be useful to take a look at a side-by-side comparison of complete MODS and Qualified Dublin Core records for the same digital resource. Table 7.2 offers such an example, taking an XML-tagged DC record example previously used in Chapter 6.

This example clearly shows the differences between the flat XML record structure used for Qualified Dublin Core and the hierarchical

Table 7.2. Side-by-Side Comparison of Qualified Dublin Core and MODS Records

Qualified Dublin Core Record	MODS Record

`<title>`The life and times of Isabella Rios: based on diaries and oral narratives as told to her daughter Maria Rios Campos`</title>`	`<titleInfo>`
	  `<nonSort>`The`</nonSort>`
	  `<title>`life and times of Isabella Rios`</title>`
	  `<subTitle>`based on diaries and oral narratives as told to her daughter Maria Rios Campos`</subTitle>`
	`</titleInfo>`

`<creator>`Campos, Maria Rios, 1923-`</creator>`	`<name` authority="naf" type="**personal**">`   `<namePart>`Campos, Maria Rios`</namePart>`   `<namePart` type="date">1923-`</namePart>`   `<role><roleTerm` type="text" authority="marcrelator">` author`</roleTerm></role>` `</name>`
`<contributor>`Alvarez, Alejandro`</contributor>`	`<name` type="personal">`   `<namePart>`Alvarez, Alejandro`</namePart>`   `<role><roleTerm` type="text" authority="marcrelator">` translator`</roleTerm> </role>` `</name>`
`<type` scheme="DCMIType">Text`</type>`	`<typeOfResource>`text`</typeOfResource>`
`<type>`biography`</type>`	`<genre` authority="marcgt">biography`</genre>`
	`<originInfo>` `<place> <placeTerm` type="text">Los Angeles`</placeTerm> </place>`
`<publisher>`Palm Press`</publisher>`	`<publisher>`Palm Press`</publisher>`
`<issued>`1960`</issued>`	`<dateIssued` keyDate="yes">1960`</dateIssued>`
`<description>`2nd ed.`</description>`	`<edition>`2nd. ed.`</edition>`
`<created` scheme="W3CDTF">2007-01-04`</created>`	`<dateCaptured` encoding="w3cdtf">2007-01-04`</<dateCaptured>` `</originInfo>`
`<extent>`137 pages; 21 cm.`</extent>`	`<physicalDescription>` `<extent>`137 pages; 21 cm.`</extent>`

`<format` scheme="IMT">image/jpeg`</format>`	`<internetMediaType>`image/jpeg`</internetMediaType>`
	  `<digitalOrigin>`reformatted digital`</digitalOrigin>`
	`</physicalDescription>`

`<identifier>`UDL-HAOC-005739`<identifier>`	`<identifier` type="local">UDL-HAOC-005739`<identifier>`
`<rights>` Use of this public-domain resource is unrestricted.`</rights>`	`<accessCondition` type="use and reproduction">Use of this public-domain resource is unrestricted.`</accessCondition>`
`<description>`A narrative of the life of Los Angeles native Isabella Rios, focusing especially on her experiences as a Hispanic American woman living in 1920s and 1930s Los Angeles and her work as an extra on the sets of film productions at the Paramount and Warner Bros. motion picture studios.`</description>`	`<abstract>`A narrative of the life of Los Angeles native Isabella Rios, focusing especially on her experiences as a Hispanic American woman living in 1920s and 1930s Los Angeles and her work as an extra on the sets of film productions at the Paramount and Warner Bros. motion picture studios.`</abstract>`

(Continued)

Table 7.2. Side-by-Side Comparison of Qualified Dublin Core and MODS Records (Continued)

Qualified Dublin Core Record	MODS Record
`<description>`One of three known surviving copies. Donated to the Hagenville University Libraries by Marco Campos, son of Maria Rios Campos, in 1995.`</description>`	`<note>`One of three known surviving copies. Donated to the Hagenville University Libraries by Marco Campos, son of Maria Rios Campos, in 1995`</note>`
`<contributor>`Hagenville University Libraries Special Collections`</contributor>`	`<location>`Hagenville University Libraries Special Collections`</location>`

`<subject>`Rios, Isabella, 1899-1976`</subject>`	`<subject authority="lcsh">`
	  `<name authority="naf" type="personal">`
	  `<namePart>`Rios, Isabella`</namePart>`
	  `<namePart type="date">`1899-1976`</namePart>`
	  `</name>`

`<subject scheme="LCSH">`Hispanic American women--California--Los Angeles--Biography`</subject>`	`<subject authority="lcsh">`
	  `<topic>`Hispanic American women`</topic>`
	  `<geographic>`California`</geographic>`
	  `<geographic>`Los Angeles`</geographic>`
	  `<genre>`Biography`</genre>`
	  `</subject>`

`<spatial scheme="TGN">`North and Central America`</spatial>`	`<subject authority="tgn">`
	  `<hierarchicalGeographic>`
	    `<continent>`North and Central America`</continent>`

`<spatial scheme="TGN">`United States`</spatial>`	`<country>`United States`</country>`
`<spatial scheme="TGN">`California`</spatial>`	`<state>`California`</state>`

`<spatial scheme="TGN">`Los Angeles`</spatial>`	`<city>`Los Angeles`</city>`
	  `</hierarchicalGeographic>`
	`</subject>`

`<temporal>`1899-1976`</temporal>`	`<subject>`
	  `<temporal point="start">`1899`</temporal>`
	  `<temporal point="end">`1976`</temporal>`
	`</subject>`

`<temporal>`Nineteen twenties`</temporal>`	`<subject>`
	  `<temporal authority="lcsh">`Nineteen twenties`</temporal>`
	`</subject>`

`<temporal>`Nineteen thirties`</temporal>`	`<subject>`
	  `<temporal authority="lcsh">`Nineteen thirties`</temporal>`
	`</subject>`

`<subject scheme="DDC">`920.7208968`</subject>`	`<classification authority="ddc">`920.7208968`</classification>`
`<isPartOf>`Hispanic Americans of California`</isPartOf>`	`<relatedItem type="host">` `<titleInfo>` `<title>`Hispanic Americans of California`</title>` `</titleInfo>`
`<isPartOf scheme="URI">`http://www.hdl.edu/HAOC/`</isPartOf>`	`<identifier type="uri">`http://www.hdl.edu/HAOC/`</identifier>`
`<publisher>`Hagenville University Digital Library`</publisher>`	`<originInfo>` `<publisher>`Hagenville University Digital Library`</publisher>` `</originInfo>` `</relatedItem>`

(Continued)

Table 7.2. Side-by-Side Comparison of Qualified Dublin Core and MODS Records *(Continued)*

Qualified Dublin Core Record	MODS Record

`<isVersionOf>`La vida y la época de Isabella Rios: basado en los diarios y narraciones orales como dijo a su hija Maria Rios Campos`</isVersionOf>`	`<relatedItem type="otherVersion">`
	  `<titleInfo>`
	    `<nonSort>`La`</nonSort>`
	    `<title>`vida y la época de Isabella Rios`</title>`
	    `<subTitle>`basado en los diarios y narraciones orales como dijo a su hija Maria Rios Campos`</subTitle>`
	  `</titleInfo>`
	`</relatedItem>`

`<source>`45097833`</source>`	`<relatedItem type="original">` `<identifier type="lccn">`45097833`</identifier>`

	`<recordInfo>`
	  `<recordCreationDate encoding="w3cdtf">`2007-05-25`</recordCreationDate>`
	  `<recordContentSource>`Hagenville Digital Library`</recordContentSource>`
	  `<languageOfCataloging>` `<languageTerm authority="iso639-2">`eng`</languageTerm>`
	  `</languageOfCataloging>`
	`</recordInfo>`

structure used in MODS. It also provides a basis for assessing how MODS is able to address many resource description needs and provide richer levels of functionality than Dublin Core, even in its qualified form. At the same time, the structural complexity of MODS, especially its use of hierarchically nested subelements, places greater demands on computer processing power and programming and makes MODS less widely interoperable than a simpler flat scheme like Dublin Core. MODS in this respect is like the majority of major cultural heritage metadata schemes, including VRA 4.0, covered in the next chapter, and Encoded Archival Description (EAD), which are complex and hierarchical XML based schemes. It should also be noted here that the 15 original simple Dublin Core elements have been widely deployed in numerous web environments beyond cultural heritage contexts alone. Many systems can read Simple DC, and it has a tremendous value as a switching language, into which metadata from richer schemes such as MODS, VRA 4.0, and EAD can be mapped for sharing in aggregated contexts. Chapter 9 delves into these topics further, all of which are related to the larger topic of metadata interoperability.

7.4. Mapping from Dublin Core to MODS

In relation to issues of metadata interoperability, Chapter 9 deals with the topic of *mapping* and *crosswalks* between different metadata schemes or element sets, including mapping from MODS as a richer scheme to Dublin Core as a simpler scheme. This current section of Chapter 7, however, introduces the topic of mapping from the simpler Dublin Core to the richer MODS, now that both of these metadata element sets have been covered in the book up to this point. Whether using this book for course study or self-study, one useful way to start working hands on with MODS and to start comparing MODS with Dublin Core is to map existing Dublin Core metadata into the MODS scheme before creating a full original MODS record. Mapping is usually done by following an established mapping table, sometimes also called a *crosswalk*, such as the one included in the next section of this chapter. It is possible to do a very simple, default-level mapping from Simple Dublin Core to MODS, or a richer mapping. The term *MODS Lite* is sometimes used to refer to MODS when using only those elements that have a correspondence to the 15 original unqualified Dublin Core elements (see http://www.loc .gov/standards/mods/userguide/lite.html).

7.4.1. Automated Mapping from Simple Dublin Core to Simple MODS

It is useful to distinguish between the kind of mapping that can be done by a computer program, which is not capable of making intelligent assessments about the values contained in a particular element, and by a human being who is able to understand and assess the nature of those values. Depending on context, either type of mapping may be desirable or practical. Computers are very limited and cannot make judgments as to how to map the actual values of many of the DC elements into different MODS elements and subelements or to make use of MODS attributes in most cases. Computers must typically be programmed to do default-level mapping because they cannot evaluate the meaning of metadata values unless those values have been explicitly tagged as having a certain meaning. The computer program needs to be provided with a default MODS element into which to map all instances of a specific DC element. For example, the value of a Dublin Core *Description* element can be mapped to MODS , <note>, or <tableOfContents>, depending on the particular type of value used in any instance of that element. A human being can assess the value and make a decision as to which MODS element is the most appropriate, but not a computer. For DC *Description*, the default mapping is to MODS <note>, because it has been judged the least likely to be incorrect.

When expressed as Simple DC, there is relatively little information about the semantic meaning of element values for a computer to work with. The default mapping from Simple DC *Date*, for example, is to MODS <dateOther>, because a computer has no way to discern what specific kind of date value in contained in the Date element. The use of a Qualified Dublin Core *Created* refinement, however, would allow for automated mapping to the more specific MODS <dateCreated> element. To understand the nature of machine mapping, you must in effect *dumb down* your own mind to the level at which a computer program could automatically map from either Simple or Qualified DC to MODS.

Remember that in mapping from Simple DC to MODS, all the computer has to work with are the Simple DC element names.

Table 7.3 replicates the official MODS website mapping from Dublin Core to MODS Version 3, current as of this writing. It is important to carefully read the notes in the mapping table and to especially notice anything designated as *default*. For the most part, a basic automated machine mapping will be able to deal only with the *defaults*. The official DC to MODS mapping also includes a table showing the conversion of *DCMI Type Vocabulary* to MODS *typeOfResource* values, as replicated in Table 7.4. Working with these mapping tables can make for an excellent exercise for students and practitioners alike.

Table 7.5 illustrates this type of mapping from Simple DC to MODS for three selected elements. These examples follow the mappings and notes given in the "Dublin Core Metadata Element Set Mapping to MODS Version 3" almost to the letter, using the *default* mapping whenever one is given in the notes. This is the way that a basic automated mapping would need to be done. As the notes in the mapping table say, distinctions in MODS are often lost when doing this kind of basic mapping. This results in a very simple set of MODS elements that does not begin to take full advantage of the richer resource description capabilities of MODS. But it is a useful exercise in direct mapping from one scheme to another.

7.4.2. Human Mapping from Qualified Dublin Core to Richer MODS

Table 7.6 illustrates a richer kind of mapping that a human being could do from Qualified DC to MODS, using the same three elements from Table 7.4.

There are several options when mapping from Qualified Dublin Core to MODS. Ideally, as much of the information conveyed by the QDC refinement and encoding scheme qualifiers will be expressed in MODS. The mappings in Table 7.6 illustrate some good options. Going beyond what can be expressed in Qualified Dublin Core (QDC), a human being could recognize that the name in the DC *Creator* element in this instance is a personal name and could add the *Type* attribute value of *personal* to the MODS <name> element. It is also possible that you could make other mapping decisions based on additional knowledge you might happen to have. For example, if you know that Matthew Brubaker is the photographer, you could use the more specific <roleTerm> *photographer* in MODS. A role/realtor code could also be used in addition to, or instead of, the text form.

In practice, it is rarely feasible for a human being to examine every record out of hundreds or thousands and map each one individually. Some kind of machine processing is the norm if converting large batches of metadata records from one scheme to another. More sophisticated automated mappings can be made from Qualified DC to MODS than from Simple DC, because the computer has more detailed tagging to work from, giving it more information about the nature of the values in the elements and encoding schemes used for those values.

Table 7.3. Simple Dublin Core Mapping to MODS Version 3

Dublin Core element	MODS element	Notes
Title	<titleInfo><title>	
Creator	<name><namePart> <role type="text">creator	1. MODS puts all names in a repeated<name> with type of contribution included in <role>. If desired to retain creator or contributor distinction, use <name><namePart><role>creator 2. MODS assumes structured form of name 3. MODS allows distinguishing name as personal, corporate, conference in type attribute. DC does not, so this information is lost. 4. MODS allows <name> subelements to be parsed: <namePart>, <displayForm>, <affiliation>, <role>, <description>. Default DC value to <namePart>.
Subject	<subject><topic> <classification>	Data in MODS may be included in a more specific subelement: <topic>, <geographic>, <temporal>, <name>, <titleInfo>, <hierarchicalGeographic>, <coordinates>. DC also uses classification schemes in Subject. These distinctions will be lost when converting from DC to MODS. Default DC value to <topic>.
Description	<note> <tableOfContents>	Multiple elements in MODS. These distinctions will be lost when converting from DC to MODS. Default DC value to <note>.
Publisher	<originInfo><publisher>	DC value may include place of publication/issuance. This distinction will be lost when converting from DC to MODS and place may be in MODS publisher.
Contributor	<name><namePart>	See notes under Creator
Date	<originInfo><dateIssued>	Multiple elements in MODS. These distinctions will be lost when converting from DC to MODS> Default DC value to <dateOther>.
	<originInfo><dateCreated>	
	<originInfo><dateCaptured>	
	<originInfo><dateOther>	
Type	<typeOfResource> <genre>	MODS uses high level types in <typeOfResource> (controlled list); more specific genre terms in <genre> (may or may not be from a controlled list). If DC value is from dc:type list, use <genre> with authority="dct" and supply a MODS enumerated typeOfResource value when possible (see mapping below). If not from dc:type list, default to <genre>.
Format	<physicalDescription> <internetMediaType>	Multiple elements in MODS. Default DC value to <physicalDescription><form>
	<physicalDescription><extent>	
	<physicalDescription><form>	
Identifier	<identifier> <location><uri>	MODS makes a distinction between a persistent identifier and a location. A type attribute specifies the identifier type, e.g. MODS <identifier type="uri">; http: URIs also go in <location><url>. Default DC value to <location><url> if it begins "http://"
Source	<relatedItem type="original"> + <titleInfo><title> or <location><url>	See notes under Relation
Language	<language>	
Relation	<relatedItem> + <titleInfo><title> or <location><url>	Data in mods:relatedItem is parsed into subelements (any MODS element may be used). Default DC value to <titleInfo><title> unless it begins "http://", in which case to <location><url>.
Coverage	<subject><temporal>	Multiple elements in MODS. May result in incorrect mapping, since there is not a way to tell if the coverage is spatial or temporal. Default coverage to <subject><geographic> (although this may result in some errors)
	<subject><geographic>	
	<subject><hierarchicalGeographic>	
	<subject><cartographics>	
Rights	<accessCondition>	

Source: "Dublin Core Metadata Element Set Mapping to MODS Version 3," December 29, 2006, http://www.loc.gov/standards/mods/dcsimple-mods.html. Network Development & MARC Standards Office, Library of Congress.

Table 7.4. Conversion of DC Resource Type Vocabulary to MODS TypeOfResource Values

DC Type value	MODS typeOfResource
Collection (use in addition to specific value below	typeOfResource collection="yes"
Dataset	software, multimedia and mods:genre="database"
Image	default to still image
InteractiveResource	software, multimedia
MovingImage	moving image
PhysicalObject	three-dimensional object
Service	software and mods:genre="online system or service"
Sound	sound recording
StillImage	still image
Software	software, multimedia
Text	text

Source: "Conversion of DC Resource Type Vocabulary to MODS TypeOfResource Values," December 29, 2006, http://www.loc.gov/standards/mods/dcsimple-mods .html. Network Development & MARC Standards Office, Library of Congress.

Table 7.5. Three Simple Dublin Core Elements Mapped to MODS Lite

DC Element	Element Value	Mapped to Simple MODS
Description	Image of raised drawbridge with Chicago River and part of downtown Chicago skyline visible.	<note>
Creator	Brubaker, Matthew	<name> <namePart>
Date	1962-09	<originInfo> <dateOther>

Table 7.6. Three Qualified Dublin Core Elements Mapped to Full MODS

DC Element	Refinement	Scheme	Value	Mapped to MODS
Description			Image of raised drawbridge with Chicago River and part of downtown Chicago skyline visible.	
Creator			Brubaker, Matthew	<name type="personal"><namePart> <roleTerm type="text" authority="marcrelator"> creator
Date	Created	W3CDTF	1962-09	<originInfo> <dateCreated encoding="w3cdtf">

7.5. Summary

This chapter has presented an overview of the Metadata Object Description Schema (MODS). The MODS scheme encompasses both a metadata element set and an XML schema. As an XML-based scheme, MODS makes use of hierarchically nested subelements to group together semantically related or similar kinds of information and uses attributes to further refine or define the values contained in certain elements. Studying MODS is useful for many reasons, even for those who do not use it in practice. Among other things, it provides a basis for informed comparison with the Dublin Core Metadata Element Set and for understanding issues involved in mapping elements and values from one metadata scheme to another. This chapter examines only selected parts of the larger MODS scheme and is based primarily on the *MODS User Guidelines, Version 3*. It is necessary to consult the actual User Guidelines and other documentation on the official MODS website in order to get a complete picture of the MODS element set and other MODS resources. This chapter has used many of the same examples given in Chapters 3 and 4 in order to demonstrate how MODS is able to address many resource description needs and provide richer levels of functionality that Simple and even Qualified Dublin Core cannot. At the same time, the complexity of MODS, especially its use of hierarchically nested subelements, makes it generally less interoperable than a simpler, flat scheme like Dublin Core. The chapter has shown some examples of MODS metadata creation software and has discussed the use of style sheets to render MODS XML for display to end users. Differences between machine and human mapping between Dublin Core and MODS were also explored.

▶ **Companion Website**

See this book's companion website at **http://www.neal-schuman.com/metadata-digital-collections** for Chapter 7 review questions, suggestions for exercises, links to online MODS documentation, and other resources.

References

DLF Aquifer Metadata Working Group. 2009. *Digital Library Federation / Aquifer Implementation Guidelines for Shareable MODS Records*, Version 1.1. March. https://wiki.dlib.indiana.edu/confluence/download/attachments/24288/DLFMODS_ImplementationGuidelines.pdf.

Library of Congress. 2010. *MODS User Guidelines (Version 3)*. Last modified October. http://www.loc.gov/standards/mods/userguide/.

Riley, Jenn, John Chapman, Sarah Shreeves, Laura Akerman, and William Landis. 2008. "Promoting Shareability: Metadata Activities of the DLF Aquifer Initiative." *Journal of Library Metadata* 8, no. 3: 221–248.

VRA Core: The Visual Resources Association Core Categories

8.1. Introduction and Overview

In the realm of cultural heritage metadata, libraries, archives, and museums are frequently grouped together as the three major types of cultural heritage institutions. This chapter takes a cursory look at two versions of the Visual Resources Association (VRA) Core Categories, a metadata scheme—also known as an element set, data set, or data structure standard—used primarily in the museum community. While VRA is sometimes used for visual resources outside of museums and is in fact built into some digital collection management software packages such as CONTENTdm, it is arguably most useful for describing works of visual art and architecture. This chapter gives only a superficial overview of VRA Core versions 3.0 and 4.0, enough to give a general sense of their structure and to allow further comparison and contrast with the Dublin Core and MODS metadata schemes.

8.1.1. Metadata for Museum Objects

Museums come in a variety of types and sizes, ranging from large to small, public to private, general to specialized, and they collect objects in areas ranging from art to natural history to science and technology to folk life, and so on. Museum culture and traditions have differed in many significant ways from those of libraries and archives, yet they also have many things in common. On the whole, museums have not had a tradition of standardization in resource description or in exchanging metadata about their collections among institutions. That makes sense given that museums usually collect unique objects. But the advent of digital representations of museum objects and online digital collections has started to alter the landscape for metadata standardization and sharing among museums.

Museums collect and display various types of objects, most often unique physical objects. Museum objects may include paintings, sculptures, decorative household items, furniture, clothing, taxidermied wildlife, rock and mineral specimens, dolls, ships, trains, signs—the list is virtually endless. This chapter focuses on metadata for museums that collect objects of art, primarily paintings and sculptures. The metadata elements included in the VRA schemes demonstrate some of the primary characteristics that art museums consider important for representation and retrieval of works of art and architecture, and of digital collections of images of those works.

Museums have always recorded and maintained information about the objects that they collect. The traditional tool for this purpose in museums was the museum *register*. Today we call that information *metadata*, whether it is handwritten, typewritten, entered into a small homemade database, or recorded in an expensive information management system. It is not uncommon for a single larger museum to have information recorded in a variety of ways in several different printed registers and electronic databases using different types of software. Many larger museums, within the past decade or so, have purchased **Content Management System (CMS)** or **Digital Asset Management System (DAMS)** software products to help manage information about their collections in a more systematic and centralized way. But there tends to be little or no standardization or compatibility among these different systems, and they are centered on each individual museum's management of its own objects and not on sharing information about museum objects among different institutions.

The information that we would now call *metadata elements*, as well as the content recorded about museum objects, has frequently varied from one museum director or curator to another. Curators have sometimes been protective of their data and their systems, and they have not always been willing to share or standardize. When a new curator comes in, he or she may establish his or her own new system. But this is beginning to change, and the drive to mount online collections of digital images of museum holdings is also driving the adoption of shared metadata standards.

In addition to the kinds of metadata elements examined in previous chapters of this book, museums will also often be interested in maintaining the following kinds of information:

- Physical material out of which an object is made
- Location of a particular object (i.e., in which museum or repository it currently resides)
- Provenance or history of ownership of an object
- Historical style and time period of an object
- Technique(s) used in creating an object

8.1.2. Metadata Standards for Museum Objects

The cultural heritage metadata landscape today includes a handful of important, well-established, and still-developing metadata standards for works of art and architecture and images of those objects. These include, most importantly:

VRA Core: The Visual Resources Association Core Categories

Element Sets (Structure Standards):

- **VRA Core 3.0**
  - Visual Resources Association, "VRA Projects - VRA Core 3.0." http://www.vraweb.org/projects/vracore3/.

- **VRA Core 4.0**
  - Library of Congress, "VRA Core Schemas and Documentation." http://www.loc.gov/standards/vracore/schemas.html.
  - Visual Resources Association, "VRA Core Home Page." http://www.vraweb.org/projects/vracore4/.

- **CDWA**
  - Baca, Murtha, and Patricia Harpring, eds. 2009. *Categories for the Description of Works of Art.* Online version. J. Paul Getty Trust. http://www.getty.edu/research/publications/electronic_publications/cdwa/index.html.

Content Standards:

- **CCO**
  - Baca, Murtha, Patricia Harpring, Elisa Lanzi, Linda McRae, Ann Whiteside, eds. 2006. *Cataloging Cultural Objects: A Guide to Describing Cultural Works and Their Images.* Chicago: American Library Association.

Value Standards:

- **AAT**
  - The Getty Research Institute, *Art & Architecture Thesaurus Online.* The J. Paul Getty Trust. http://www.getty.edu/research/tools/vocabularies/aat/index.html.

- **TGN**
  - The Getty Research Institute, *Getty Thesaurus of Geographic Names Online.* The J. Paul Getty Trust. http://www.getty.edu/research/tools/vocabularies/tgn/index.html.

- **ULAN**
  - The Getty Research Institute, *Union List of Artist Names Online.* The J. Paul Getty Trust. http://www.getty.edu/research/tools/vocabularies/ulan/index.html.

CDWA contains a much richer and more complex set of categories or elements than those in VRA. This chapter, however, looks only at VRA Core. Previous chapters have already referenced the AAT, TGN, and ULAN vocabularies. By looking at VRA Core, you can get a good introductory sense of the kinds of metadata important for art museums and of some of the resource description issues that arise when describing museum objects and images of those objects.

Crosswalk for Cultural Heritage Metadata. Readers may be interested in looking over the "Metadata Standards Crosswalk" on the Research at the Getty website (http://www.getty.edu/research/conducting_ research/standards/intrometadata/crosswalks.html). It consists of a single table presenting mappings between multiple metadata schemes: CDWA,

CCO, CDWA Lite, VRA 4.0 XML, MARC/AACR, MODS, Dublin Core, DACS, EAD, and other metadata schemes.

8.2. VRA 3.0 Overview

The VRA Core Categories Version 3.0 metadata scheme bears some similarities to Dublin Core in its relative simplicity, number of elements, and use of qualifiers. Like Dublin Core and MODS for that matter, in VRA 3.0 all elements and qualifiers are optional and repeatable and may be given in any order. It is assumed that local implementers will make their own application decisions about element requirements, repeatability, vocabularies, content guidelines, and the like, and document these in some form. The use of controlled vocabularies, especially the Getty vocabularies, is recommended.

The VRA 3.0 website (http://www.vraweb.org/projects/vracore3/) contains all of the official documentation for the scheme, including a short introduction; a list of the categories (elements) with their definitions, qualifiers, specifications for data values, and mapping to Dublin Core; a compendium of examples; and a MARC mapping table. The VRA Core 3.0 documentation is quite brief compared to the MODS documentation.

VRA closely adheres to the *One-to-One Principle*, that is, "only one object or resource may be described within a single metadata set" (Visual Resources Association, 2011). It makes a sharp distinction between **works** and **images** of those works and assumes that separate metadata description sets (records) will be created for each and linked to each other in a local database. The structure of the local database and the method of linking are local application issues.

The VRA 3.0 *Record Type* element may contain one of two values, *work* or *image*, thereby indicating whether the metadata record represents a work or an image of a work. While this sharp distinction might not make as much sense in non-museum contexts, in the museum world it provides a clear way to distinguish between an art object that a museum owns versus a documentary image of that art object. It is in this sense that the distinction between *work* and *image* is made in VRA. It does not mean that an image cannot also itself be regarded as a *work* from a different perspective. It means that for purposes of this particular metadata scheme, based on its underlying conceptual model, the term *work* is used in this specialized sense. Even within VRA, however, there are special cases in which an image itself may be regarded as a *work*. An example could be an instance in which a famous photographer photographs the museum object. But this is relatively rare.

The VRA Core 3.0 scheme contains 17 elements, technically called *categories*. Like Dublin Core, VRA 3.0 is *not* an inherently XML-based element set and does not have an established XML schema, although the metadata *could* be expressed in an XML format. Table 8.1 lists each of the VRA elements, along with any applicable qualifiers, specifications on data values, and mapping to Dublin Core.

Works and Images in VRA 3.0

What Is a Work?

"In the context of the VRA Core 3.0, a work is a physical entity that exists, has existed at some time in the past, or that could exist in the future. It might be an artistic creation such as a painting or a sculpture; it might be a performance, composition, or literary work; it might be a building or other construction in the built environment; or it might be an object of material culture. Works may be single items, or they may consist of many parts."

What Is an Image?

"An image is a visual representation of a work. It can exist in photomechanical, photographic and digital formats. In a typical visual resources collection, an image is a reproduction of the work that is owned by the cataloging institution and is typically a slide, photograph, or digital file. A visual resources collection may own several images of a given work."

(Visual Resources Association, 2011.)

VRA Core: The Visual Resources Association Core Categories

_	_	_	_
Table 8.1. VRA 3.0 Categories, Qualifiers, Data Values, and DC Mappings			
VRA Category	**Qualifiers**	**Data Values (controlled)**	**Dublin Core**
Record Type	[none]	work, image	Type
Type	[none]	recommend AAT	Type
Title	Title.Variant Title.Translation Title.Series Title.Larger Entity	formulated according to data content rules for titles of works of art	Title
Measurements	Measurements.Dimensions Measurements.Format Measurements.Resolution	formulated according to standards for data content (e.g., AACR, etc.)	Format
Material	Material.Medium Material.Support	AAT	Format
Technique	[none]	AAT	Format
Creator	Creator.Role Creator.Attribution Creator.Personal name Creator.Corporate name	recommend ULAN and AAAF (LC authority files)	Creator Contributor
Date	Date.Creation Date.Design Date.Beginning Date.Completion Date.Alteration Date.Restoration	formulated according to standards for data content (e.g., AACR, DC dates, etc.)	Date Coverage
Location	Location.Current Site Location.Former Site Location.Creation Site Location.Discovery Site Location.Current Repository Location.Former Repository	BHA index, AAAF (LC), Grove's Dictionary of Art Location Appendix	Contributor Coverage
ID Number	ID Number.Current Repository ID Number.Former Repository ID Number.Current Accession ID Number.Former Accession	——	Identifier
Style/Period	Style/Period.Style Style/Period.Period Style/Period.Group Style/Period.School Style/Period.Dynasty Style/Period.Movement	recommend AAT	Coverage Subject
Culture	[none]	recommend AAT, LCSH	Coverage
Subject	[none]	recommend AAT, TGM, ICONCLASS, Sears Subject Headings	Subject
Relation	Relation.Identity Relation.Type	——	Relation
Description	[none]	——	Description
Source	[none]	——	Source
Rights	[none]	——	Rights
Source: Composite based on "VRA Core Categories, Version 3.0," http://www.vraweb.org/projects/vracore3/categories.html. Data Standards Committee, Visual Resources Association.			

8.3. VRA 3.0 Record Examples

The examples in Tables 8.2 and 8.3 illustrate two related VRA *data sets* representing an etching in a museum collection and a digital image of that etching.

Table 8.2. VRA 3.0 Data Set for an Etching (Work Record)	
Record Type	work
Type	print
Title	This is how it happened
Title.Variant	As Sucedi
Measurements.Dimensions	24.5 x 35 cm
Material.Medium	ink
Material.Support	paper
Technique	etching
Technique	drypoint
Creator.Personal Name	Francisco Jose de Goya y Lucientes
Creator.Role	printmaker
Date.Creation	ca. 1810-1814
Location.Current Repository	Ann Arbor (MI,USA), University of Michigan Museum of Art
Location.Creation Site	Madrid (ESP)
ID Number. Current Accession	1977/2.15
Style/Period	Romanticism
Culture	Spanish
Subject	war
Relation.Part of	Part of Disasters of war
Description	This is how it happened is No. 47 (33) from the series "The Disasters of War", 4th edition, plates for the series ca. 1810-14, 1820, 4th edition was published 1906.
Rights	Weber family trust

Source: Adapted from the VRA Core 3.0 "Compendium of Examples," http://www.vraweb.org/projects/vracore3/examples.html. Data Standards Committee, Visual Resources Association.

Table 8.3. VRA 3.0 Data Set for an Image of the Etching (Image Record)	
Record Type	image
Type	digital
Title	general view
Measurements.Dimensions	72 dpi
Measurements.Format	jpeg
Technique	scanning
Creator	Fred Technician
Date.Creation	1999
Location.Current Repository	Ann Arbor (MI,USA), University of Michigan Museum of Art
ID Number.Current Repository	PCD5010-1611-1037-27
ID Number.Current Repository	1977_2.15.jpeg
Description	For more information, see http://www.si.umich.edu/Art_History/demoarea/details/1977_2.15.html
Source	University of Michigan Museum of Art
Rights	University of Michigan Museum of Art

Source: See Table 8.2.

8.4. VRA 4.0 Overview

The VRA Core Version 4.0 metadata standard is a newer, expanded, XML-based scheme for the cultural heritage community, developed by the Visual Resources Association's Data Standards Committee. In terms of the standardized metadata schemes covered in this book, VRA 4.0 bears a good deal of similarity to MODS, as VRA 3.0 does to Dublin Core. VRA 4.0 includes a formal XML schema and makes use of hierarchically-nested elements and subelements, as well as element attributes, all expressed in an XML syntax. The official VRA Core Schemas and documentation, including an "Introduction," "Element Outline," detailed "Element Description and Tagging Examples," and two formal XML schemas, are now hosted by the Library of Congress Standards website at http://www.loc.gov/standards/vracore/schemas.html. Readers are strongly encouraged to look over the "Introduction" and "Element Description and Tagging Examples," documents. The VRA Core Four website (http://www.vraweb.org/projects/vracore4/index.html) contains some important information about the scheme, including a number of very useful "Cataloging Examples" (http://www.vraweb.org/projects/vracore4/vracore_examples.html) that illustrate a wide range of types of works and collections. For each example, you can view the display metadata in table form or in its native XML form.

VRA Core 4.0 has 19 top-level elements. Actually, the first one is a *wrapper* or container element used to contain the other 18 elements. Some of the elements have subelements and attributes, structured very much like those in MODS. All elements in VRA 4.0 are optional and repeatable, except for the *Work*, *Collection*, or *Image* element, which is required and non-repeatable. After working through MODS in XML, the basic structure of VRA should look fairly familiar to readers, even if the specific elements and attributes are new. Table 8.4 gives a summary overview listing of the VRA 4.0 Elements, Subelements, and Attributes. In this table, attributes are given in parentheses and italics. The scheme also includes the following Global Attributes that can be used with any element or subelement: *dataDate, extent, href, pref, refid, rules, source, vocab, xml:lang*.

The remainder of this section gives an overview of a few noteworthy aspects of the VRA 4.0 scheme. Most of this information is a distillation and summary of selected information in the VRA Core 4.0 "Introduction" (http://www.loc.gov/standards/vracore/VRA_Core4_Intro.pdf). This document is essential reading for anyone interested in VRA Core 4.0.

Agent **Element**. VRA 4.0 has eliminated the *Creator* element used in VRA 3.0 and instead has an *agent* element. The *type* attribute is used to specify the specific type of agent, such as artist, painter, sculptor, donor, commissioner, builder, etc.

Works, Images, and Collections. Like VRA 3.0, VRA 4.0 makes a critical distinction between *works*, which are built or created objects, usually residing in a museum, and *images*, which are visual surrogates of such objects. VRA 4.0 adds the term *collections*, which are aggregates of such objects. It is vital in VRA to connect records for works and their

Table 8.4. VRA 4.0 Elements, Subelements, and Attributes

Elements	Subelements and Attributes
work, collection, or image	*(id)*

agent	attribution
	culture
	dates *(type)*
	   earliestDate *(circa)*
	   latestDate *(circa)*
	name *(type)*
	role

culturalContext	—-
date	*(type)* earliestDate *(circa)* latestDate *(circa)*
description	—-
inscription	author position text *(type)*
location	*(type)* name *(type)* refid *(type)*
material	*(type)*
measurements	*(type, unit)*
relation	*(type, relids)*
rights	*(type)* rightsHolder text
source	name *(type)* refid *(type)*
stateEdition	*(count, num, type)* description name
stylePeriod	—-
subject	term *(type)*
technique	
textref	name *(type)* refid *(type)*
title	*(type)*
worktype	—-

Source: Composite based on VRA Core 4.0 Outline, http:// www.loc.gov/standards/vracore/ VRA_Core4_Outline.pdf, February 28, 2007. Network Development & MARC Standards Office, Library of Congress; Data Standards Committee, Visual Resources Association.

images by using ID numbers to reference each from the other. VRA 4.0 recommends that work IDs begin with "**w_**" (for example, "w_018288"), image IDs with "**i_**", and collection IDs with "**c_**". This is illustrated in the record examples in Section 8.5. VRA 4.0 has a wrapper element that contains all of the other elements in an individual record. The generic element is called *work, collection, or image*, but the actual element name is one of those three terms, depending on which of the three types is being described in the individual metadata record. For a digital image, for example, the element is <image>. The element also contains an *id* attribute, and the value of that attribute is the ID number as discussed above. For example, <image id="i_002874">.

Set **Wrapper Elements**. For every element inside of a *Work, Collection, or Image* element, VRA uses *set* wrapper elements to bind together sets of elements and subelements. For example, everything related to the *Agent* element is put inside of an *AgentSet* wrapper element, as illustrated below.

```
<agentSet>
    <display>Jasper Francis Cropsey (American painter, 1823-
    1900)</display>
    <agent>
        <name type="personal" vocab="ULAN" refid="500012491">
         Cropsey, Jasper Francis</name>
        <dates type="life">
            <earliestDate>1823</earliestDate>
            <latestDate>1900</latestDate>
        </dates>
        <culture>American</culture>
        <role vocab="AAT" refid="300025136">painter</role>
    </agent>
</agentSet>
```

Display, Indexing, and Annotation. VRA allows for the distinction between data for *display* and data for *indexing*. Within each *set* wrapper element, there may be a **display** element containing the metadata to be displayed to the public. The preceding example for *AgentSet* illustrates this. The remaining elements in the set are intended for indexing. The **indexing** elements are formatted to facilitate retrieval, browsing, searching, and so forth. They are tagged in such a way as to make them machine-processable for these purposes. There is also an optional *Notes* subelement that may be used for free-text annotation of element-specific information not already covered in other attributes.

Required/Minimal Elements. Technically, the only required element in VRA is the *Work, Collection,* or *Image* wrapper element. But, in practice, VRA recommends that a minimum-level work record contain the following elements, which provide vital information about the what, who, where, and when of the work: *Work type* (what), *Title* (what), *Agent* (who), *Location* (where), *Date* (when).

Restricted and Unrestricted Schemas. The VRA 4.0 XML Schema actually exists in two versions, one *unrestricted* and the other *restricted*. The **unrestricted** version imposes no restrictions on what values may be entered into any of the elements, subelements, or attributes. The

restricted version of the schema imposes restrictions on the data values which may be entered into the *type* attributes for various elements. The *VRA Core 4.0 Restricted Schema Type Values* document (http://www.loc .gov/standards/vracore/VRA_Core4_Restricted_schema_type_values .pdf) lists of allowable *Type* values for the various elements. The restricted schema is an extension of the unrestricted schema and should be used in addition to it, rather than in place of it.

8.5. VRA 4.0 Record Examples

The example below is a minimal level VRA 4.0 record (adapted and simplified from VRA Core 4.0 Examples, #5 XML, http://www.vraweb.org/ projects/vracore4/xml/example026.xml). It includes only the recommended minimum elements from the VRA Core 4.0 Introduction.

```xml
<?xml version="1.0" encoding="UTF-8" ?>
<vra xmlns="http://www.vraweb.org/vracore4.htm"
 xmlns:xsi="http://www.w3.org/2001/XMLSchema-instance"
 xsi:schemaLocation="http://www.vraweb.org/vracore4.htm
 http://gort.ucsd.edu/escowles/vracore4/vra-4.0-
 restricted.xsd">
 <work id="w_000777">
 <agentSet>
     <agent>
         <name>Cropsey, Jasper Francis, 1823-1900</name>
     </agent>
 </agentSet>
 <dateSet>
     <date>
         <earliestDate>1860</earliestDate>
         <latestDate>1860</latestDate>
     </date>
 </dateSet>
 <locationSet>
     <location>
         <name type>National Gallery of Art (Washington,
         DC, USA</name>
     </location>
 </locationSet>
 <titleSet>
     <title>Autumn - On the Hudson River</title>
 </titleSet>
 <worktypeSet>
     <worktype>oil painting</worktype>
 </worktypeSet>
 </work>
</vra>
```

The preceding example illustrates how an organization can use the VRA 4.0 element set very simply. The following example (pp. 222–224) provides an instance of a detailed XML record for the same work, along with records for two related images, all in a single XML file. Comparing the minimal and full records demonstrates the flexibility of VRA in allowing implementers to decide on the level of detail they want to include in their local applications of this scheme. They are free to select whichever elements, subelements, and attributes they deem valuable for their institution or project and for which they have the time, staff, and software to make feasible.

Detailed VRA 4.0 XML Record Example

```xml
<?xml version="1.0" encoding="UTF-8" ?>

<vra xmlns="http://www.vraweb.org/vracore4.htm"
xmlns:xsi="http://www.w3.org/2001/XMLSchema-
instance"
xsi:schemaLocation="http://www.vraweb.org/vrac
ore4.htm
http://gort.ucsd.edu/escowles/vracore4/vra-
4.0-restricted.xsd">

<work id="w_000777" refid="000597"
source="History of Art Visual Resources
Collection, UCB">

<agentSet>
    <display>Jasper Francis Cropsey (American
    painter, 1823-1900</display>
    <agent>
        <name type="personal" vocab="ULAN"
        refid="500012491">Cropsey, Jasper
        Francis</name>
        <dates type="life">
            <earliestDate>1823</earliestDate>
            <latestDate>1900</latestDate>
        </dates>
        <culture>American</culture>
        <role vocab="AAT" refid="300025136">
        painter</role>
    </agent>
</agentSet>

<dateSet>
    <display>1860</display>
    <date type="creation">
        <earliestDate>1860</earliestDate>
        <latestDate>1860</latestDate>
    </date>
</dateSet>

<descriptionSet>
    <display>Monumental view of the Hudson
    River Valley painted from memory in the
    artist's London studio.</display>
    <description>Monumental view of the Hudson
    River Valley painted from memory in the
    artist's London studio.</description>
</descriptionSet>

<inscriptionSet>
    <display>lower center: Autumn on the Hudson
    River / J. F Cropsey / London
    1860</display>
    <inscription>
        <author vocab="ULAN" refid="500012491">
        Cropsey, Jasper Francis</author>
        <position>lower center</position>
        <text>Autumn on the Hudson River /
        J. F Cropsey / London 1860</text>
    </inscription>
</inscriptionSet>

<locationSet>
    <display>National Gallery of Art
    (Washington, DC, USA) 1963.9.1</display>
    <location type="repository">
        <name type="corporate">National Gallery
        of Art</name>
        <name type="geographic" vocab="TGN"
        refid="7013962">Washington</name>
        <name type="geographic" vocab="TGN"
        refid="7015717">District of
        Columbia</name>
        <name type="geographic" vocab="TGN"
        refid="7012149">United
        States</name>
        <refid type="other">1963.9.1</refid>
    </location>
    <location type="creation">
        <name type="geographic" vocab="TGN"
        refid="7011781">London</name>
        <name type="geographic" vocab="TGN"
        refid="7002445">England</name>
    </location>
</locationSet>

<materialSet>
    <display>oil paint on canvas</display>
    <material type="medium" vocab="AAT"
    refid="300015050">oil
    paint</material>
    <material type="support" vocab="AAT"
    refid="300014078">canvas</material>
</materialSet>
```

(Continued)

Detailed VRA 4.0 XML Record Example *(Continued)*

```
<measurementsSet>
    <display>151.8 x 274.9 cm (59 3/4 x 108
    1/4 in)</display>
    <measurements type="height" unit="cm"
    extent="overall">151.8</measurements>
    <measurements type="width" unit="cm"
    extent="overall">274.9</measurements>
    <measurements type="height" unit="in"
    extent="overall">59.75</measurements>
    <measurements type="width" unit="in"
    extent="overall">108.25</measurements>
</measurementsSet>

<relationSet>
    <relation type="imageIs" relids="i_099890"
    source="History of Art Visual Resources
    Collection, UCB">Full view</relation>
    <relation type="imageIs" relids="i_099989"
    href="http://www.nga.gov/cgi-
    bin/pimage?46191+0+0">Full view</relation>
</relationSet>

<rightsSet>
    <display>Copyright (c)2005 National Gallery
    of Art, Washington, DC</display>
    <rights>
        <text>The contents of this site, including
        all images and text, are for personal,
        educational, non-commercial use only. The
        contents of this site may not be reproduced
        in any form without the permission of the
        National Gallery of Art. National Gallery
        of Art, 4th and Constitution Avenue,
        NW, Washington, D.C. 20565</text>
    </rights>
</rightsSet>

<sourceSet>
    <display>National Gallery of Art Online
    (accessed 7 September 2005)</display>
    <source>
        <name type="electronic">National
        Gallery of Art Online</name>
        <refid type="URI" dataDate="2005-09-
        07">http://www.nga.gov/cgi-bin/pinfo?
        Object=46191+0+none</refid>
    </source>
</sourceSet>

<stylePeriodSet>
    <display>Hudson River School</display>
    <stylePeriod>Hudson River School</stylePeriod>
    <stylePeriod vocab="AAT"
    refid="300172863">Romantic</stylePeriod>
</stylePeriodSet>
```

```
<subjectSet>
    <display>Hudson River (New York, USA); Storm
    King Mountain (Orange county, New York, USA);
    peace; man in harmony with nature</display>
    <subject>
        <term type="geographicPlace"
        vocab="TGN" refid="7013729">Hudson
        River (New York, USA)</term>
        <term type="geographicPlace" vocab="TGN"
        refid="2697783">Storm King Mountain
        (Orange county, New York, USA</term>
        <term type="descriptiveTopic" vocab="AAT"
        refid="300015636">landscapes</term>
        <term type="conceptTopic">man in
        harmony with nature</term>
        <term type="conceptTopic" vocab="AAT"
        refid="300260027">peace</term>
    </subject>
</subjectSet>

<techniqueSet>
    <display>oil painting</display>
    <technique vocab="AAT"
    refid="300178684">oil painting</technique>
</techniqueSet>

<titleSet>
    <display>Autumn - On the Hudson River</display>
    <title type="inscribed" pref="true">Autumn -
    On the Hudson River</title>
</titleSet>

<worktypeSet>
    <display>oil painting</display>
    <worktype vocab="AAT" refid="300033799">oil
    painting</worktype>
</worktypeSet>
</work>

<image id="i_099890" refid="500381" source="History
of Art Visual Resources Collection, UCB">

<locationSet>
    <display>History of Art Visual Resources
    Collection, UCB 500381</display>
    <location type="repository">
        <name type="corporate">History of Art
        Visual Resources Collection, UCB</name>
        <name type="geographic" vocab="TGN"
        refid="7013386">Berkeley</name>
        <name type="geographic" vocab="TGN"
        refid="7007147">California</name>
        <refid type="accession">500381</refid>
    </location>
</locationSet>
```

(Continued)

Detailed VRA 4.0 XML Record Example *(Continued)*

```
<measurementsSet>
    <measurements type="width" unit="mm"
    extent="overall">35</measurements>
    </measurementsSet>

<relationSet>
    <relation type="imageOf"
    relids="w_000777">Autumn - On the Hudson
    River</relation>
</relationSet>

<sourceSet>
    <display>Metropolitan Museum of Art,
    American Paradise: The World of the Hudson
    River School, New York: Abrams, 1987, p.
    207</display>
    <notes>p. 207</notes>
    <source>
        <name type="book">American Paradise:
        The World of the Hudson River
        School</name>
        <refid type="ISBN">0870994964</refid>
    </source>
</sourceSet>

<titleSet>
    <display>Full view</display>
    <title type="descriptive" pref="true">Full
     view</title>
    </titleSet>

<worktypeSet>
    <display>color transparency</display>
    <worktype vocab="AAT" refid="300128364">
     color transparency</worktype>
</worktypeSet>

</image>

<image id="i_099989" refid="c500381" source=
"History of Art Visual Resources Collection,
UCB">

<locationSet>
    <display>History of Art Visual Resources
     Collection, UCB c500381</display>
    <notes>c500381=Image ID number</notes>
    <location type="repository">
        <name type="corporate">History of Art
        Visual Resources Collection,
        UCB</name>
        <refid type="other">c500381</refid>
        <name type="geographic" vocab=
        "TGN" refid="7013386">
        Berkeley</name>
```
```
        <name type="geographic" vocab="TGN"
        refid="7007147">California</name>
    </location>
</locationSet>

<relationSet>
    <relation type="imageOf"
    relids="w_000777">Autumn - On the Hudson
    River</relation>
</relationSet>

<rightsSet>
    <display>Copyright (c)2005 National Gallery
    of Art, Washington, DC</display>
    <rights>
        <text>The contents of this site,
        including all images and text, are for
        personal, educational, non-commercial
        use only. The contents of this site
        may not be reproduced in any form
        without the permission of the National
        Gallery of Art. National Gallery of
        Art, 4th and Constitution Avenue, NW,
        Washington, D.C. 20565</text>
    </rights>
</rightsSet>

<sourceSet>
    <display>National Gallery of Art Online
    (accessed 7 September 2005)</display>
    <source>
        <name type="electronic">National
        Gallery of Art Online (accessed 7
        September 2005)</name>
        <refid
        type="URI">http://www.nga.gov/cgi-
        bin/pimage?46191+0+0</refid>
    </source>
</sourceSet>

<titleSet>
    <display>Full view</display>
    <title type="generalView" pref="true">Full
view</title>
</titleSet>

<worktypeSet>
    <display>digital image</display>
    <worktype vocab="AAT"
     refid="300215302">digital image</worktype>
</worktypeSet>

</image>

</vra>
```

(VRA Core Four Cataloging Examples, Example 26, Landscape painting, XML Record: http://www.vraweb.org/projects/vracore4/xml/example026.xml. Data Standards Committee, Visual Resources Association.)

Notice that this lengthy example is one XML file containing three separate records: one work and two image records. Each record has an ID in its opening <work> or <image> element which is referenced in the <relation> element in the other records, thereby creating a link among them. The <worktype> element tells what kind of work or image is being described: in this case an oil painting, a color transparency, and a digital image, respectively. These records illustrate the most complete use of the <display> elements, which are distinguished from all of the other elements used for indexing. Bold font has been used to highlight some of the main VRA 4.0 elements and subelements, as well as examples of some common attributes. Note especially the use of references to a controlled vocabulary and to the ID number of the specific entry in that vocabulary.

8.6. Summary

This chapter has given a cursory summary overview of the Visual Resources Association Core Categories Versions 3.0 and 4.0, enough to get a general sense of the basic structure of these schemes, the types of elements they contain, some of their important characteristics, and how they compare with Dublin Core and MODS. VRA 3.0 is a relatively simple, non-XML-based scheme with several characteristics in common with Dublin Core. VRA 4.0 is a more elaborate XML-based scheme with several characteristics in common with MODS. Yet each has its own unique characteristics and includes some elements of special interest to museums and of special value to describing works of art and architecture.

Both versions of VRA adhere strictly to the *One-to-One Principle*, creating a single record for each manifestation of an object and linking those records together in a database. Both versions of VRA make a distinction between a *work*, which can encompass many types of creations, but often equates to an object held by a museum, and an *image*, which is a visual, documentary representation of a work. Separate records are created for works and one or more images and are linked together. In VRA 4.0, one method of linking is through the use of ID numbers in the opening <work>, <image>, or <collection> element. VRA 4.0 makes use of *Set* wrapper elements and allows for the option of including separate elements used for public display in addition to elements used for indexing within each set. VRA 4.0 includes a recommended minimal set of elements, but requires only the *Work, Collection,* or *Image* wrapper element. Both versions of VRA allow implementers great latitude in the level of detail, or granularity, at which they choose to implement VRA in their own applications.

▶ Companion Website

See this book's companion website at **http://www.neal-schuman.com/ metadata-digital-collections** for Chapter 8 review questions, suggestions for exercises, links to online VRA documentation, and other resources.

Reference

Visual Resources Association. 2011. "VRA Core 3.0." Accessed January 10. http://www.vraweb.org/projects/vracore3/.

Metadata Interoperability, Shareability, and Quality

9.1. Interoperability

This chapter deals with a set of interrelated topics all having to do with the usability of your local metadata outside of its original closed-system context. This includes viability of metadata for future system migration; sharing metadata within an institution or consortium or with a third-party aggregator; issues of metadata harvesting, especially the use of the OAI harvesting protocol; metadata processing, conversion, and aggregation within a repository of metadata from multiple sources; crosswalks and mapping among different element sets; and metadata quality indicators and assessment methods.

Most of these topics fall under the umbrella term of **interoperability**. "Interoperability is the ability of multiple systems with different hardware and software platforms, data structures, and interfaces to exchange data with minimal loss of content and functionality" (NISO, 2004: 2). The concept of metadata interoperability in its broadest sense encompasses the topics of metadata sharing, harvesting, conversion, and aggregation.

9.2. Short- and Long-Term Metadata Viability

Although this chapter focuses primarily on issues of interoperability in the context of current and future metadata sharing, harvesting, and aggregating, many of the same issues that pertain to these contexts also apply to the context of interoperability between current local systems and future local systems. In most metadata projects, the focus of your work is necessarily on digitizing resources, creating metadata for them using current system software, and making the collections available online in a timely fashion with limited time, staff, and budget. But it is also important to think ahead to the future. How will your metadata fare with upgrades and changes to your current digital collection management software or system? Are you certain that you will always use the same software, system, or vendor product? What if a superior product is developed and critical mass of institutions like your own moves to that platform? How well will your current metadata be migratable into the new system? Will a new system be able to ingest and use any of your nonstandard local elements, or will it import only elements from a standardized scheme, such as Qualified or Simple Dublin Core?

If you are currently using Dublin Core, will you always use it? What if MODS or some other richer scheme becomes the widely preferred metadata element set of choice for digital library collections in the near future? How well will your current metadata map into that scheme? Will your nonstandard local element names be usable? Have you correctly used DC elements and qualifiers such that your metadata values will map into a new system or element set correctly, meaningfully, and usably, making your resources findable and interpretable by your users? What if the Linked Data/Semantic Web movement takes off in the near future within cultural heritage communities? Will your metadata play well in that environment?

For the most part, designing local metadata schemes and creating current metadata with an eye toward future interoperability will entail the same awareness and practices that make for interoperable, good quality, and sharable metadata in the current harvesting and aggregating context discussed in the following sections of this chapter.

9.3. Metadata Sharing, Harvesting, and Aggregating

In addition to its original context, which is often designed for a specific collection, cultural heritage metadata is also often shared among multiple collections within an institution, among different institutions, and among various external metadata services and repositories.

Users may access your digital resources in several overlapping ways. First, they may explore the resources within each of your individual collections in the context of its own unique web interface, with its own set of unique field names and search and browse options. But, secondly, they may also search across all of your institution's diverse digital collections, which might have very different types of resources and subject content. For example, users may search or browse the University of Washington Libraries' Ethnomusicology Musical Instrument Collection in its own interface at http://content.lib.washington.edu/ethnomusic web/index.html, but they may also access and search across all of the University of Washington Libraries' digital collections at http://content .lib.washington.edu/.

Furthermore, not all digital collections are created by, or stored in, an individual institution. Some collections are built as collaborative enterprises among several contributing institutions. Another common scenario is for individual institutions to create their own local digital collections and metadata but to also make these available as part of a larger consortium.

Such a consortium may be at the state level, or it may be established among a group of institutions from a group of neighboring states or among those with similar interests across the country or the world. Among a plethora of examples are the North Carolina ECHO (Exploring Cultural Heritage Online) collaborative at http://www.ncecho.org, the Mountain West Digital Library at http://mwdl.org/, and the National Science Digital Library at http://www.nsdl.org/.

In many of these cases, an individual institution exposes its own local metadata for automated harvesting by the consortium into a shared metadata repository, where it is aggregated with metadata from many other institutions. The most common method of doing this is by means of the Open Archives Initiative Protocol for Metadata Harvesting (OAI, 2008), covered in the next section in this chapter. The OAI-PMH requires, at minimum, a set of Simple Dublin Core metadata elements encoded in XML. This may be accompanied by a richer set of metadata, such as Qualified Dublin Core, MODS, or VRA. But in many, perhaps most, current cases, only the metadata harvested as Simple Dublin Core is used.

Once local metadata is harvested and aggregated into an external repository, the rich, collection-specific local element names, along with most of the original context of the metadata itself, are lost. This complicates the process of metadata design and creation. It is very important to keep metadata harvesting and aggregation in mind when designing a local metadata scheme for a digital collection. This is also one reason why it is important for most projects to include a mapping of each local metadata element or field to one of the 15 Simple Dublin Core elements.

9.4. OAI Metadata Harvesting

The **Open Archives Initiative (OAI)** is an initiative to develop and promote interoperability standards to facilitate the dissemination of web-accessible content through interoperable repositories for metadata sharing (Open Archives Initiative website, http://www.openarchives.org/). It originally arose out of the e-prints community, which needed a simple interoperability framework for accessing electronic scholarly papers, called e-prints, especially in the sciences. The OAI has since expanded to many other information communities that realized the value of the open archives approach. Many digital libraries, archives, and museums today use OAI's protocol to expose their digital collections metadata for harvesting.

The **OAI Protocol for Metadata Harvesting (OAI-PMH)** is a mechanism developed by the OAI for harvesting metadata records from diverse repositories. It is based on HTTP (Hypertext Transfer Protocol) and XML (Extensible Markup Language), which are both open standards. It provides a relatively simple method for data providers to make their internal metadata available to external information services. The OAI-PMH allows metadata from many sources to be *aggregated*: that is, gathered together in one database by a service provider. Service providers can provide search and navigation interfaces to provide access to the aggregated metadata. Note that the OAI-PMH does not provide

---

OAI Participants

Participation in OAI harvesting and aggregating is purely voluntary and involves two broad categories of participants.

- **Data Providers** are the owners of the digital resource content and creators of the original metadata for those resources. They maintain one or more repositories (web servers) that support the OAI protocol as a means of exposing the metadata about their content. They may choose to register and publicize the fact that they have adopted the OAI protocol. CONTENTdm and other digital content management systems have a built-in capability of exposing metadata in Simple Dublin Core XML format for OAI harvesting.

- **Service Providers** are outside agencies that harvest and aggregate metadata from selected data providers to serve communities of interest. Their harvesting systems issue machine-processable OAI-PMH requests to data providers' exposed metadata and use the ingested metadata as a basis for building value-added services. These institutions may choose to register and publicize their existence as OAI service providers.

OAI Metadata Formats

The OAI protocol supports several metadata formats, including Qualified Dublin Core, MODS, MARC, and TEI, but it always requires a set of Simple Dublin Core metadata elements encoded in XML, regardless of whether or not a richer metadata format is included in addition. Simple Dublin Core in XML provides a basic level of interoperability for all service providers. Mapping among multiple metadata formats would place too great a burden on many service providers. The 15 simple DC elements have developed as a de facto standard for simple cross-discipline metadata and have therefore been selected as the common metadata set for OAI.

Local repositories, as has been shown previously in this book, often use their own local DC element labels, extensions, and qualifiers; their own unique nonstandard collection specific element names; and/or other metadata schemes such as MODS or VRA. If they are to share their metadata through the OAI-PMH, these institutions must be able to internally map their metadata to the 15 simple DC elements in order to make them accessible for harvesting by the OAI protocol.

Each data provider is also free to offer metadata in one or more other schemes in addition to simple DC from its server. A harvester can request that metadata be provided in a scheme other than DC as part of the harvest request. This works only when both a particular data provider and a particular service provider use that metadata scheme, and it still requires that all metadata sets be structured as XML data with a corresponding XML schema for validation.

An excellent resource is the brief, two-page "Summary of OAI Metadata Best Practices" available at http://www.diglib.org/architectures/oai/imls2004/training/MetadataFinal.pdf.

the ability to perform *federated searching* across diverse metadata or databases. It only makes it possible to bring the data together into one centralized repository. Figure 9.1 offers a rough graphical depiction of OAI harvesting at its simplest level.

The following example contains an example of the portion of an OAI message that contains Simple Dublin Core metadata in **OAI DC XML**:

```
<metadata>

<oai_dc:dc
    xmlns:oai_dc="http://www.openarchives.org/OAI/2.0/oai_dc/"
    xmlns:dc="http://purl.org/dc/elements/1.1/"
    xmlns:xsi="http://www.w3.org/2001/XMLSchema-instance"
    xsi:schemaLocation="http://www.openarchives.org/OAI/2.0/oai_dc/
    http://www.openarchives.org/OAI/2.0/oai_dc.xsd">

  <dc:title>Using Structural Metadata to Localize
    Experience of Digital Content</dc:title>
  <dc:creator>Dushay, Naomi</dc:creator>
  <dc:subject>Digital Libraries</dc:subject>
  <dc:description>With the increasing technical
    sophistication of both information consumers and
    providers, there is increasing demand for more
    meaningful experiences of digital information. We
    present a framework that separates digital object
    experience, or rendering, from digital object storage
    and manipulation, so the  rendering can be tailored to
    particular communities of users.</dc:description>
  <dc:description>Comment: 23 pages including 2
    appendices, 8 figures</dc:description>
  <dc:date>2001-12-14</dc:date>
  <dc:type>e-print</dc:type>
  <dc:identifier>http://arXiv.org/abs/cs/
    0112017</dc:identifier>

</oai_dc:dc>

</metadata>
```

(OAI, 2008.)

The OAIster database is one of the best-known national OAI service providers, containing several million harvested and aggregated metadata

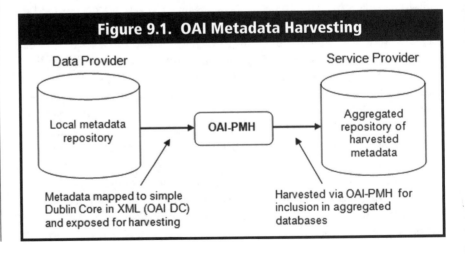

Figure 9.1. OAI Metadata Harvesting

Data Provider

Service Provider

Local metadata repository → OAI-PMH → Aggregated repository of harvested metadata

Metadata mapped to simple Dublin Core in XML (OAI DC) and exposed for harvesting

Harvested via OAI-PMH for inclusion in aggregated databases

records for digital resources from thousands of contributors (http://www.oclc.org/oaister/).

> OAIster began at the University of Michigan in 2002 funded by a grant from the Andrew W. Mellon Foundation and with the purpose of establishing a retrieval service for publicly available digital library resources provided by the research library community. OAIster has since grown to become one of the largest aggregations of records pointing to open archive collections in the world. In 2009, OCLC formed a partnership with the University of Michigan to provide continued access to open archive collections through the OAIster database. ("History of OAIster," http://www.oclc.org/us/en/oaister/about/default.htm. Reprinted with permission.)

The OAIster database can be searched at http://oaister.worldcat.org/. Figures 9.2 and 9.3 show OAIster advanced search functions for fielded searching and limiting searches by Resource Type.

9.5. Metadata Mapping and Crosswalks

Mapping metadata elements and their values from one scheme or element set to those in another scheme can be done by humans or by machines. Element mapping provides a means for some level of semantic interoperability among diverse metadata schemes. But in roughly the same way that

Figure 9.2. OAIster Advanced Search: Fielded Search Options

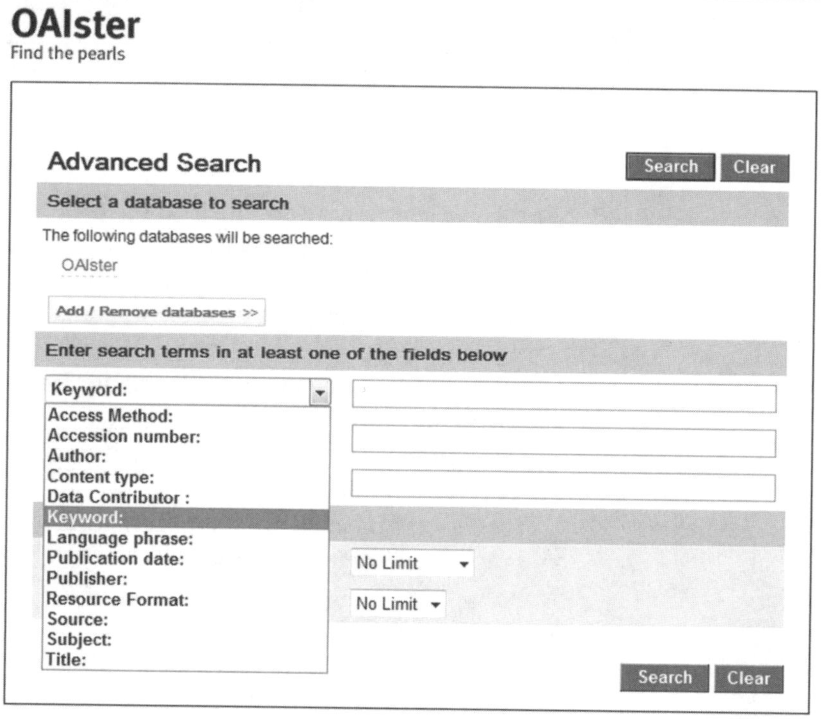

Source: http://oaister.worldcat.org/advancedsearch. OCLC Online Computer Library Center, Inc. Reproduced with permission.

Figure 9.3. OAIster Advanced Search: Resource Type Limit Options

Advanced Search   Search | Clear

Select a database to search

The following databases will be searched:

OAIster

Add / Remove databases >>

Enter search terms in at least one of the fields below

Keyword: ▼ [   ]

Title: ▼ [   ]

Author: ▼ [   ]

Limit results by (optional)

Language Phrase Limiter: No Limit ▼

Resource Type Phrase: No Limit ▼

                             No Limit
                             Audio
                             Dataset   Search | Clear
                             Image
                             Text
                             Video

Source: See Figure 9.2.

you can never make an exact translation of a text in one human language into another, you cannot map from one metadata scheme to another with a precise one-to-one correspondence and without some loss of meaning.

The terms *mapping* and *crosswalks* are most often used interchangeably. But some people use the term *crosswalks* to refer specifically to visual representations, usually in the form of tables, that show the element correlations between two or more different schemes. In contrast, they use the term *mapping* to refer to the intellectual process of examining two schemes and deciding which elements in one scheme map to which in the other. *Mapping* may also refer to the process of actually converting a set of metadata from one scheme to another, whether by a human being or by a machine. In this usage, *crosswalks* are the documents of those mappings or the programs that make them happen. Crosswalks are specifications for mapping one metadata standard to another: the source standard to the target standard. There are limits to how far this verbal distinction should be pressed, because far more often than not, the terms *mappings* and *crosswalks* are used in metadata literature and practice to refer to essentially the same thing.

Several metadata element mappings/crosswalks have been developed. Some are official, some nonofficial. The MODS, VRA, and MARC websites offer a number of mapping tables (or crosswalks). The MODS "Conversions" page (http://www.loc.gov/standards/mods/mods-conversions .html) includes the following MODS Mappings: MARC to MODS, MODS to MARC, RDA to MODS, Dublin Core (simple) to MODS, and MODS to Dublin Core (simple). These are textual documents, not machine-readable programs for automated mapping. The MODS XSLT style sheets available from the same MODS "Conversions" page, however, can be used for machine transformation of XML metadata documents, if you have the right XML processing software. The "VRA Core Categories, Version 3.0" document (http://www.vraweb.org/projects/vracore3/categories.html) includes a mapping of each VRA 3.0 element to Dublin Core. The "VRA Core 4.0 Element Description" document (http://www.loc.gov/standards/vracore/VRA_Core4_Element_Description.pdf) includes mappings from each VRA 4.0 element to VRA Core 2.0, VRA Core 3.0, CDWA, Dublin Core, and CCO. For a list of MARC mappings, see: http://www.loc.gov/marc/marcdocz.html. Another useful source is "Metadata: Mapping between Metadata Formats" by Michael Day, UKOLN (the UK Office for Library and Information Networking): http://www.ukoln.ac.uk/metadata/interoperability/.

Metadata schemes lie on a wide spectrum of richness and detail, from the extremely simple and general to the extremely complex and specialized, and many levels in between. Mapping from one scheme to another is virtually impossible without metadata degradation. This happens especially when mapping from a richer scheme to a simpler one and when mapping from a specialized scheme to a general one. It is useful to consider mapping from a richer local scheme to Simple Dublin Core for purposes of harvesting as OAI DC XML. Table 9.1 shows a set of relatively richer local metadata elements and their mapping to Qualified Dublin Core,

Semantic Element Mapping Problems

1. Single versus multiple elements for the same concept
   - One-to-many
   - Many-to-one

2. Specific versus generic elements for the same concept
   - Free text to controlled vocabulary
   - Controlled vocabulary to free text
   - Different controlled vocabularies

3. No equivalence for a concept
   - Extra elements in source
   - Unresolved mandatory elements in target

4. Data intended for display versus data intended for hidden indexing and retrieval

5. Combinations of the above for a single element mapping

(Adapted from St. Pierre and LaPlant, 1998.)

Table 9.1. Local Metadata with Mapping to Dublin Core

Local Element	DC Element	Value
Title / Name of Bridge	Title	Manchester Street Bridge, Sauk County, Wisconsin
Date of Construction	Date Created	1896
Architect or Firm	Creator	Lassig Bridge and Iron Works
Type of Bridge	Subject	Truss bridges
Bridge Dimensions	Format Extent	128.9 ft. long; 13.7 ft. deck width
County	Coverage Spatial	Sauk County
Resource Type	Type	Still Image
Photographer	Creator	Kramer, Paul Jacob
Date of Photograph	Date Created	1955
Original Photograph Size	Format Extent	35 mm
Original Photograph Medium	Format Medium	Black & white slide
Original Photograph ID Number	Identifier	171, 33b-765
Original Photograph Collection	Relation Is Part Of	Paul J. Kramer Archival Photograph Collection
Original Photograph Repository	Contributor	Hagenville University Archives
Digital Collection	Relation Is Part Of	Bridges of Wisconsin
Digital Image Copyright	Rights	Copyright © 2009 Hagenville University
Digital Image Publisher	Publisher	Hagenville University
Digital File Format	Format	image/jpeg
Digital File Number	Identifier	WB0078736
Date Digitized	Date Created	2008-12-15

Thomas Baker and Pete Johnston have written about Dublin Core as a useful kind of *pidgin* language (Baker, 2000; Johnston, 2006). That is, it is a highly simplified kind of language that allows people speaking different languages to communicate with one another using an extremely limited shared vocabulary and syntax for purposes such as basic commercial transactions, without having to know the full richness of each individual language. In this sense, Dublin Core serves as a kind of *lowest common denominator* set of metadata elements. Metadata from other richer and more specialized schemes can be mapped into and out of Dublin Core for purposes of metadata sharing.

The simplicity of Dublin Core and its widespread adoption in many cultural heritage, e-commerce, and other web environments make it highly interoperable. In many respects Dublin Core was designed to complement other resource descriptions, not to replace them. Dublin Core is not necessarily to be always used instead of other more specialized or complex metadata schemes—but rather to be used in addition to them, serving as a common metadata language with a common, core set of descriptive elements, so that elements from these other schemes can be automatically translated to and from DC and thus be understood by a common user interface.

The OAI metadata harvesting protocol is in effect using Dublin Core this way. OAI content providers may submit their own richer metadata elements, but they must also supply a set of Simple Dublin Core elements as a minimum requirement for interoperability, and these must be encoded in XML.

Dublin Core may also be further used as a kind of *switching* language between various more complex metadata standards, a middle language for translation from one language to another.

Table 9.2. Local Metadata after Mapping to Simple Dublin Core

DC Element	Value
Title	Manchester Street Bridge, Sauk County, Wisconsin
Date	1896
Creator	Lassig Bridge and Iron Works
Subject	Truss bridges
Format	128.9 ft. long; 13.7 ft. deck width
Coverage	Sauk County
Type	Still Image
Creator	Kramer, Paul Jacob
Date	1955
Format	35 mm
Format	Black & white slide
Identifier	171, 33b-765
Relation	Paul J. Kramer Archival Photograph Collection
Contributor	Hagenville University Archives
Relation	Bridges of Wisconsin
Rights	Copyright © 2009 Hagenville University
Publisher	Hagenville University
Format	image/jpeg
Identifier	WB0078736
DateCreated	2008-12-15

and Table 9.2 shows the resulting metadata after mapping to Simple Dublin Core.

Chapter 7 included the topic of mapping from Simple Dublin Core to MODS as an introduction to the larger topic of element mapping and as an aid to moving from the study of Dublin Core to the study of MODS. That was an instance of mapping from a simpler scheme to a richer one, and the mapping could make use of only a small number of MODS elements and a limited level of detail. This chapter turns now to look at the reverse mapping, from MODS to Simple Dublin Core, as a further example of mapping from a richer, hierarchical scheme to a simpler, flat scheme. Table 9.3 presents the official MODS to Dublin Core Mapping Table, and Table 9.4 presents the official <typeOfResource> conversion table.

9.6. Metadata Conversion and Processing

Harvesting and aggregating agencies often need to perform machine conversion and processing of the metadata they ingest so that it conforms to their internal element set and metadata value specifications. They may, for example, *normalize* content to remove pieces of punctuation that will interfere with indexing in their aggregated repository. Or they might make automated corrections to, say, any DC *Type* element values

Table 9.3. MODS to Dublin Core Metadata Element Set Mapping

MODS element	Dublin Core element	Notes
<titleInfo><title>	Title	1. For multiple MODS titles use multiple instances of dc:title. 2. MODS allows <titleInfo> subelements to be parsed: <nonSort>, <title>, <subTitle>, <partNumber>, <partName> MODS subelements should be concatenated in Dublin Core, separated by a space or other form of punctuation.
<name><namePart>	Creator Contributor	1. MODS puts all names in a repeated<name> with type of contribution indicated in <role>. It does not make the explicit distinction between creator and contributor in terms of primary vs. secondary roles. An application may wish to designate use of Creator or Contributor for all MODS names or use the role value to determine which DC element is used. 2. MODS allows <name> subelements to be parsed: <namePart>, <displayForm>, <affiliation>, <role>, <description> MODS subelements should be concatenated in Dublin Core, separated by a space or other form of punctuation.

<subject>
  <topic>
  <name>
  <occupation>
<classification>
	Subject	

 <note> <tableOfContents>	Description	
<originInfo><publisher>	Publisher	
<originInfo><dateIssued> <originInfo><dateCreated> <originInfo><dateCaptured> <originInfo><dateOther>	Date	
<typeOfResource> <genre>	Type	1. Use separate instances of Type for each MODS element value. 2. If converting MODS typeOfResource values to Dublin Core Resource Type values, see conversion details below. If MODS <genre> contains authority="dct", that may be used in dc:type and typeOfResource dropped.
<physicalDescription> <internetMediaType> <extent> <form>	Format	Use separate instances of Format for each MODS element value.
<identifier> <location> <URL>	Identifier	It is suggested that the identifier type be retained and associated with the identifier value.
<language>	Language	
<relatedItem>	Relation	<relatedItem> data is parsed into subelements in MODS (any MODS element may be used). Implementations may wish to consider the relatedItem type to determine mapping. If type= "constituent", a full description may be given under relatedItem and conversion may result in an incomprehensible value. Alternatively, an application may wish to map only some elements under <relatedItem>, e.g., <titleInfo> and <identifier> or <location> if a full MODS description is given. For example, if giving a reference to a resource fully described in MODS relatedItem, one could use: <relatedItem><identifier> *and/or* title of a resource: <relatedItem><titleInfo><title>

<subject>
  <geographic>
  <temporal>
  <hierarchicalGeographic>
  <cartographics>
	Coverage	

<accessCondition>	Rights	
<recordInfo>		

Source: MODS to Dublin Core Metadata Element Set Mapping, Version 3, June 7, 2005: http://www.loc.gov/standards/mods/mods-dcsimple.html. Network Development & MARC Standards Office, Library of Congress.

Table 9.4. Conversion of MODS TypeOfResource Values to DC Resource Type Vocabulary

MODS typeOfResource	DC Type value
typeOfResource collection="yes"	Collection (use in addition to specific value below)
software and mods:genre="database"	Dataset
cartographic material	Image
multimedia	InteractiveResource
moving image	MovingImage
three-dimensional object	PhysicalObject
software and mods:genre="online system or service"	Service
sound recording, sound recording-musical, sound recording-nonmusical	Sound
still image	StillImage
software	Software
text, notated music	Text

Source: "MODS to Dublin Core Metadata Element Set Mapping," Version 3, June 7, 2005: http://www.loc.gov/standards/mods/mods-dcsimple.html. Network Development & MARC Standards Office, Library of Congress.

that do not conform to the DCMI Type Vocabulary scheme. They might change the mapping of some elements to ones that conform to their repository's usage. For example, they might decide that the kind of data that they put into their DC *Source* element would be better put into a *Relation* element within their repository.

Being able to look at your local documentation can help aggregating agencies make such determinations, because they know how you interpreted the elements, what kind of values you put into them, whether or not you applied any controlled vocabularies to those values, and so forth. You may, for example, have decided to handle data entry for uncertain dates and date ranges following a particular pattern. As long as the metadata values have been entered consistently, the harvesting agency may be able to write a program to perform data conversion. This goes as well for mapping, processing, or converting metadata into a future system or richer element set. For example, if you have used a convention such as *circa 1940* for approximate dates, a script could be written to strip out the *circa_* and to map the remaining value of *1940* into a field designated as an approximate date or into an XML schema with a type attribute of *approximate*, as in MODS, or some other variation of this sort.

It is also theoretically possible to make use of current nonstandard, collection-specific local element names for future mapping and processing purposes. For example, if in your local scheme you have designed separate elements to contain metadata values applicable to the original resource and to the digital resource, it could be possible to write a script to map these values to new element and data structures that better accommodate original versus digital information and better uphold the *One-to-One Principle*. A local element such as *Date Original* or *Format Original* could be mapped to a separate record for the original item, and *Date Digital* or *Format Digital* to a separate record for the digital item, and these records linked together, if such a system became widely available and normative in the cultural heritage metadata world. Or mapping could theoretically be made into a MODS or MODS-like <relatedItem> structure, with all of the information about the original item included as subelements inside of a <relatedItem type="original"> container or wrapper element.

Some institutions, such as digital libraries, may take over responsibility for collections previously created by some other agency. For example, a library's digitization unit might take over the management of a digital slide collection originally created by the university's art history department. The department may have created metadata for these slides using their own home-grown set of metadata fields and standards for data input. The digital library will need to decide how to map the existing element into its own scheme and/or into Dublin Core or another standard element set. They may also need to do various kinds of normalization, manipulation, or *massaging* of the metadata values in order for them to *play well* with other metadata in the local environment, which becomes in effect a kind of aggregated environment.

9.7. Example of Metadata Harvesting, Processing, and Aggregating

This section presents an actual instance of two different ways in which local metadata, residing in a CONTENTdm digital collection, has been harvested as Simple Dublin Core and differently processed and mapped to two different aggregators' specifications. The metadata represents the digital image shown in Figure 9.4. Take a careful look at the metadata in

Figure 9.4. Digital Image

Source: From the Archives Department and Digital Collections, University of Wisconsin–Milwaukee Libraries. Image reproduced with permission.

the following three examples and compare what is done with local fields before and after harvesting, and how the two different service providers handle the same metadata fields. These three examples illustrate (1) the metadata in its original local context with local element names, (2) the metadata after OAI harvesting as Simple Dublin Core into a statewide repository, and (3) the metadata after OAI harvesting as Simple Dublin Core into an international repository.

Table 9.5 depicts the original local metadata in the Milwaukee Repertory Theater Photographic History digital collection (http://www.uwm.edu/Library/digilib/milrep/index.htm).

Table 9.6 depicts the same metadata after having been harvested, processed, and aggregated into the Wisconsin Heritage Online (WHO) statewide digital collections repository (http://www.wisconsinheritage.org/).

Table 9.7 depicts the same metadata after having been harvested, processed, and aggregated into the OAIster international metadata repository (http://oaister.worldcat.org/).

Table 9.5. Original Local Metadata

Performance	1977-1978: A Christmas Carol
Description	From left: Larry Shue as Bob Cratchit, the Cratchit family, Henry Strozier as Ebenezer Scrooge, and Durward McDonald as Spirit of Christmas Present
Actor(s)	Shue, Larry
Strozier, Henry	McDonald, Durward
Play Title	A Christmas Carol
Author	Dickens, Charles
Season	1977-1978
Stage	Pabst Theater
Director	Berman, Norman L.
Set Designer	Idoine, Christopher M.
Costume Designer	Covey, Elizabeth
Lighting Designer	Winkler, Richard
Subject	Theater--Wisconsin--Milwaukee; Milwaukee Repertory Theater
Type	Image
Original Collection	Avery Mark Photography. Photographs, 1977-1994
Photographer	Avery, Mark
Date	1977
Original Item Location	UWM Manuscript Collection 155. Box 1, vol. 2, Assign. D, file no. A77070, row 1, no. 2
Original Item Dimensions	35 mm
Original Item Medium	Negative
Repository	Archives. University of Wisconsin-Milwaukee Libraries
Finding Aid	http://www.uwm.edu/Library/arch/findaids/uwmmss155.htm
Digital ID	av00053
Rights	The Board of Regents of the University of Wisconsin System
Digital Publisher	University of Wisconsin-Milwaukee Libraries

Source: Digital Collections, University of Wisconsin–Milwaukee Libraries. Reproduced with permission.

Table 9.6. Harvested Metadata in Statewide Consortial Repository	
Title:	1977-1978: A Christmas Carol
Creator:	Shue, Larry / Strozier, Henry / McDonald, Durward / Dickens, Charles / Berman, Norman L. / Avery, Mark
Contributor:	Idoine, Christopher M. / Covey, Elizabeth / Winkler, Richard
Date:	1977-1978
Date:	1977
Place/Time:	Pabst Theater
Publisher:	University of Wisconsin-Milwaukee Libraries
Description:	From left: Larry Shue as Bob Cratchit, the Cratchit family, Henry Strozier as Ebenezer Scrooge, and Durward McDonald as Spirit of Christmas Present
Subjects:	Theater--Wisconsin--Milwaukee / Milwaukee Repertory Theater
Type:	Image
Format:	35 mm / Negative
Identifier:	av00053
Is Part Of:	Milwaukee Repertory Theater Photographic History
Related Items:	http://www.uwm.edu/Library/arch/findaids/uwmmss155.htm
Related Items:	Avery Mark Photography. Photographs, 1977-1994 UWM Manuscript Collection 155. Box 1, vol. 2, Assign. D, file no. A77070, row 1, no. 2 Archives. University of Wisconsin-Milwaukee Libraries
Rights:	The Board of Regents of the University of Wisconsin System
Submitter:	UWM Libraries Digital Collections
Local Identifier:	WHO.MkeRepertory.93.bib
Source: Wisconsin Heritage Online Digital Collections: http://www.wisconsinheritage.org/.	

In the examples in Tables 9.6, and 9.7, the metadata from Table 9.5 has been harvested as Simple Dublin Core in OAI DC XML. The nonstandard local element names have not been picked up by the aggregating service providers. Each aggregator has done its own unique kinds of mapping and processing of the metadata to conform to its own local metadata element set and specifications.

In the Wisconsin Heritage Online instance in Table 9.6, names entered into the local *Actor(s)*, *Author*, *Director*, and *Photographer* elements appear in a single *Creator* element, separated by a space-slash-space. Each of these local elements was mapped in University of Wisconsin–Milwaukee's local CONTENTdm database to the Dublin Core *Creator* element, and this is the metadata that the harvesting agency ingested. The Wisconsin Heritage Online database uses the space-slash-space as the machine-readable designator to instruct the computer to index each name separately even though they appear in a single *Creator* field. The *Set Designer*, *Costume Designer*, and *Lighting Designer* elements were mapped internally to the Dublin Core *Contributor* element, and they have been harvested as such in the Wisconsin Heritage Online database. The *Season* and *Date* elements were both mapped to DC *Date*, and have been harvested into two separate *Date* elements in Wisconsin Heritage Online. *Original Item Dimensions* and *Original Item Medium* were both mapped to DC *Format*. Close

Table 9.7. Harvested Metadata in International OAIster Repository	
1977-1978: A Christmas Carol;	
Author:	Mark Avery; Christopher M Idoine; Elizabeth Covey; Richard Winkler; Larry Shue; All authors
Publisher:	University of Wisconsin-Milwaukee Libraries 1977-1978; 1977;
Edition/Format:	Visual material : Clipart/images/graphics : Picture : English
Database:	OAIster
Summary:	From left: Larry Shue as Bob Cratchit, the Cratchit family, Henry Strozier as Ebenezer Scrooge, and Durward McDonald as Spirit of Christmas Present.
Details:	
Title:	1977-1978: A Christmas Carol;
Database Name:	OAIster
All Authors / Contributors:	Mark Avery; Christopher M Idoine; Elizabeth Covey; Richard Winkler; Larry Shue; Henry Strozier; Durward McDonald; Charles Dickens; Norman L Berman
Notes:	Negative. Mode of access: World Wide Web. The Board of Regents of the University of Wisconsin System.
Description:	35 mm.
Other Titles:	A Christmas Carol;; Milwaukee Repertory Theater Photographic History.
Year:	1977-1978; 1977;
Publisher:	University of Wisconsin-Milwaukee Libraries 1977-1978; 1977;
Details:	Mode of access: World Wide Web.
Access:	http://collections.lib.uwm.edu/u?/mkerep,93
General Info:	The Board of Regents of the University of Wisconsin System.
Abstract:	From left: Larry Shue as Bob Cratchit, the Cratchit family, Henry Strozier as Ebenezer Scrooge, and Durward McDonald as Spirit of Christmas Present.
Identifier:	Theater--Wisconsin--Milwaukee Milwaukee Repertory Theater
Source: OAIster Database: http://oaister.worldcat.org/. OCLC Online Computer Library Center, Inc. Reproduced with OCLC's permission.	

examination of the Wisconsin Heritage Online harvested metadata reveals other mappings and combinations of metadata values, with some values not harvested, and a new *Submitter* element added, possibly automatically generated based on a consortial required element for the member institution submitting the metadata.

The same local metadata, as mapped to Simple Dublin Core, has been harvested, mapped, and processed in yet different ways in the OAIster database, according to its own internal harvesting and processing rules and methods of aggregating, labeling, and displaying metadata harvested from thousands of different contributors. The first section of Table 9.7 shows the initial abbreviated display, and the second section the detailed display. Notice the OAIster field names *Author*, *Edition/Format*, *Summary*, *Year*, *Details*, *General Info*, and the like, and the metadata values that have been mapped into these fields. Tables 9.5, 9.6, and 9.7 provide concrete examples of different ways in which the same Simple Dublin Core metadata is processed and labeled by two different metadata harvesting and aggregating agencies.

9.8. Good Quality and Shareable Metadata

Metadata quality and shareability have been the topics of a number of studies and papers within the past decade (Bruce and Hillmann, 2004; Dushay and Hillmann, 2003; Han et al., 2009; Hutt and Riley, 2005; Jackson et al., 2008). Bruce and Hillmann (2004) discuss seven characteristics of quality metadata, presented here in a highly abbreviated list format.

1. **Completeness**. Choose an element set for describing resources as completely as is economically feasible and apply that element set as completely as possible.

2. **Accuracy**. Metadata is correct and factual and conforms to syntax of the element set in use.

3. **Provenance**. Provide information about the expertise of the person(s) creating the original metadata and its transformation history.

4. **Conformance to expectations**. Metadata elements, use of controlled vocabularies, and robustness should match the expectations of the user community. This may be particularly problematic for OAI data providers because sharing metadata via OAI allows it to be used by a wider variety of communities than previously targeted.

5. **Logical consistency and coherence**. Element usage matches standard definitions and is consistently applied.

6. **Timeliness**. "Currency": metadata is kept up to date up with changes to the resource it describes. "Lag": it is problematic when a resource is made available prior to the availability of its metadata.

7. **Accessibility**. Proper association of metadata with the resource it describes and readability by target users.

One notable attempt to articulate widely applicable, general guidelines for sharable metadata is an outcome of a joint initiative between the Digital Library Federation (DLF) and the National Science Digital Library (NSDL) called "Best Practices for OAI Data Provider Implementations and Shareable Metadata." The primary result is a collaborative, user-editable wiki (DLF, 2007). A related outcome is a document of the same name (DLF/NSDL Working Group on OAI PMH Best Practices, 2007). The wiki makes the point that "quality metadata may or may not be shareable metadata" (DLF, 2008). It also lists a number of benefits of creating shareable metadata, as follows:

Benefits of creating shareable metadata

Creating shareable metadata requires an investment of time. However, there are many benefits gained from making this investment.

The first and perhaps most significant benefit to creating shareable metadata is that it will be interoperable, or meaningful when combined with metadata from other sources. By using metadata schemas and rules for creating metadata values similar to those used by others, your resources can meaningfully appear in search results alongside related resources from other metadata providers.

When creating true shareable metadata, your resources are more likely to be found when pooled together with resources from other providers, rather than not being retrieved by searchers due to inconsistencies or gaps in description. Your resources therefore will receive more exposure, and end-users will have the opportunity to make previously unseen connections between your resources and those from other metadata providers.

Finally, creating shareable metadata increases the number of access points for your resources available to end-users. Aspects of a resource not previously explicitly described are often added when metadata creators think in terms of shareable metadata. (DLF, 2008)

9.9. Assessing Metadata Quality

Bruce and Hillmann (2004) include in their article a list of *compliance indicators* for assessing metadata quality. They make a point of saying that these are not exact and serve more as a set of general guidelines. Not all of them will apply equally well in all contexts. Most metadata quality assessment is qualitative rather than quantitative. Nonetheless, there are software tools which can assist with this and which have at least a partially quantitative aspect. One example of a fairly expensive software package is *Spotfire* (Dushay and Hillmann, 2003). Another new tool that may hold promise is *Google Refine*. It is possible, however, to use a tool as commonplace as Microsoft Excel to do some substantial metadata quality analysis. Excel can be used to detect such problems as missing elements, missing values, disparate values, and so forth. Many metadata database systems allow metadata records to be exported into comma-delimited file format, which can then be viewed using spreadsheet software such as Excel. Table 9.8 offers an example of a small partial set of selected metadata records from an imaginary Architecture of North America digital collection. The records have been exported in a comma-delimited format and can be viewed in table format in Excel or any other spreadsheet software.

Using spreadsheet sorting capabilities, you can sort the table by each element and easily find instances of records lacking values for any given element. For example, sorting on the *Type of Resource* or *Digital Format* columns will arrange all blank cells together. You can then shade these cells with a particular color you've chosen to indicate incomplete data, then go on to perform sorts on other columns. This process also reveals some instances of incorrect element values, especially for fields that require the use of a relatively small number of controlled values. Table 9.9 illustrates the results of sorting on the *Type of Resource* element, revealing records lacking a value for that element and records containing incorrect values. The correct value for that element in this collection has been specified in the local application profile as the DCMI Type term *Still Image*. The values *Image*, *image/jpeg*, and *Jpeg image* are not valid.

						Table 9.8. Metadata Records Viewed in Spreadsheet Table
Title	Architect	Building Name	Building Type	Date of Construction	Type of Resource	Digital Format
Des Moines Public Library, South Face	Chipperfield, David.	Des Moines Public Library (Des Moines, Iowa)	Public Library	2006	Still Image	image/jpeg
Dulles International Airport, Chantilly, Virginia	Saarinen, Eero, 1910-1961	Dulles International Airport	Airport	1962	Still Image	image/jpeg
Fallingwater at Ohiopyle (Bear Run), Pennsylvania	Wright, Frank Lloyd, 1867-1959	Fallingwater (Pa.)	Residence	1934-1937	Stillmage	image /jpeg
Fallingwater(Edgar J. Kaufmann Sr. Residence), Mill Run, Pennsylvania	Wright, Frank Lloyd, 1867-1959	Fallingwater (Edgar J. Kaufmann Sr. Residence)	Residence	1937	Image	image/jpeg
Fallingwater, Mill Run, Pennsylvania	Wright, Frank Lloyd, 1867-1959	Fallingwater	Residence	1936-1938	Still Image	image/jpeg
Farnsworth House, Plano, Illinois	Van der Rohe, Ludwig Mies, 1886-1969	Farnsworth House	Residence	1951		image
Fredrick R. Weisman Art Museum (Minneapolis, MN)	Gehry, Frank. O, 1929-	Frederick R. Weisman Art Museum	Art Museum	1993-11-21	Still Image	image/jpeg
Goldblatt Bros. Department Store, Chicago, Illinois	Alschuler, Alfred S. (Alfred Samuel), 1876-1940	Goldblatt Bros. Department Store	Department Store	1928	Still Image	image/jpeg
Grand Opera House, Oshkosh, Wisconsin	Waters, William, 1843-1917	Grand Opera House, Oshkosh, Wisconsin	Theater	1883	Image	image/jpeg
Guggenheim Museum of Art, New York, New York	Wright, Frank Lloyd, 1867-1959	Solomon R. Guggenheim Museum	Art Museum	1959-10-21	Still Image	image/jpeg

A quick glance at the *Digital Format* column reveals similar issues, which can be seen by grouping them together by sorting on that column. The same holds true both for missing dates and for dates entered in an incorrect format. If you have mandated use of the W3CDTF scheme in the Date of Construction field, you would find incorrect values such as *Oct. 20, 1979* and *10/20/09*. Table sorts on personal names may reveal the use of names not conforming to the specified format or not taken from the specified authority file. For example, most of the records for works by Frank Lloyd Wright will contain the value *Wright, Frank Lloyd, 1867-1959*. Any forms of name that differ from that value string will sort in a separate place in the table.

Identifying missing and incorrect values helps to address metadata quality issues of completeness and consistency. The identified problems may be corrected in each record, or you may have batch editing software to make many changes at once. You may also have the ability to make the corrections in the spreadsheet, resave it as a comma-delimited file, and reimport it into your digital collection database software. In Excel you can click and drag to automatically fill in cells that will have the same values, such as *Still Image*, thereby supplying missing data and overwriting incorrect data. These are relatively quick and easy ways to

Table 9.9. Spreadsheet Table Sorting to Reveal Missing and Disparate Values					
Architect	**Building Name**	**Building Type**	**Date of Construction**	**Type of Resource**	**Digital Format**
Van der Rohe, Ludwig Mies, 1886-1969	Farnsworth House	Residence	1951		image
Meier, Richard, 1934-	The Getty Center	Art Museum	1997		image/jpeg
Wright, Frank Lloyd, 1867-1959	Unitarian Church (Shorewood Hills, Wisconsin)	Church	1947		image/jpeg
Gehry, Frank O., 1929-	Frederick R. Weisman Art Museum	Art Museum	1993		image/jpeg
Gehry, Frank O., 1929-	Walt Disney Concert Hall (Los Angeles, Calif.)	Art museum	2003-10-23		image/jpeg
Wright, Frank Lloyd, 1867-1959	Fallingwater (Edgar J. Kaufmann Sr. Residence)	Residence	1937	**Image**	image/jpeg
Waters, William, 1843-1917	Grand Opera House, Oshkosh, Wisconsin	Theater	1883	**Image**	image/jpeg
Thornton, William, 1759-1828	United States Capitol	Capitol Building	1824	**Image**	jpeg
Solomon R. Guggenheim Museum	Art Museum		1959-10-21	**image/jpeg**	
Wright, Frank Lloyd, 1867-1959	Solomon R. Guggenheim Museum	Art Museum	1959-10-21	**Jpeg image**	
Chipperfield, David.	Des Moines Public Library (Des Moines, Iowa)	Public Library	2006	**Still Image**	image/jpeg
Saarinen, Eero, 1910-1961	Dulles International Airport	Airport	1962	**Still Image**	image/jpeg
Wright, Frank Lloyd, 1867-1959	Fallingwater	Residence	1936-1938	**Still Image**	image/jpeg
Gehry, Frank. O, 1929-	Frederick R. Weisman Art Museum	Art Museum	1993-11-21	**Still Image**	image/jpeg
Alschuler, Alfred S. (Alfred Samuel), 1876-1940	Goldblatt Bros. Department Store	Department Store	1928	**Still Image**	image/jpeg

identify and correct some metadata quality problems without purchasing expensive data analysis software.

9.10. Five Ways to Improve Your Metadata Quality and Interoperability

Given everything covered in this chapter thus far, what precautions can you take now to *future-proof* your current metadata: that is, to make it likely to be more interoperable with future systems and needs, as well as to make your metadata more shareable in an OAI and other harvesting and aggregating contexts, and to increase its general quality? Although there are many factors to take into account, the following aspects stand out as especially important. A number of articles and research studies have dealt with issues and problem areas in OAI harvested metadata and the shareability of metadata in that context, especially metadata harvested as Simple Dublin Core (Hutt and Riley, 2005; Shreeves, 2005; Jackson et al., 2008; Han et al., 2009). These articles, in addition to the other sources already cited in this chapter, support the following areas of special concern.

1. Use Dublin Core and other standard elements correctly. Whether creating your metadata directly in a standardized element set such as Dublin Core or MODS, or mapping your own nonstandard local elements to the standardized set, be certain that you understand the intended meaning, scope, and usage of the elements in that standardized scheme. Enter or map metadata values into those elements accordingly. Even when using a richer scheme such as MODS, be aware that many aggregators will harvest only Simple Dublin Core, and that you will need to map your metadata into simple DC. Chapters 3 and 4 of this book can hardly claim to be the definitive source on this, but they attempt to go a long way towards giving guidance on the correct usage of Dublin Core elements. *Pay special attention to the correct use of Dublin Core Source and Relation, Type versus Format, and Date versus Temporal Coverage.*

2. Include sufficient contextual information and access points. Shreeves (2005) has written about information loss when mapping from complex metadata schemes to Simple Dublin Core and when metadata is taken out of its local context. Remember that, after harvesting into an aggregated repository, your metadata becomes disassociated from its original context. This includes the loss of any nonstandard local element names used to give context and meaning to data values. It also includes the loss of any contextual information implied or discernable by users of the particular collection, such as the collection name and subject matter.

This latter problem has often been referred to as the *"on a horse" problem*, in reference to a situation described by Robin Wendler of Harvard University (Wendler, 2004: 64). Harvard's Visual Image Access catalog ingested metadata for a collection of resources about Theodore Roosevelt. A subject heading "on a horse" in the original context would be understood to be about Roosevelt, but once the record is taken outside of that context, the subject heading loses its meaning. Along these same lines, suppose that some metadata records for resources in a collection about Abraham Lincoln lack any reference to Lincoln himself, such as in titles or subject access points. After OAI harvesting into an aggregated repository, the record will likely become largely meaningless and useless.

These issues may apply in local system cross-collection searching as well as in third-party service provider aggregations.

Five Ways to Improve Your Metadata Quality and Interoperability: Summary Overview

1. **Use Dublin Core and other standard elements correctly.**
   a. Understand the intended meaning, scope, and usage of the elements in any standardized scheme.
   b. Enter or map metadata values into those elements accordingly.
   c. Pay special attention to the correct use of Dublin Core *Type* versus *Format*, *Source* and *Relation*, and *Date* versus *Coverage Temporal*.

2. **Include sufficient contextual information and access points.**
   a. Be sure to include sufficient descriptive information and access points in your metadata to make your resources findable and understandable after harvesting as Simple Dublin Core and taken outside of their original context.
   b. Avoid the *On a Horse problem* (see point 2 in Section 9.10).

3. **Enter data values that are machine-processable and linkable.**
   a. Understand the distinction between fields that contain free text and fields that are used for computer processing.
   b. Enter values that computers can process for hyperlinking, indexing, browsing, search limiting, and navigation in these fields.
   c. In most cases, use data values from controlled vocabularies or that follow a standardized encoding scheme.

4. **Distinguish administrative and technical metadata from descriptive metadata.**
   a. Consider which fields contain metadata that has administrative and technical value but are not of use to end users, such as dates of digitization, digital file names and identifiers, and technical digitization specifications.
   b. Exclude this type of information from exposure for OAI harvesting, and consider removing it from the descriptive metadata altogether, or else suppressing it from indexing and/or display.

5. **Document your local practices.**
   a. Document your decisions, practices, and local scheme for your colleagues, successors, and others.
   b. Documentation also provides information needed for future metadata system migration and for current metadata harvesting in order to effectively process and convert your metadata to function in new environments.

See Section 9.10 for more detailed explanations of each of these points.

In many if not most aggregated repositories, the metadata also becomes disassociated from the digital image or other resource surrogate that helps give meaning and context if displayed with the metadata in the original local context. Here also the value of giving a Resource Type element becomes evident, even when every resource in a collection has the same type. In a cross-collection and aggregated environment, that element becomes highly useful for users to be able to limit searches, while its omission guarantees the loss of that functionality for users, and resources will be missed when a user applies such limits.

The best way to test for sufficient context and access points is to take a sample of records at the start of any new project, strip away any locally created, nonstandard element names, and examine the records with only their Qualified DC element names, and then especially with only their Simple DC element names. Do the individual elements and their values, and the records as a whole, stand well on their own without your local element names? Will they make sense in an aggregated environment? Where is there ambiguity, and how can you address that? Is there sufficient metadata content and contextual information to make each resource intelligible? Are there sufficient access points to make each findable by common methods users are likely to employ for resource discovery?

3. Enter data values that are machine-processable and linkable. Understand the distinction between fields that are purely descriptive, not used for processing, and containing free text data, on the one hand, and fields that are used for processing and indexing, on the other hand. In these latter types of fields, enter data values in ways that are usable by computers and systems to serve user needs and functionality such as hyperlinking, indexing, browsing, and search limiting. In most cases, this means using data values taken from a controlled vocabulary, such as a standardized list of resource types or a subject thesaurus, or entered following a standardized encoding scheme, such as the *W3CDTF* format for dates. Avoid adding extraneous data that break character string matching, hyperlinking, and indexing. Avoid the addition of *pseudo-qualifiers* such as role terms in creator and contributor fields and type of date designations in date fields. Avoid inconsistent entry of dates in formats not able to be consistently processed by machines, such as *October 15, 2009* and *10/15/09*.

Several journal articles on the topic and best practice guides for shareable metadata also recommend not putting multiple values into a single field: for example, multiple personal names in a *Creator* or *Contributor* field, or multiple subject terms in a *Subject* field. Not all systems will understand that these are actually separate data values. Not all systems will be able to process the punctuation conventions used in your local system for demarcating separate data values in the same field. This is a more difficult point for many implementers to adhere to, because digital library management system software may default to multiple values per field. This is a classic case in which harvesting agencies may need to understand your local conventions, often by using your local documentation, as the basis for converting multiple values in a single field into multiple instances of the same field, each containing the separate data values.

4. Distinguish administrative and technical metadata from descriptive metadata. Some kinds of metadata have a primarily administrative and technical value and are not of interest or use to the majority of end users. Information about dates of digitization and resource updating, technical specifications used in digitization, and digital file names and identifiers fall into this category. While such information may be important or necessary to include in the descriptive metadata in the current local context, it may not be important or useful in an aggregated context. It may in fact add to the *noise* of the metadata in these contexts, increasing the number and ambiguity of data values. This type of information is usually best excluded from exposure for OAI and other types of harvesting by consortial aggregators and other third-party service providers. In the local context, it might be excluded from indexing and/or public display.

5. Document your local practices. Document your decisions and practices for each collection or project so that you and/or your colleagues and successors can understand what standards and practices were followed. This can be done in the form of a table or other documentation, which may be a data dictionary or application profile for your institution as a whole and/or for each individual collection. Include such information as: (a) mappings of local element names to Dublin Core, along with qualifiers, controlled vocabularies and encoding schemes, whether locally devised or standardized, that have been used for the values in any elements; (b) level of obligation or requirement for every element; and (c) general input or content guidelines for metadata creators, such as sources of information, use of capitalization and abbreviations, forms of names, handling of uncertain dates and date ranges, and the like. Chapter 10 on Metadata Design and Documentation covers this in greater detail. Such documentation can be critical for harvesters to be able to ingest, process, manipulate, convert, and massage your metadata to function well with other metadata in the aggregated repository. These same things apply for processing your current metadata for use in your own future systems and metadata schemes. Consider also the potential value of using separate local element names for original versus digital manifestations, and clearly labeling them as such, as shown in the examples given in Chapter 2. By having these values in separate fields, explicitly labeled, the potential is open for mapping into more sophisticated derivate resource relationship structures in the future.

9.11. Summary

Interoperability is the ability to exchange data among different systems without special processing and without loss of meaning and functionality. Metadata interoperability encompasses several interrelated issues related to the usability of your local metadata outside of its original closed-system context. This includes viability of metadata for future system migration;

sharing metadata within an institution or consortium or with a third-party aggregator; metadata harvesting, processing, conversion, and aggregation; and mapping among different element sets. Metadata quality, both within the local system and when shared outside of that system, is a closely related issue. Metadata designers and creators have many reasons to care about the interoperability, shareability, and quality of their metadata. These issues should be taken into account when designing a local metadata scheme and when creating metadata for every digital collection.

The most common current method of sharing cultural heritage metadata is by means of the Open Archives Initiative Protocol for Metadata Harvesting (OAI-PMH). OAI participants consist of both data providers and service providers. The OAI-PMH is capable of harvesting metadata in many different formats or element sets, but also requires that all metadata be exposed for harvesting as Simple Dublin Core encoded in XML as a lowest common denominator, interoperable format. Many metadata service providers harvest only Simple Dublin Core, perform various conversion processes on it, and incorporate it into their aggregated repositories, which have their own user interfaces.

Mapping from one element set to another is fraught with difficulties because no two element sets align exactly with one another. Metadata schemes lie on a spectrum of complexity and differ in various ways. Data loss inevitably occurs, especially when mapping from a richer scheme to a simpler scheme. Among the most common challenges in metadata mapping are multiple elements for a concept in one scheme versus a single element in another scheme, elements for a similar concept in one scheme using controlled vocabularies but not in another, and schemes using different controlled vocabularies for roughly the same element, an element in one scheme having no equivalent element in another, and elements intended for display in one scheme versus those intended for hidden indexing and retrieval in another. Mapping from Dublin Core to MODS, and from MODS to Dublin Core, illustrates all of these issues. Mapping between these schemes and VRA 3.0 and 4.0 gives further evidence.

Several characteristics of metadata quality and shareability have been identified in the cultural heritable metadata literature. Both aspects should be taken into account when designing a local metadata scheme and creating local metadata. Among good practices for creating quality and shareable metadata are using Dublin Core and other standard elements correctly, including sufficient contextual information and access points to make the metadata meaningful and usable outside of its original context, entering data values that are machine processable and linkable in those elements that require them, distinguishing administrative and technical metadata from descriptive metadata, and documenting local practices.

▶ **Companion Website**

See this book's companion website at **http://www.neal-schuman.com/ metadata-digital-collections** for Chapter 9 review questions, suggestions for exercises, and other resources.

References

Baker, Thomas. 2000. "A Grammar of Dublin Core." *D-Lib Magazine* 6, no. 10 (October). http://mirrored.ukoln.ac.uk/lis-journals/dlib/dlib/dlib/october00/baker/10baker.html.

Bruce, Thomas R., and Diane I. Hillmann. 2004. "The Continuum of META-DATA Quality: Defining, Expressing, Exploiting." In *Metadata in Practice*, edited by Diane Hillmann and Elaine Westbrooks, 238–256. Chicago: ALA.

DLF (Digital Library Federation). 2007. "Best Practices for OAI Data Provider Implementations and Shareable Metadata." Last modified July 10. http://webservices.itcs.umich.edu/mediawiki/oaibp/index.php/Main_Page.

———. 2008. "Introduction to Best Practices for Shareable Metadata." Last modified January 17. http://webservices.itcs.umich.edu/mediawiki/oaibp/index.php/IntroductionMetadataContent.

DLF/NSDL Working Group on OAI PMH Best Practices. 2007. "Best Practices for OAI PMH Data Provider Implementations and Shareable Metadata." Digital Library Federation. http://www.diglib.org/pubs/dlf108.pdf.

Dushay, Naomi, and Diane Hillmann. 2003. "Analyzing Metadata for Effective Use and Re-Use." In *DC-2003—Proceedings of the International DCMI Metadata Conference and Workshop, September 28–October 2, 2003, Seattle, Washington, USA*. http://dcpapers.dublincore.org/ojs/pubs/article/view/744/740.

Han, Myung-Ja, Christine Cho, Timothy W. Cole, and Amy S. Jackson. 2009. "Metadata for Special Collections in CONTENTdm: How to Improve Interoperability of Unique Fields Through OAI-PMH." *Journal of Library Metadata* 9, no. 3/4: 213–238.

Hutt, Arwen, and Jenn Riley. 2005. "Semantics and Syntax of Dublin Core Usage in Open Archives Initiative Data Providers of Cultural Heritage Materials." In *Proceedings of the 5th ACM/IEEE-CS Joint Conference on Digital Libraries, Denver, CO, USA, June 7–11, 2005*, 262–270. New York: ACM Press.

Jackson, Amy S., Myung-Ja Han, Kurt Groetsch, Megan Mustafoff, and Timothy W. Cole. 2008. "Dublin Core Metadata Harvested Through OAI-PMH." *Journal of Library Metadata* 8, no. 1: 5–21.

Johnston, Pete. 2006. "Metadata Sharing and XML." In *Good Practice Guide for Developers of Cultural Heritage Web Services*. Bath, UK: UKOLN. Last modified January. http://www.ukoln.ac.uk/interop-focus/gpg/Metadata/.

NISO (National Information Standards Organization). 2004. "Understanding Metadata." Bethesda, MD: NISO Press. http://www.niso.org/publications/press/UnderstandingMetadata.pdf.

OAI (Open Archives Initiative). 2008. "OAI-PMH (The Open Archives Initiative Protocol for Metadata Harvesting) Protocol Version 2.0 of 2002-06-14." Document Version 2008-12-07T20:42:00Z. http://www.openarchives.org/OAI/2.0/openarchivesprotocol.htm.

Shreeves, Sarah L. 2005. "The Open Archives Initiative Protocol for Metadata Harvesting." In *Technology for the Rest of Us: A Primer on Computer Technologies for the Low-Tech Librarian*, edited by Nancy Courtney, 85–108. Westport, CT: Libraries Unlimited.

St. Pierre, Margaret, and William P. LaPlant. 1998. "Issues in Crosswalking: Content Metadata Standards." NISO Standards White Paper. October 15. http://www.niso.org/publications/white_papers/crosswalk/.

Wendler, Robin. 2004. "Eye of the Beholder: Challenges of Image Description and Access at Harvard." In *Metadata in Practice*, edited by Diane Hillmann and Elaine Westbrooks, 51–69. Chicago: American Library Association.

Designing and Documenting a Metadata Scheme

10.1. Metadata Scheme Design and Documentation

10.1.1. Introduction

A critical aspect of metadata for digital collections is designing and documenting metadata schemes for individual collections or for groups of collections within an individual institution or a consortium of institutions. Unlike the world of library cataloging, for example, where almost everyone uses a relatively small number of the same sets of structure, content, value, and encoding standards, the cultural heritage metadata world entails making many local decisions about each of these types of standards, usually including many local specifications in addition to the adoption of widespread formal standards. In its broadest sense, a *scheme* can mean any kind of "systematic or organized configuration" (Merriam-Webster, 2009). In the metadata context, the term is often used in two different ways. First, the term *metadata scheme* is often used to refer to a formally standardized metadata element set (or data structure standard), such as the Dublin Core Metadata Element Set, the VRA 3.0 Core Categories, and the set of MODS elements, subelements, and attributes. Second, the term *metadata scheme* may also be used to refer to a locally established element set or an interconnected suite of local metadata specifications. This may include local application specifications for a formally established element set, such as Dublin Core, for a set of locally established elements, or for a combination of both, as well as specifications about local element requirements, content guidelines, controlled vocabularies, and the like. It is in this second sense that the term *metadata scheme* is used in this section of Chapter 10. When documented, a metadata scheme in this sense is for all intents and purposes the same thing as what is variously called an *application profile, data dictionary, best practice guide*, or local metadata *usage guide*, taken in their broadest scope.

Chapter 1 made the point that metadata scheme design is one part of a larger process, including selection, curation, and compiling of the resources to be digitized; digitization and processing of digitized files; web design, information architecture, and programming; database or retrieval system design; and metadata design, cataloging, and indexing. The design of the metadata scheme and the selection or creation of controlled vocabularies usually, and ideally always, go hand-in-hand with the design of the search, browse, and navigation functions and of the record displays in the user interface. Each is dependent on the other and informs the other. And each of these should go hand-in-hand with the identification of key pieces of information that the primary users of the collection will need to identify and access the objects in the collection. Chopey (2005) does an excellent job of discussing how all of these aspects are intertwined with one another. Foulonneau and Riley (2008) also provide excellent and detailed coverage of metadata scheme design. Good metadata scheme design is also dependent on a solid understanding of the meaning and intended scope of the underlying metadata element set standard, such as Dublin Core or MODS; the value and use of controlled vocabularies; and issues of interoperability. These topics have been covered in previous chapters. A good grasp of those topics and issues will help a metadata designer make more intelligent, informed decisions when designing a local metadata scheme.

Metadata scheme design, like all other aspects of metadata for digital collections, varies tremendously depending on the specific type and size of institution, the specific type and scope of digital content being covered by the scheme, the number of staff and their level of expertise, and many other factors. It is therefore difficult to generalize, and the aspects covered in this chapter in a somewhat step-by-step fashion do not constitute the only way to approach the process of metadata scheme design. Several of the steps covered in this chapter could be grouped together into a single step or, alternatively, many could be further subdivided into more detailed components. Nor are they strictly chronological, and in fact most of them usually overlap with one another in practice. Nonetheless, all digital collection projects will need to include each of the components covered in this chapter in one form or another, whether formally or informally.

The points made in Section 10.1 are intended to go hand-in-hand with the concrete examples given in Section 10.2. Those examples include brief selections from four general metadata application profile documents, selections from three different collection-specific application profile documents, and screen captures from the CONTENTdm digital collection management software system in order to illustrate various aspects of metadata scheme design.

10.1.2. Analyze Context, Content, and Users and Determine Functional Requirements

The first logical step in designing a local metadata scheme or application profile is to analyze the content, determine the users, and decide on functional requirements. The triad of *context, content*, and *users* is frequently used in the field of information architecture, and Morville and Rosenfeld (2006) discuss it throughout their foundational book on the topic. This triad applies equally well to the context of metadata scheme design.

Context. Metadata design does not take place in a vacuum. It always takes place within the context of a particular organization or institution, with its own unique *corporate culture*, priorities, needs, strengths, and weaknesses. It also takes place within many other institutional and professional contexts, such as librarianship, with its own professional culture and community. These considerations, among many other aspects of the context within which a digital collection is created, necessarily impact the specifics of the metadata scheme design.

Content. Even more centrally, the design of a metadata scheme, especially when it is collection-specific, depends on the particular content of the digital collection, including the specific types of digital objects included, the subject matter they cover, and the focus of the collection. For example, a collection might consist exclusively of digital still images, or exclusively of some other resource type, or of a mix of different types. It might be focused on the work of a particular photographer, or the original photographer may be of no importance. It might be focused on the type of original resource, such as a slide collection, or a collection of letters and diaries by and about a particular person. All of these aspects will play a role in how the metadata scheme is designed.

Users. Ultimately a digital collection exists to provide information to users and should be centered on user needs and information seeking behaviors. It is important to identify your anticipated users, noting likely primary and secondary user groups and their known or likely information identification and retrieval needs. In some cases, this may be fairly clear. For example, a slide collection intended for use by undergraduate students in an art history class has a clear primary user group. In other cases, the potential user groups may be more diffuse. Furthermore, once a collection is made public on the Internet, unanticipated and sometimes surprising types of users may emerge. To the extent possible, work to identify important attributes of the digital objects by which various types of users will want and need to find and identify those objects. These attributes will usually become metadata elements in your scheme. Principles and practices of user-centered design, usability, and iterative and cyclical usability testing go beyond the scope of this book, but should be incorporated into the metadata scheme design process to the highest degree that is realistically possible. Even a small amount of modest and inexpensive usability testing is infinitely preferable to none (Krug, 2006).

Functional Requirements. Based on the results of the content and user analysis, determine a set of functional requirements. Functional requirements center on the functions that the database, retrieval system, and user interface will need to be able to perform in order to support those functions that users will want and need to perform. Asking and answering questions such as the following will help you determine functional requirements for a metadata application context or project:

- How will your users want to search and browse for the content of this collection? By what attributes of the digital objects or by what access points will they search?

- What information will your users want to know about each digital object in the collection? What pieces of information will be important for them to be able to identify and interpret the resources in this particular collection?

- How will your users want to sort and group objects in the collection? What kinds of sets of related items will they likely want to retrieve? How will they want to limit their search results?

- What are the common attributes or properties of the objects in the collection that will allow users to accomplish the tasks above? These are candidates for metadata elements.

- How do the values of those elements need to be entered and structured to enable those functions? Which elements will need standardized encoding schemes and controlled vocabularies in order to fulfill identified user needs?

- How will these elements conform and map to the standardized element set selected?

To take a more specific example, a metadata designer working with subject experts or curators may determine that the users of a particular collection will need to be able to do the following:

- Browse and search by geographic location and time period.

- Browse by a selected set of subject categories relevant to the particular collection.

- Limit searches by date ranges.

- Limit searches by primary resource type (text, still image, moving image, sound, etc.).

These functions can then be used to develop the local metadata element set and the specification of content and value standards needed to accomplish those functions. Although not everyone develops a formal list of functional requirements, doing so can be quite useful to clarify the desired functionality and to have a good basis for the remaining steps in the metadata scheme design process. As part of the functional requirements development, an initial "wish list" of desired metadata elements may be developed before moving into more formal element set decisions.

Some metadata elements will be used simply to provide information about a digital resource, helping users to identify, understand, and interpret it and distinguish it from other similar objects. Other elements will provide active search and browse functionality, allowing users to search by specific fields, limit searches by specific values, and/or browse through specific categories or other attributes of the objects in the collection. Some elements may provide for both aspects at the same time. When developing a list of functional requirements, the focus is often on the searching and browsing functionality. But functions such as identification may also be included. For example, you might determine that you want users of a particular online collection to be able to identify each resource by a title, a content description, a physical description, and the like. These may be free-text fields in the database, not used directly for searching or browsing, but still be important to identify the content and characteristics of digital images, for example. These can also then translate into a list of desired metadata elements.

10.1.3. Select and Develop an Element Set

The second logical step in designing a local metadata scheme or application profile is to decide on an element set. This is your data structure standard, whether it is an internationally established standard, a purely local one, or a combination of both. The element set lies at the core of the larger metadata scheme. It includes a set of element names with definitions and perhaps additional comments and specifications. The element set should be based on the resource attributes and functional requirements identified in the previous step. One option, theoretically, would be to develop an original, purely local element set, without reference to an existing standard. This option is somewhat common in the business world and other non–cultural heritage application contexts in which there is no current or future need to make metadata interoperable and sharable. Almost all cultural heritage institutions, however, choose to use an existing standardized element set, such as Dublin Core, VRA Core, or MODS, either on its own or as the base scheme to which their local schemes are mapped.

The first thing to do, then, is to select a standardized element set that will enable the functionality you need and/or to develop your own local element set mapped to a standardized set to enable such functionality. Some institutions may use more than one standardized element set for different types of collections. For example, they might use Dublin Core for most of their digital collections, but VRA for a set of art slides, EAD for their archival finding aids, and CSDGM for their digital geospatial data sets. In any event, selecting and developing an element set always takes place within constraints such as metadata interoperability and shareability needs, community norms, and local software requirements and limitations. Metadata designers have several options, and this chapter subsumes them into two broad methods or models of metadata design: general/cross-collection metadata scheme design and collection-specific metadata scheme design.

10.1.3.1. General/Cross-Collection Metadata Scheme Design

Design a single, general element set and element specifications that will apply to all of the collections in your institution. This also applies to consortial repositories harvesting or ingesting metadata from multiple collections coming from different institutions. Adopt an existing, standardized element set, such as Dublin Core, MODS, VRA, or others, and decide whether to adopt it in whole, without additions or modification, or in part, with the addition of elements from another standardized

---

Standardized Metadata Element Sets (aka Schemes or Schemas)

General Element Sets

Schemes intended to describe a wide variety of resource types for a variety of information communities, or intended for institutions that collect a wide variety of resource types in various formats and covering a wide variety of subject matter. For example:

- DC: Dublin Core Metadata Element Set
- MODS: Metadata Object Description Schema

Domain-Specific Element Sets

Schemes intended to describe a specific type of resource or a narrower range of resources specific to a given domain or information community, such as museum objects, archival collections, educational resources and learning objects, social science or geospatial data sets, moving images, and so on. For example:

- VRA Core: Visual Resources Association Core Categories
- CDWA: Categories for the Description of Works of Art
- EAD: Encoded Archival Description
- TEI: Text Encoding Initiative Standard for Text Interchange
- IEEE LOM: Learning Object Metadata
- MPEG-7 and MPEG-21: Moving Picture Experts Group Multimedia Metadata
- FGDC/CSDGM: Federal Geospatial Data Committee's Content Standard for Digital Geospatial Metadata
- DDI: Data Documentation Initiative for social science data sets

scheme and/or some locally established elements. The adoption of a standardized scheme with the addition of some locally established elements is quite common among cultural heritage institutions and consortia. Recall from previous chapters that in Dublin Core, MODS, and VRA 3.0, all elements are optional, repeatable, and may be used in any order. VRA 4.0 is the only scheme covered in this book that has one required element and recommends use of a minimal set of core elements, but aside from that, it likewise gives great flexibility in the application of the scheme.

The Dublin Core, MODS, and VRA standardized schemes have been developed with the understanding that that local institutions and consortia will develop their own application profiles for implementing the schemes. This is a critical point to understand. Application profile development commonly entails such decisions as the following:

- Which elements, qualifiers, subelements, and attributes will you use, and what order will you put them in?
- Which of these will you make required, recommended, or optional?
- Which will you make repeatable or nonrepeatable?
- What local comments will you add and constraints you will make on the definitions and application of the standardized elements (as long as you do not violate the original meaning)?
- What specifications for controlled vocabularies and encoding schemes will you make for specific elements?
- What content or input guidelines or other requirements will you develop for the element values?
- What local names might you give to any of these elements?
- What additional local elements might you add if needed when not present in the standardized base element set?

When devising local names for elements from the standardized base scheme, each element specification normally includes a mapping to one of the elements from that scheme, such as Dublin Core. There is a wide variety in the manner in which Dublin Core application profiles are implemented in practice, illustrated by the three examples given in Section 10.2.1 of this chapter.

10.1.3.2. Collection-Specific Metadata Scheme Design

Develop a set of local elements for a specific collection and map them to a standardized element set. This is the common CONTENTdm model of metadata design. Some of the local element names may be identical to those in the standardized base scheme while others will be unique to the specific collection. For example, you might have your own *Title* and *Description* elements, which are Dublin Core element names, but you might also have a *Photographer* or *Architect* element, which would be specific to a collection of photographs or architectural drawings. The local elements would both be mapped to the Dublin Core *Creator* element.

You may work out your collection-specific element set based on the content of your particular collection and the necessary functional requirements, and document these in a Word or Excel table or some other method, then subsequently work out the mapping to Dublin Core or VRA, for example. Or you might work out the two in tandem, which is wise since the collections-specific elements must always conform to the meaning and scope of the standardized element to which they are mapped, especially for long term viability, interoperability, shareability, and data quality.

The examples given in section 10.2.2 of this chapter illustrate selected elements from three collection-specific application profiles used for collections created in CONTENTdm. When setting up a collection-specific scheme in the CONTENTdm system, the metadata designer starts with the selected underlying base scheme, such as Dublin Core, and subsequently renames the selected elements with local collection-specific names, thereby mapping each to a DC element for cross-collection searching, OAI harvesting, and other potential reuse. This requires a good knowledge of the base scheme, and the meaning and scope of each local collection-specific element must remain within the meaning and scope of the underlying base element to which it is mapped. The local scheme may, however, include some elements not mapped to the base scheme and thus not exposed for harvesting or sharing. Section 10.2.3 of this chapter presents several examples of CONTENTdm screens, illustrating some of the more important aspects of metadata design and creation using that software.

10.1.3.3. Factors in Choice of Metadata Element Set

Whether following the general or the collection-specific method of metadata design, the choice of metadata element set should be based on the results of the content and user analysis and the functional requirements. But this will also depend, as previously noted, on the following factors, among others:

1. Your local system software and what schemes it supports. For example, CONTENTdm currently includes Simple and Qualified Dublin Core and VRA 3.0 as base schemes, as well as EAD.

2. The community of institutions to which your institution belongs. For example, many large university libraries have adopted MODS as their base metadata element set, and sister institutions may wish to follow suit, while some museums have adopted VRA Core, a standard especially suited to art and architecture resources.

3. Issues of metadata interoperability, shareability, future viability, and reuse also come into play in selecting a metadata element set. It is best to design a scheme for both local needs, on the one hand, and for interoperability and shareability, on the other hand, as much as possible. Although designing for current needs and users takes precedence, metadata scheme designers may face a certain tension between these two aspects, and they will need to maintain a reasonable balance between them.

10.1.4. Establish Element and Database Specifications

Another step in designing a local metadata scheme or application profile is to develop specifications for each element and its corresponding database field. In addition to an element name and its definition, each metadata element requires further specifications for local application. Every metadata element also becomes a field in the database, and each field requires that certain specifications be made in the database software. While in some cases element and database field specifications differ, in many cases they overlap. These kinds of specifications commonly include the following.

Obligation. Is the element or field required, required if applicable, recommended, or optional? There is no one set of standardized terms used to designate obligation. Some implementers use the term *mandatory*, while others use *required*. At minimum, most will have the following three levels of obligation or requirement.

1. **Mandatory** or **Required**: Every metadata record in the database absolutely must contain this element or field with a value filled in; no exceptions. A Title element of some kind is a common mandatory element.

2. Mandatory or Required **If Applicable**, or sometimes **If Available**: The element or field must be used if it applies to a particular resource and/or if the information is available to the metadata creator. For example, some resources may not have a Creator or a Language, in which case the element is left blank. Or perhaps the creator, date of creation, or some other element might not be known for every resource. In those cases, the appropriate metadata elements may be left blank. But when the information is known, it is mandatory or required to fill them in.

3. **Optional** usually means that the use of the element is up to the individual metadata creator, or, more commonly, to the member institution of a consortium or to the individual metadata scheme designer for a local collection. In some cases, particularly in consortial environments in which many different institutions will be contributing metadata and these institutions will differ in size, staffing and expertise, some elements may be designated as **Recommended**, and sometimes also **Recommended If Applicable**. This means that they should be used if possible, but they are not absolutely mandated or required.

Within a database, it is usually possible to enforce by machine only one of two options: mandatory/required or optional; that is, a particular database field must always contain a value in every record or not.

Cardinality, also often called *Repeatability* or *Occurrence*. Is the element or field repeatable or non-repeatable: that is, can there be more than one instance of the field in a single metadata record? This is a fundamental aspect of database design. For example, it would be common to make a *Subject* element or field repeatable, because you would want to allow more than only one subject term per record. You might, however, want to allow only one instance of a *Title* element per record, or only one *Date of Publication*, or the like. In some digital content management systems, like CONTENTdm, the system default is to include multiple values in a single field, separated by some piece of punctuation that tells the system to treat them as separate values for computer indexing, searching, hyperlinking, and so forth. That is, there may be only one *Subject* field into which multiple subject terms may be entered, demarcated by a punctuation convention such as a semicolon followed by a space. Even in these contexts, however, you may want to specify whether or not a field may contain only one or more than one data value.

Data value specification: controlled vocabularies and encoding schemes. Are there any constraints on the type of value or content that can go into the element or field? Can it be completely free text? Must it conform to an encoding scheme such as a particular format for recording dates? Must it be taken from a specific list, thesaurus, or other kind of other controlled vocabulary? This is a critical aspect of metadata design, and its implications have been explored throughout the book, especially in Chapters 2–5. Some schemes may designate the type of data value for every single element, including those that have uncontrolled values. In such cases, the metadata designer might use terms such as *free text* or *transcribed text*.

Size of field designation. In the database, how many characters can be entered into the field? In some database software, a category such as *large* or *small* is selected, the meaning of each being specified somewhere in the software documentation. Sometimes it simply refers to the size of the input box that appears to metadata creators working behind the scenes.

Searchability, indexing, and/or hyperlinking. Is the content of the element or field to be made searchable or suppressed from search results? Will the value of a given element become an active hyperlink in the user interface for retrieving sets of related resources? Or is it unlinked, unindexed text?

Visibility. Will the field and its content appear to users in the public display or appear only to staff members using the underlying database and metadata creation interface?

10.1.5. Establish Controlled Vocabularies and Encoding Schemes

Another step in designing a local metadata scheme or application profile is to decide which controlled vocabularies and syntax encoding schemes will be used for the values of individual elements/fields. In order to facilitate consistency in information retrieval, as well as for grouping, sorting, and hyperlinking, constraints are often put on the values that can be entered into a particular element. These are data value standards. For a *Resource Type* element, for example, the allowable values may be limited to those taken from a small list of established terms. For a Subject element, allowable values may be limited to those taken from a particular thesaurus or subject heading list. For a *Language* element, allowable values may be limited to an internationally established list of language codes. These are all forms of what are broadly called *controlled vocabularies*. For a *Date* element, values may be required to conform to a particular syntax encoding scheme, such as 2010-07-21 as a consistent, computer-processable form of date for July 21, 2010. Chapters 3, 4, and especially 5 dealt with the topic of controlled vocabularies and encoding schemes in some detail.

Decisions about particular vocabularies will be based on an analysis of the subject content of your collection, the presence of vocabularies built into a digital library management software package, and an awareness of vocabularies commonly used in your institutional or consortial community or larger professional community. For example, many museums use the Getty *Art and Architecture Thesaurus* (AAT) and *Union List of Artist Names* (ULAN), while many libraries use the Library of Congress *Thesaurus for Graphic Materials* (LCTGM or TGM), *Library of Congress Subject Headings* (LCSH), and the Library of Congress/NACO *Name Authority File* (NAF or LCNAF). If an established controlled vocabulary does not adequately meet local needs, in whole or in part, the institution may develop one or more of its own local vocabularies, as described in Chapter 5.

10.1.6. Develop Content Guidelines

A further step in designing a local metadata scheme or application profile is to develop input or content guidelines. This is a form of *data content standard*, whether it consists of a small handful of general guidelines, more detailed specifications for each element, or a following formally established content standard such as the *Anglo-American Cataloguing Rules* or *Cataloging Cultural Objects*. Sometimes these specifications are called *input guidelines*. They provide directions for metadata creators in how to handle issues that arise when entering metadata in fields that are not automatically filled in or when no controlled vocabulary or encoding scheme applies. For example, they may specify how to handle capitalization, abbreviations, acronyms, variant forms of title, various forms of personal, corporate, and geographic names, variant dates, date ranges, uncertain or approximate dates, missing or incomplete information, and the like. They may also specify preferred sources of information: for example, that a title should be taken from a title page of a published book. Some digital libraries specify the use of the *Anglo-American Cataloguing Rules* (*AACR2*), with some adaptations, as their primary content guidelines for digital collections. Museums might specify the use of *Cataloging Cultural Objects* (*CCO*). Local documentation normally includes some general content or input guidelines that will apply generally to all or most elements, as well as element-specific guidelines that address issues for inputting metadata content into those particular elements. The application profile examples in the second part of this chapter include several good instances of input or content guidelines for specific elements.

10.1.7. Document the Scheme

The logically final step in designing a local metadata scheme or application profile is to document it, including the element set, element and database specifications, controlled vocabularies and encoding schemes, and content guidelines. Metadata scheme documentation is a critical aspect of metadata design. As with all of the other aspects of metadata design, documentation may range from the informal to the formal, from the general to the specific, from a simple table to a document of several dozen or several hundred pages. Scheme documentation serves several important purposes:

1. It serves as a set of guidelines for local metadata creators (catalogers/indexers) to use when creating metadata for digital objects.

2. It stands as a record of local decisions and practices for your institution and your staff in the present and especially in the future.

3. It may serve as a resource for migration of your metadata to a new software system or element set in the future, or for current and future metadata harvesters to use in interpreting your application of metadata elements so that they can process your data and appropriately map it into their aggregated repository.

4. It may be of use to other institutions that could benefit from your decisions and not have to reinvent the wheel.

In the world of cultural heritage metadata practice today, you will find many different terms used to name metadata scheme documentation. Common names include **metadata guidelines**, **best practice guides**, **data dictionaries**, and **metadata application profiles** (sometimes abbreviated as MAPs), or other variations on these types of names. Often these terms are used interchangeably with one another by different institutions and communities, while in some environments they may have different meanings. Sometimes the term *data dictionary* is restricted to a table format and/or to a set of element names and guidelines for a specific collection. The term *application profile* has had an interesting history. In its broadest sense it can refer to any specification of the application of a metadata element set for a local use, including all of the aspects covered in this section. Some authors have restricted its meaning to the combination of elements from two or more established schemes, such as an application that uses the 15 Dublin Core elements and adds a few elements from another scheme, such as the IEEE Learning Object Metadata scheme. The Dublin Core Metadata Initiative has been developing a much more complex and exacting meaning of a *Dublin Core Application Profile* (DCAP) compatible with metadata implemented in a Semantic Web environment, which will be outlined in Chapter 11.

In their article on the OhioLINK Metadata Application Profile, authors Hicks, Perkins, and Maurer make some interesting points:

Application profiles can be created at different levels of abstraction, ranging from community of practice guidelines to project level implementations. Three levels are in common use:

- Discipline- or format-based communities of practice seeking to establish a standard set of guidelines specific to a certain discipline or format. Examples include the DCMI, the CanCore Learning Resource Metadata Initiative, and the Video Development Initiative.

- Consortiums or other collaborative groups seeking to establish a common set of guidelines for their members. Examples include the CDP and Canadian Culture Online.

- Local project implementers needing to document local practice, track project specific details, and ensure compliance with other standards. At this level, application profiles are often called data dictionaries and are somewhat different than a full application profile. These local level application profiles include less detail and are more prescriptive since they document all the final choices made for a specific instantiation. Examples include the University of Washington and Miami University. (Hicks, Perkins, and Maurer, 2007: 120)

For purposes of this book, however, it is understood that all of these terms refer to metadata scheme documentation of some kind. In practice there is little difference found in the nature and scope of documentation that some call a *best practice guide* and others call a *metadata application profile*. The same can be true of what others call a *data dictionary*. Such documentation may be collection-specific, as in the case of documenting the local elements for a specific CONTENTdm collection, their mapping to Dublin Core, and other specifications. Or it may be general and intended to apply to a range of collections created by a single institution; a consortium of institutions; a particular type of community, such as the library community; or a particular type of work, such as scholarly works. This chapter will use the term *metadata application profile* in its broadest sense to include the full range of metadata scheme design and documentation, regardless of the name used if the documentation itself. The term *application profile* is used here with full awareness of the more restricted and Semantic Web–oriented use of the term within the Dublin Core Metadata Initiative today.

10.2. Metadata Design Examples

This second section of the chapter presents a small selection of examples from different application profiles or metadata scheme documentation. In looking over these examples, it is hoped that readers will take away the following especially important points.

1. Different institutions, consortia, and communities develop application profiles to meet their own metadata application needs.
2. There is a wide range of level of detail and complexity in different types of application specifications and documentation.

3. Some documentation is specific to a particular digital collection, using nonstandard local element names mapped to standard elements such as Dublin Core, while other documentation is intended to apply across the full range of all digital collections created within, or contributed to, an institution or consortium.

4. Application profiles developed for specific collections document decisions about local element names selected specifically for that collection, in order to label the specific types of information for users and to provide search and browse names that will best serve the content, users, and functional requirements for that specific collection.

10.2.1. General Application Profile Examples

This subsection of the chapter offers a small number of selected screen captures from metadata documentation developed by consortia or other groups of institutions that provide general, cross-collection elements and application specifications. Note the differences in the local element names and their mapping to standard Dublin Core, differences in length and detail of the documentation, and differences in what the creators call these documents. For the sake of consistency, each of the figures in this section is labeled as an *MAP* (metadata application profile).

10.2.1.1. Collaborative Digitization Program Dublin Core Metadata Documentation

Figures 10.1 through 10.8 consist of a selection of pages from the Collaborative Digitization Program's *Dublin Core Metadata Best Practices* (CDP Metadata Working Group, 2006). This documentation was originally developed for a collaborative of western states. Note that this document calls itself *Dublin Core Best Practices*, but compare and contrast it with the other two examples of metadata documentation given in this section of the chapter. Figure 10.1 shows the table of contents and illustrates the scope of the document, as well as its length of 67 pages.

Figure 10.2 shows the list of elements, divided into Mandatory and Optional.

Figure 10.3 shows an example of general input guidelines, a basic type of local content standard applicable across many elements in the scheme.

Figure 10.4 shows the beginning of the element specifications for the *Title* element, including a Term Name, Label, DC Definition and Comment, CDP Comment, specifications on obligation and repeatability, applicable DC Qualifiers, and Input Guidelines specific to the *Title* element.

Figure 10.5 shows the continuation of the specifications for the *Title* element, including Examples for titles created by the creator or publisher, on the one hand, and titles supplied by the metadata creators in the institutions contributing metadata records to the collaborative, on the other hand.

Figures 10.6 through 10.8 show the specifications for the *Coverage* element. Note the further explanation of the meaning of the element in the CDP Comment, the inclusion of specifications on Spatial and

Figure 10.1. CDP MAP Table of Contents Page

CDP Dublin Core Metadata Best Practices Version 2.1

 CDPDCMBP Last Modified 2006-09-15

Page 1 of 67

Source: CDP, 2006. Used with permission of the BCR's CDP. After January 1, 2011, the CDP Dublin Core Metadata Best Practices will be available through the Lyrasis website at http://www.lyrasis.org.

Figure 10.2. CDP MAP List of Mandatory and Optional Elements

CDP Dublin Core Metadata Best Practices Version 2.1

Digitization Specifications may also contain technical or preservation metadata for other digital formats, such as audio, video, or text encoding, according to emerging standards.

2.3.1.3. Contributing Institution

Contributing Institution (formerly *Holding Institution*), records information about the institutions or administrative units involved in the creation of a digital resource. This element is particularly important for collaborative projects where records from multiple institutions are combined in a shared database. Since the *Contributing Institution* is not necessarily the same as the copyright holder (*Rights Management*) or the *Publisher,* the Working Group felt it necessary to record this information separately.

2.3.2. Mandatory and Optional Elements

The Dublin Core record as developed by the CDP Metadata Working Group includes eighteen elements, each of which is repeatable. To assure success in a collaborative environment where consistent description of digital resources is critical for interoperability, the CDP Metadata Working Group has designated the following ten mandatory elements:

- *Title*
- *Creator (if available)*
- *Subject*
- *Description*
- *Date Digital*
- *Date Original (if applicable)*
- *Format*
- *Digitization Specifications*
- *Resource Identifier*
- *Rights Management*

The remaining eight elements are optional, but recommended. Richer, more complete records increase the likelihood that database users will locate the desired digital resource.

- Publisher
- Contributor
- Type
- Source
- Language
- Relation
- Coverage
- Contributing Institution

CDPDCMBP Last Modified 2006-09-15

Source: See Figure 10.1.

Figure 10.3. CDP MAP General Input Guidelines

CDP Dublin Core Metadata Best Practices Version 2.1

- Language
- Relation
- Coverage
- Contributing Institution

3.4. General Input Guidelines

Metadata creators should follow the general grammatical rules of the language involved when entering descriptive information about resources. In addition, it may be useful to consult the latest version of the *Anglo-American Cataloging Rules (AACR2), Describing Archives: A Content Standard (DAC)*,[16] or *Cataloging Cultural Objects (CCO)* for more information and details on general rules and guidelines for data entry. The following are a few brief comments:

3.4.1. Punctuation

Avoid ending punctuation unless it is part of the content of the resource.

3.4.2. Abbreviations

In general, the following abbreviations are allowed: common or accepted abbreviations (such as "St." for "Saint"); designations of function (such as "ed." for "Editor"); terms used with dates (b. or fl.); and distinguishing terms added to names of persons, if they are abbreviated on the item (such as "Mrs."). We suggest that abbreviations not be used if they would make the record unclear. In case of doubt, spell out the abbreviation.

3.4.3. Capitalization

In general, capitalize the first word (of a title, for example) and proper names (place, personal, and organization names). Capitalize content in the description element according to normal rules of writing. Acronyms should be entered in capital letters.

3.4.4. Initial Articles

Omit initial articles at the beginning of the title such as: the, a, an, le, la, los, el, der, die, das, etc.

3.4.5. Character Encoding

Have a clear understanding of how the database handles nonstandard characters and diacritics (such as ü, é, ñ, etc.) and input them so that they display and retrieve effectively.[17]

---

[16] Published in 2004, *Describing Archives: A Content Standard* is intended to supersede *Archives, Personal Papers and Manuscripts (APPM)*

[17] For additional information on Character Encoding see: "Character Encoding," Wikipedia. <http://en.wikipedia.org/wiki/Character_encoding>. Implementation of character encoding is also discussed in section *2.4.5 Character Encoding*.

CDPDCMBP Last Modified 2006-09-15

Source: See Figure 10.1.

Figure 10.4. CDP MAP *Title* Element Specifications, First Page

CDP Dublin Core Metadata Best Practices Version 2.1

4.1.   *Title*

Term Name: title
Label: Title
Dublin Core Definition: The name given to the resource.
Dublin Core Comment:
    Typically, a *Title* will be a name by which the resource is formally known.
CDP Comment:
    The name given to the resource by the creator or publisher; may also be an identifying
    phrase or name of the object supplied by the contributing institution.
Mandatory: Yes
Repeatable: Yes
Qualifiers:
    Refinements:

Refinement Name	Refinement Label	Definition
alternative	Alternative	Any form of the title used as a substitute or alternative to the formal title of the resource

    Schemes: None

Input Guidelines:
1. Enter multiple titles in the order in which they appear on the resource or in order of their importance. Use separate *Title* elements to enter multiple titles or *clearly separate each entry* by a semicolon and a space within an element. Use separate elements to enter more than one title if necessary for access i.e., "caption title, former title, spine title, collection title, series title, artist's title, object name, etc." or if in doubt about what constitutes the title.
2. Transcribe the title, if there is one, from the resource itself, such as a caption from a photograph or a title on a map.
3. When no title is found on the resource itself, use a title assigned by the contributing institution or found in reference sources. For more guidance in constructing titles, consult established cataloging rules such as *Anglo-American Cataloging Rules (AACR2), Describing Archives: A Content Standard (DAC)*, or *Cataloging Cultural Objects (CCO)*.
4. Make the title as descriptive as possible, avoiding simple generic titles such as "Papers" or "Annual report."
5. When possible, exclude initial articles from title. Exceptions might include when the article is an essential part of the title or when local practice requires use of initial articles.
6. Capitalize only the first letter of the first word of the title or of any proper names contained within the title.
7. In general, transcribe titles and subtitles from the source using the same punctuation that appears on the source. If the holding institution has created the title, then use punctuation that would be appropriate for English language. Some institutions may wish to apply consistent guidelines prescribed by the Modern Language Association (MLA), *Chicago Manual of Style*, etc.

CDPDCMBP Last Modified 2006-09-15

Source: See Figure 10.1.

Figure 10.5. CDP MAP *Title* Element Specifications, Second Page

CDP Dublin Core Metadata Best Practices Version 2.1

8. File names, accession numbers, call numbers, or other identification schemes should be entered in the *Identifier* element.
9. Collections:
    a) If multiple items are being described as a collection by one record and no collection title already exists, create a collective title that is as descriptive as possible of the contents.
    b) If each item in such a collection is itself worthy of being described by its own record (i.e., item-level record), refer back to the collection-level title in the *Relation* element. Likewise, list any titles for subordinate item-level records in the *Relation* element of the collection-level record.

Notes: None.

Examples:

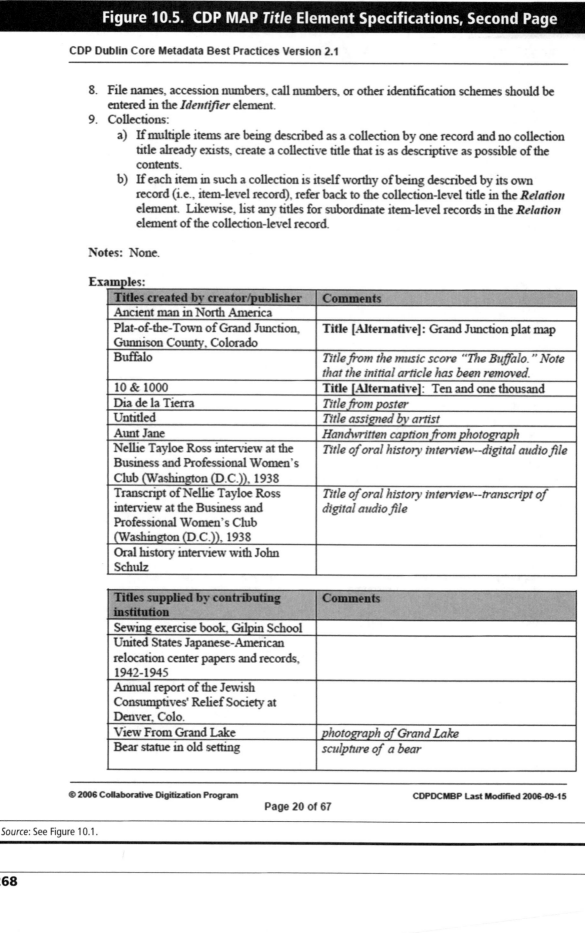

Titles created by creator/publisher	Comments
Ancient man in North America	
Plat-of-the-Town of Grand Junction, Gunnison County, Colorado	**Title [Alternative]:** Grand Junction plat map
Buffalo	*Title from the music score "The Buffalo." Note that the initial article has been removed.*
10 & 1000	**Title [Alternative]:** Ten and one thousand
Dia de la Tierra	*Title from poster*
Untitled	*Title assigned by artist*
Aunt Jane	*Handwritten caption from photograph*
Nellie Tayloe Ross interview at the Business and Professional Women's Club (Washington (D.C.)), 1938	*Title of oral history interview--digital audio file*
Transcript of Nellie Tayloe Ross interview at the Business and Professional Women's Club (Washington (D.C.)), 1938	*Title of oral history interview--transcript of digital audio file*
Oral history interview with John Schulz	

Titles supplied by contributing institution	Comments
Sewing exercise book, Gilpin School	
United States Japanese-American relocation center papers and records, 1942-1945	
Annual report of the Jewish Consumptives' Relief Society at Denver, Colo.	
View From Grand Lake	*photograph of Grand Lake*
Bear statue in old setting	*sculpture of a bear*

© 2006 Collaborative Digitization Program   CDPDCMBP Last Modified 2006-09-15

Page 20 of 67

Source: See Figure 10.1.

Figure 10.6. CDP MAP *Coverage* Element Specifications, First Page

CDP Dublin Core Metadata Best Practices Version 2.1

4.16. *Coverage*

Term Name: coverage
Label: Coverage
Dublin Core Definition: The extent or scope of the content of the resource.
Dublin Core Comment:
  Coverage will typically include spatial location (a place name or geographic coordinates), temporal period (a period label, date, or date range) or jurisdiction (such as a named administrative entity). Recommended best practice is to select a value from a controlled vocabulary (for example, the *Thesaurus of Geographic Names* [TGN]) that, where appropriate, uses named places or time periods in preference to numeric identifiers such as sets of coordinates or date ranges.
CDP Comment:
  Coverage describes the spatial or temporal characteristics of the intellectual content of the resource. Spatial refers to the location(s) covered by the intellectual content of the resource (i.e., place names, longitude and latitude, celestial sector, etc.) *not* the place of publication. Temporal coverage refers to the time period covered by the intellectual content of the resource (e.g., Jurassic, 1900-1920), *not* the publication date. For artifacts or art objects, the spatial characteristics usually refer to the place where the artifact/object originated while the temporal characteristics refer to the date or time period during which the artifact/object was made.
Mandatory: No. Currently recommended only for use in describing maps, globes, and cartographic resources or when place or time period cannot be adequately expressed using the *Subject* element.
Repeatable: Yes
Qualifiers:
  Refinements:

Refinement Name	Refinement Label	Definition
spatial	Spatial	Spatial characteristics of the intellectual content of the resource
temporal	Temporal	Temporal characteristics of the intellectual content of the resource

  Schemes:

Spatial Schemes		
Scheme Name	Scheme Label	Definition
TGN	TGN	*Thesaurus of Geographic Names* http://www.getty.edu/research/conducting_research/vocabularies/tgn/
Point	DCMI Point	Encoding for geographic coordinates to locate a point in space http://dublincore.org/documents/dcmi-point/

Source: See Figure 10.1.

Figure 10.7. CDP MAP *Coverage* Element Specifications, Second Page

CDP Dublin Core Metadata Best Practices Version 2.1

| Box | DCMI Box | Encoding for geographic limits to define a region of space http://dublincore.org/documents/dcmi-box/ |
| ISO3166 | ISO 3166 | Codes for the representation of names of countries and their subdivisions http://www.iso.org/iso/en/ISOOnline.frontpage |

Temporal Schemes		
Scheme Name	**Scheme Label**	**Definition**
Period	DCMI Period	DCMI Period http://dublincore.org/documents/dcmi-period/

Other Spatial Schemes available, but not recommended by DCMI		
Scheme Name	**Scheme Label**	**Definition**
GNIS	GNIS	Geographic Name Information System http://geonames.usgs.gov/index.html
OSGRS	OSGRS	Ordnance Survey Grid Reference System http://sewhgpgc.co.uk/os.php

Other schemes available, but not recommended by DCMI
Terms from controlled vocabularies such as *Library of Congress Subject Headings* for recording time periods (Example: *Middle Ages*).

Input Guidelines:

1. Multiple places, physical regions, dates, and time periods may be associated with the intellectual content of the resource. No hierarchy is implied. Use separate *Coverage* elements to enter multiple spatial and temporal values or *clearly separate each entry* by a semicolon and a space within an element.
2. If using place names, select terms from a controlled vocabulary to identify place names (e.g., *Geographic Names Information System (GNIS)*, *Getty Thesaurus of Geographical Names*, *Library of Congress Subject Headings*, etc.).
3. If using latitude/longitude, enter according to GNIS standards:
    "A variable-length alphanumeric field that contains geographic coordinate pairs locating the feature. Each coordinate pair is compressed into and fixed at 15 characters. Latitude and longitude values are in degrees, minutes, and seconds followed by a one-character directional indicator. If the degrees of longitude are less than 100, a leading zero is present. The first coordinate pair listed in this element is termed the primary coordinates. In the case of areal features *[i.e., covering a broad area, such as a mountain range]*, they represent the location of the approximate geographic center of the feature, whereas the primary coordinates of linear features *[i.e., long & narrow as in a river]* represent the location of the mouth of the feature."— (*GNIS User Guide 6*, Reston, VA. 1996. http://geonames.usgs.gov/gnis_users_guide_descripdbs.html).

    Enter coordinates as "DDDMMSSXDDDMMSSX" with D=degrees, M=minutes; S=seconds, X=Directional indicator (N, S, E, or W); citing the latitude first, following by the longitude. Note that two

Source: See Figure 10.1.

Figure 10.8. CDP MAP *Coverage* Element Specifications, Third Page

CDP Dublin Core Metadata Best Practices Version 2.1

spaces are provided for latitude and three spaces for longitude degrees. Use leading zeros if needed to fill up allotted spaces.

Example:
To represent coordinates for Washington Monument in Washington, D.C., cite as "385322N0770208W," which translates as latitude 38 degrees, 53 minutes, 22 seconds north and longitude of 77 degrees, 2 minutes, 8 seconds west.

4. Use free text to input B.C.E. dates, as in "200 B.C.E."
5. For a range of dates, enter the dates on the same line, separating them with a space, hyphen, and space as in "1900 - 1950."
6. Follow dates with a question mark ("1997?") to show a date is approximate, or a circa date.

Notes: None

Examples:

Coverage [Spatial]	Comment
394916N0771325W	Latitude/Longitude for *Gettysburg National Military Park*
390254N0954040W	Latitude/Longitude for *Topeka, Kansas*
290903N0891512W	Latitude/Longitude for *Mississippi River*, at its mouth (end) in Pilottown, Louisiana
442830N084430W	Latitude/Longitude, *Higgins Lake* in Mich.
SN 045 055	A place in Wales, using the UK Ordnance Survey Grid System
North America	Place name
Paris	Place name
Rocky Mountains	Place name
Coverage [Temporal]	**Comment**
1776-07-04	Date for July 4, 1776
Colonial America	Time Period
Ming	Time Period
1840?	Approximate date or circa date
1900-1901	Date range
15th century	Time period
96 B.C.E.	Free text B.C.E. date

Maps to: Dublin Core *Coverage*
CDPDC Term Modified: 2004-07-21

CDPDCMBP Last Modified 2006-09-15

Source: See Figure 10.1.

Temporal Schemes as well as Refinements, separate examples for *Spatial* and *Temporal Coverage*, and the mapping of the CDP *Coverage* element to the Dublin Core *Coverage* element.

10.2.1.2. OhioLINK Dublin Core Metadata Documentation

Figures 10.9 through 10.14 consist of selected pages from the Ohio LINK Digital Resources Commons (DRC) Metadata Application Profile Version 1.2 (OhioLINK Digital Resources Management Committee (DRMC) Metadata Subcommittee, 2010). Figure 10.9 shows the table of contents and the scope of this 39-page document.

Figure 10.10 shows a snapshot of the OhioLINK DRC Element Set, including those elements that are Mandatory, and the beginning of their General Input Guidelines, and Figure 10.11 shows a continuation of those guidelines on the following page.

Figures 10.12 through 10.14 show the specifications for the OhioLINK *Title*, *Creator*, and *Subject* elements, respectively, including definition, mapping to Dublin Core elements, obligation, occurrence, recommended schemes, specific input guidelines, and examples.

10.2.1.3. Indiana Memory Dublin Core Metadata Documentation

Figures 10.15 through 10.18 consist of selected pages from the Indiana Memory Project's *Dublin Core Metadata Guide* (Indiana Memory Project, 2007). This 13-page document gives the specifications for its elements in order of those that are Required, followed by those that are Recommended, and concluding with those that are Optional. A set of answers to Frequently Asked Questions constitutes pages 9–13 of the document. Figure 10.15 shows the first page of the document, including its introduction, a statement that it is based on the CDP Dublin Core Metadata Best Practices document, the beginning of the Required elements, with their definition of what *Required* means, and the specifications for the *Title* element.

Figure 10.16 shows the Indiana Memory specifications for the *Subject* element. Note the Cataloging Notes, lists of Recommended Thesauri and Other Example Thesauri codes and names, with URLs when applicable.

Figure 10.17 shows the conclusion of the *Subject* element specifications, followed by those for their *Date.Original* element and the beginning of their *Date.Digital* element. Note the examples section for the *Subject* element, and the Cataloging Notes for the two date elements.

Figure 10.18 shows the conclusion of the specifications for *Date.Digital* and the beginning of their set of Recommended Elements, with their definition of the meaning of *Recommended*, the specifications for the *Creator* element, and beginning of the specifications for the *Publisher* element.

10.2.1.4. DLF/Aquifer MODS Metadata Documentation

Figures 10.19 through 10.23 consist of a few selected pages from the 117-page *Digital Library Federation/Aquifer Implementation Guidelines for Shareable MODS Records* (DLF Aquifer Metadata Working Group, 2009). These guidelines have also now been incorporated into the

Figure 10.9. OhioLINK MAP Table of Contents

Table of Contents

Figure 10.10. OhioLINK MAP Core Element Set and General Input Guidelines

DRC Metadata Application Profile
p. 6

Snapshot of DRC Core Element Set

The following list provides an at-a-glance view of the DRC Core Element set in the same order as presented later in the document in detail. **Mandatory elements appear in bold.**

> - **Title**
> - **Creator**
> - Date created
> - Description
> - Subject Keywords
> - Coverage Spatial
> - Coverage Temporal
> - Language
> - Type
> - Repository Name
> - Publisher
> - Digital Publisher
> - **Date digitized**
> - Digitizing Equipment
> - Rights
> - Collection Name
> - **OhioLINK Institution**
> - **Identifier**
> - Format
> - Size
> - Date Issued
> - Date Accessioned
> - Date Available

General Input Guidelines

Input guidelines are provided for all non-system supplied elements, including guidelines for commonly encountered anomalies or otherwise ambiguous situations. While it is impossible to anticipate all situations, every effort has been made to assist contributors in metadata creation. Recommended best practice is to select or establish content standards prior to project implementation and to apply them consistently across elements as appropriate. Examples of established content standards include: Anglo-American Cataloguing Rules (AACR2), Describing Archives: a Content Standard (DACS), and Cataloging Cultural Objects (CCO). Select terms from controlled vocabularies, thesauri and heading lists; establish new terms and headings using the same standards. Employing terminology from these types of sources ensures consistency, reduces spelling errors and can improve the quality of search results. In some cases, this document refers to specific external content standards such as the date/time standard ISO 8601. Full citations for text-based standards or URLs for those that are Internet accessible are provided in the References.

1. **Repeatable Values.** For elements that allow repeatable values, follow guidelines in the software interface. The interface may require multiple values to be added to an element by delimiting them with a semi-colon and space or the interface may provide separate text entry fields for each value to be entered.

Source: See Figure 10.9.

Figure 10.11. OhioLINK MAP General Input Guidelines, Continued

DRC Metadata Application Profile
p. 7

2. **Names.** Apply the same rules or guidelines to format names of creators, digital publishers, contributors, and names entered as subjects. If not following established rules such as Anglo-American Cataloguing Rules (AACR2), then use these guidelines:

    a. Determine correct form of the name when possible. The Library of Congress Authority File (http://authorities.loc.gov) or other locally specified bibliographic utility (OCLC, RLIN, etc.) should be consulted.

    b. Enter personal names in inverted form in most cases: last name, first name, middle name or initial.. If it is not obvious how to invert or structure the name, use the name form given in an authority list or enter it as it would be in the country of origin. Birth and/or death dates, if known, can be added, in accordance with the authorized form of name.

    c. Enter group or organization names in full, direct form. In the case of a hierarchy, list the parts from the largest to smallest, separated by a period and space. You may input an entire group name in the "last name" box in the default DRC/DSpace submission for.

    d. If there is doubt as to how to enter a name and the form of name cannot be verified in an authority list, enter it as it appears and do not invert (Example: Sitting Bull -- n.b. enter this type of name in the "Last name" box).

3. **Dates.** Enter dates in the form YYYY-MM-DD in accordance with the date/time standard ISO 8601 defined in http://www.w3.org/TR/NOTE-datetime.html. Use a single hyphen to separate year, month, and date components:

    a. Year:
       YYYY (1997 for the year 1997)

    b. Year and month:
       YYYY-MM (1997-07 for July 1997)

    c. Complete date:
       YYYY-MM-DD (1997-07-16 for July 16, 1997)

    d. For a range of dates, enter the dates on the same line, separating them with a space hyphen space (1910 – 1920)

    e. To show date is approximate, follow the date with a question mark (1890?)

    f. Input B.C.E. dates (200 B.C.E.) and time periods (Jurassic) as needed.

    g. The default DRC/DSpace default submission form precludes direct entry of some of the formats listed above. You may use DRC editing mode to reformat you date entries.

Source: See Figure 10.9.

Figure 10.12. OhioLINK MAP *Title* Element Specifications

DRC Metadata Application Profile
p. 11

Title

Definition: A name given to a resource. Typically a title will be a name by which the resource is known. It may also be an identifying phrase or object name supplied by the holding institution.

Maps to DC Element: dc:title
Obligation: Mandatory
Occurrence: Non-Repeatable

Recommended Schemes: None.

Input Guidelines:
1. Identify and enter one Title element per record according to the guidelines that follow.
2. Transcribe title from the resource itself, such as book title, photograph caption, artist's title, object name, etc., using same punctuation that appears on the source.
3. When no title is found on the resource itself, use a title assigned by the holding institution or found in reference sources. If title must be created, make the title as descriptive as possible, avoiding generic terms such as Papers or Annual report. Use punctuation appropriate for English writing. For additional guidance on composing titles see DACS.
4. When possible, exclude initial articles from title. Exceptions might include when the article is an essential part of the title or when local practice requires use of initial articles.
5. Capitalize only the first letter of the first word of the title and of any proper names contained within the title.
6. Consult established cataloging rules such as Anglo-American Cataloguing Rules (AACR2) or Archives, Personal Papers, and Manuscripts (APPM) for more information.
7. Multiple titles: The DRC default submissions page offers a checkbox for multiple titles. When that box is checked, the "Other Titles" field is then shown with the other metadata fields in the DSpace submission form. Any additional titles entered in the "Other Titles" text box are mapped to dc.title.alternative (repeatable)

> **Examples:**
> 1. Channel crew poling ice blocks
> 2. DH-4 battle plane and Wright Model C Flyer share air space
> 3. Exhibition flight over Lake Erie
> 4. Great Ballcourt

Source: See Figure 10.9.

Figure 10.13. OhioLINK MAP *Creator* Element Specifications

DRC Metadata Application Profile
p. 12

Creator

Definition: An entity primarily responsible for making the content of the resource. Examples of creators include authors of written documents, artists, illustrators, photographers, collectors of natural specimens or artifacts, organizations that generate archival collections, etc.

Maps to DC element: dc:contributor.author
Comments: Use the DC qualifier that is most appropriate for the role of the creator. dc:contributor.author is the default. You may contact your local systems administrator or OhioLINK DRC staff to customize the submission form for input of additional qualified fields, e.g., dc:contributor.photographer. N.B. dc:creator is not used due to current DSPACE system specific limitations.
Obligation: Mandatory
Occurrence: Repeatable

Recommended Schemes: Library of Congress Authority File.

Input Guidelines:
1. Enter the name(s) of the creator(s) of the object. Construct names according to General Input Guidelines. Enter multiple primary creators in the order in which they appear on the resource or in order of their importance. Secondary authors, editors, etc. should be entered using the Contributor element.
2. Use "unknown" if a creator cannot be determined.
3. Repeat the names of creators in the subject element only if the object is also about the creator in some way. (Example: A record for a self portrait of Picasso would list Picasso, Pablo, 1881-1973 as both creator and subject; a record for a work by Picasso would list Picasso, Pablo, 1881-1973 only in the creator element).

Examples:
1. Niebergall, Ernst
2. Dayton Wright Airplane Company
3. United States. Army. Air Corps.
4. Grimm, Linda T.
5. unknown

Author:

Last name, *e.g. Smith*   First name(s) + "Jr", *e.g. Donald Jr*
Add
Enter group or organization name in full, direct form in the "Last name" box.

Source: See Figure 10.9.

Figure 10.14. OhioLINK MAP *Subject* Element Specifications

DRC Metadata Application Profile
p. 15

Subject Keywords

Definition: A topic of the content of the resource. Typically, Subject will be expressed as keywords, or thesaurus terms or classification codes that describe a topic of the resource. Recommended best practice is to select a value from a controlled vocabulary, name authority file or formal classification scheme. *Comments: If a controlled vocabulary is used, it is recommended that the local systems administrator or OhioLINK DRC staff customize the submission form to specify the vocabulary as an extension, e.g. dc:subject.lcsh Specific geographic subjects or time periods should be described elsewhere: use Coverage Spatial (geographic subject) and Coverage Temporal (time period).*

Maps to DC Element: dc:subject
Obligation: Required (if available)
Occurrence: Repeatable

Recommended Schemes: It is strongly recommended that subject words and phrases come from established thesauri or discipline-related word lists, e.g. LCSH, Mesh, TGM.

Input Guidelines:
1. Determine subject terms using the resource itself, including title and description. Use words or phrases from established thesauri or construct new subject terms following the rules of an established thesaurus if available terms do not adequately describe content of resource. Construct names according to General Input Guidelines.
2. Enter multiple subjects in order of their importance, often determined by how much of the entire content is devoted to a particular subject.
3. Subjects may be personal or organization names as well as topics, places, genres, forms, and events. Subject elements may describe not only what the object is, but also what the object is about.
4. Repeat the names of creators in the subject element only if the object is also about the creator in some way. (Example: A record for a self portrait of Picasso would list Picasso, Pablo, 1881-1973 as both creator and subject; a record for a work by Picasso would list Picasso, Pablo, 1881-1973 only in the creator element).

Examples:
1. Gliding and soaring
2. Campaigns & battles
3. Kill Devil Hills (N.C.)
4. African Americans -- Civil rights -- History

15 of 39

Figure 10.15. Indiana Memory MAP Introductory and *Title* Element Documentation

Dublin Core Metadata Guide**
Indiana Memory Project
February 8, 2007

This document provides information on the application of published standards and best practices for Dublin Core metadata creation. It includes a list of required metadata elements, recommended metadata elements, and optional metadata elements for Indiana Memory metadata records. Required elements must be included in any item-level Indiana Memory metadata record. Recommended elements should be included if those creating the metadata have enough information to describe the elements accurately. Optional elements may be included at the discretion of those creating the metadata. An FAQ section providing information on the Indiana Memory program, Dublin Core metadata, and other metadata standards starts on page 9 of this document.

Based on the Collaborative Digitization Program's (CDP) Dublin Core Metadata Best Practices Version 2.1 (http://www.cdpheritage.org/cdp/documents/CDPDCMBP.pdf) and Indiana University's "Metadata Best Practices For Use of Qualified Dublin Core" (www.dlib.indiana.edu/workshops/indl04/handout7.pdf).

REQUIRED ELEMENTS		
The following elements must be included in the metadata of all projects or collections created with state-licensed CONTENTdm acquisition stations and/or LSTA funding that are shared on Indiana Memory.		
Element Name	**DC Definition**	**Comments**
Title (Maps to Title)	A name given to the resource.	Typically, the **title** will be a name by which the resource is formally known. The title may be a name given to the resource by the creator or publisher. If the item does not have a title, assign one that is brief but descriptive.

Cataloging Notes:
- If the resource does not have a title, create a title for it.
- Make the title as descriptive as possible while still keeping it fairly brief. Avoid simple generic titles, though this is not always possible.
- Bring out the unique qualities of an item.
- Capitalization: First word of any title should be capitalized; all other words are lower-case except for proper nouns
- Include format (i.e. papers, portrait) in the title only when you feel it is required to properly convey the nature of the title. Remember that the "Item Type" field, a required field on page 3, is the proper place for format information.

Examples:
- Little orphan Annie
- Tourist's pocket map of the state of Indiana
- 12 ways to get to 11
- Jacob Piatt Dunn papers
- Portrait of Abraham Lincoln
- Aerial view of South Bend, Indiana, 1899
- Mrs. John Smith at birthday party
- 15th annual report / Charity Organization Society of the City of New York.

Page 1 of 13

Source: Indiana State Library Indiana Memory Program.

Figure 10.16. Indiana Memory MAP *Subject* Element Documentation, Beginning

Element Name	DC Definition	Comments
Subject (Maps to Subject)	The topic of the content of the resource.	Typically, a **subject** will be expressed as keywords, key phrases or classification codes that describe a topic of the resource. Recommended best practice is to select a value from a controlled vocabulary or formal classification scheme. Generally, this field will contain terms that describe what is depicted in an image, or terms that describe what a text is about. May also include terms for significantly associated people, places, events, genres, forms, etc. This field will not contain item type descriptions, such as "photographic print," because this data will be described in the Item Type field, a required metadata element.

Cataloging Notes:
- This field is repeatable, so feel free to enter more than one subject.
- If including names of people, places, groups, or events consult the Library of Congress Authority File for Authorized Headings. Use Authorized Heading if found.
- If an Authorized Heading is not found create the name based on AACR2 rules.
- Make sure to include a subject heading that describes the county, city, or geographic area covered by your resource. "Indiana" alone is too general. For example, the Starke County Historical Society and the Starke County Public Library have included the LC subject heading "Starke County (Ind.)" in the subject field for items in their collection that relate specifically to that county. If users search for Starke County as a keyword or a subject, this ensures that they will retrieve items related to that geographic area.

Recommended Thesauri

These are commonly used and easily accessible thesauri that provide a wide range of controlled subject headings. They should suffice for most collections:

Code	Name of Thesaurus
LCAF	Library of Congress Authorities File: http://authorities.loc.gov
LCSH	Library of Congress Subject Headings: http://authorities.loc.gov/cgi-bin/Pwebrecon.cgi?DB=local&PAGE=First
LCTGM	Thesaurus for Graphic Materials: TGM I, Subject Terms: http://lcweb.loc.gov/rr/print/tgm1/

Other Example Thesauri

These may also prove useful for certain collections:

Code	Name of Thesaurus
AAT	Art and Architecture Thesaurus http://www.getty.edu/research/tools/vocabulary/aat/
AASL	Asian American Studies Library subject headings
AMG	Audiovisual Materials Glossary (AMG)
CHT	Chicano Thesaurus for Indexing Chicano Materials
DDC	Dewey Decimal Classification http://www.oclc.org/dewey/
FAST	Faceted Application of Subject Terminology
RBGENR	Genre Terms: A Thesaurus for Use in Rare Books and Special Collections
GEOREFT	GEORef Thesaurus
TGN	Getty Thesaurus of Geographic Names http://www.getty.edu/research/tools/vocabulary/tgn/
GSAFD	Guidelines on Subject Access to Individual Works of Fiction, Drama, etc.
LCC	Library of Congress Classification http://lcweb.loc.gov/catdir/cpso/lcco/lcco.html
LCSHAC	Library of Congress Subject Headings: Annotated Card Program (Children's headings)
Local	Locally controlled list of terms

Page 2 of 13

Source: Indiana State Library Indiana Memory Program.

Figure 10.17. Indiana Memory MAP *Subject*, *Date.Original*, and *Date.Digital* Elements

a specific statement for each resource.
- Make sure that the rights statement corresponds to the digital resource; for example, link to a copyright statement for the digital resource instead of the original resource.

Examples:
- Original Contributions, Copyright 2006, the Trustees of Indiana University. The extent to which IUPUI University Library has the authority, we grant permission to view and print items from the Digital Collections of IUPUI University Library for personal use, study, research or classroom teaching without permission. Any commercial use is prohibited without permission. Any fair use, as defined by copyright law, is acceptable, though IUPUI University Library leaves the interpretation of said use to the user. For additional information or for requests for permission to use, please contact the IUPUI Digital Library Summit or consult The Copyright Management Center. Consulting your own institution's copyright lawyer is also suggested.
- Copyright 2002-2004. The Trustees of Indiana University. This material may be protected by U.S. Copyright Law (Title 17, U.S. Code), which governs reproduction, distribution, display, and certain other uses of protected works. The user of this material is responsible for compliance with the Law.
- Digital image © 2004 Indiana Historical Society. All Rights Reserved.

DC Element	DC Definition	Comments
Date.Original (Maps to Date)	Date of the creation of the resource.	Date of publication if known. If item never published enter the date of creation.

Cataloging Notes: When a precise date is known, use the format YYYY-MM-DD, supplying as much information as possible. Use a single hyphen to separate the year, moth, and date components.
> Year 1942
> Year + month 1942-03
> Year + month + day 1942-03-09

> For date ranges, enter the dates in the same date field. (Example: 1901-1907)

Libraries and archives have traditionally recorded dates according to the rules of AACR2 and APPM. Dates in these forms may be used when an exact year is not known or it is important to distinguish between a copyright date and a publication date. Example dates in these formats include:
> [ca. 1940]
> 18--?
> c1920
> 1907?
> Be aware that formatting dates using brackets, question marks, ca., etc. makes it difficult for
systems to use the date for searching and browsing purposes.

Suggested practice if no date is known, enter n.d./unknown.

DC Element	DC Definition	Comments
Date.Digital (Maps to Date)	Digital Date	Date the item was added to digital content management tool. This date is can be automatically generated by Content DM and many other digital content management tools.

Cataloging Notes: When a precise date is known, use the format YYYY-MM-DD, supplying as much information as possible. Use a single hyphen to separate the year, moth, and date components.
> Year 1942
> Year + month 1942-03
> Year + month + day 1942-03-09

> For date ranges, enter the dates in the same date field. (Example: 1901-1907)

Libraries and archives have traditionally recorded dates according to the rules of AACR2 and

Page 5 of 13

Figure 10.18. Indiana Memory MAP Recommended, *Creator*, and *Publisher* Elements

APPM. Dates in these forms may be used when an exact year is not known or it is important to distinguish between a copyright date and a publication date. Example dates in these formats include:
>[ca. 1940]
>18--?
>c1920
>1907?
>Be aware that formatting dates using brackets, question marks, ca., etc. makes it difficult for
systems to use the date for searching and browsing purposes.

Suggested practice if no date is known, enter n.d./unknown.

RECOMMENDED ELEMENTS

If the information required to accurately describe each of the following metadata elements is available to the cataloger, the element should be included in the metadata of projects or collections created with state-licensed CONTENTdm acquisition stations and/or LSTA funding that are shared on Indiana Memory.

Element Name	DC Definition	Comments
Creator (Maps to Creator)	Identifies anyone responsible in some way for the content of the resource.	The person or group responsible for the intellectual or artistic content of the original item. Examples include: author, artist, sculptor, photographer, etc.

Cataloging Notes:
- This element is repeatable.
- When including names of people, groups, or events consult the Library of Congress Authority File for Authorized Headings (http://authorities.loc.gov). Use Authorized Heading if found.
- If an Authorized Heading is not found create the name based on AACR2 rules.
- This field can contain more than one name separated by a semi colon (;).

Examples:
- Lincoln, Abraham, 1809-1865
- Riley, James Whitcomb, 1849-1916
- Toulouse-Lautrec, Henri de, 1864-1901
- Clinton, Bill, 1946-
- Chesney, Kenny
- Indiana State Library
- United States. Army. Indiana Infantry Regiment, 9th (1861-1865)
- Walt Disney Company; Clinton, Bill, 1946-; Chesney, Kenny

DC Element	DC Definition	Comments
Publisher (Maps to Publisher)	An entity responsible for making the resource available.	Sometimes a publisher cannot be determined from the information provided on the resource. If that is the case, do not use this element.

Cataloging Notes:
- When including names of people, groups, or events consult the Library of Congress Authority File for Authorized Headings (http://authorities.loc.gov). Use Authorized Heading if found.
- If an Authorized Heading is not found create the name based on AACR2 rules.
- If the publisher is the same as the creator, do not repeat the name in the Publisher field.

Examples:
- Indiana Historical Society
- Microsoft Corporation
- United States. Government Printing Office
- University of Virginia Press

Page 6 of 13

Source: Indiana State Library Indiana Memory Program.

MODS User Guidelines, Version 3. This is for all intents and purposes a MODS metadata application profile for this collaborative. Figures 10.19 and 10.20 show the first two pages of the Summary of Requirements and Recommendations, which give a broad overview of the specifications, before proceeding to the detailed specifications for each individual MODS element, subelement, and attribute as they are implemented for the DLF/Aquifer Digital Library Federation initiative. Note the designations for required, required if applicable, recommended, and recommended if applicable; repeatability; and controlled content.

Figures 10.21 through 10.23 show the detailed specifications for the MODS <typeOfResource> element, including summary of requirements, definitions from the MODS User Guidelines, Discussion of Use, Examples, Use By Aggregators, and Mapping to Dublin Core.

Figure 10.19. DLF/Aquifer MAP Summary, First Page

DLF/Aquifer Implementation Guidelines for Shareable MODS Records – November 2006

Summary of Requirements and Recommendations

Element	Element Requirement Level	Subelement(s)/Attributes required if element used	Subelement(s)/Attributes recommended or recommended if applicable	Repeat-able	Content Controlled
`<titleInfo>` (page 14)	Required	- `<title>`	- `type` attribute - `authority` attribute - `<subTitle>` - `<partName>` - `<partNumber>` - `<nonSort>`	Yes	Recommended authority attribute limits content
`<name>` (page 18)	Required if applicable	- `<namePart>`	- `type` attribute - `authority` attribute - `<role><roleTerm>`	Yes	Recommended authority attribute limits content
`<typeOfResource>` (page 24)	Required	None	- `Collection` attribute - `manuscript` attribute	Yes	Yes
`<genre>` (page 28)	Recommended	- `authority` attribute	N/A	Yes	Recommended authority attribute limits content
`<originInfo>` (page 30)	Required	- `<placeTerm>` and `type` attribute when `<place>` used - `authority` attribute when `<placeTerm type="code">` used - At least one date subelement - At least one date subelement must have attribute `keyDate="yes"`	- `<publisher>` - `encoding` attribute for date - `point` attribute for date - `qualifier` attribute for date - `<edition>`	Yes	Recommended authority and encoding attribute limits content

10 of 117

Figure 10.20. DLF/Aquifer MAP Summary, Second Page

DLF/Aquifer Implementation Guidelines for Shareable MODS Records – November 2006

Element	Element Requirement Level	Subelement(s)/Attributes required if element used	Subelement(s)/Attributes recommended or recommended if applicable	Repeat -able	Content Controlled
`<language>` (page 36	Required, if language is primary to resource	- `<languageTerm>` - each `type` attribute - `authority` attribute when `type="code"`	N/A	Yes	Required `authority` attribute limits content
`<physical Description>` (page 40)	Required	- `<digitalOrigin>` - `<internetMediaType>`	- `<form>` and `authority` attribute - `<extent>` - `<note>`	No	Yes (see guidelines)
`<abstract>` (page 44)	Recommended	N/A	N/A	Yes	No
`<tableOfContents>` (page 46)	Recommended if applicable	none	- `xlink` attribute	Yes	No
`<targetAudience>` (page 48)	Recommended if applicable	none	- `authority` attribute	Yes	Recommended `authority` attribute limits content
`<note>` (page 50)	Recommended if applicable	none	none	Yes	No
`<subject>` (page 54)	Required if applicable	At least one subelement is required as `<subject>` is a wrapper element.	- `authority` attribute - `<topic>` - `<geographic>` - `<temporal>` with encoding, point attributes - `<titleInfo>` - `<name>` - `<hierarchicalGeographic>` - `<geographicCode>` with `authority` attribute	Yes	Recommended `authority` attribute limits content

11 of 117

Source: Network Development & MARC Standards Office, Library of Congress.

10.2.2. Collection-Specific Application Profile Examples

This section of the chapter contains three examples of *collection-specific* Dublin Core metadata scheme documentation. Each of these schemes was designed for a specific collection created using the CONTENTdm digital content management system. These examples illustrate the wide range of nonstandard element or field names tailored to each collection and its specific subject content. This type of documentation is sometimes called a *data dictionary*, but it also fits into the scope of *application profile* taken in its broadest sense. Notice the diversity of local element names and their mapping to standard Dublin Core, as well as the kinds of information given in each document. The first two examples come

Figure 10.21. DLF/Aquifer MAP <typeOfResource> Element, First Page

DLF/Aquifer Implementation Guidelines for Shareable MODS Records – November 2006

<typeOfResource>

MODS Element	Attributes	Subelements
<typeOfResource>	collection manuscript	None

SUMMARY OF REQUIREMENTS

The *DLF/Aquifer Implementation Guidelines for Shareable MODS Records* require the use in all records of at least one <typeOfResource> element using the required enumerated values. This element is repeatable.

DEFINITION FROM *MODS USER GUIDELINES*

A term that specifies the characteristics and general type of content of the resource.

DISCUSSION OF USE

For the purposes of records created according to these guidelines, information in <typeOfResource> is about the original item. For example, in the case of a digitized photograph, <typeOfResource> would apply to the analog original; in born-digital materials, it would apply to the original digital format.

The <typeOfResource> element is required by these guidelines and is used to categorize the resource at a fairly high level. <typeOfResource> has no subelements, but does require the use of an enumerated list of values. There are two possible attributes in addition to the common attributes described at the end of these guidelines [see page 100].

Repeat this element as necessary.

<u>Attributes:</u>

collection [RECOMMENDED IF APPLICABLE]

Use this attribute (collection="yes") to indicate whether the resource described is a collection. A collection is defined as a multi-part group of resources. If there are multiple resource types within the collection, these should be enumerated in separate <typeOfResource> elements.

manuscript [RECOMMENDED IF APPLICABLE]

Use this attribute (manuscript="yes") to indicate whether the resource described is handwritten or typescript.

<u>Values:</u>

24 of 117

Source: Network Development & MARC Standards Office, Library of Congress.

Figure 10.22. DLF/Aquifer MAP <typeOfResource> Element, Second Page

DLF/Aquifer Implementation Guidelines for Shareable MODS Records – November 2006

The values for <typeOfResource> are restricted to those in the following list. These should be used in accordance with the guidelines offered in the MODS *User Guidelines*.[15]

> text
> cartographic
> notated music
> sound recording [if not possible to specify "musical" or "nonmusical"]
> sound recording-musical
> sound recording-nonmusical
> still image
> moving image
> three dimensional object
> software, multimedia
> mixed material

EXAMPLES OF <typeOfResource> USE

```
<typeOfResource>text</typeOfResource>
<typeOfResource>still image</typeOfResource>

<typeOfResource>cartographic</typeOfResource>

<typeOfResource collection="yes">text</typeOfResource>

<typeOfResource manuscript="yes">text</typeOfResource>
```

USE BY AGGREGATORS

Due to its utility for determining research value (for example, a researcher looking specifically for cartographic material), aggregators may choose to include this field in a brief display to end users, and may also index it to allow limiting or refining by this data. Aggregators may also use this field to determine suitability for harvesting based on their perception of end users' needs.

MAPPING TO DUBLIN CORE

The *MODS to Dublin Core Metadata Element Set Mapping Version 3.0 (June 7, 2005)* recommend mapping <typeOfResource> to <dc:type>. In addition, these guidelines recommend that when mapping the values found in <typeOfResource> to Dublin Core Type values[16], include both the MODS value and the DC value if they are substantially different. Similarly, the attributes of collection and manuscript should be included as an additional, separate <dc:type> value.

```
<dc:type>text</dc:type>
<dc:type>still image</dc:type>

<dc:type>cartographic</dc:type>
```

---

[15] http://www.loc.gov/standards/mods/v3/mods-userguide-elements.html#typeofresource
[16] http://dublincore.org/documents/dcmi-type-vocabulary/

25 of 117

Source: Network Development & MARC Standards Office, Library of Congress.

Figure 10.23. DLF/Aquifer MAP <typeOfResource> Element, Third Page

DLF/Aquifer Implementation Guidelines for Shareable MODS Records – November 2006

```
<dc:type>StillImage</dc:type>

<dc:type>collection</dc:type>
<dc:type>text</dc:type>

<dc:type>manuscript</dc:type>
<dc:type>text</dc:type>
```

RELATIONSHIP TO DLF/NSDL BEST PRACTICES FOR SHAREABLE METADATA

Related information is discussed in the Types of Resource[17] and the Describing Versions and Reproductions[18] sections of the DLF/NSDL *Best Practices for Shareable Metadata*.

---

[17] http://oai-best.comm.nsdl.org/cgi-bin/wiki.pl?TypesofResources
[18] http://oai-best.comm.nsdl.org/cgi-bin/wiki.pl?DigitalTactileResource

26 of 117

Source: Network Development & MARC Standards Office, Library of Congress.

from the University of Washington Libraries Digital Collections and include only a selected subset of the fields in the complete scheme documentation. All of the University of Washington's data dictionaries or metadata application profiles are available for viewing online, as of the time of this writing, at http://www.lib.washington.edu/msd/mig/datadicts/. The UW's Metadata Implementation Group has also posted some fairly extensive additional Dublin Core and CONTENTdm documentation at http://www.lib.washington.edu/msd/mig/advice/default.html. As of this writing, this documentation includes a basic template for a metadata application profile following their local practices, and more detailed information about, and content guidelines for, each Dublin Core element.

10.2.2.1. University of Washington's Architecture Collection Metadata Documentation

Table 10.1 consists of selected elements for an Architecture Collection created for the University of Washington Libraries Digital Collections (University of Washington Libraries Metadata Implementation Group, 2006). The complete application profile can be found at http://www.lib .washington.edu/msd/mig/datadicts/default.html.

This documentation consists of a table with four columns. The first column contains the local, collection-specific element name. This list of elements constitutes the data structure standard for this collection. The second column contains the Dublin Core element to which each local element is mapped, which is also an aspect of the data structure standard, along with designations for CONTENTdm settings for field searchability and public display. It also contains the Obligation designation of *required* when it applies to a specific element. The third column specifies controlled vocabularies that apply to certain elements. These are data value standards. The fourth column consists of detailed comments that explain the application of the element, what kinds of information should go into each, how it should be structured, and in some cases includes examples. The content of this fourth column constitutes the local data content standard for this particular digital collection.

10.2.2.2. University of Washington's Musical Instruments Collection Metadata Documentation

Table 10.2 shows selected metadata elements from a very different digital collection at the University of Washington (University of Washington Libraries Metadata Implementation Group, 2003). This document follows the same format as that for the Architecture Collection shown in Table 10.1. Notice the differences and similarities between the two, especially the local element names specific to this particular collection and its content.

10.2.2.3. University of Wisconsin–Milwaukee's Transportation Collection Metadata Documentation

Table 10.3 provides a third example of collection-specific metadata documentation from another institution (University of Wisconsin–Milwaukee Libraries Digital Collections, 2009).

Table 10.1. Architecture of the Pacific Northwest Data Dictionary: Selections

Field name	DC mapping	Authority file	Comments
Title	Title: searchable, public; required		Descriptive title of work to be assigned by the cataloger based on subject of the drawing. It should include information in the following order: name of structure taken from the artifact (architectural drawing or rendering), the location in parentheses (Seattle, Wash.) and parts represented. If the specific name of the structure is unidentified, the title may include other identifiers, such as building type, location, or anything else of significance in identifying the subject. Titles belonging to a group of images from the same drawing set should begin with the same character set (e.g. Northern Life Tower, ...) in order to group the thumbnails for Contentdm presentation. Examples: Northern Life Tower (Seattle, Wash.), south elevation Residence with carriage house (Seattle, Wash.), first and second floor plans
Architectural firm	Creator: searchable, public	LC Authority	The name of the corporate body responsible for the creation of the design of the item. Use LC Authority File for form of name, if available. For unknown creators, enter Unknown. The names of the individual architects belonging to the firm can be entered into the additional "Creator" fields. If the Creator is determined from a resource other than the item, create a Note. Familiar names or variation of names of corporate bodies should be noted in the Notes Field.
Architects	Creator: searchable, public	LC Authority File	The name (s) of the individual (s) responsible for the creation of the design of the item. Input lastname, firstname or the corporate body name. Use LC Authority File for form of name, if available. Multiple names are okay; separate multiple names with . For unknown creators, enter Unknown. If the Creator is determined from a resource other than the item, create a Note. Familiar names or variation of names of corporate bodies should be noted in the Notes Field.
Engineers	Creator: searchable, public	LC Authority File	Name of the engineer or firm responsible for creating the item. Input lastname, firstname or the corporate body name. Use LC Authority File for form of name, if available. Multiple names are okay; separate multiple names with . If none, leave blank.
Date of drawing execution	Date: searchable, public		The time period the drawing was made. Enter span dates which are inclusive of all revisions represented on item. Dates are recorded as single years. If undated, input circa date. (ca. 1900). Months and days are noted in the Descriptive Notes Field.
Building location	Coverage: searchable, public/staff field		The spatial characteristics of the intellectual content of the resource. Spatial coverage refers to a physical region. Places names are taken from the LC Authority File or another controlled list. Input in hierarchical format. United States--Washington (State)--Seattle
Building style	Subject: searchable, public		Use terminology from AAT if possible. Otherwise use vocabulary terms from: A visual inventory of buildings & urban design resources for Seattle Washington / Historic Seattle Preservation and Development Authority, consultants: Folke Nyberg, Victor Steinbrueck , [Seattle, Wash.] : The Authority, 1975
Subject (LCTGM)	Subject: searchable, public	TGM	Terms in this field are taken from the LC Thesaurus for Graphic Materials I: Subject Terms (LC TGM I). Subject terms and phrases are displayed as a list in this field, with no blank lines between terms. Examples: Space Needle (Seattle, Wash.) Buildings--Washington (State)--Seattle

Source: University of Washington Libraries Special Collections Division, Architecture of the Pacific Northwest Data Dictionary: Selections. Courtesy: UW Libraries Metadata Implementation Group. Used with permission.

The first column gives the local, collection-specific field name, with the Dublin Core mapping in the second column. The third column contains examples of the type of content to be used in most of the fields, and the fourth column specifies any controlled vocabularies to be used for a given field. Because this collection has a strong geographic focus, and

Table 10.2. Musical Instruments in the University of Washington Ethnomusicology Division Data Dictionary: Selections

Field name	DC mapping	Authority file	Comments
Instrument title	**Title:** Searchable, public; *required*		A short descriptive phrase in English describing what is depicted in the image. This field will be used as the thumbnail caption and will be used for sorting the thumbnails. When the collection includes more than one example of an instrument, the instrument title will contain a number to make it unique, for example, Sho 1, Sho 2, etc. A consistent pattern here will lead to better sorting of thumbnails in CONTENTdm.
Sound of instrument	None		Contains link to audio clip of instrument sound if available
Performance clip	None		Contains link to audio clip of instrument performance, either solo or in ensemble, if available
Instrument name	**Subject:** Searchable, public	**Grove**	Contains name of musical instrument as found in New Grove Dictionary of Musical Instruments (1984). Variant forms/spellings of the instrument name given in variant instrument name.
Variant instrument name	**Subject:** Searchable, public		Includes alternate forms and spellings for instrument names.
Country/area	**Coverage:** Searchable, public	**LCAF**	Enter <Country>. Derive place names from LC headings. If no authorized version of the place can be found, the cataloging supervisor will be alerted and a name may be established in the LC file. Example: *Japan East Asia*
Culture area	**Subject:** Searchable, public	**LCAF**	Language or ethnic based provenance.
Hornbostel-Sachs No.	**Subject:** Searchable, public	**Hornbostel-Sachs Classification of Musical Instruments**	A system of classifying musical instruments according to the means of sound production.
Keyword	**Subject:** Searchable, public		Includes musical genre terms and contexts in which music is performed.
Materials	**Subject:** Searchable, public	**AAT**	Example: *bamboo lacquer metal*

Source: Musical Instruments in the Collection of the University of Washington, School of Music, Ethnomusicology Division Data Dictionary: Selections. Courtesy UW Libraries Metadata Implementation Group. Used with permission.

includes images from all over the world, the metadata designer included separate elements for *Continent, Country/Region, State/Province*, and *City/Place*, all mapped to Dublin Core *Spatial Coverage*. If mapped into MODS, the content of each of these elements could go into a specific subelement in a <subject><hierarchicalGeographic> element.

The metadata design, including the specific local elements and the use of controlled vocabulary terms, makes possible certain types of functionality for users of the collection in its public web interface. For example, Figure 10.24 shows a clickable map that allows users to browse images by continent. When the user clicks on *Asia*, for example, the software executes a search matching on the controlled value *Asia* in

Table 10.3. Transportation Around the World Database Fields

Field	Mapped to DC	Content Examples	Vocabulary
Title	Title	Auckland Harbor Bridge in Auckland, New Zealand	Free text
Photographer's Note/Description	Description	New bridge across Auckland harbor	Transcribed text
Photographer	Creator	Forman, Harrison	
Transportation Type	Subject	Land Transportation; Water Transportation	Controlled Voc. **Transportation Research Thesaurus**
Transportation Mode	Subject		Controlled Voc. **Library of Congress Thesaurus for Graphic Materials**
Transportation Facilities	Subject	Bridges; Harbors	Controlled Voc. **Library of Congress Thesaurus for Graphic Materials**
Alternate terms	Subject	Cantilever bridges; Ports	Free text
Continent	Spatial Coverage	Oceania	Controlled Voc. **Getty Thesaurus of Geographic Names**
Country/Region	Spatial Coverage	New Zealand	Controlled Voc. **Getty Thesaurus of Geographic Names**
State/Province	Spatial Coverage		Controlled Voc. **Getty Thesaurus of Geographic Names**
City/Place	Spatial Coverage	Auckland	Controlled Voc. **Getty Thesaurus of Geographic Names**
Geographic Feature	Spatial Coverage		Controlled Voc. **Getty Thesaurus of Geographic Names**
Time	Temporal Coverage	1969	
Type	Type	Image	
Collection	Source	Harrison Forman Collection	
Original Item Size	Format	35 mm	
Original Item Medium	Format	Color slide	Controlled Voc **Art & Architecture Thesaurus**
Original Item ID	Source	45 c, 15-1-20	Transcribed text
Provenance	Contributor	Donated by Sandra Forman, Harrison Forman's wife.	Free Text
Repository	Relation-Is-Part-Of	American Geographical Society Library, University of Wisconsin-Milwaukee Libraries	
Rights	Rights	The Board of Regents of the University of Wisconsin System.	
Publisher	Publisher	University of Wisconsin-Milwaukee Libraries	
Digital ID	Identifier	fr000247	

Source: University of Wisconsin–Milwaukee Libraries Digital Collections. Used with permission.

the *Continent* field in every metadata record in the database and delivers the results.

Figure 10.25 shows another browse screen available to users of this collection. Notice that the metadata scheme documented in Table 10.3 includes separate fields called *Transportation Mode* and *Transportation*

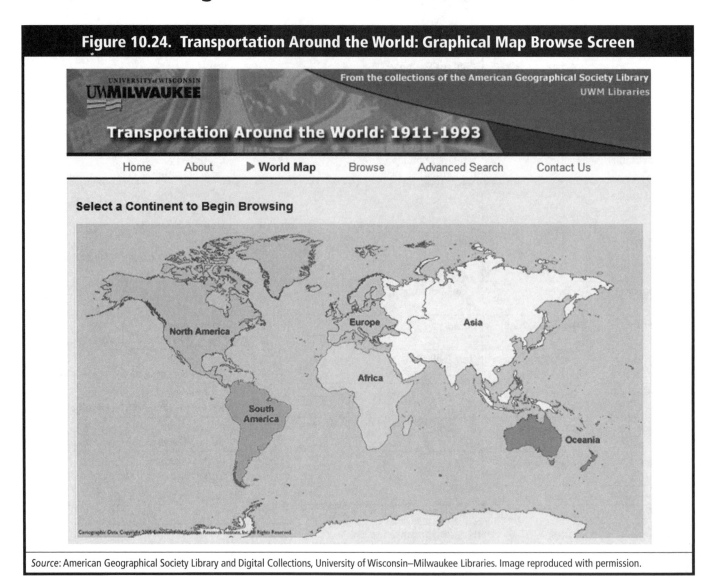

Figure 10.24. Transportation Around the World: Graphical Map Browse Screen

Source: American Geographical Society Library and Digital Collections, University of Wisconsin–Milwaukee Libraries. Image reproduced with permission.

Facilities, and that each allows only terms from a controlled vocabulary. A selected number of those terms are presented to users here. When a user clicks on *Train Stations* under *Browse by Transportation Facilities*, the software is again executing a query to find all instances of that term in that field in the underlying metadata for the collection.

10.2.3. CONTENTdm Examples

This section of Chapter 10 provides a number of examples of screens from the CONTENTdm digital content management system software that are used when designing a new metadata scheme for a new digital collection and when subsequently creating metadata for a digital object in that collection. This section may be especially helpful for those who have never seen such a system, in order to get a more concrete sense of how metadata design and creation can work in practice when using this widely used software package.

Designing and Documenting a Metadata Scheme

Figure 10.26 shows a CONTENTdm screen for adding a new collection and selecting an existing metadata scheme for that collection. Notice that the first three choices in the drop-down menu in this example are standardized schemes: Simple Dublin Core, Qualified Dublin Core, and VRA 3.0. The other selections are collection-specific schemes previously created within the CONTENTdm system by this institution. In this example, Qualified Dublin Core has been selected as the base element

Figure 10.26. CONTENTdm Add Collection Screen

CONTENTdm Administration

admin home | server | collections | items

:: collections : settings : viewers : users : reports : about : help ::

Add collection

A CONTENTdm collection consists of a set of files that are stored in a directory on the server. Creating a new collection entails creating a new directory and assigning permissions on the server.

After you add the collection, you need to edit the collection configuration settings to enable functionality such as full text searching, PDF file processing, and full resolution image format.

Tip: Use short aliases to avoid browser limitations when searching across a large number of collections.

- ⦿ **Create a new collection using** [Qualified Dublin Core ▾] **template**
- ◯ **Import an existing CONTENTdm**

Simple Dublin Core
Qualified Dublin Core
VRA Core 3.0
AGSL Digital Photo Archive - Asia and Middle East
Afghanistan - Images from the Harrison Forman Collection
American Geographical Society Library Digital Map Collection
Architectural Drawings of Willis and Lillian Leenhouts
Archives Digital Collections
Art Slides
Aviation History Collection - Selections from the George Hardie Collection
Cities Around The World
Digital Sanborn Maps of Milwaukee, 1894 and 1910
Greetings from Milwaukee
Images of Russia and Caucasus Region 1929-1933 from the W.O. Field Collection
March On Milwaukee - Civil Rights History Project
Milwaukee Neighborhoods
Milwaukee Repertory Theater Photographic History
Nazi Invasion of Poland in 1939 - Images and Documents from the Harrison Forman
Picturing Golda Meir
Polar Expeditions - Images from the American Geographical Society Library

Collection name

Collection alias

Directory name

[add]

powered by CONTENTdm® | ©2001—2009

^ to top ^

Source: CONTENTdm screenshots are used with OCLC's permission. CONTENTdm® is a registered trademark of OCLC Online Computer Library Center, Inc.

set upon which the customized collection-specific element set will be built.

Figure 10.27 shows the next step in the process. The default screen from which the metadata designer starts is a list of the 15 Dublin Core elements or fields. Each of the fields can be edited to rename the field, to set its mapping to a Dublin Core element, and to set the data type, field size, searchability, visibility, requirement level, and controlled vocabulary specification. Additional fields can be added, existing fields deleted, and fields moved into any order desired. Note that the name of this collection is *Polar Expeditions - Images from the American Geographical Society Library*, appearing in the Current Collection box near the top of the screen.

Figure 10.28 shows the screen for editing a specific field. In this example, the metadata designer is working with a Qualified Dublin Core *Coverage-Spatial* element and has renamed the field to *Continent*, retaining its mapping to DC *Coverage-Spatial*. This is where the designer sets each of the field properties by making selections from drop-down menus. When selecting *Yes* for Controlled Vocabulary, the designer can work in the *Select and share controlled vocabulary* section. In this example, The *Thesaurus for Graphic Materials: TGM1, Subject Terms* has been selected from a drop-down list as the controlled vocabulary

Figure 10.27. CONTENTdm Metadata Fields Screen Before Customizing

CONTENTdm Administration

admin home — server

:: configuration : fields

Current collection: Polar Expeditions - Images from the American Geographical Society Library [v] [change]

Metadata fields

View and configure collection and administrative fields.

Collection field properties

View, add, edit and delete fields. Enable full text searching and controlled vocabulary. After you have added, changed, or deleted fields, index the collection to update changes.

	Field name	DC map	Data type	Large	Search	Hide	Required	Vocab		add field
1	Title	Title	Text	No	Yes	No	Yes	No	move to [v]	edit | delete
2	Subject	Subject	Text	No	Yes	No	No	No	move to [v]	edit | delete
3	Description	Description	Text	Yes	Yes	No	No	No	move to [v]	edit | delete
4	Creator	Creator	Text	No	No	No	No	No	move to [v]	edit | delete
5	Publisher	Publisher	Text	No	No	No	No	No	move to [v]	edit | delete
6	Contributors	Contributors	Text	No	No	No	No	No	move to [v]	edit | delete
7	Date	Date	Text	No	No	No	No	No	move to [v]	edit | delete
8	Type	Type	Text	No	No	No	No	No	move to [v]	edit | delete
9	Format	Format	Text	No	No	No	No	No	move to [v]	edit | delete
10	Identifier	Identifier	Text	No	No	No	No	No	move to [v]	edit | delete
11	Source	Source	Text	No	No	No	No	No	move to [v]	edit | delete
12	Language	Language	Text	No	No	No	No	No	move to [v]	edit | delete
13	Relation	Relation	Text	No	No	No	No	No	move to [v]	edit | delete
14	Coverage	Coverage	Text	No	No	No	No	No	move to [v]	edit | delete
15	Rights	Rights	Text	No	No	No	No	No	move to [v]	edit | delete

Source: See Figure 10.26.

that will be used for the *Continent* (DC *Coverage-Spatial*) element for this collection. Notice the other options available, including the ability to import a controlled vocabulary from a file or to use a controlled vocabulary from another field or collection previously used in CONTENTdm.

Figure 10.29 shows some vocabularies available for this particular institution in the drop-down list. This includes several widely used standardized vocabularies such as AAT, DCMI *Type*, MeSH, TGN, TGMI, and ULAN, all covered in previous chapters of this book.

Figure 10.30 shows how the metadata designer can select or enter default values to be used for one or more fields for a particular collection. For the collection in this example, the *Type* element will always contain

Figure 10.28. CONTENTdm Edit Field Screen

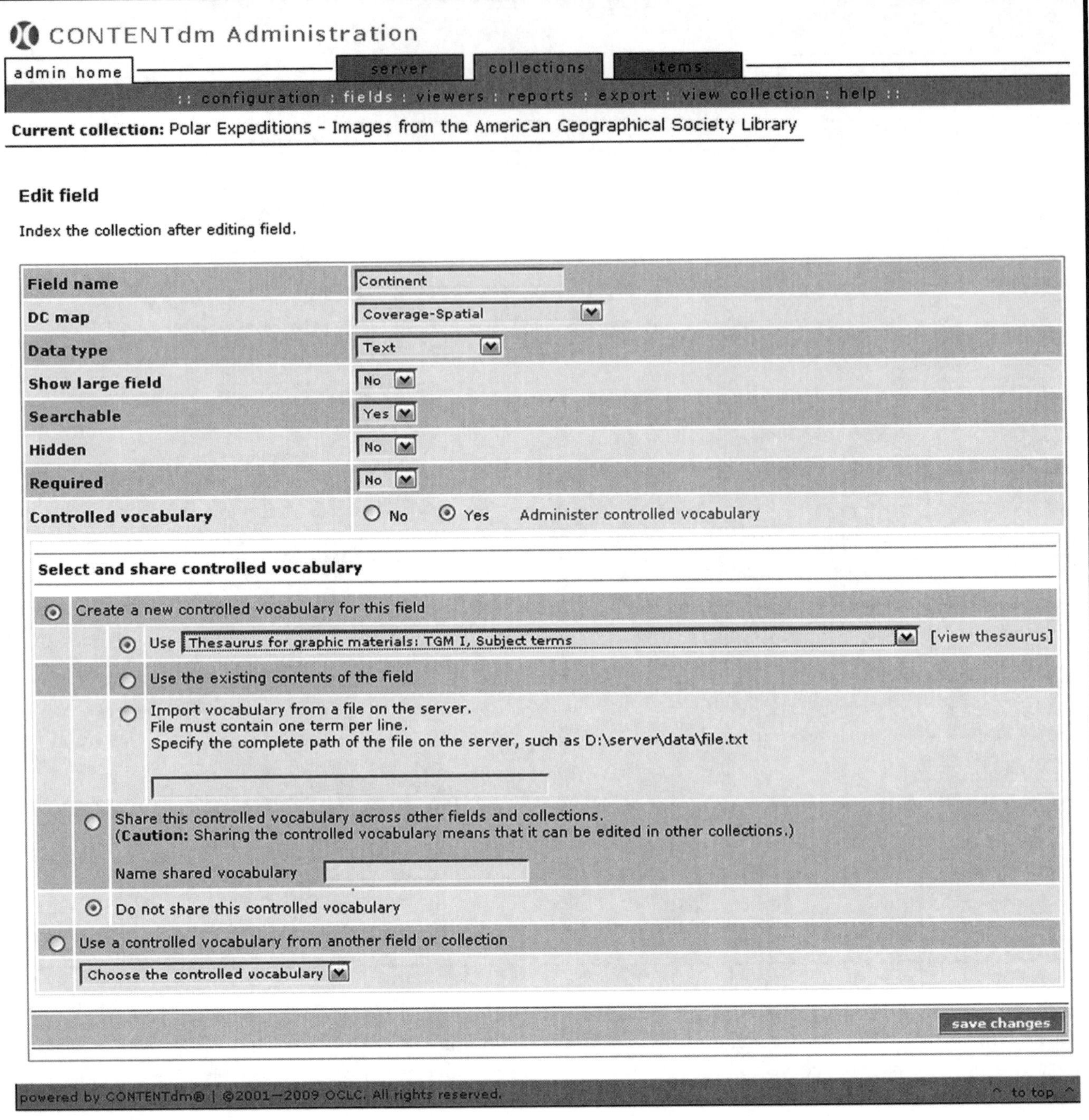

CONTENTdm Administration

admin home | server | collections | items

:: configuration : fields : viewers : reports : export : view collection : help ::

Current collection: Polar Expeditions – Images from the American Geographical Society Library

Edit field

Index the collection after editing field.

Field name	Continent
DC map	Coverage-Spatial
Data type	Text
Show large field	No
Searchable	Yes
Hidden	No
Required	No
Controlled vocabulary	○ No ● Yes Administer controlled vocabulary

Select and share controlled vocabulary

● Create a new controlled vocabulary for this field

    ● Use [Thesaurus for graphic materials: TGM I, Subject terms] [view thesaurus]

    ○ Use the existing contents of the field

    ○ Import vocabulary from a file on the server.
    File must contain one term per line.
    Specify the complete path of the file on the server, such as D:\server\data\file.txt

○ Share this controlled vocabulary across other fields and collections.
(Caution: Sharing the controlled vocabulary means that it can be edited in other collections.)

    Name shared vocabulary

● Do not share this controlled vocabulary

○ Use a controlled vocabulary from another field or collection

[Choose the controlled vocabulary]

save changes

powered by CONTENTdm® | ©2001—2009 OCLC. All rights reserved.   ^ to top ^

Source: See Figure 10.26.

the value *Image*. By setting these default constant values here, every time a screen is opened for creating a new record, these fields will automatically be populated with these values. This saves time for the people creating the metadata for each individual digital object and also ensures accuracy of the data for that field.

Designing and Documenting a Metadata Scheme

Figure 10.29. CONTENTdm Select Controlled Vocabulary Screen

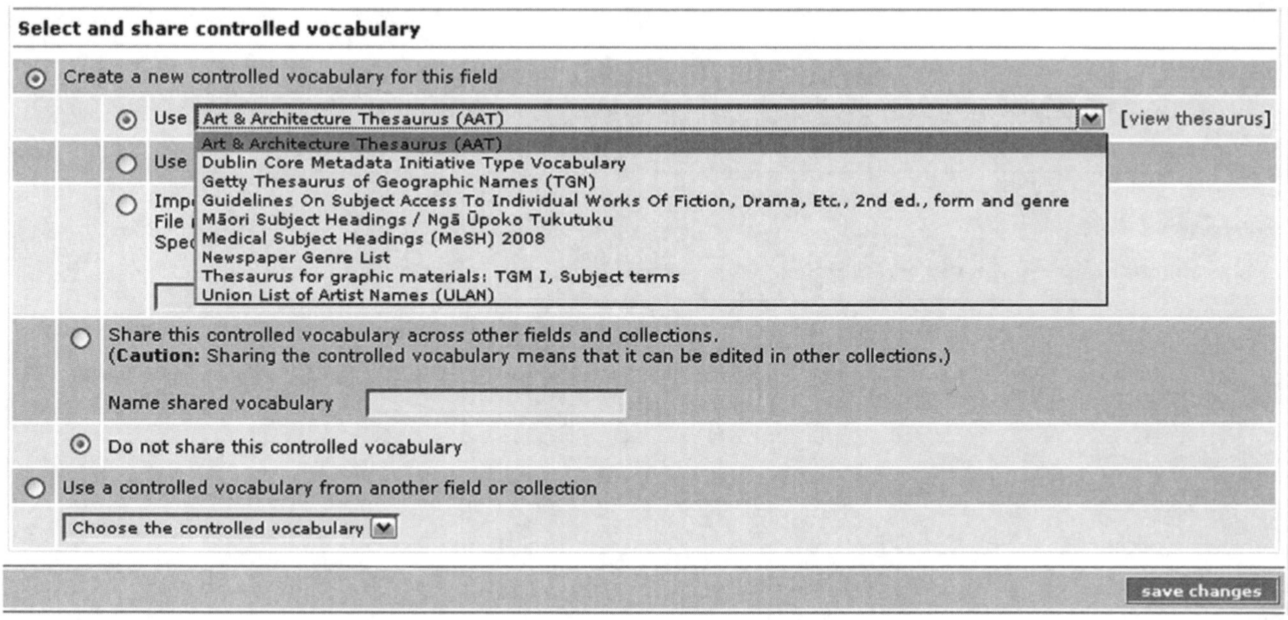

Select and share controlled vocabulary

- ◉ Create a new controlled vocabulary for this field
  - ◉ Use Art & Architecture Thesaurus (AAT) ▼ [view thesaurus]

    Art & Architecture Thesaurus (AAT)
    Dublin Core Metadata Initiative Type Vocabulary
    Getty Thesaurus of Geographic Names (TGN)
    Guidelines On Subject Access To Individual Works Of Fiction, Drama, Etc., 2nd ed., form and genre
    Māori Subject Headings / Ngā Ūpoko Tukutuku
    Medical Subject Headings (MeSH) 2008
    Newspaper Genre List
    Thesaurus for graphic materials: TGM I, Subject terms
    Union List of Artist Names (ULAN)

  - ○ Use
  - ○ Impo File
    Spec

  - ○ Share this controlled vocabulary across other fields and collections.
    (**Caution:** Sharing the controlled vocabulary means that it can be edited in other collections.)

    Name shared vocabulary [   ]

  - ◉ Do not share this controlled vocabulary
- ○ Use a controlled vocabulary from another field or collection
  - Choose the controlled vocabulary ▼

[save changes]

Source: See Figure 10.26.

Figure 10.30. CONTENTdm Set Default Values Screen

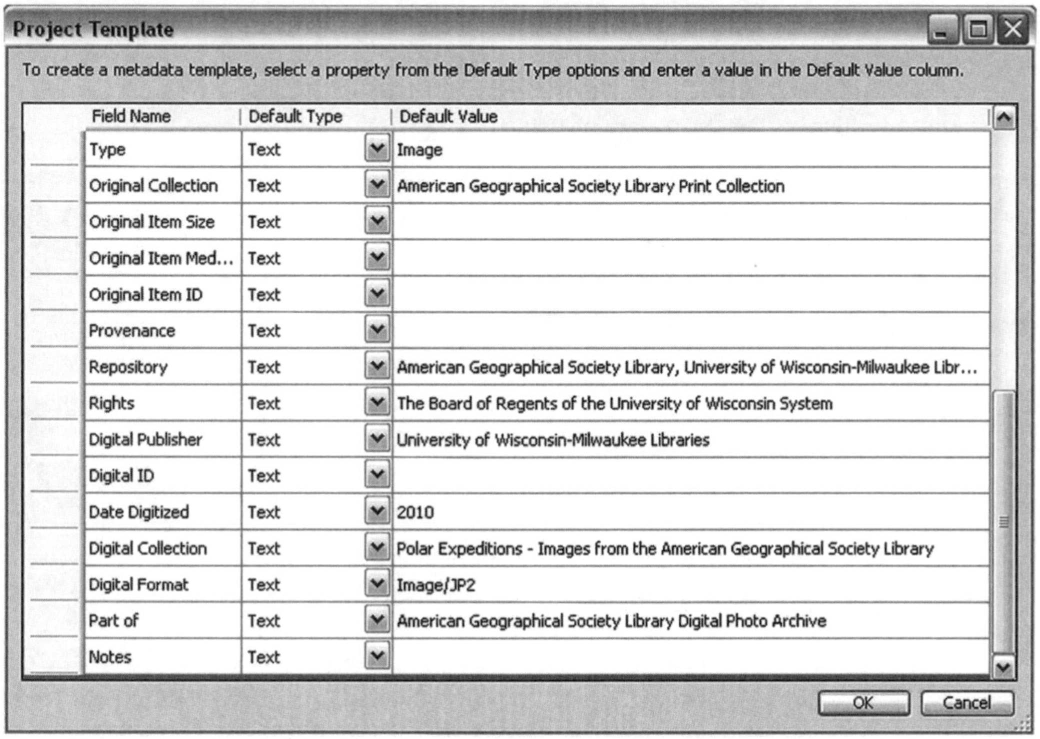

Project Template

To create a metadata template, select a property from the Default Type options and enter a value in the Default Value column.

Field Name	Default Type	Default Value
Type	Text ▼	Image
Original Collection	Text ▼	American Geographical Society Library Print Collection
Original Item Size	Text ▼	
Original Item Med...	Text ▼	
Original Item ID	Text ▼	
Provenance	Text ▼	
Repository	Text ▼	American Geographical Society Library, University of Wisconsin-Milwaukee Libr...
Rights	Text ▼	The Board of Regents of the University of Wisconsin System
Digital Publisher	Text ▼	University of Wisconsin-Milwaukee Libraries
Digital ID	Text ▼	
Date Digitized	Text ▼	2010
Digital Collection	Text ▼	Polar Expeditions - Images from the American Geographical Society Library
Digital Format	Text ▼	Image/JP2
Part of	Text ▼	American Geographical Society Library Digital Photo Archive
Notes	Text ▼	

[OK] [Cancel]

Source: See Figure 10.26.

Figure 10.31. CONTENTdm Metadata Fields Screen After Customizing

CONTENTdm Administration

admin home — server — collections — items

:: configuration : fields : viewers : reports : export : view collection : help ::

Current collection: Polar Expeditions - Images from the American Geographical Society Library ▼ | change

Metadata fields

View and configure collection and administrative fields.

Collection field properties

View, add, edit and delete fields. Enable full text searching and controlled vocabulary. After you have added, changed, or deleted fields, index the collection to update changes.

	Field name	DC map	Data type	Large	Search	Hide	Required	Vocab	add field	
1	Title	Title	Text	No	Yes	No	Yes	No	move to ▼	edit | delete
2	Date of Photograph	Date-Created	Text	No	Yes	No	No	No	move to ▼	edit | delete
3	Caption	Description	Text	No	Yes	No	No	No	move to ▼	edit | delete
4	Verso Description	Description	Text	No	Yes	No	No	No	move to ▼	edit | delete
5	Photographer	Creator	Text	No	Yes	No	No	No	move to ▼	edit | delete
6	Source of Descriptive Information	Description	Text	No	Yes	No	No	No	move to ▼	edit | delete
7	Subject TGM	Subject	Text	No	Yes	No	No	Yes	move to ▼	edit | delete
8	Expedition	Subject	Text	No	Yes	No	No	No	move to ▼	edit | delete
9	Subject LC	Subject	Text	No	Yes	No	No	Yes	move to ▼	edit | delete
10	Continent	Coverage-Spatial	Text	No	Yes	No	No	Yes	move to ▼	edit | delete
11	Country	Coverage-Spatial	Text	No	Yes	No	No	No	move to ▼	edit | delete
12	Region	Coverage-Spatial	Text	No	Yes	No	No	No	move to ▼	edit | delete
13	State/Province	Coverage-Spatial	Text	No	Yes	No	No	No	move to ▼	edit | delete
14	City or Place	Coverage-Spatial	Text	No	Yes	No	No	No	move to ▼	edit | delete
15	Geographic Feature	Coverage-Spatial	Text	No	Yes	No	No	No	move to ▼	edit | delete
16	Type	Type	Text	No	No	No	No	Yes	move to ▼	edit | delete
17	Original Collection	Relation-Is Part Of	Text	No	Yes	No	No	No	move to ▼	edit | delete
18	Original Item Size	Format-Extent	Text	No	Yes	No	No	No	move to ▼	edit | delete
19	Original Item Medium	Format-Medium	Text	No	Yes	No	No	No	move to ▼	edit | delete
20	Original Item ID	Identifier	Text	No	Yes	No	No	No	move to ▼	edit | delete
21	Provenance	Contributors	Text	No	No	No	No	No	move to ▼	edit | delete
22	Repository	Relation-Is Part Of	Text	No	No	No	No	No	move to ▼	edit | delete
23	Rights	Rights	Text	No	No	No	No	No	move to ▼	edit | delete
24	Digital Publisher	Publisher	Text	No	No	No	No	No	move to ▼	edit | delete

Source: See Figure 10.26.

Designing and Documenting a Metadata Scheme

Figure 10.31 (see facing page) shows the finalized metadata scheme for a specific collection. Note the variety of collection-specific field names, each mapped to a standard DC element, and different values selected for the Search, Required, and Vocab specifications.

Figure 10.32 shows what a metadata creator or cataloger sees when creating a new record for a digital object in a specific collection. This is where he or she enters the descriptive metadata for that object. Note that in this example the digital image being described appears as a thumbnail in the left-hand viewing pane. Some fields, such as *Type*, may be pre-populated with default values selected by the metadata scheme designer. In this example, the metadata creator has clicked inside of the *Subject LC* field. Because a controlled vocabulary was specified for that field, all of the available values from that vocabulary appear in the viewing pane on the right side of the screen. The metadata creator needs only to browse and select one or more terms from the controlled list. When clicking on a term, it automatically pops over into the Field Values box. This makes the process of selecting and entering controlled vocabulary terms much faster and easier for the metadata creator, also ensuring accuracy in data entry because the term does not need to be typed in by hand. In CONTENTdm it is possible for the metadata designer to select only a small subset of values from a larger vocabulary, only those values that the designer has decided will apply to, or be used for, a particular collection.

Figure 10.32. CONTENTdm Metadata Entry/Record Creation Screen

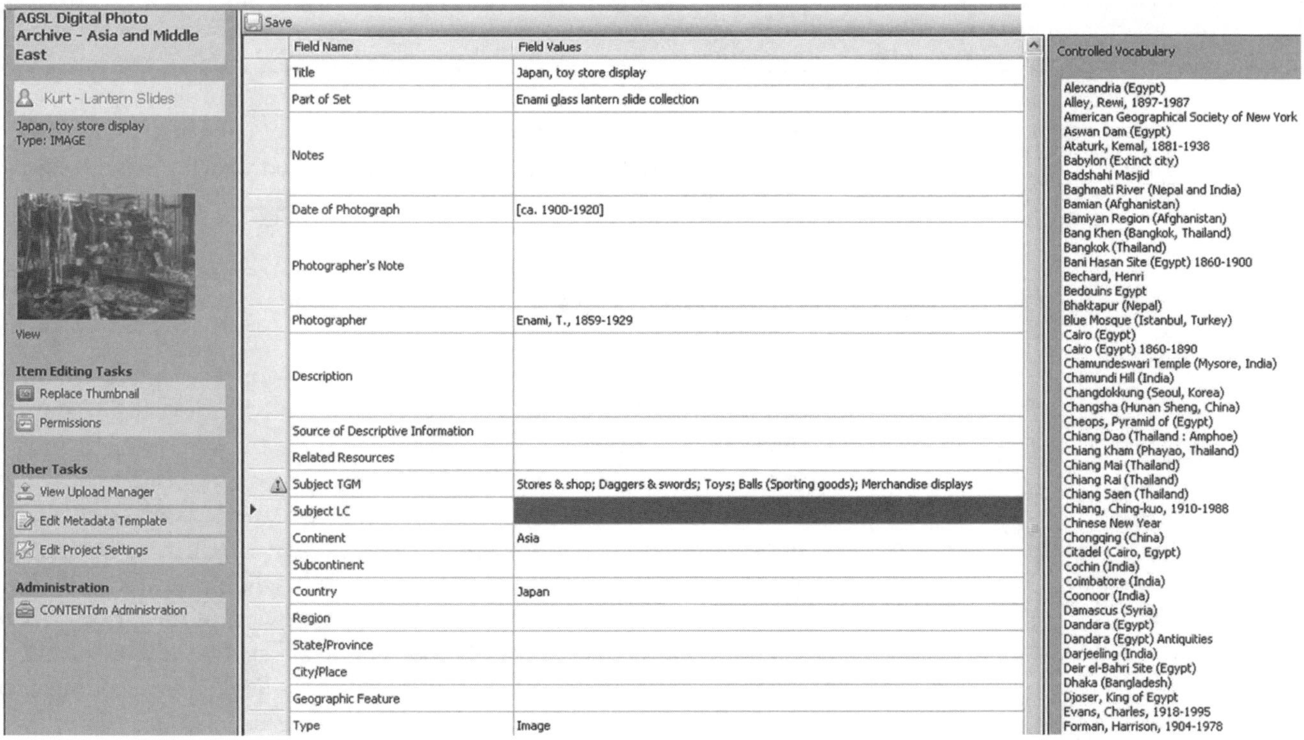

Source: See Figure 10.26.

Figure 10.33. CONTENTdm Export Metadata Screen

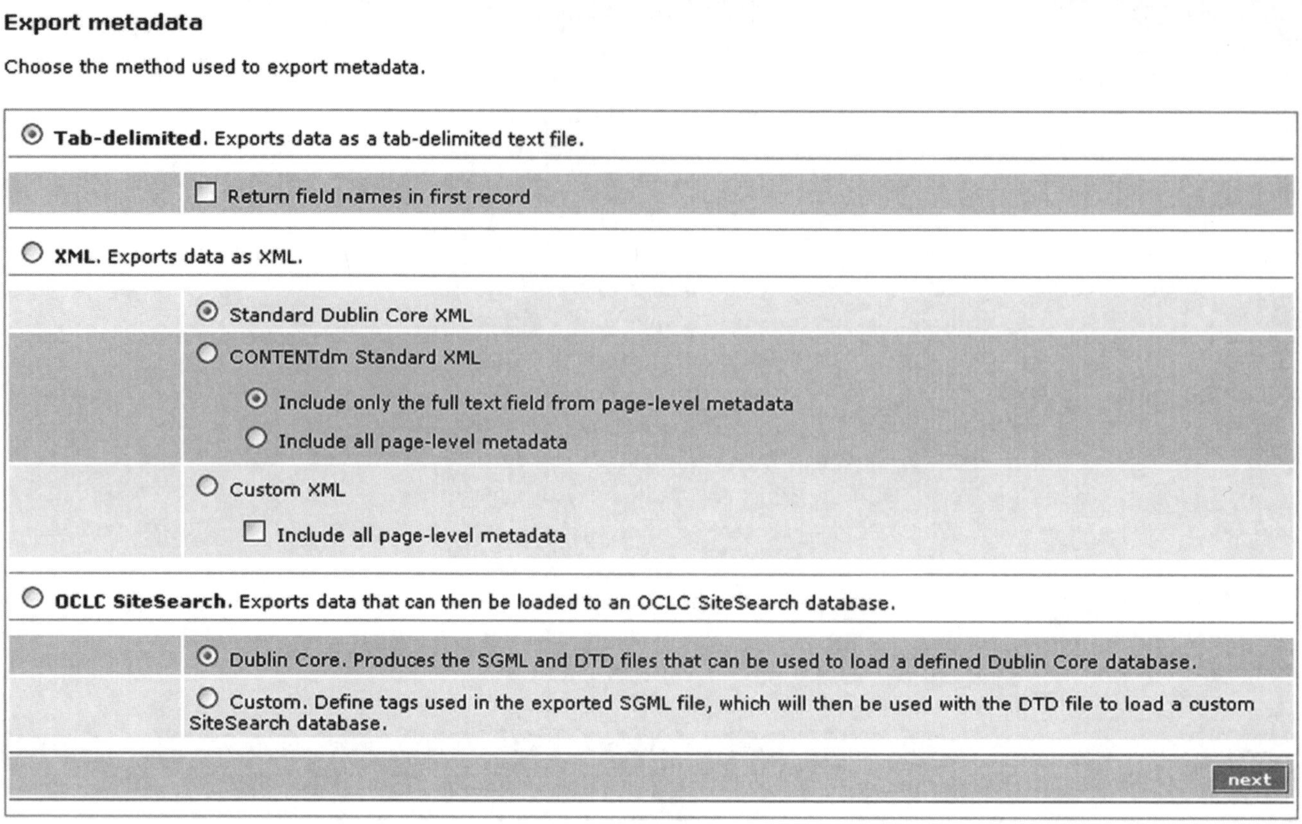

Export metadata

Choose the method used to export metadata.

⊙ **Tab-delimited**. Exports data as a tab-delimited text file.

  ☐ Return field names in first record

○ **XML**. Exports data as XML.

  ⊙ Standard Dublin Core XML

  ○ CONTENTdm Standard XML

    ⊙ Include only the full text field from page-level metadata
    ○ Include all page-level metadata

  ○ Custom XML

    ☐ Include all page-level metadata

○ **OCLC SiteSearch**. Exports data that can then be loaded to an OCLC SiteSearch database.

  ⊙ Dublin Core. Produces the SGML and DTD files that can be used to load a defined Dublin Core database.

  ○ Custom. Define tags used in the exported SGML file, which will then be used with the DTD file to load a custom SiteSearch database.

  [next]

Source: See Figure 10.26.

Figure 10.33 shows various options for exporting metadata records after their creation, including as a tab-delimited text file or as Standard Dublin Core in XML.

10.3. Summary

A critical aspect of metadata for digital collections is designing and documenting metadata schemes for individual collections or for groups of collections within an individual institution or a consortium of institutions. Developers of standardized schemes such as Dublin Core, MODS, and VRA understand and expect local implementers to make their own application decisions and to develop their own application profiles for implementing these schemes locally. Metadata scheme design and record creation are only one aspect, albeit a critical aspect, of the larger process of digital collection creation. Good metadata scheme design should go hand-in-hand with assessing the content to be included in a collection and the attributes of that content needed for users to search browse, limit, navigate, understand, interpret, and identify the digital objects in the collection, by themselves and in relation to one another. Good metadata scheme design should also go hand-in-hand with the design of the user interface, the search and browse mechanisms available, the display of the metadata records, and the like, insofar as these are customizable.

Good metadata scheme design can therefore begin with an analysis of the institutional or consortial context of a digital collection or shared collections, the type of digital content objects included in the collection(s), and the anticipated users of the collection(s). This analysis, whether formal or informal, documented or not, provides a basis for determining a set of functional requirements for metadata design, database design, and user interfaces design, all of which are ideally interrelated. Functional requirements in turn lead to decisions about specific elements to be included and the specifications for each element. First, a standardized element set needs to be selected, one that best suits the context, content, users, and functional requirements for a specific collection or type of institution or consortium. Next, decisions need to be made about how that scheme will be applied locally. This may entail creating local element names and mapping them to the base standardized scheme. It will also necessarily entail decisions about the requirement and cardinality of each element, application of controlled vocabularies, content or input guidelines, and other specifications. The resulting scheme may be general—that is, intended to apply to multiple collections within an institution or consortium, in which case it will have widely applicable, generic element names—or it may be collection-specific, in which case it will have element names tailored for a specific collection. Decisions about collection-specific element names and specifications are a critical aspect of metadata design when following this model.

Metadata schemes, whether general or collection-specific, should be documented in some form. There are no standardized terms or formats for these kinds of documents. The terms *application profile, data dictionary, user guide, metadata guidelines, best practice guide,* and others have been used. This book uses the term *metadata application profile* (MAP) for all of these types of documentation and types of metadata design. Within the Dublin Core Metadata Initiative (DCMI), the term and concept of application profile has been developed during recent years to become more exactingly used, in order to conform to models of metadata usage and interoperability in a Semantic Web and Linked Data context. This book acknowledges this fact, but does not restrict the term application profile to DCMI usage, which continues to change over time. This chapter presents a few real-world examples of general and collection-specific metadata application profiles, most of them based on Dublin Core, as well as examples of how collection-specific metadata schemes are designed in the CONTENTdm digital collection management system.

▶ Companion Website

See this book's companion website at **http://www.neal-schuman.com/metadata-digital-collections** for Chapter 10 review questions, suggestions for exercises, and other resources.

References

CDP Metadata Working Group. 2006. "CDP Dublin Core Metadata Best Practices." Version 2.1.1. September. http://www.lyrasis.org/Products-and-Services/Digital-and-Preservation-Services/Digital-Toolbox/Metadata.aspx.

Chopey, Michael A. 2005. "Planning and Implementing a Metadata-Driven Digital Repository." *Cataloging & Classification Quarterly* 40, no. 3/4: 255–287.

DLF Aquifer Metadata Working Group. 2009. "Digital Library Federation/ Aquifer Implementation Guidelines for Shareable MODS Records." Version 1.1. March. https://wiki.dlib.indiana.edu/confluence/download/attachments/ 24288/DLFMODS_ImplementationGuidelines.pdf.

Foulonneau, Muriel, and Jenn Riley. 2008. *Metadata for Digital Resources: Implementation, Systems Design and Interoperability.* Oxford, UK: Chandos.

Hicks, Emily A., Jody Perkins, and Margaret Beecher Maurer. 2007. "Application Profile Development for Consortial Digital Libraries: An OhioLINK Case Study." *Library Resources and Technical Services* 51, no. 2: 33–43.

Indiana Memory Project. 2007. "Dublin Core Metadata Guide." Last modified February. http://www.in.gov/library/files/dig_metast.pdf.

Krug, Steve. 2006. *Don't Make Me Think: A Common Sense Approach to Web Usability.* 2nd ed. Berkeley, CA: New Riders Press.

Merriam-Webster. 2009. *Merriam-Webster's Collegiate Dictionary.* 11th ed. Springfield, Massachusetts.

Morville, Peter, and Louis Rosenfeld. 2006. *Information Architecture for the World Wide Web.* 3rd ed. Sebastopol, CA: O'Reilly.

OhioLINK Digital Resources Management Committee (DRMC) Metadata Subcommittee. 2010. "OhioLINK Digital Resources Commons (DRC) Metadata Application Profile." Version 1.2. OhioLINK. October 1. https://sites.google.com/a/ohiolink.edu/drmc/Home/Subcommittees/ Metadata/drmc_metadataprofile--10-5-10.pdf.

University of Washington Libraries Metadata Implementation Group. 2003. "Musical Instruments in the Collection of the University of Washington Ethnomusicology Division Data Dictionary." Last modified November 5. http://www.lib.washington.edu/msd/mig/datadicts/ethnomus.html.

University of Washington Libraries Metadata Implementation Group. 2006. "Architecture Collection Data Dictionary." Last modified February 26. http://www.lib.washington.edu/msd/mig/datadicts/archcolldd.html.

University of Wisconsin–Milwaukee Libraries Digital Collections. 2009. "Transportation around the World: 1911–1993." Last modified January 6. http:// www4.uwm.edu/libraries/digilib/transport/.

Metadata, Linked Data, and the Semantic Web

11.1. What Are Linked Data and the Semantic Web and Why Care about Them?

Within the cultural heritage metadata and cataloging communities, there has been an increasing amount of interest in the Linked Open Data movement and the Semantic Web (Coyle, 2010; ALCTS, 2010; Hillmann et al., 2010). The Dublin Core Metadata Initiative has made these an increasingly important focus of interest and activity (NISO/DCMI, 2010). This chapter explores selected aspects of these, focusing on some basic structures needed for metadata to function in the Linked Data and Semantic Web contexts. The content of much of this chapter is heavily influenced by and indebted to Coyle (2010) and NISO/DCMI (2010).

What are *Linked Data* and the *Semantic Web*? The Linked Data website states the following:

> **Linked Data** is about using the Web to connect related data that wasn't previously linked, or using the Web to lower the barriers to linking data currently linked using other methods. More specifically, Wikipedia defines Linked Data as "a term used to describe a recommended best practice for exposing, sharing, and connecting pieces of data, information, and knowledge on the Semantic Web using URIs and RDF. This site exists to provide a home for, or pointers to, resources from across the Linked Data community. (Linked Data website, http://www.linkeddata.org/, accessed September 28, 2010)

Figure 11.1 is a screen capture of part of the Linking Open Data (LOD) cloud diagram that "shows datasets that have been published in Linked Data format, by contributors to the Linking Open Data community project and other individuals and organizations" (Cyganiak and Jentzsch, 2010).

The Wikipedia article on Linked Data states: "Linked Data is a sub-topic of the Semantic Web. The term Linked Data is used to describe a method of exposing, sharing, and connecting data via dereferenceable URIs on the Web" (Wikipedia, 2010a). The Wikipedia article on the

Figure 11.1. The Linking Open Data Cloud Diagram: Selection

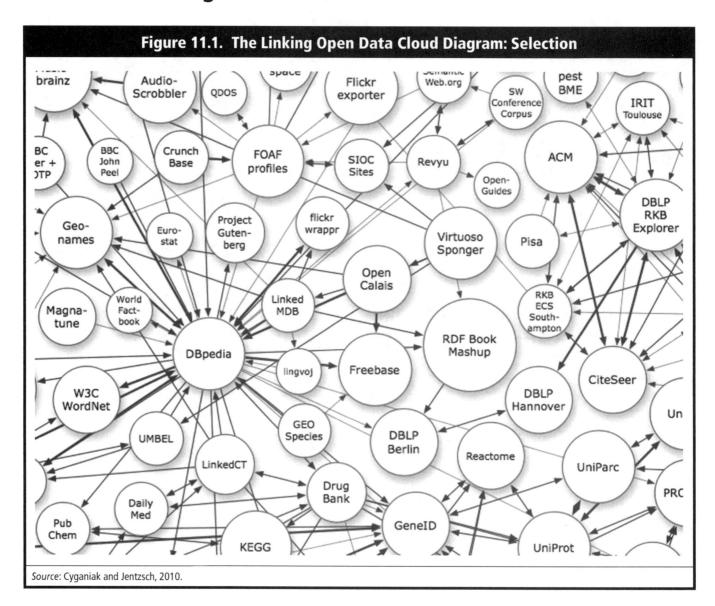

Source: Cyganiak and Jentzsch, 2010.

Semantic Web states:

> Semantic Web is a group of methods and technologies to allow machines to understand the meaning—or "semantics"—of information on the World Wide Web.... While the term "Semantic Web" is not formally defined it is mainly used to describe the model and technologies proposed by the W3C. These technologies include the Resource Description Framework (RDF), a variety of data interchange formats (e.g. RDF/XML, N3, Turtle, N-Triples), and notations such as RDF Schema (RDFS) and the Web Ontology Language (OWL), all of which are intended to provide a formal description of concepts, terms, and relationships within a given knowledge domain. (Wikipedia, 2011)

Across various web communities and among various individuals, there has been some disagreement about the relationship between the concepts of Linked Data and the Semantic Web. Some people use the terms more or less synonymously, while others make sharp distinctions between them. This book takes the approach that Linked Data, and specifically Linked Open Data, is one aspect of, or one method of realizing important aspects of, the larger Semantic Web vision. To a large extent, both have not yet been widely realized and remain visions of the future. Many people have great enthusiasm about their potential and are actively engaged in early implementations, while others remain highly skeptical. Linked Data and Semantic Web models and technologies can be used internally within an organization and are being so used today, but it is their application within an open web environment that is the primary concern in this chapter.

The Dublin Core Metadata Initiative is taking Linked Data very seriously and has been increasingly moving away from the 1990s focus on the Dublin Core Metadata Element Set as a core set of elements for the web, and toward a focus on a core vocabulary and metadata structures for Linked Data (DCMI, 2011a). Within the library cataloging community, the new *Resource Description and Access* (RDA) cataloging standard is Linked Data and Semantic Web compatible, employing Linked Data/Semantic Web concepts, terminology, and structures (Joint Steering Committee for Development of RDA, 2009a, 2009b). The RDA elements and vocabularies are being formally registered in Linked Data/Semantic Web ready ways (Open Metadata Registry, 2011b). The Library of Congress is making many of its vocabularies, including TGM and LCSH, available in Linked Data/Semantic Web structures (Library of Congress, 2011). Obviously, then, Linked Data and the Semantic Web are being taken very seriously within the cultural heritage metadata and cataloging communities. This chapter focuses on giving a very simple partial introduction to some of the basic concepts of Linked Open Data, especially as they relate to cultural heritage metadata, with a primary focus on expressing metadata in the Resource Description Framework, one of the foundational data models for Linked Data and Semantic Web.

11.2. Linked Open Data and the Resource Description Framework

The three words that make up the term **Linked Open Data** point to three important aspects of the concept and why so many people are excited about its potential. The current World Wide Web is basically a web of linked *documents*: that is, resources linked to each other by hyperlinks. The links themselves have no other meaning than *link* (Coyle, 2010: 18). Search engines retrieve documents by matching users' keywords to words contained in the documents. This is quite different from searching a database of metadata, which consists of structured statements about a resource, statements that have a level of semantic meaning and allow meaningful querying of the database. For example, a query could be make to retrieve all items created by a specific person, within a specific time range, about a specific topic, in a specific genre or format, by each of these parameters separately or all of them combined in a single query. Web search engines like Google do not work this way. The Linked Open Data movement is about taking semantically meaningful metadata and making it openly available for searching in the open web environment, beginning to build a web of linked *data* instead of a web of linked *documents*.

Most metadata currently resides in databases, such as library catalogs, CONTENTdm systems, and the like. The metadata therefore exists in numerous separate *data silos*, and cannot be linked and queried together. The web search engines usually cannot find and index this content. It is usually part of the *Deep Web*, also called the *Hidden Web* or *Invisible Web*. Even if they could access this content, the search engines could do nothing more than match on keywords. Computers are very literal and cannot understand or extract semantic meaning from text, unless pieces of data are explicitly tagged as having a certain meaning, which is metadata. Web search engines do not execute structured queries on structured metadata. How, then, can current metadata be made searchable and linkable in an open web environment? It needs to be expressed in a shared, structured format that new Linked Data and Semantic Web applications can query. This structured format, most sources seem to agree, is the **Resource Description Framework (RDF)**.

11.2.1. Statements, Properties, Values, and RDF Triples

The *Resource Description Framework* provides a framework for structuring metadata as **statements** composed of a **subject**, a **predicate**, and an **object**. In RDF the *subject* is called a **resource**, the *predicate* is called a **property**, and the *object* is called a **value**. In RDF each statement is also called a **triple**, because it consists of these three components. The basic structure of the RDF statement or triple is often rendered as a graphical illustration, called a **graph**, as shown in Figure 11.2. In the terminology used with these graphs, each circle is a **node** and the arrowed line is an **arc** connecting the two nodes and indicating a typed relationship between the two entities represented by each node.

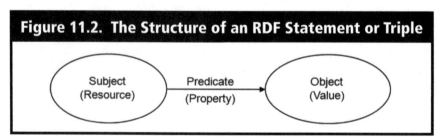

Figure 11.2. The Structure of an RDF Statement or Triple

Subject (Resource) → Predicate (Property) → Object (Value)

Most current metadata resides in separate **records** in databases. This has been the model used throughout the previous chapters. Records may be encoded in proprietary database software or in XML or other formats. Regardless the format, each metadata record can be understood to consist of a set of *statements* about the resource being described in that metadata record. Take the examples in Tables 11.1 and 11.2.

Each row in Table 11.1 and each XML element in Table 11.2 constitutes a *statement* consisting of a *property* and a *value*, to use RDF terminology. In RDF, what has traditionally been called an *element* is called a *property*. Each statement about the described resource contains a *property-value pair*. The first statement in both versions of the record in Tables 11.1 and 11.2 is declaring, in effect, that *this digital image* (subject) *has the title* (predicate) *Manchester Street Bridge, Sauk County, Wisconsin* (object). Other statements are made about the subject and creator of the image, which can be rendered as shown in Table 11.3.

The first statement, about the subject of the resource, can be rendered as the graph shown in Figure 11.3. In this graph, the arrowed line (arc) connecting the two nodes indicates a typed subject relationship between the two entities represented by each node. That is, the relationship has been specified to be of a certain type, and that type is *has subject*.

11.2.2. URIs: Uniform Resource Identifiers

Another core principle of the Resource Description Framework is that resources, properties, and values should be unambiguously identified whenever possible. RDF specifies the use of **Uniform Resource Identifiers (URIs)**, and the specific kind or format of URI is the hypertext transfer protocol (HTTP) form of **Uniform Resource Locator (URL)**, the

Table 11.1. Dublin Core Metadata Record in Table Format

Property	Value
Title	Manchester Street Bridge, Sauk County, Wisconsin
Date	1896
Creator	Lassig Bridge & Iron Works
Subject	Truss bridges
Format	128.9 ft. long; 13.7 ft. deck width
Coverage	Sauk County
Type	Still Image
Creator	Kramer, Paul Jacob
Date	1955
Format	35 mm.
Format	Black & white slide
Identifier	171, 33b-765
Relation	Paul J. Kramer Archival Photograph Collection
Contributor	Hagenville University Archives
Relation	Bridges of Wisconsin
Rights	Copyright © 2009 Hagenville University
Publisher	Hagenville University
Format	image/jpeg
Identifier	WB0078736
Date	2008-12-15

Table 11.2. Dublin Core Metadata Record in XML Format

```
<dc:title>Manchester Street Bridge, Sauk County, Wisconsin</dc:title>
<dc:date>1896</dc:date>
<dc:creator>Lassig Bridge and Iron Works</dc:creator>
<dc:subject>Truss bridges</dc:subject>
<dc:format>128.9 ft. long; 13.7 ft. deck width</dc:format>
<dc:coverage>Sauk County</dc:coverage>
<dc:type>Still Image</dc:type>
<dc:creator>Kramer, Paul Jacob</dc:creator>
<dc:date>1955</dc:date>
<dc:format>35 mm.</dc:format>
<dc:format>Black & white slide</dc:format>
<dc:identifier>171, 33b-765</dc:identifier>
<dc:relation>Paul J. Kramer Archival Photograph Collection</dc:relation>
<dc:contributor>Hagenville University Archives<dc:contributor>
<dc:relation>Bridges of Wisconsin</dc:relation>
<dc:rights>Copyright (c)2009 Hagenville University</dc:rights>
<dc:publisher>Hagenville University</dc:publisher>
<dc:format>image/jpeg</dc:format>
<dc:identifier>WB0078736</dc:identifier>
<dc:date>2008-12-15</dc:date>
```

Table 11.3. Statements about a Digital Image

Resource (subject)	Property (predicate)	Value (object)
Digital Image WB0078736	hasSubject	Truss bridges
Digital Image WB0078736	hasCreator	Kramer, Paul Jacob

Figure 11.3. Subject Statement Shown as Graph

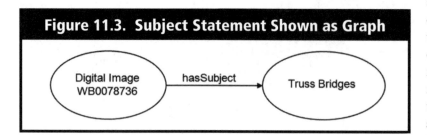

current method of locating resources on the World Wide Web. In RDF, a URL may be used as an identifier even when it is not used as a location. That is, the *http://...* format may be used to identify a resource, property, or value, even when it is not an actual address or location on the web. But in most cases the URI will also be **dereferenceable**: that is, able to reference an actual location on the web. In RDF, linking among resources is made actionable by software matching URIs and creating links between them. This is in contrast to matching on text strings, as is the case in most metadata databases, including library catalogs. In current MARC-based library catalogs, for example, a hyperlink is created among all forms of a person's name or a subject term only if the string of characters, including spaces and punctuation, is exactly the same in each instance. In an open web environment, it becomes critical to use unique URIs to disambiguate between terms, names, numbers, and the like that come from different vocabularies, authority files, and local systems.

For example, the identifier for the digital image represented by the metadata record in Table 11.1 is **WB0078736**. In the fictional Hagenville Digital Library's local system, this string of characters constitutes a unique identifier for that digital image. But if exposed in an open web environment, there is no guarantee that some other institution could not also use this same string as an identifier for a completely different resource. If expressing a statement about this resource in RDF for use in a Linked Open Data environment, a unique URI would need to be used. The invented URI **http://www.hdl.edu/WisBridges/WB0078736** provides such an example, in which *www.hdl.edu* stands for Hagenville Digital Library and its web domain, and *WisBridges* is the subdirectory for the Bridges of Wisconsin digital collection. The local identifier follows as the last part of this URI. But that identifier is now given a context that makes it truly globally unique in the web environment. (It is also possible that Hagenville Digital Library could have a permanent location for the digital image itself at *http://www.hdl.edu/WisBridges/WB0078736.html*, although this is not strictly required in RDF.) Table 11.4 offers an example using a unique URI identifier for the digital image in contrast to of the format used in Table 11.3.

Most of the real linking power of RDF and of the Linked Open Data environment will come from institutions using common, shared URIs

Table 11.4. URIs Used as Subjects in RDF Triples

Resource (subject)	Dublin Core Property (predicate)	Value (object)
http://www.hdl.edu/WisBridgres/WB0078736	Subject	Truss bridges
http://www.hdl.edu/WisBridgres/WB0078736	Creator	Kramer, Paul Jacob

Table 11.5. URIs Used as Properties in RDF Triples

Resource (subject)	Property (predicate)	Value (object)
http://www.hdl.edu/WisBridgres/WB0078736	http://purl.org/dc/elements/1.1/subject	Truss bridges
http://www.hdl.edu/WisBridgres/WB0078736	http://purl.org/dc/elements/1.1/creator	Kramer, Paul Jacob

for resources, properties, and values. This means that elements from standardized element sets such as Dublin Core need to be formally registered on the web with a unique URI for each property (element). This has been done in the DCMI Metadata Terms namespace at http://www.dublincore.org/documents/dcmi-terms/. All aspects of Dublin Core metadata are now expressed in terms compatible with RDF, Linked Data, and the Semantic Web. In Table 11.5 (above), URIs have now been used instead of text strings for the Resources and the Properties in each statement. The property URIs in this example are the actual, real-world URIs for these two Dublin Core properties.

Forms of personal names and subject terms also need to be formally registered with unique URIs in order to facilitate linking in an RDF, Linked Open Data context. The Library of Congress is making many of its controlled vocabularies available in a Linked Data/Semantic Web ready format at http://id.loc.gov/. As of this writing, this includes terms from the *Thesaurus of Graphic Materials*, the *Library of Congress Subject Headings*, and the *MARC List for Relators*, among several others. For example, the URI for the term *Truss bridges* in the *Thesaurus of Graphic Materials* is http://id.loc.gov/vocabulary/graphicMaterials/tgm011115. Figure 11.4 shows the webpage documenting the use of this URI and formally registering it on the web. By clicking on one of the Alternate Formats listed at the bottom of the screen, users can view different coded forms of the RDF.

In Table 11.6, this URI has been used instead of a text string as the value. A URI has also been used in this table for the personal name, in this case an imaginary one based on a scenario of Hagenville Digital Library having its own local name authority file and formally registering its names with a URI.

The statements in Tables 11.3 through 11.6 are identical in terms of their semantic meaning, but

Figure 11.4. *Thesaurus of Graphic Materials Term in RDF*

Truss bridges

From **Thesaurus of Graphic Materials**

Details	Visualization

🏴 Truss bridges

URI
<http://id.loc.gov/vocabulary/graphicMaterials/tgm011115>

Parent Vocabulary
> Thesaurus for Graphic Materials

Broader Terms:
> Bridges

Related Terms:
> Trusses

Scope Notes
> 🏴 Main Term

Example:
> Applied within MARC as: Subject (MARC 150/650)
> Geographic faceting note: --[country or state]--[city]

History Notes
> Former control number from TGM I: lctgm011084
> Former usage note: Formerly TGMI term.

Change Notes
> 2007-08-02: Updated
> 1995-10-27: Creation

Term Status
stable

Instance Of
> SKOS Concept ↗

Alternate Formats
> RDF/XML
> N-Triples
> JSON

Source: Thesaurus of Graphic Materials, Authorities & Vocabularies, Library of Congress: http://id.loc.gov/. Term record: http://id.loc.gov/vocabulary/graphicMaterials/tgm011115.

Table 11.6. URIs Used as Values in RDF Triples

Resource (subject)	Property (predicate)	Value (object)
http://www.hdl.edu/Wis Bridges/ WB0078736	http://purl.org/dc/elements/ 1.1/subject	http://id.loc.gov/vocabulary/graphicMaterials/tgm011115
http://www.hdl.edu/Wis Bridges/ WB0078736	http://purl.org/dc/elements/ 1.1/creator	http://www.hdl.edu/nameauthority/938475

only the fourth has the ability to make full use of RDF's linking capabilities and to function unambiguously in a Linked Open Data environment.

11.2.3. Literals, Strings, and Things

Publishing or exposing metadata in RDF gives RDF-based software applications the ability to automatically create links among triples from many different sources by matching identical URIs. The following examples provide a simple illustration. In the first set of examples, the resource being described is the Project Gutenberg e-book of *Narrative of the Life of Frederick Douglass*, by Frederick Douglass. Table 11.7 represents a set of three triples about the title, creator, and subject of this e-book.

This and the following examples also explore the distinction between *strings* and *things* in Linked Data. A **string** is a string of lexical characters that, in most cases, points to nothing beyond itself and does not link to anything else. In contrast, a *resource* in the RDF sense is a **thing** that can link to other resources/things. This distinction ties in with the RDF concept of **literals** and anything that is not a literal, called **nonliterals** in some sources. Although there is not an exact equation between literals and strings, most strings are literals. "Literal values are raw text that can be used instead of objects in RDF triples. Unlike names (i.e. URIs) which are stand-ins for things in the real world, literal values are just raw text data inserted into the graph. Literal values could be used to relate people to their names, books to their ISBN numbers, etc." (Tauberer, 2008). In Table 11.7, the three triples are expressed as literals or strings, whereas in Table 11.8, all but one of the components of the three triples have been expressed as nonliteral *things* or *resources* in the form of linkable URIs. The title, in contrast, consists of a *literal string* of characters.

The URIs in Table 11.8 are all real-world, dereferenceable URIs (as of this writing). The Project Gutenberg e-book is located at http://www .gutenberg.org/files/23/23-h/23-h.htm. The Virtual International

Table 11.7. Three Triples Expressed as Literals/Strings

Resource (subject)	Property (predicate)	Value (object)
EBook 23/23-h/23-h	DC Title	Narrative of the Life of Frederick Douglass
EBook 23/23-h/23-h	DC Creator	Douglass, Frederick, 1817-1895
EBook 23/23-h/23-h	DC Subject	African American abolitionists--Biography

Table 11.8. Two Triples Expressed as URIs/Things

Resource (subject)	Property (predicate)	Value (object)
http://www.gutenberg.org/files/ 23/23-h/23-h.htm	http://purl.org/dc/elements/ 1.1/title	Narrative of the Life of Frederick Douglass
http://www.gutenberg.org/files/ 23/23-h/23-h.htm	http://purl.org/dc/elements/ 1.1/creator	http://www.viaf.org/viaf/10088/
http://www.gutenberg.org/files/ 23/23-h/23-h.htm	http://purl.org/dc/elements/ 1.1/subject	http://id.loc.gov/authorities/sh2007100462#concept

Authority File (VIAF) has established the VIAF ID:10088 for Frederic Douglass at http://www.viaf.org/viaf/10088/, which is rendered as *Douglass, Frederick, 1817-1895* for use in the majority of national libraries participating in this project. One subject of the resource, using the Library of Congress Subject Headings, is *African American abolitionists--Biography.* This heading has been assigned the following URI by the Library of Congress: http://id.loc.gov/authorities/sh2007100462#concept.

Figure 11.5 represents the three literal string triples from Table 11.7 in graph form. Figure 11.6 then represents the triples from Table 11.8 and shows how the three are linked by matching on the identical URI for the e-book resource. Figure

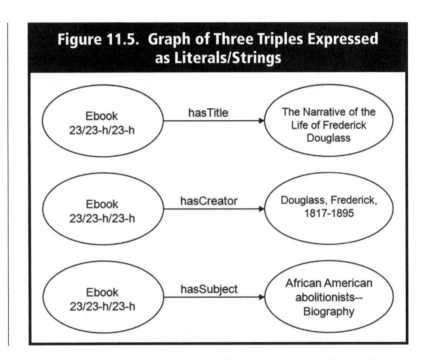

Figure 11.5. Graph of Three Triples Expressed as Literals/Strings

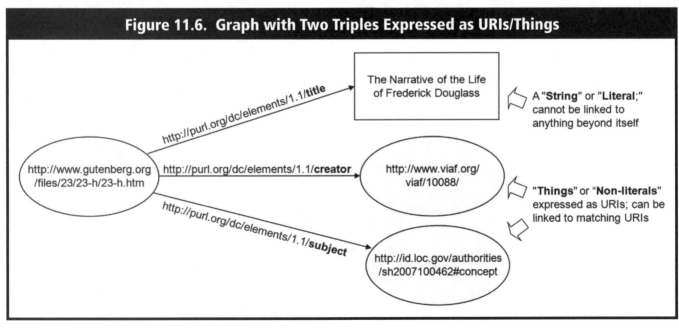

Figure 11.6. Graph with Two Triples Expressed as URIs/Things

11.6 also uses a square box instead of an oval to represent the string or literal that is not a linkable URI, like the other nonliterals in the graph.

It should be noted that there is not always a one-to-one equation of strings with literals. It is possible for a string to function as a nonliteral when it stands as a surrogate for a resource or thing. This may be the case, for example, when a string comes from a vocabulary encoding scheme, and that scheme is specified in the RDF statement. This gets into a level of detail outside the scope of this chapter, but it is important to realize that there are more nuances than what are covered in this simplified, introductory overview.

11.2.4. The Power of Linking and Querying in the Linked Data Cloud

Figure 11.7 consists of three triples for a new resource (related to the resource represented in the previous example), a printed book titled *Frederick Douglass and the Fourth of July* by James A. Colaiaco, first edition, published by Palgrave Macmillan in 2006. The Library of Congress's online catalog includes the following LCCN permalink for this book: http://lccn.loc.gov/2005051520. This URI has been used to represent the resource in Figure 11.7.

The resource represented in Figure 11.7 is *about* Frederick Douglass, and the VIAF URI for Frederick Douglass has been used as the value of the object in the triple that is making a statement about the subject of the resource. RDF software can then match this URI to the URI used in Figure 11.6, and the result is **Linked Data**: the two sets of triples now linked to each other, as depicted in Figure 11.8.

The power of Linked Open Data is to create link after link in this fashion, linking more and more resources based on matching URIs, as

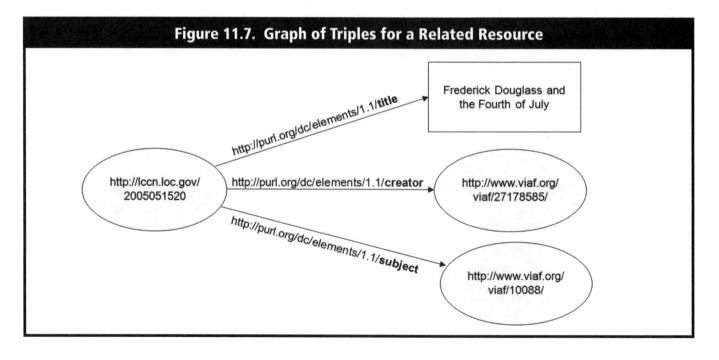

Figure 11.7. Graph of Triples for a Related Resource

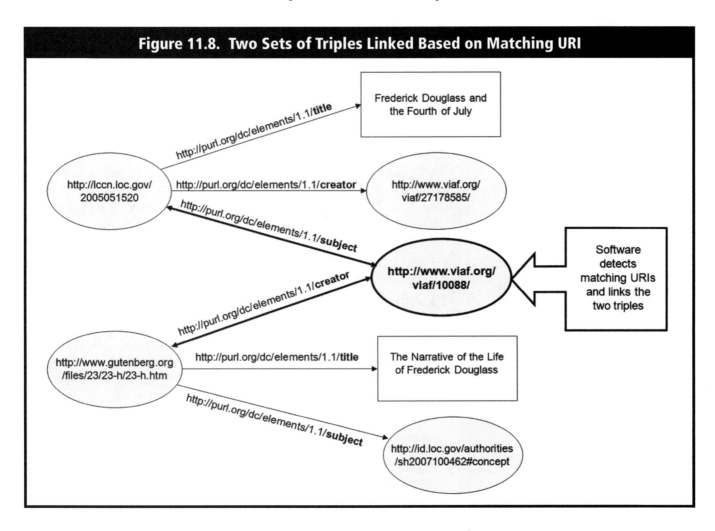

Figure 11.8. Two Sets of Triples Linked Based on Matching URI

more and more people publish or expose their data in a machine-actionable RDF syntax. One can imagine, for example, linking to other resources by and about Frederick Douglass, such as the Wikipedia article at http://en.Wikipedia.org/wiki/Frederick_Douglass. This Wikipedia article includes a great deal of additional information that could be expressed as RDF triples: Douglass's dates and places of birth and death; occupations; spouses; children; parents; works of scholarship and works for young readers about Douglass, including their ISBNs (which are themselves a type of identifier); and documentary films about him.

DBpedia is a Linked Data/Semantic Web compatible version of Wikipedia. The "About DBpedia" webpage offers the following brief description:

> DBpedia is a community effort to extract structured information from Wikipedia and to make this information available on the Web. DBpedia allows you to ask sophisticated queries against Wikipedia, and to link other data sets on the Web to Wikipedia data. We hope this will make it easier for the amazing amount of information in Wikipedia to be used in new and interesting ways, and that it might inspire new mechanisms for navigating, linking and improving the encyclopaedia itself. (DBpedia, 2010a)

This description points to a principal goal of the Linked Data movement: to allow for more powerful, semantically meaningful, and creative queries of web-based information in ways that web search engines, matching keywords against words in documents, cannot do. The following example illustrates one type of very specific query that could be made based on Linked Open Data. According to the DBpedia website, the existing LOD application, called the Berlin SNORQL query explorer, allows a user to ask for and retrieve very precise information such as "All soccer players, who played as goalkeeper for a club that has a stadium with more than 40.000 seats and who are born in a country with more than 10 million inhabitants" (DBpedia, 2010b). This query indicates the level of detail and number of parameters that can be used in querying structured metadata about information resources, in contrast to matching words in unstructured full text information resources.

11.2.5. RDF/XML

For these RDF statements or triples to function, they need to be expressed in a machine-readable RDF syntax or *serialization* format. **RDF/XML** is one such syntax. Other non-XML RDF serialization formats include Notation 3 (N3), Turtle, and N-Triples. The following example shows a possible way of expressing the RDF triples from Table 11.8 in RDF/XML syntax:

```
<?xml version="1.0" encoding="UTF-8"?>
<rdf:RDF xmlns:rdf="http://www.w3.org/1999/02/22-rdf-syntax-ns#"
    xmlns:dc="http://purl.org/dc/elements/1.1/">

  <rdf:Description rdf:about="http://www.gutenberg.org/
  files/23/23-h/23-h.htm">

    <dc:title>Narrative of the Life of Frederick
    Douglass</dc:title>
    <dc:creator rdf:resource="http://www.viaf.org/viaf/10088/" />
    <dc:subject rdf:resource="http://id.loc.gov/authorities/
    sh2007100462#concept" />

  </rdf:Description>

</rdf:RDF>
```

Notice that this is an **XML** record by the XML declaration at the start of the record. Two namespaces have been declared, establishing a prefix code for each: *rdf:* for RDF and *dc:* for Dublin Core. The root tag is **RDF**. This RDF/XML example is an RDF description about the resource identified with its URI. The Dublin Core *Title* element contains the value that is a literal string. The Dublin Core *Creator* and *Subject* elements are here expressed as *empty elements* that do not contain a string of characters between two tags. An XML *empty element* is indicated by a start tag that concludes with an internal forward slash and no matching end tag. In this case the meaning of the element is conveyed by means of an RDF *resource* attribute within in Dublin Core subject and creator tags. This convention is used because the value is a nonliteral URI, pointing to an RDF *resource* or *thing,* instead of a literal character string.

The following example presents the RDF/XML record in Library of Congress Authorities and Vocabularies for the LCSH heading *African American abolitionists--Biography*. The URI for the webpage is http://id.loc.gov/authorities/sh2007100462#concept.

```
<?xml version="1.0" encoding="UTF-8"?>
<rdf:RDF
    xmlns:dcterms="http://purl.org/dc/terms/"
    xmlns:owl="http://www.w3.org/2002/07/owl#"
    xmlns:rdf="http://www.w3.org/1999/02/22-rdf-syntax-ns#"
    xmlns:skos="http://www.w3.org/2004/02/skos/core#"
>
    <rdf:Description rdf:about="http://id.loc.gov/authorities/sh2007
    100462#concept">
      <skos:prefLabel xml:lang="en">African American abolitionists--
      Biography</skos:prefLabel>
      <owl:sameAs rdf:resource="info:lc/authorities/
      sh2007100462"/>
      <skos:inScheme rdf:resource="http://id.loc.gov/authorities
      #topicalTerms"/>
      <skos:inScheme rdf:resource="http://id.loc.gov/authorities
      #conceptScheme"/>
      <dcterms:created
      rdf:datatype="http://www.w3.org/2001/XML
      Schema#dateTime">2007-09-26T00:00:00-04:00</dcterms:
      created>
      <dcterms:modified
      rdf:datatype="http://www.w3.org/2001/XML
      Schema#dateTime">2007-10-17T07:55:53-04:00</dcterms:
      modified>
      <rdf:type rdf:resource="http://www.w3.org/2004/02/skos/
      core#Concept"/>
      <dcterms:source xml:lang="en">Work cat.: Narrative of
      the life of Frederick Douglass, an American slave,
      [2000]</dcterms:source>
    </rdf:Description>
</rdf:RDF>
```

Notice that this is an **XML record**, as shown by the XML declaration at the start of the record. The root tag is again **RDF**. Notice especially the first three elements after the opening tag. The first element states that this is an RDF record about the concept represented with the URI http://id.loc.gov/authorities/sh2007100462#concept. The second element is a SKOS element. **SKOS** stands for *Simple Knowledge Organization System* and is basically an RDF/Semantic Web syntax for encoding traditional controlled vocabulary data, including the three types of semantic relationships covered in Chapter 5. In this case, it is declared that the preferred label in English for the concept identified by this URI is *African American abolitionists--Biography*.

The third element is an OWL element. **OWL** stands for *Web Ontology Language*. Ontologies are usually regarded as critical components of the Semantic Web, but it is beyond the scope of this chapter to go into them. The significant thing to notice here is that the subject heading identified at this URI is declared to be the *SameAs* that located at another URI. This is another important aspect of Linked Data: the ability to state that two different URIs represent the same entity. In the Linked Open Data environment, it is expected that a variety of different individuals and organizations will make their RDF triples available to RDF software applications and that they will not always use the same URIs to identify the same things. It is therefore important to be able to make these equations, thereby creating links among different URIs representing the same information resource, person, object, subject concept, and so on. Using the *SameAs* equation can be fairly clear-cut when it comes to persons, corporate bodies, known objects, and the like, but much more ambiguous when it comes to abstract concepts, and must be used with great care.

11.3. Linked Data and Digital Collections

Section 11.2.4 gave a simple introductory overview of the power of linking data and of querying that linked data in the Linked Open Data Cloud. How might this apply to metadata for digital collections? First of all, existing metadata in the form of database and XML records would need to be converted into RDF triples and openly exposed to RDF applications, perhaps in a manner not unlike current OAI harvesting. The metadata could remain in its native format within its own database but be made available for harvesting in RDF format. Another option is for metadata implementers to convert their existing data into an RDF triple store as its native metadata format and make those triples available to RDF applications. Some tools for accomplishing this kind of conversion have already been developed, with more being developed in the present and near future.

Once exposed as RDF, the kind of linking demonstrated in Figure 11.8 could take place. Metadata representing digital images, texts, audio and video resources that are about particular subjects, people, places, time periods, objects, and so forth would be available for linking to other resources. The ability to do this lies in using common vocabularies that can be matched to registered URIs for such concepts, persons, etc. Someone searching for information about bridges located in the southeastern United States or in Southeast Asia, built during a particular span of years, or by architects working during a particular time period, and/or bridges of a specific type of construction or material, could discover digital images of, and other information resources about, the bridges that meet their search parameters. The unique local resources digitized and made available in online digital collections could be made discoverable in much more precise and useful ways in an open web environment when their metadata is exposed in RDF. Someone searching for information on a particular World War II battle could discover local oral history interviews of veterans who participated in that battle in addition to Wikipedia articles, books, journal articles, and other online resources. The possibilities are theoretically endless. At the present time this is largely a dream, a vision for the future, but one taken very seriously by the metadata and cataloging communities.

The vision of free Linked Open Data across the open web is a powerful and attractive one, but its ability to be realized in practice remains open to some question. A possibly more realistic or realizable alternative could be the implementation of Linked Data in a controlled environment, such as an international digital library or digital cultural heritage RDF data repository, with contributions of RDF triples made by trusted members.

11.4. Dublin Core: From a Core Metadata Element Set for the Web to a Core Vocabulary for Linked Data

Dublin Core has gradually changed "from a 'core metadata element set' for the web to a 'core vocabulary' for Linked Data" (Dekkers, 2010: slide 14). The Dublin Core Metadata Initiative has evolved over time and has increasingly turned its focus to the Linked Data/Semantic Web environment for metadata implementation.

> Early Dublin Core workshops popularized the idea of "core metadata" for simple and generic resource descriptions. The fifteen-element "Dublin Core" achieved wide dissemination as part of the Open Archives Initiative Protocol for Metadata Harvesting (OAI-PMH) and has been ratified as IETF RFC 5013, ANSI/NISO Standard Z39.85-2007, and ISO Standard 15836:2009.
>
> Starting in 2000, the Dublin Core community focused on "application profiles"—the idea that metadata records would use Dublin Core together with other specialized vocabularies to meet particular implementation requirements. During that time, the World Wide Web Consortium's work on a generic data model for metadata, the Resource Description Framework (RDF), was maturing. As part of an extended set of DCMI Metadata Terms, Dublin Core became one of most popular vocabularies for use with RDF, more recently in the context of the Linked Data movement.
>
> The consolidation of RDF motivated an effort to translate the mixed-vocabulary metadata style of the Dublin Core community into an RDF-compatible DCMI Abstract Model (2005). The DCMI Abstract Model was designed to bridge the modern paradigm of unbounded, linked data graphs with the more familiar paradigm of validatable metadata records like those used in OAI-PMH. A draft Description Set Profile specification defines a language for expressing constraints in a generic, application-independent way. The Singapore Framework for Dublin Core Application Profiles defines a set of descriptive components useful for documenting an application profile for maximum reusability. (DCMI, 2011a)

11.4.1. The DCMI Abstract Model (DCAM)

One important development in the DCMI's increasing move towards fostering implementation of metadata in a LOD/Semantic Web environment was the development of the **DCMI Abstract Model** (Powell et al., 2007), or **DCAM**. The authors state the following information about the documentation and model:

> The primary purpose of this document is to specify the components and constructs used in Dublin Core metadata. It defines the nature of the components used and describes how those components are combined to create information structures. It provides an information model which is independent of any particular encoding syntax.... The DCMI Abstract Model builds on work undertaken by the World Wide Web Consortium (W3C) on the Resource Description Framework (RDF). (Powell et al., 2007: para. 1)

The DCMI Abstract Model actually consists of three parts: the *DCMI Resource Model*, the *DCMI Description Model*, and the *DCMI Vocabulary Model*. The following is a textual definition of the **DCMI Resource Model**:

> The abstract model of the *resources* described by *descriptions* is as follows:
> - Each *described resource* is described using one or more *property-value pairs*.
> - Each *property-value pair* is made up of one *property* and one *value*.
> - Each *value* is a resource—the physical, digital or conceptual entity or *literal* that is associated with a *property* when a *property-value pair* is used to describe a *resource*. Therefore, each value is either a *literal value* or a *nonliteral value*:
>   - A *literal value* is a *value* which is a *literal*.
>   - A *nonliteral value* is a *value* which is a physical, digital or conceptual entity.
> - A *literal* is an entity which uses a Unicode string as a lexical form, together with an optional language tag or datatype, to denote a *resource* (i.e. "literal" as defined by RDF). (Powell et al., 2007)

The *DCMI Resource Model* is represented in a graphical form, using Unified Modeling Language (UML) as shown in Figure 11.9. After having read previous sections of this chapter, the model should look quite familiar to readers.

The **DCMI Description Set Model** builds on the Resource Model and puts it in the context of what is called a *description set*. A **description set** is a set of one or more *descriptions*, each of which describes a single resource. A *description* is made up of one or more *statements*, each statement consisting of a *property-value pair*. Basically, a description set is another name for a *record*. The DCMI Description Set Model is more or less a way to conceptually understand and model traditional metadata database records in the terminology and conceptual framework of RDF, Linked Data, and the Semantic Web. An exploration of the DCMI Description Set Model lies outside the scope of this chapter. But the concepts covered herein should assist those approaching the model for the first time to better understand it. Similarly, this chapter does not delve into the DCMI Vocabulary Model, which includes the RDF and

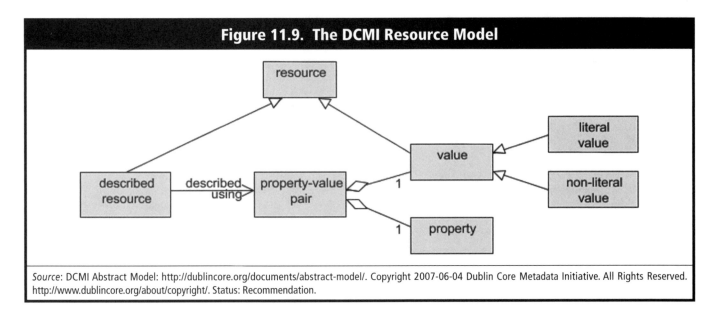

Figure 11.9. The DCMI Resource Model

ontology concepts of *classes, ranges,* and *domains* that lie outside the scope of this book.

11.4.2. Dublin Core Application Profiles

Metadata application profiles have been mentioned in various places throughout this book and covered in some detail in Chapter 10. This book uses the term *metadata application profile* in a broad, generic way as a term for virtually any kind of documentation of an institution's local application of a metadata element set or scheme. Within the DCMI, however, a more rigorous framework has been developed for designing a formal **Dublin Core Application Profile (DCAP)** that follows the DCMI Abstract Model with the intent of promoting metadata that will integrate with a Semantic Web of Linked Data (Coyle and Baker, 2009). The Guidelines for Dublin Core Application Profiles are based on the Singapore Framework for Dublin Core Application Profiles, illustrated graphically in Figure 11.10 (Nilsson, Baker, and Johnston, 2008).

The purpose of including mention of the DCMI Abstract Model, the Dublin Core Application Profile Guidelines, and the Singapore Framework in this chapter is simply to make readers aware of these models, frameworks, and guidelines, and not to delve into them in any detail. The important points for the purposes of this book are that the DCMI is developing models and frameworks explicitly intended to facilitate the creation of metadata that will be able to operate within a Linked Data/Semantic Web context.

11.5. Metadata Registries

"A **metadata registry** is a central location in an organization where metadata definitions are stored and maintained in a controlled method"

Figure 11.10. The Singapore Framework for DCAPs

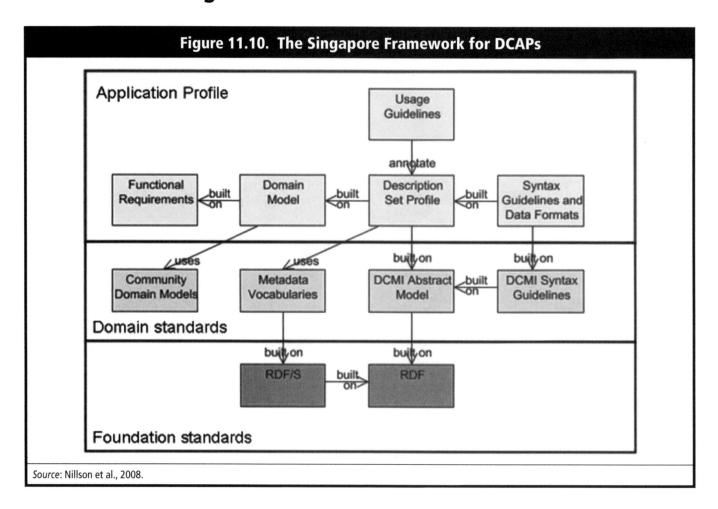

Source: Nillson et al., 2008.

(Wikipedia, 2010b). In most cases, metadata registries are locations on the web that formally document metadata elements and controlled vocabularies and are maintained by authorized persons within organizations. In the language of RDF, these are all *vocabularies*, with some terms being *properties*, others *classes*, and so forth. The Dublin Core Metadata Element Set is, for example, a vocabulary consisting of properties, their definitions, and the like. The types of registries of interest in the context of this chapter are those that formally register each property and class with a URI, as has been shown is the case with the Dublin Core elements earlier in this chapter.

In addition to the DCMI namespace references in the examples given previously in this chapter, there is also a **Dublin Core Metadata Registry** located at http://dcmi.kc.tsukuba.ac.jp/dcregistry/. "The Dublin Core Metadata Registry is designed to promote the discovery and reuse of properties, classes, and other types of metadata terms. It provides an up-to-date source of authoritative information about DCMI metadata terms and related vocabularies. The registry aids in the discovery of terms and their definitions and shows relationships between terms" (DCMI, 2011b).

Among many registries in existence, one is of special interest in the context of current developments associated with **Resource Description**

and Access (RDA), the Anglo-American cataloging community's new set of cataloging rules or metadata content standard. Implied within the standard is a set of metadata elements and subelements. This is evident, among other sources, in the "RDA Element Analysis," which states, "The RDA Element Analysis (including both the table and the accompanying notes) provides a detailed analysis of the relationship between RDA and the two metadata models that are referenced in the RDA Scope and Structure document (i.e., The <indecs> Metadata Framework, and the DCMI Abstract Model)" (Joint Steering Committee for Development of RDA. 2009a). Terminology and concepts from RDF and the DCAM are also evident in the "RDA Scope and Structure" document, which "defines the scope and structure of RDA in relation to its underlying conceptual models (FRBR and FRAD) and to two related metadata models (the DCMI Abstract Model and The <indecs> Metadata Framework)" (Joint Steering Committee for Development of RDA, 2009b: 1).

In terms of metadata registries, work has been done in the **Open Metadata Registry** to formally register all of the RDA elements and subelements (properties and subproperties) and associated controlled vocabularies in Semantic Web–enabled form, including the use of URIs for each term (Open Metadata Registry, 2011a). "The Metadata Registry provides services to developers and consumers of controlled vocabularies and is one of the first production deployments of the RDF-based Semantic Web Community's Simple Knowledge Organization System (SKOS)" (Open Metadata Registry, 2011a). Hillmann et al. (2010) have described this Semantic Web–enabled RDA registration activity.

11.6. What Does All of This Have to Do with Me?

What do RDF, Linked Data, and Semantic Web have to do with the majority of current implementers of digital collections? Not much, if anything, at the present time, other than having an awareness of the basic concepts and vision. This awareness may also help shape the way that you design your metadata schemes, especially the idea that in the Linked Data context, *statements* are the basic unit of metadata rather than *records*. Metadata statements (property-value pairs) currently residing in database records might one day be harvested and processed separately (apart from their current collection into a record structure) in a Linked Data environment.

Some implementers might want to establish a formal registry for their local elements, assigning each a URI and making a commitment to maintain those URIs indefinitely. In the future it might become relatively more common for a larger number of institutions to register their elements, or, preferably, for many institutions to share a number of elements needed for digital collections but not part of a standardized scheme such as Dublin Core or MODS. Most digital collection application profiles for consortial contexts include a few elements that are more or less the same, in that they are intended to record the same kind of information, but at present each uses their own element names and definitions. An element called *Submitter, Submitting Institution, Contributing Agency*, and the like is a good example. A number of implementers might come together to establish a registry of common elements needed for metadata sharing in an OAI or other consortial harvesting context. But this is still looking toward the future.

It remains to be seen to what extent the vision and hopes for Linked Open Data are taken up in practice, software applications created, and metadata structured as RDF widely deployed. Insofar as this happens, as many within the cultural heritage metadata communities desire and expect, there will no doubt be institutions that are early adopters, taking the plunge to implement before there are guarantees that the investment will pay off in the long run. If and when Linked Data begins to prove itself, there will likely be a large number of mainstream middle adopters, who gradually convert to Linked Data implementations over a long period of time. And there will be late adopters, usually smaller institutions with fewer staff and less expertise. Perhaps the move from card catalogs to MARC-based online catalogs provides a useful analogy here. The next step in that evolution may be, as many currently hope, to move library bibliographic metadata into RDF structures and Linked Data applications. Metadata for digital collections would be part of this next evolutionary stage.

11.7. Summary

This chapter has offered an introductory overview of selected aspects of the Linked Open Data and Semantic Web movements as they apply to metadata structures. Most of the chapter focused on the Resource Description Framework (RDF) data model and its applicability to cultural heritage metadata. In RDF, metadata consists of statements. Statements are made up of *triples* consisting of a *subject*, a *predicate*, and an *object*, also called a *resource*, a *property*, and a *value*. RDF uses URIs, in an open web context, to uniquely identify resources, properties, and as many values as possible. RDF uses URIs in the form of HTTP-structured URLs. URIs represent linkable *resources* or *things*, in contrast to *strings* of characters or *literals* that represent nothing other than themselves and do not create links. When RDF triples are exposed for processing by RDF/Linked Data software applications, the software can detect matching URIs and create links between them, thereby engendering a web of *Linked Data*. This has the potential to allow for richer, more precise, structured, semantically-meaningful queries and search results than is possible with search engines that use keyword matching algorithms. The Linked Data cloud becomes like a large, distributed metadata database, a web of structured *data* rather than a web of *documents*.

Many within the current cultural heritage metadata and cataloging communities are investing in RDF, Linked Data, and Semantic Web models and structures. The Dublin Core Metadata Initiative has increasingly moved during the past decade or more in this direction. The development of the DCMI Abstract Model and the Singapore Framework for Dublin Core Application Profiles, among others, are evidence of this. The Library of Congress is registering and making available many of its controlled vocabularies, including the *Thesaurus for Graphic Materials* and *Library of Congress Subject Headings*, in RDF/SKOS formats with URIs for each term. The new library cataloging rules, *Resource Description and Access* (RDA), have been designed to be Linked Data/Semantic Web compatible, and there has been an effort to register RDA elements and vocabularies in RDF/SKOS as well. The future of the Linked Data/Semantic Web vision remains uncertain as of this writing, but many have invested in it and are looking toward future implementations. At the present time this is having little or no practical effect of the majority of cultural heritage metadata implementers, but it is important to be aware of what is happening, to keep abreast of ongoing developments, and to be prepared to take part when the right time comes.

> ▶ **Companion Website**
>
> See this book's companion website at **http://www.neal-schuman.com/ metadata-digital-collections** for Chapter 11 review questions, suggestions for exercises, and other resources.

References

ALCTS. 2010. "Linked Data: Making Library Data Converse with the World." Presentations at ALCTS Preconference, June 24, 2010, Washington, DC. http://presentations.ala.org/index.php?title=Thursday%2C_June_24.

Coyle, Karen. 2010. *Understanding the Semantic Web: Bibliographic Data and Metadata*. Library Technology Reports, vol. 46, no. 1. Chicago: American Library Association.

Coyle, Karen, and Thomas Baker. 2009. "Guidelines for Dublin Core Application Profiles." May 18. http://dublincore.org/documents/profile-guidelines/index.shtml.

Cyganiak, Richard, and Anja Jentzsch. 2010. "The Linking Open Data Cloud Diagram." Last modified September 22. http://richard.cyganiak.de/2007/10/lod/.

DBpedia. 2010a. "About DBpedia." Accessed September 27. http://www.dbpedia.org/about/.

DBpedia. 2010b. "Accessing the DBpedia Data Set over the Web." Accessed November 28. http://wiki.dbpedia.org/OnlineAccess/.

DCMI. 2011a. "DCMI Metadata Basics." Accessed February 2. http://dublincore.org/metadata-basics/.

DCMI. 2011b. "The Dublin Core Metadata Registry." Accessed February 24. http://dcmi.kc.tsukuba.ac.jp/dcregistry/.

Dekkers, Max. 2010. "Dublin Core in the Early Web Revolution." Presentation at Joint NISO/DCMI Webinar, August 25. http://dublincore.org/resources/training/NISO_Webinar_20100825/dcmi-webinar-01.pdf.

Hillmann, Diane, Karen Coyle, Jon Phipps, and Gordon Dunsire. 2010. "RDA Vocabularies: Process, Outcome, Use." *D-Lib Magazine* 16, no. 1/2 (January/February). http://www.dlib.org/dlib/january10/hillmann/01hillmann.html.

Joint Steering Committee for Development of RDA. 2009a. "RDA Element Analysis." Rev/3, July 1. http://www.rda-jsc.org/docs/5rda-elementanalysisrev3.pdf.

Joint Steering Committee for Development of RDA. 2009b. "RDA—Resource Description and Access: Scope and Structure." Rev/4, July 1. http://www.rda-jsc.org/docs/5rda-scoperev4.pdf.

Library of Congress. 2011. "Authorities and Vocabularies: About." Accessed February 2. http://id.loc.gov/authorities/about.html.

Nilsson, Mikael, Thomas Baker, and Pete Johnston. 2008. "The Singapore Framework for Dublin Core Application Profiles." Issued January 14. http://dublincore.org/documents/2008/01/14/singapore-framework/.

NISO/DCMI. 2010. "Dublin Core: The Road from Metadata Formats to Linked Data." Joint NISO/DCMI Webinar, August 25. Presentation slides by Makx Dekkers and Thomas Baker. http://www.dublincore.org/resources/training/.

Open Metadata Registry. 2011a. "Home." Accessed February 24, 2011. http://www.metadataregistry.org/.

Open Metadata Registry. 2011b. "The RDA (Resource Description and Access) Vocabularies." Accessed February 24. http://metadataregistry.org/rdabrowse.htm.

Powell, Andy, Michael Nilsson, Ambjörn Naeve, Pete Johnston, and Thomas Baker. 2007. "DCMI Abstract Model." June 4. http://dublincore.org/documents/abstract-model/.

Tauberer, Joshua. 2008. "What Is RDF and What Is It Good For?" RDF: About. Last modified January. http://www.rdfabout.com/intro/.

Wikipedia. 2010a. "Linked Data." Accessed September 28. http://en.wikipedia.org/wiki/Linked_data.

Wikipedia. 2010b. "Metadata Registry." Accessed September 28. http://en.wikipedia.org/wiki/Metadata_registry.

Wikipedia. 2011. "Semantic Web." Accessed February 1. http://en.wikipedia.org/wiki/Semantic_Web.

Bibliography

Alexander, Arden, and Tracy Meehleib. 2001. "The Thesaurus for Graphic Materials: Its History, Use, and Future." *Cataloging & Classification Quarterly* 31, no. 3/4: 189–212.

Arms, Caroline. "Some Observations on Metadata and Digital Libraries." Discussion paper presented at the Library of Congress Bicentennial Conference on Bibliographic Control for the New Millennium, November 15–17, 2000. http://lcweb.loc.gov/catdir/bibcontrol/arms_paper.html.

Arms, Caroline R., and William Y. Arms. 2004. "Mixed Content and Mixed Metadata: Information Discovery in a Messy World." In *Metadata in Practice*, edited by Diane Hillmann and Elaine Westbrooks, 223–237. Chicago: ALA.

Baca, Murtha, ed. 2008. *Introduction to Metadata*, 2nd ed., v. 3.0. Los Angeles: Getty Research Institute. http://www.getty.edu/research/publications/electronic_publications/intrometadata/index.html.

Baca, Murtha, et al. 2008. "Practical Principles for Metadata Creation and Maintenance." In *Introduction to Metadata*. 2nd ed., v. 3.0, edited by Murtha Baca. Los Angeles: Getty Research Institute. http://www.getty.edu/research/publications/electronic_publications/intrometadata/index.html.

Baca, Murtha, Patricia Harpring, Elisa Lanzi, Linda McRae, and Ann Baird Whiteside, ed. 2006. *Cataloging Cultural Objects: A Guide to Describing Cultural Works and Their Images.* Chicago: American Library Association.

Baker, Thomas. 2000. "A Grammar of Dublin Core." *D-Lib Magazine* 6, no. 10 (October). http://mirrored.ukoln.ac.uk/lis-journals/dlib/dlib/dlib/october00/baker/10baker.html.

Bauer, Charlie. 2005. "Institutional Repositories." In *Technology for the Rest of Us: A Primer on Computer Technologies for the Low-Tech Librarian*, edited by Nancy Courtney, 109–122. Westport, CT: Libraries Unlimited.

Berners-Lee, James Hendler, and Ora Lassila. 2001. "The Semantic Web." *Scientific American*, May 17. http://www.scientificamerican.com/article.cfm?id=the-semantic-web.

Bishoff, Liz, and Elizabeth S. Meagher. 2004. "Building Heritage Colorado: The Colorado Digitization Experience." In *Metadata in Practice*, edited by Diane Hillmann and Elaine Westbrooks, 17–36. Chicago: ALA.

Bishoff, Liz, and William A. Garrison. "Metadata, Cataloging, Digitization and Retrieval: Who's Doing What to Whom: The Colorado Digitization Project Experience." Discussion paper presented at the Library of Congress Bicentennial Conference on Bibliographic Control for the New Millennium, November 15–17, 2000. http://lcweb.loc.gov/catdir/bibcontrol/bishoff_paper.html.

Boiko, Bob. 2010. "Defining Data, Information, and Content: A CM Domain White Paper." Accessed November 1. http://www.metatorial.com/downloads/Boiko_Wp_DefiningDataInformationContent.pdf.

Boughida, Karim. 2005. "CDWA Lite for Cataloging Cultural Objects (CCO): A New XML Schema for the Cultural Heritage Community." In *Humanities, Computers and Cultural Heritage: Proceedings of the XVI International Conference of the Association for History and Computing, = September 14–17.* Amsterdam: Royal Netherlands Academy of Arts and Sciences. http://www.knaw.nl/publicaties/pdf/20051064.pdf.

Bowen, Jennifer. 2008. "Metadata to Support Next-Generation Library Resource Discovery: Lessons from the eXtensible Catalog, Phase 1." *Information Technology and Libraries*, June: 6–19.

Bray, Tim. 1998. "RDF and Metadata." O'Reilly XML.com, June 9. http://www.xml.com/xml/pub/98/06/rdf.html.

Brisson, Roger. 1999. "The World Discovers Cataloging: A Conceptual Introduction to Digital Libraries, Metadata and the Implications for Library Administrations." *Journal of Internet Cataloging* 1, no. 4: 3–30.

Bruce, Thomas R., and Diane I. Hillmann. 2004. "The Continuum of META-DATA Quality: Defining, Expressing, Exploiting." In *Metadata in Practice*, edited by Diane Hillmann and Elaine Westbrooks, 238–256. Chicago: American Library Association.

Burnard, Lou, and C. M. Sperberg-McQueen. 2002. *TEI Lite: An Introduction to Text Encoding for Interchange.* Last modified May. Sections 1–3, 20. http://www.tei- c.org/Guidelines/Customization/Lite/teiu5_en.html.

Burnett, Kathleen, Kwong Bor Ng, and Soyeon Park. 1999. "A Comparison of the Two Traditions of Metadata Development." *Journal of the American Academy for Information Science* 50, no. 13: 1209–1217.

Butterfield, Kevin L. 1996. "Catalogers and the Creation of Metadata Systems." Proceedings of the OCLC Internet Cataloging Project Colloquium, San Antonio, Texas, January 19. http://www.worldcat.org/arcviewer/1/OCC/2003/07/21/0000003889/viewer/file22.html.

Campbell, D. Grant. 2005. "Metadata, Metaphor, and Metonymy." In *Metadata: A Cataloger's Primer*, edited by Richard P. Smiraglia, 57–73. Binghamton, NY: Haworth Press.

Cantara, Linda. 2005. "METS: The Metadata Encoding and Transmission Standard." *Cataloging & Classification Quarterly* 40, no. 3/4: 237–253.

Caplan, Priscilla. 1995. "You Call It Corn, We Call It Syntax-Independent Metadata for Document-Like Objects." *The Public-Access Computer Systems Review* 6, no. 4. http://info.lib.uh.edu/pr/v6/n4/caplan.6n4.

———. 1997. "To Hel(sinki) and Back for the Dublin Core." *The Public-Access Computer Systems Review* 8, no. 4. http://info.lib.uh.edu/pr/v8/n4/capl8n4.html.

———. 2000. "International Metadata Initiatives: Lessons in Bibliographic Control." Paper presented at the Library of Congress Bicentennial Conference on Bibliographic Control for the New Millennium, November 15–17. http://lcweb.loc.gov/catdir/bibcontrol/caplan_paper.html.

———. 2003. *Metadata Fundamentals for All Librarians.* Chicago: American Library Association.

Caplan, Priscilla, and Rebecca Guenther. 1996. "Metadata for Internet Resources: The Dublin Core Metadata Elements Set and Its Mapping to USMARC." *Cataloging & Classification Quarterly* 22, no. 3/4: 43–58.

CDP Metadata Working Group. 2006. "CDP Dublin Core Metadata Best Practices." Version 2.1.1 (September). http://www.lyrasis.org/Products-

and-Services/Digital-and-Preservation-Services/Digital-Toolbox/Metadata
.aspx.

Chopey, Michael A. 2005. "Planning and Implementing a Metadata-Driven Digital Repository." In *Metadata: A Cataloger's Primer*, edited by Richard P. Smiraglia, 255–287. Binghamton, NY: Haworth Press.

Coyle, Karen. 2005a. "Descriptive Metadata for Copyright Status." *First Monday* 10, no. 10. http://www.uic.edu/htbin/cgiwrap/bin/ojs/index .php/fm/article/view/1282/1202 (accessed October 28, 2010).

———. 2005b. "Understanding Metadata and its Purpose." *Journal of Academic Librarianship* 31, no. 2 (March): 160–163.

———. 2010. *Understanding the Semantic Web: Bibliographic Data and Metadata.* Library Technology Reports, vol. 46, no. 1. Chicago: American Library Association.

Coyle, Karen, and Thomas Baker. 2009. "Guidelines for Dublin Core Application Profiles." Dublin Core Metadata Initiative. http://dublincore.org/documents/ profile-guidelines/index.shtml.

Day, Michael. 2002. "Metadata: Mapping between Metadata Formats." *UKOLN.* Last modified May 22. http://www.ukoln.ac.uk/metadata/inter operability/.

Desmarais, Norman. 2000. *The ABCs of XML: The Librarian's Guide to the eXtensibile Markup Language.* Houston: New Technology Press.

DLF (Digital Library Federation). 2005. "Summary of OAI Metadata Best Practices." Last modified November 29. http://www.diglib.org/architectures/ oai/imls2004/training/MetadataFinal.pdf.

———. 2007. "Best Practices for OAI Data Provider Implementations and Shareable Metadata." Last modified July 10. http://webservices.itcs.umich .edu/mediawiki/oaibp/index.php/Main_Page.

DLF Aquifer Metadata Working Group. 2009. "Digital Library Federation / Aquifer Implementation Guidelines for Shareable MODS Records." Version 1.1. March. https://wiki.dlib.indiana.edu/confluence/download/attachments/ 24288/DLFMODS_ImplementationGuidelines.pdf.

DLF/NSDL Working Group on OAI PMH Best Practices. 2007. "Best Practices for OAI PMH Data Provider Implementations and Shareable Metadata." Edited by Sarah L. Shreeves, Jenn Riley, and Kat Hagedorn. Digital Library Federation. http://www.diglib.org/pubs/dlf108.pdf.

Dushay, Naomi, and Diane Hillmann. 2003. "Analyzing Metadata for Effective Use and Re-Use." In *DC-2003—Proceedings of the International DCMI Metadata Conference and Workshop, September 28–October 2, 2003, Seattle, Washington, USA.* http://dcpapers.dublincore.org/ojs/pubs/article/view/ 744/740/.

Duval, Erik, Wayne Hodgins, Stuart Sutton, and Stuart L. Weibel. 2002. "Metadata Principles and Practicalities." *D-Lib Magazine* 8, no. 4 (April). http://www.dlib.org/dlib/april02/weibel/04weibel.html.

Elings, Mary W. and Günter Waibel. 2007. "Metadata for All: Descriptive Standards and Metadata Sharing across Libraries, Archives and Museums." *First Monday* 12, no. 3 (March). http://firstmonday.org/issues/issue12_3/ elings/index.html.

Fiander, David J. 2001. "Applying XML to the Bibliographic Description." *Cataloging & Classification Quarterly* 33, no. 2: 17–28.

Foulonneau, Muriel, and Jenn Riley. 2008. *Metadata for Digital Resources: Implementation, Systems Design and Interoperability.* Oxford, UK: Chandos.

Gill, Tony. 2008. "Metadata and the Web." In *Introduction to Metadata.* 2nd ed., v. 3.0, edited by Murtha Baca. Los Angeles: Getty Research Institute.

http://www.getty.edu/research/publications/electronic_publications/intro metadata/index.html.

Gilliland, Anne J. 2008. "Setting the Stage." In *Introduction to Metadata*. 2nd ed., v. 3.0, edited by Murtha Baca. Los Angeles: Getty Research Institute. http://www.getty.edu/research/publications/electronic_publications/intro metadata/index.html.

Glogoff, Stuart J., and Garry J. Forger. 2001. "Metadata Protocols and Standards: Bringing Order to Our Digital Objects." *Internet Reference Services Quarterly* 5, no. 4: 5–14.

Gourkova, Helen. 2005. "International Yearbook of Library and Information Management 2003–2004: Metadata Applications and Management." *Library Management*, 26, no. 6/7: 413–415.

Greenberg, Jane. 2005. "Understanding Metadata and Metadata Schemes." In *Metadata: A Cataloger's Primer*, edited by Richard P. Smiraglia, 17–36. Binghamton, NY: Haworth Press.

Guenther, Rebecca S. 2003. "MODS: The Metadata Object Description Schema." *Libraries and the Academy* 3, no.1 (January): 137–150.

———. 2004. "Using the Metadata Object Description Schema (MODS) for Resource Description: Guidelines and Applications." *Library Hi Tech* 22, no. 2: 89–98.

Guenther, Rebecca, and Sally McCallum. 2003. "New Metadata Standards for Digital Resources: MODS and METS." *Bulletin of the American Society for Information Science and Technology* 29, no. 2 (Dec/Jan): 12–15.

Han, Myung-Ja, Christine Cho, Timothy W. Cole, and Amy S. Jackson. 2009. "Metadata for Special Collections in CONTENTdm: How to Improve Interoperability of Unique Fields Through OAI-PMH." *Journal of Library Metadata* 9, no. 3/4: 213–238.

Harpring, Patricia. 2002. "The Language of Images: Enhancing Access to Images by Applying Metadata Schemas and Structured Vocabularies." In *Introduction to Art Image Access Issues, Tools, Standards, Strategies*, edited by Murtha Baca. Los Angeles: Getty Research Institute. http://www.getty.edu/research/conducting_research/standards/intro_aia/harpring.pdf.

Haynes, David. 2004. *Metadata for Information Management and Retrieval*. London: Facet.

Heery, Rachel. 1998. "What is . . . RDF?" *Ariadne* 14 (March). http://www.ariadne.ac.uk/issue14/what-is/.

Hicks, Emily A., Jody Perkins, and Margaret Beecher Maurer. 2007. "Application Profile Development for Consortial Digital Libraries: An OhioLINK Case Study." *Library Resources and Technical Services* 51, no. 2: 33–43.

Hillmann, Diane. 2005. "Using Dublin Core." Dublin Core Metadata Initiative. November 7. http://dublincore.org/documents/usageguide/.

Hillmann, Diane I., and Elaine L. Westbrooks. 2004. *Metadata in Practice*. Chicago: American Library Association.

Hillmann, Diane et al. 2010. "RDA Vocabularies: Process, Outcome, Use." *D-Lib Magazine* 16, no. 1/2 (January/February). http://www.dlib.org/dlib/january10/hillmann/01hillmann.html.

Hodge, Gail. 2000. *Systems of Knowledge Organization for Digital Libraries: Beyond Traditional Authority Files*. The Digital Library Federation. http://www.diglib.org/pubs/dlf090/dlf090.pdf.

Hudgins, Jean, Grace Agnew, and Elizabeth Brown. 1999. *Getting Mileage Out of Metadata: Applications for the Library*. Chicago: American Library Association.

Hutt, Arwen, and Jenn Riley. 2005. "Semantics and Syntax of Dublin Core Usage in Open Archives Initiative Data Providers of Cultural Heritage

Materials." In *Proceedings of the 5th ACM/IEEE-CS Joint Conference on Digital Libraries, Denver, CO, June 7–11, 2005,* 262–270. New York: ACM Press.

Ianella, Renato. 1998. "An Idiot's Guide to the Resource Description Framework." *The New Review of Information Networking* 4. http://renato.iannella.it/paper/rdf-idiot/.

IFLA Study Group on the Functional Requirements for Bibliographic Records. 2010. *Functional Requirements for Bibliographic Records.* Accessed November 24. http://www.ifla.org/en/publications/functional-requirements-for-bibliographic-records.

Indiana Memory Project. 2007. *Dublin Core Metadata Guide.* http://www.in.gov/library/files/dig_metast.pdf.

Intner, Sheila S., Susan S. Lazinger, and Jean Weihs. 2005. *Metadata and Its Impact on Libraries.* Library and Information Science Text Series. Westport, CT: Libraries Unlimited.

Jackson, Amy S., Myung-Ja Han, Kurt Groetsch, Megan Mustafoff, and Timothy W. Cole. 2008. "Dublin Core Metadata Harvested Through OAI-PMH." *Journal of Library Metadata* 8, no. 1: 5–21.

Johnston, Pete. 2006. "Metadata Sharing and XML." In *Good Practice Guide for Developers of Cultural Heritage Web Services.* Bath, UK: UKOLN. Last modified January. http://www.ukoln.ac.uk/interop-focus/gpg/Metadata/.

Joint Steering Committee for Development of RDA. 2009a. "RDA Element Analysis." Rev/4, July 1. http://www.rda-jsc.org/docs/5rda-elementanalysis-1.pdf.

Joint Steering Committee for Development of RDA. 2009b. "RDA—Resource Description and Access: Scope and Structure." Rev/4, July 1. http://www.rda-jsc.org/docs/5rda-scoperev4.pdf.

Kalbach, James. 2008. "Navigating the Long Tail." *Bulletin of the American Society for Information Science and Technology* 34, no.2 (December/January): 36–38. http://www.asis.org/Bulletin/Dec-07/kalbach.html.

Lagoze, Carl. 2000. "Business Unusual: How 'Event-Awareness' May Breathe Life Into the Catalog?" Paper presented at the Library of Congress Bicentennial Conference on Bibliographic Control for the New Millennium (November 15–17). http://lcweb.loc.gov/catdir/bibcontrol/lagoze_paper.html.

———. 2001. "Keeping Dublin Core Simple: Cross-Domain Discovery or Resource Description?" *D-Lib Magazine* 7, no. 1 (January). http://www.dlib.org/dlib/january01/lagoze/01lagoze.html.

Layne, Sara Shatford. 1994. "Some Issues in the Indexing of Images." *Journal of the American Society for Information Science* 45, no. 8: 583–588.

———. 2002. "Subject Access to Art Images." In *Introduction to Art Image Access Issues, Tools, Standards, Strategies,* edited by Murtha Baca. Los Angeles: Getty Research Institute. http://www.getty.edu/research/conducting_research/standards/intro_aia/layne.pdf.

Layne, Sara Shatford, Patricia Harpring, Colum Hourihane, and Christine L. Sundt. 2002. *Introduction to Art Image Access Issues, Tools, Standards, Strategies,* edited by Murtha Baca. Los Angeles: Getty Research Institute. http://www.getty.edu/research/conducting_research/standards/intro_aia/index.html.

Lee-Smeltzer, Kuang-Hwei. 2000. "Finding the Needle: Controlled Vocabularies, Resource Discovery, and the Dublin Core." *Library Collections, Acquisitions, & Technical Services* 24: 205–215.

Leise, Fred, Karl Fast, and Mike Steckel. 2002. "What Is a Controlled Vocabulary?" Boxes and Arrows. Last modified April 7. http://www.boxesandarrows.com/view/creating_a_controlled_vocabulary_.

Library of Congress. 1995. "II. Indexing Images: Some Principles." In *Thesaurus for Graphic Materials I: Subject Terms (TGM I)*. http://www.loc.gov/rr/print/tgm1/.

"Linked Data: Making Library Data Converse with the World." 2010. Presentation at ALCTS Preconference, June 24, Washington, D.C. http://presentations.ala.org/index.php?title=Thursday%2C_June_24.

Lynch, Clifford. 1997. "Searching the Internet." *Scientific American* 276, no. 3 (March): 52–56.

———. 1998. "The Dublin Core Descriptive Metadata Program: Strategic Implications for Libraries and Networked Information Access." *ARL* 196 (February): 5–10.

Matusiak, Krystyna K. 2006. "Towards User-centered Indexing in Digital Image Collections." *OCLC Systems & Services* 22, no. 4: 283–298.

"Metadata Standards Crosswalk." 2009. Research at the Getty. Last modified June 9. www.getty.edu/research/conducting_research/standards/intrometadata/crosswalks.html.

Miller, Eric. 1998. "An Introduction to the Resource Description Framework." *D-Lib Magazine* (May). http://www.dlib.org/dlib/may98/miller/05miller.html.

Miller, Steven J. 2010. "The One-to-One Principle: Challenges in Current Practice." In *Proceedings of the International Conference on Dublin Core and Metadata Applications*, edited by Diane I. Hillmann and Michael Lauruhn, 150–164. http://dcpapers.dublincore.org/ojs/pubs/article/view/1043.

Milstead, Jessica, and Susan Feldman. 1999a. "Metadata: Cataloging by Any Other Name." *Online* 23, no. 1 (January): 24–31.

———. 1999b. "Metadata Projects and Standards." *Online* 23, no. 1 (January): 32–40.

Moody, Glyn. 1998. "A New Dawn." *New Scientist* (May 30). http://xml.coverpages.org/newScientistXML9805.html.

Morgan, Eric Lease. 2004. *Getting Started with XML: A Workshop.* http://www.infomotions.com/musings/getting-started/.

Morville, Peter. 2005. "The Sociosemantic Web." In *Ambient Findability*, 119–154. Sebastopol, CA: O'Reilly.

Morville, Peter, and Louis Rosenfeld. 2006. *Information Architecture for the World Wide Web.* 3rd edition. Sebastopol, CA: O'Reilly.

National Science Digital Library. 2004. "Ten Commandments For Metadata Quality." In *Getting a Leg Up on the Open Archives Initiative Protocol for Metadata Harvesting (OAI-PMH)*, 5–7. http://www.ideals.uiuc.edu/bitstream/2142/75/4/2620_National_Science_Digital_Library_Conference.doc.pdf.

Nevile, Liddy, and Sophie Lissonnet. 2006. "Dublin Core and Museum Information: Metadata as Cultural Heritage Data." *International Journal of Metadata, Semantics and Ontologies* 1, no. 3: 198–206.

Nilsson, Mikael, Thomas Baker, and Pete Johnston. 2008. "The Singapore Framework for Dublin Core Application Profiles." http://dublincore.org/documents/2008/01/14/singapore-framework/.

NINCH (National Initiative for a Networked Cultural Heritage). 2002. *NINCH Guide to Good Practice in the Digital Representation and Management of Cultural Heritage Materials.* http://www.nyu.edu/its/humanities/ninchguide/index.html.

NISO (National Information Standards Organization). 2004. "Understanding Metadata." Bethesda, MD: NISO Press. http://www.niso.org/publications/press/UnderstandingMetadata.pdf.

———. 2005. *ANSI/NISO Z39.19-2005 - Guidelines for the Construction, Format, and Management of Monolingual Controlled Vocabularies.* Bethesda, Maryland: NISO Press. http://www.niso.org/kst/reports/standards?step=2&gid=None&project_key=7cc9b583cb5a62e8c15d3099e0bb46bbae9cf38a.

———. 2007. *A Framework of Guidance for Building Good Digital Collections,* 3rd edition. NISO. http://framework.niso.org/.

NISO/DCMI. 2010. "Dublin Core: The Road from Metadata Formats to Linked Data." Joint NISO/DCMI Webinar, August 25. Presentation slides by Makx Dekkers and Thomas Baker available: http://dublincore.org/resources/training/.

OAI (Open Archives Initiative). 2008. *OAI-PMH (The Open Archives Initiative Protocol for Metadata Harvesting)* Protocol Version 2.0 of 2002-06-14. Document Version 2008-12-07T20:42:00Z. http://www.openarchives.org/OAI/2.0/openarchivesprotocol.htm.

"Obtain the Getty Vocabularies." 2010. The Getty. Last modified March 23. http://www.getty.edu/research/conducting_research/vocabularies/license.html.

OhioLINK Database Management and Standards Committee (DMSC) Metadata Task Force 2006. *OhioLINK Digital Media Center (DMC) Metadata Application Profile.* Columbus, OH: OhioLINK. Issued August 21. http://silver.ohiolink.edu/dms/dmccontribution/DMC_AP.pdf.

Powell, Andy, Mikael Nilsson, Ambjörn Naeve, Pete Johnston, and Thomas Baker. 2007. "DCMI Abstract Model." Dublin Core Metadata Initiative. http://dublincore.org/documents/2007/04/02/abstract-model/.

Rettig, Patricia J. 2002. "Administrative Metadata for Digital Images: A Real World Application of the NISO Standard." *Library Collections, Acquisitions, & Technical Services* 26: 173–179.

Riley, Jenn, John Chapman, Sarah Shreeves, Laura Akerman, and William Landis. 2008. "Promoting Shareability: Metadata Activities of the DLF Aquifer Initiative." *Journal of Library Metadata* 8, no. 3: 221–248.

Rhyno, Art. 2005. "Introduction to XML." In *Technology for the Rest of Us: A Primer on Computer Technologies for the Low-Tech Librarian,* edited by Nancy Courtney, 71–84. Westport, CT: Libraries Unlimited.

RLG. 2005. "Terminology." In *Descriptive Metadata Guidelines for RLG Cultural Materials,* 3–5. Mountain View, CA: RLG. http://www.oclc.org/programs/ourwork/past/culturalmaterials/RLG_desc_metadata.pdf.

Shreeves, Sarah L. 2005. "The Open Archives Initiative Protocol for Metadata Harvesting." In *Technology for the Rest of Us: A Primer on Computer Technologies for the Low-Tech Librarian,* edited by Nancy Courtney, 85–108. Westport, CT: Libraries Unlimited.

Shreeves, Sarah L., Jenn Riley, and Liz Milewicz. 2006. "Moving Towards Shareable Metadata." *First Monday* 11, no. 8. http://firstmonday.org/htbin/cgiwrap/bin/ojs/index.php/fm/article/view/1386/1304.

Smiraglia, Richard P., ed. 2005. *Metadata: A Cataloger's Primer.* Binghamton, NY: Haworth Press. Copublished simultaneously as *Cataloging & Classification Quarterly* 40, no. 3/4 (2005).

St. Pierre, Margaret, and William P. LaPlant. 1998. "Issues in Crosswalking: Content Metadata Standards." NISO Standards White Paper. October 15. http://www.niso.org/publications/white_papers/crosswalk/.

Sutton, Stuart. 2007. "Tutorial 1: Basic Semantics." Presentation at DC-2007: International Conference on Dublin Core and Metadata Applications, Singapore, August 27–31. http://dublincore.org/resources/training/dc-2007/T1-BasicSemantics.pdf.

Tauberer, Joshua. 2008. "What Is RDF and What Is It Good For?" RDF: About. Last modified January. http://www.rdfabout.com/intro/.

TDL (Texas Digital Library) Metadata Working Group. 2005. "MODS Application Profile for Electronic Theses and Dissertations," Version 1, December. http://www.tdl.org/wp-content/uploads/2009/04/etd_mods_profile.pdf.

———. 2008. "Texas Digital Library Descriptive Metadata Guidelines for Electronic Theses and Dissertations," Version 1.0, June. http://www.tdl.org/wp-content/uploads/2009/04/tdl-descriptive-metadata-guidelines-for-etd-v1.pdf.

Thurman, Alexander C. 2005. "Metadata Standards for Archival Control: An Introduction to EAD and EAC." *Cataloging & Classification Quarterly* 40, no. 3/4: 183–212.

Tillett, Barbara B. 1991. "A Taxonomy of Bibliographic Relationships." *Library Resources & Technical Services* 35, no. 2 (April): 150–158.

———. 2001. "Bibliographic Relationships." In *Relationships in the Organization of Knowledge*, edited by Carol A. Bean and Rebecca Green, 19–35. *Information Science and Knowledge Management*, v. 2. Dordrecht, Netherlands: Kluwer Academic Publishers.

Vellucci, Sherry L. 1997. "Options for Organizing Electronic Resources: The Coexistence of Metadata." *Bulletin of the American Society for Information Science* 24, no. 1 (October/November): 14–17.

———. 1998. "Metadata." *Annual Review of Information Science and Technology* 33: 187–222.

———. 1999. "Metadata and Authority Control." *Library Resources and Technical Services* 44, no. 1: 33–43.

Weibel, Stuart. 1995. "Metadata: The Foundation of Resource Description." *D-Lib Magazine* (July). http://www.dlib.org/dlib/July95/07weibel.html.

———. 1997. "Q&A: The 'News' Talks with Metadata Expert Weibel." In *Metadata: Connecting Researchers with Relevant Resources. The Research Libraries Group News* 44 (Fall): 6, 8.

Wendler, Robin. 2004. "Eye of the Beholder: Challenges of Image Description and Access at Harvard." In *Metadata in Practice*, edited by Diane Hillmann and Elaine Westbrooks, 51–69. Chicago: American Library Association.

Whalen, Maureen. 2008. "Rights Metadata Made Simple." In *Introduction to Metadata*. 2nd ed., v. 3.0, edited by Murtha Baca. Los Angeles: Getty Research Institute. http://www.getty.edu/research/publications/electronic_publications/intrometadata/index.html.

Woodley, Mary. 2008. "Crosswalks, Metadata Harvesting, Federated Searching, Metasearching: Using Metadata to Connect Users and Information." In *Introduction to Metadata*. 2nd ed., v. 3.0, edited by Murtha Baca. Los Angeles: Getty Research Institute. http://www.getty.edu/research/publications/electronic_publications/intrometadata/index.html.

Wool, Gregory. 1998. "A Meditation on Metadata." *The Serials Librarian* 33, no. 1/2: 167–178.

Xu, Amanda. 1998. "Metadata Conversion and the Library OPAC." *The Serials Librarian* 33, no. 1/2: 179–198.

Yott, Patrick. 2005. In *Metadata: A Cataloger's Primer*, edited by Richard P. Smiraglia, 213–235. Binghamton, NY: Haworth Press.

Zeng, Marcia Lei, and Jian Qin. 2008. *Metadata*. New York: Neal-Schuman.

Index

Page numbers followed by the letter "f" indicate figures; those followed by the letter "t" indicate tables.

About the Author

Steven J. Miller is a senior lecturer at the University of Wisconsin–Milwaukee School of Information Studies. He teaches graduate courses in metadata, cataloging, and information architecture, and has given many continuing education workshops and conference presentations on metadata and other topics. He has served as a member of the Editorial Board of the *Journal of Library Metadata*, the chair of the ALA ALCTS Metadata Interest Group, a cochair of the Wisconsin Heritage Online Metadata Working Group, and a member of the DCMI User Guide and Glossary Task Groups. He presented a paper at the DC-2010 International Conference on Dublin Core and Metadata Applications. He is a recipient of the Excellence in Online Teaching Award from the Web-based Information Science Education Consortium (WISE) for both 2010 and 2006. Prior to his current position, he was a professional cataloger and later head of the monographs cataloging department at the University of Wisconsin–Milwaukee Libraries. He received his MLIS from the University of Wisconsin–Milwaukee in 1990, in addition to a previous MA and all but dissertation for a PhD from Marquette University.